THE BOOK OF LIFE

THE BOOK OF LIFE

A COMPENDIUM OF THE BEST
AUTOBIOGRAPHICAL AND MEMOIR WRITING

EDITED BY

EVE CLAXTON

EBURY PRESS

First published in Great Britain 2005

1 3 5 7 9 10 8 6 4 2

Introductory and biographical text © Eve Claxton 2005

Eve Claxton has asserted her right to be identified as the author of this
work under the Copyright, Designs and Patents Act 1988.

Ebury Press, an imprint of Ebury Publishing.
Random House, 20 Vauxhall Bridge Road, London SW1V 2SA

Random House Australia (Pty) Limited
20 Alfred Street, Milsons Point, Sydney, New South Wales 2061, Australia

Random House New Zealand Limited
18 Poland Road, Glenfield, Auckland 10, New Zealand

Random House South Africa (Pty) Limited
Isle of Houghton, Corner Boundary Road & Carse O'Gowrie,
Houghton, 2198, South Africa

The Random House Group Limited Reg. No. 954009

www.randomhouse.co.uk

A CIP catalogue record for this book is available from the British Library.

Cover design by Two Associates
Text design and typesetting by Richard Evans Design & Art

ISBN 0 091 90033 6

Papers used by Ebury Press are natural, recyclable products made from
wood grown in sustainable forests.

Printed and bound in the UK by Clays of St Ives PLC

'I would rather be well-versed about myself than about Cicero. In the experience I have of myself I find enough to make me wise if I were a good scholar.'

MICHEL DE MONTAIGNE,
'OF EXPERIENCE', 1588

'It is a hard and nice subject for a man to write of himself, it grates his own heart to say anything of disparagement, and the reader's ears to hear anything of praise from him.'

ABRAHAM COWLEY,
'OF MYSELF', 1668

'The three essentials for an autobiography are that its compiler shall have had an eccentric father, a miserable misunderstood childhood and a hell of a time at his public school, and I enjoyed none of these advantages. My father was as normal as rice pudding, my childhood went like a breeze from start to finish, with everybody I met understanding me perfectly, while as for my schooldays at Dulwich they were just six years of unbroken bliss. It would be laughable for me to attempt a formal autobiography. I have not got the material.'

P.G. WODEHOUSE,
OVER SEVENTY: AN AUTOBIOGRAPHY
WITH DIGRESSIONS, 1957

ACKNOWLEDGMENTS

The editor would like to thank: Hannah MacDonald,
Emma Parry, Jackie Krendal and Ken Barlow;
Ros Claxton, John Claxton, Ruth Claxton and
Hannah Claxton; Hannah Weaver and David Nicholls.
Thanks to Kristina Blagojevitch for arranging the
permissions. With special thanks to Chris Durrance for
his translation help and much-valued support.

~ CONTENTS ~

~ INTRODUCTION ~

THIS COMPENDIUM OF AUTOBIOGRAPHICAL and memoir-writing is meant for general reading, as a kind of sampler of some of the great personal literature already in existence. No new works have been commissioned for it, as there was such a wealth of material to draw upon. By including the many voices and diverse styles of authors from every age, it is hoped that this book will open up the breathtaking variety of the genre to curious readers.

As with any compendium, anthology or miscellany, there are many ways that the material can be arranged. Early on in the project, I decided that it seemed to make the most poetic sense to order the entries by the period of life they described, following the course of a lifetime. This *Book of Life* begins with earliest memories of childhood and moves age by age, phase by phase, through the span of years, encompassing adolescence, mid-life and old age. The first entry is from St Augustine, reflecting on his infancy; the last is by the English archaeologist Margaret Murray, who wrote her autobiography when she was 100 years old. Writers on childhood describe early intimations of consciousness and heartbreaking losses of innocence; the writers on adolescence recount their first sexual stirrings and struggles with self-definition; in middle age, there are deaths and births to contend with, and all the many muddling challenges of adulthood; and while old age brings a diminishing of physical capabilities, it also lends a vital clarity of perception as the end comes into sight.

It is a vast subject, autobiography, and I wanted a structure that did not attempt to rein things in too much. And the present arrangement came closest, I felt, to corresponding to the spirit of the genre, which has to do with human experiences, with the individual's quest for self-determination, with the undergoing of existence. I also felt that this matched most closely to how I might approach a single autobiography or memoir, tracing the movement of narrative through the life of another, instinctively drawing the lines of connection and contrast between my own experiences and the author's. I find it is impossible to read descriptions of someone else's childhood, for example, without memories of my own formative experiences flickering through.

Although the entries could have been placed next to one another in historical and chronological order, beginning with the ancients like St Augustine and finishing up with moderns such as Lorna Sage, I was not convinced that this would be as inviting or helpful to the reader. With all the early authors clustered together at the beginning and the more recent ones together at the end, contemporary writing would have to provide a grand culmination of 17 centuries of human experience, and I am not certain it does. Also, by ordering the material as a historical survey in this way, it would have left giant gaps that I would have felt obliged to fill, even if the writing itself was not completely compelling. (Instead, I hope the brief historical survey in this introduction will suffice to give readers enough of a sense of the development of the genre.) Equally, arranging the entries according to style, theme or sub-genre would have seemed more of an artifice.

The great pleasure of ordering by phase of life, at least for its editor, has been the degree of randomness and unexpectedness it allows, the opportunity for odd contrasts and inadvertent echoes that would not have been otherwise possible. It has meant that film stars can keep company with Roman emperors, factory workers with aristocrats, and mystics with modern secularists. The 160-odd authors included here come from manifold backgrounds, ethnicities and belief systems. Such a loose and universally identifiable structure ultimately seemed the right arrangement for this most democratic of genres. From the start, personal writers have used the experiences of a single lifetime to represent the experiences of many. Here, by way of reversal, the experiences of many are used to stand in for a single lifetime.

With the many hundreds of autobiographies and memoirs that have appeared in our bookshops over the past decade – by authors from every walk of life and sort of lifestyle – it is easy to forget that the genre has an extremely long and fascinating history. Taken in the broadest sense of the word – to mean a non-fiction account of a life written by the person it describes – personal writing is extremely ancient, getting a head start on the novel by many centuries. The word 'memoir' – from the French word for memory – made its first appearance in the English language in the 16th century. The word 'autobiography' was not coined until 1797, and represents an amalgam of the Greek roots for 'self', 'life' and 'writing'. Today, the usual way of distinguishing between autobiographies and memoirs – and the distinction is slippery – is that an autobiography is the whole of a life, whereas memoirs relate to a portion of a life, or particular group of people and events.

What is clear is that the act of writing one's life story is a much older phenomenon than the terms we now use to describe it. At almost every point in the history of literature there have been those who have written about their own experiences in the hope that they could benefit either themselves or their readers. Equally, there have always been those who derive especial pleasure from reading autobiographies and memoirs. There is something eternally seductive about a book that invites you to eavesdrop on an intimate universe.

That autobiographers should provide readers with revealing information is immediately suggested in the title of the first full-length 'autobiography' ever written: *The Confessions of St Augustine*. The book was produced between 397 and 400, in Roman North Africa, by the newly consecrated Bishop of Hippo, Aurelius Augustinus, later known as St Augustine. *The Confessions* forms an extended prayer of praise as well as a plea for mercy and forgiveness, addressed directly to God. But woven into all the praying and pleading is a very compelling story of sinfulness. There are long and vivid portrayals of Augustine's youthful misdemeanours – stealing pears from orchards, giving into pre-marital carnal cravings, cheering on the barbaric games at the Coliseum and generally pursuing the empty goals and hedonistic urges of a Roman pagan. Eventually, at the age of 32, Augustine converts to Christianity – the great turning-point in his life – and in the narrative from here on, he devotes himself to musing on religious matters. At this point, less theologically minded readers tend to lose a certain amount of interest.

As much as *The Confessions* remains one of the most influential books in the Christian canon, critical in the establishment of the Catholic Church where confession became a central tenet, it has also had an enduring influence on personal writing. St Augustine's story, reduced to its essential components, will sound all too familiar to modern readers: from difficult beginnings the author confronts various obstacles and challenges, followed by a gradual realization of the need for change, culminating in a turning-point that allows him to be liberated from his past problems and to move forward in a new spirit. Contemporary memoirists and autobiographers might include more than one epiphany, and their narratives might not necessarily be spiritual, but even so, the act of making sense of one's past and formative experiences through writing owes its very rhythms to Augustine's *Confessions*.

Although St Augustine is the person almost always cited as the originator of the 'autobiography' – and certainly he is the first to write about himself at such length – there were certainly those who came before him. In the writings of the great Greeks and Romans there was plenty of self-scrutinizing to provide Augustine with precedents. Included in this compendium, by way of example, are the famous opening lines from *The Meditations of Emperor Marcus Aurelius Anthoninus* (167), where he lists the principal influences on his personal development. Marcus's jottings were a very private exercise – he dedicated *The Meditations* 'To himself' and never intended that they be read by others. Nonetheless, his notebook – a testing ground for his theories on life, leadership, philosophy, good citizenship and how to live well – has survived, offering us insights not only into the emperor's own existence, but also our own (*The Meditations* has been described as an ancient self-help manual of sorts). Although it would be another two centuries before St Augustine wrote the first 'true autobiography', Marcus, along with other leaders and philosophers of antiquity, had already shown that a written record of an individual's struggles could prove illuminating to many.

After Augustine, Western personal writing continued in a spiritual vein. Throughout the Middle Ages, a time when the Church was at the very centre of both private and public life, autobiographical accounts were written by those who defined themselves in terms of their relationship to God. In 14th-century England, Julian of Norwich, a cloistered nun, wrote the first known book by a woman in English. Although not a revealing life story in the manner of St Augustine, *Showings* (c.1393) is nevertheless Julian's very personal story. It tells of a woman utterly dedicated to religious contemplation and devotion, describing both her powerful religious visions and her reflections on them.

For examples of early personal writing of a secular nature it is possible to look to medieval Japan, where from the 8th to 11th centuries, in the courts of the Heian emperors, prominent courtiers were keeping memoir-notebooks (*nikki bungaku*) that they would present as gifts to their masters and mistresses. Those that have survived provide us with startlingly intimate accounts of lives and times. The best known of these, *The Pillow Book of Sei Shōnagon* (written between 994 and 1000 or thereabouts), is a particularly audacious and gossipy account of a long-vanished world. Shōnagon, an attendant to the Empress Sadako Teshi, describes in delightful detail the infighting and intrigue of the court, and lists at length her very particular likes and dislikes. Much of Shōnagon's writing reads as if it had been put on the page just yesterday, not 11 centuries ago.

For St Augustine, as for Julian, the impetus to write a life story stemmed from needing to declare one's piety. During the period of the European Renaissance, writers of poems, plays and prose in general began to place a greater store by the earthier and more individualistic possibilities of human experience. In 16th-century Italy, both the scientist Girolamo Cardano and the sculptor Benvenuto Cellini wrote frank personal accounts that mark a quantum leap from the spiritual narratives of their predecessors. Although Cardano's life story was not published until the 17th century and Cellini's not until the 18th, both books demonstrate the wide world view from within which these Renaissance men thought and operated. Cellini's *My Life*, which he began writing in 1558, might include a description of the author's mid-life religious conversion, but it is better remembered as a rip-roaring tale of a philanderer, a murderer and an egotist, a man who appears to be anything but a humble servant of God. Cardano was an accomplished astronomer, mathematician, physicist and philosopher, and *The Book of My Life*, written in 1576, reveals the many facets of his person, his life experiences and learning, right down to the exact details of his physiognomy.

In this time of rebirth and rediscovery, writers and thinkers were looking beyond the writers of the Middle Ages to the works of classical antiquity for their models. In 1572, from the seclusion of his chateau in the French countryside, the philosopher Michel de Montaigne began to compose his famous *Essays*, embarking on them as exercises in moral argument in the classical manner. Montaigne would take a subject and set out to expound on it, but he almost immediately strayed from the point, and the essays record the meandering of his thoughts as much as they do any coherent argument. Readers of Montaigne will learn about all sorts of intimate subjects – the author's dietary preferences and his physical ailments, for instance – before they gain any idea of his political and moral positions. Of all the great Renaissance writers, Montaigne is the one who lastingly demonstrated that a personal record could serve as a record for all – 'Every man has within himself the entire human condition,' he wrote. He is truly the first writer to reveal the workings of his thoughts so extensively, allowing the reader to overhear his inner dialogue, laying bare the kind of conversations that had previously only taken place between two ears.

Montaigne is also credited with helping to inspire the flourishing of the essay form that took place in England in the 16th and 17th centuries. In 1668 the English poet Abraham Cowley, writing under the spell of the French writer, produced an essay called 'Of Myself', one of the earliest and most intimate of short personal pieces in the English language. Cowley begins with a dilemma that will haunt many a memoirist in the future – how to write about oneself without either resorting to excessive self-deprecation or seeming too vain: 'It is a hard and nice subject for a man to write of himself; it grates his own heart to say anything of disparagement, and the reader's ears to hear anything of praise from him ... '

The 18th century saw the rise of another factor which helped to redefine personal writing in English – namely the novel. When the novel was new and novelists still had to prove their relevance to readers, writers would often pass their narratives off as 'true stories', in the hope that their readership would take them more seriously. The first novel in English, *Robinson Crusoe* by Daniel Defoe, was originally published anonymously under the title *The Life and Strange and Surprising Adventures of Robinson Crusoe, told by himself* (1719). Defoe drew on actual accounts by mariners and castaways to create what is, in effect, not only the first novel but also the first fabricated autobiography – readers were meant to think that Crusoe was the book's author as well as its narrator. The titles of so many of the novels that followed then tended, in their turn, to convey the impression that the subject-matter was a self-penned portrait of the hero or heroine: *The Fortunes and*

Misfortunes of the Famous Moll Flanders (1722), *The History of Tom Jones, A Foundling* (1749), *The Life and Opinions of Tristram Shandy* (1759–1767), to name but three.

Just as novelists were inspired by the memoir, these same novelists were providing inspiration to contemporary memoirists. In 18th-century England, scandalous true stories penned by 'fallen' women began to appear, with heroines that were every bit as intriguing as Defoe's Moll. The actress Charlotte Charke published her life story – *A Narrative of the Life of Mrs Charlotte Charke* (1755) – in which she described her adventures and misadventures. Forced to carve out a career for herself as a businesswoman and travelling player, after her powerful actor-manager father disowned her, Charke relates how she suffered one round of bad luck after another. Even her hopes of making her fortune from writing her memoirs were thwarted, and she died soon after their completion, quite penniless. Charke's father, Colley Cibber, had already produced one of the earliest actor-memoirs, *An Apology for the Life of Mr Colley Cibber, written by himself*, in 1740. His rambling account mostly serves to promote the author as the greatest actor-manager of his times, but Cibber also provides a fascinating insight into London's burgeoning theatrical world in the period after the Restoration. The first courtesan memoir appeared as early as 1748 and although *Harriette Wilson's Memoirs*, excerpted in this compendium, was not published until 1825, the book was very much a product of this age of glamorous adventuresses pleading their virtue despite all evidence to the contrary.

Although begun in England, where its author had fled punishment for his writings, the most important autobiography of the 18th century was published in France between 1782 and 1789. It was the French philosopher Jean-Jacques Rousseau's *The Confessions*, and although it shares a name with St Augustine's book, it was written in direct opposition to the saint's insistence on subservience to a higher power. From first sentence to last, Rousseau took as his subject himself – his emotions, his sensibilities and even his sexuality – and he did so in terms that were purely secular, without any sense of deference to God. As another autobiographer, the Irish writer Oscar Wilde, later wrote in his essay 'The Critic as Artist' (1891), Rousseau confessed his sins 'not to a priest, but to the world'.

The book includes Rousseau's famous opening declaration of his intention to portray himself and none other. It contrasts his inner life with the public masks he feels society has forced him to adopt, and he describes his sense of alienation from society. Throughout, he places emphasis on the emotions and the imagination above any other qualities, directly anticipating and inspiring the Romantics who follow him and, by extension, the self-obsessions of our own era. Just as Rousseau used his novels and philosophical writings to promote his point of view, *The Confessions* is a profound political statement. To follow the dictates of personal experience rather than any external edict – either from God, the Church, the King, or one's aristocratic superiors – is a radical directive. In *The Confessions* we witness nothing less than the emergence of the modern democratic sense of self.

Across the Atlantic, in the new colonies of America, the act of telling one's life story served an important if more religious purpose. For the 17th- and 18th-century settlers, many of whom were escaping persecution in the Old World, recounting the story of your spiritual conversion in front of other church members was a way of being fully accepted into your community. This tradition of testifying in public was later translated into written form. In his 'Personal Narrative' (written sometime after 1739), the Puritan preacher Jonathan Edwards demonstrated the kind of deeply felt religious devotion he expected from the members of his congregation. Although in most churches testifying was usually left to men, the Quaker preacher Elizabeth Ashbridge is one woman who produced a written life story. *Some Account of the Fore-part of the Life of Elizabeth Ashbridge* (written in 1746) is particularly rich in personal incident and detail.

After the colonies declared their independence from Britain in 1776, the act of writing about one's life took on a further resonance. A new democracy cherishes, and depends on, the vigour of its members. Writers of personal histories in their assertions of the individual's experience played a prominent role in establishing the American sense of self and, by extension, of nationhood. Benjamin Franklin's *The Autobiography* – first given that title and published after the founding father's death in 1790 – demonstrates the American paradigm of the self-made man *par excellence*. *The Autobiography* tells the story of the son of a humble soap- and candle-maker who ran away from home at the age of 17 to make his way in the world, becoming the hugely successful and distinguished businessman, scientist, inventor, founding father and statesman of legend. His memoirs, written initially as a letter to his son, were deliberately meant to provide an example to young American males. Through his own story, Franklin demonstrates that with a combination of hard work, rational thinking and hearty self-reliance, any man can make something of his life. It is possible to read Franklin's autobiography as an allegory for the story of a nation itself: a New World son finding his feet and earning his hard-won independence from his Old World father.

Equally, for early African-American writers, the autobiographical form was both a political tool and means of self-definition. From the late 18th century until the time of the Civil War, narratives written by former and escaped slaves were immensely popular with readers, not only in America but also in Europe. These narratives – hundreds of which were published during this period – were used in the cause of the abolitionists who were instrumental in their sponsoring and distribution. One of the earliest of these, *The Interesting Narrative of the Life of Olaudah Equiano, or Gustavus Vassa, the African, written by himself* (1789), had its first printing in England where its author had settled after buying his freedom from his American owner. *The Interesting Narrative* tells Equiano's story, from his boyhood in Nigeria to his capture by British slavers, his transportation to the colonies, and his subsequent struggle for freedom and betterment through education. The book ran into eight editions over a period of five years and Equiano became something of a celebrity, lecturing all round Britain – an early instance of an author who achieves fame through writing his memoirs.

With the growing popularity of memoir writing and also of the novel in both America and Europe came the need to distinguish between literary forms in a way that had not been necessary before. The word 'biography' first appears in English around 1800, and 'autobiography' finally comes into use around the turn of the 19th century. The coining of the word 'autobiography' is often credited to the English poet Robert Southey in a review written in 1809, and it would be gratifying to think that this honour belonged to a Romantic who, along with Samuel Taylor Coleridge and William Wordsworth, was so concerned with matters of individual sensibility and experience. But, in fact, the word seems to have appeared 12 years earlier, in 1797, in a review of the English critic Isaac D'Israeli's *Miscellanies, or Literary Recreations* (1796). The reviewer, 'William Taylor of Norwich', discusses D'Israeli's use of the term 'self-biography' to describe the act of writing about oneself. Taylor, evidently something of a pedant, points out that self-biography is a Saxon-Greek hybrid, and D'Israeli may have been better off using the all-Greek-rooted word autobiography. *Auto* for 'self', *bios* for 'life' and *graphein* for 'to write'.

Nonetheless, the Romantics were bound to exploit and extend the possibilities of personal writing. While Wordsworth was exploring his childhood and formative experiences in the famous autobiographical poem, *The Prelude* (written and published in various versions between 1799 and 1850), his fellow Romantic, the Scotsman Thomas De Quincey, was creating his *Confessions of an English Opium-Eater* (first published in 1822). This autobiographical work, written in a richly poetic prose, effectively expanded the literary prospects of the form. At the time of completion, the author reassured readers that he had shaken off his addiction to opium, a habit he had acquired while a student at Oxford – making *Confessions of an English Opium-Eater* one of the earliest of 'drug recovery' memoirs, now so familiar to modern readers. Prior to his death in 1856, it should be noted, De Quincey published a revised version of the *Confessions*, in which he admitted that he had repeatedly fallen back into addiction in later life.

Many 19th-century autobiographers maintained a much stiffer upper lip than De Quincey. At the request of his biographer, Charles Dickens began to write the story of his childhood in 1847, but became too distraught to continue. The pain of recollecting his family's descent into debt and his time working as a child labourer in a shoe-polish factory was too unsettling for the author. Instead, he took the material and turned it into his most autobiographical novel, *David Copperfield* (1849). While Dickens was alive, he never informed his readers as to the circumstances of his childhood, which were only revealed when Dickens' fragment of autobiography was published in John Forster's *The Life of Charles Dickens* (1872). Later in the century another novelist, Anthony Trollope, informed readers that he had no intention of offering any insight into his 'inner life' in *An Autobiography*, published posthumously, in 1883, at the author's request in 1883. 'If the rustle of a woman's petticoat has ever stirred my blood, if a cup of wine has been a joy to me, if I have thought tobacco at midnight in pleasant company to be one of the elements of an earthly paradise, if now and again I have somewhat recklessly fluttered a £5 note over a card table, of what matter is that to any reader?' he asked.

Such dignified reticence would soon seem antiquated. At the turn of the 20th century, the Austrian psychoanalyst Sigmund Freud published *The Interpretation of Dreams* (1900), in which he described the role of the subconscious in determining human behaviour. By putting his patients on the couch and asking them to reveal the details of their dreams and memories, and by writing about his own dream-life, Freud effectively transformed the art of autobiography into a science. Much of 20th-century autobiographical writing, in a certain sense, has to do with transforming that science back into art. In 1907, the English poet and critic Edmund Gosse published an extraordinary memoir of his relationship with his father (*Father and Son*), exploring the conflicts between the elder Gosse's rigorous Christianity and his own more modern sceptical outlook. This beautifully crafted memoir made a definitive leap in its exposure of a complex family dynamic. Gosse evidently felt a degree of discomfort in laying bare his family history, as he originally published the book anonymously, only revealing himself as its author when *Father and Son* went into its fourth edition.

In 1913 Gosse's friend, the American novelist Henry James, produced one of the first modernist memoirs: *A Small Boy and Others*. Although the work began as a portrait of his brother, the philosopher William James, *A Small Boy and Others* quickly developed beyond its author's original intentions. What James eventually created was a book that is as much an attempt to render 'tiny particles of history' in prose – evoking the flow of consciousness itself and even James's dream life – as it is a recounting of people and events. The same year, the French novelist Marcel Proust published the first volume of *Remembrance of Times Past*. Soon afterwards *A Portrait of the Artist As A Young Man* (1914-1915), by the Irish writer James Joyce, appeared. Although both Proust and Joyce were writing fiction, their concerns were identical to James's – trying to reconcile how we can recapture the past, how memory can be made into art. James continued his own experiments in two further volumes of memoirs, the third left unfinished at the time of his death in 1916.

Throughout the 1920s and 1930s literary writers, in general, continued to move beyond the limits of convention in order to explore the ways in which past experiences had shaped them and could, in turn, be reshaped through writing. Stream of consciousness took the place of omniscient authorial voices in fiction; writers made use of unreliable narrators – protagonists who might not be trustworthy – a technique that autobiographers had long since inadvertently perfected. The American writer Gertrude Stein produced a book that remains the most inventive of autobiographies: *The Autobiography of Alice B. Toklas* (1933) is Stein's famous version of her life written as if by her partner, Alice B. Toklas. The English writer Virginia Woolf and the Irish poet W.B. Yeats both left behind fragmentary autobiographies, careful to question their own versions of events, acknowledging memory and experience as shifting, variable, diffuse.

Yet during this same period, the First and then the Second World Wars necessitated and reinforced the power of testimonial, of the eyewitness account and the binding of a writer's word to an experience. As Woolf observed, in times of great transition autobiographies tend to proliferate: 'the only thing that remains stable is oneself'. In the English poet Robert Graves' *Good-bye to All That* (1929), with its vivid description of trench life, the poet made his 'bitter leave-taking' of England and expressed his outrage at the hypocrisy of his elders and officers. The English pacifist Vera Brittain wrote her *Testament of Youth* (1933) about her own experience of the First World War, precisely so that there would be a woman's record to stand alongside those of Graves and his comrades. Autobiography had become a means of exorcising atrocity, of helping to inspire moral outrage in the hope that such horrors would never be allowed to occur again. Some of the most powerful of wartime testimonials appeared after the Second World War, written by Jewish Holocaust survivors. The earliest of these are also the most extraordinary. *If This is A Man* (1947), by the Italian chemist and author Primo Levi, was written immediately after his release from Auschwitz in 1945. The Romanian-born writer Elie Wiesel's *Night* appeared in 1958 – the author had vowed to wait ten years until he wrote about what he had witnessed in the death camps. That these experiences were conveyed as non-fiction was essential: Levi and Wiesel were rightly concerned that Nazi atrocities might fail to be believed.

For authors displaced by the wars and revolutions of the 20th century, the writing of memoirs became a means of salvaging and preserving the past. In *Speak, Memory: An Autobiography Revisited* (1966), the Russian *émigré* writer Vladimir Nabokov meticulously re-created the St Petersburg of his childhood and the early experiences of his European exile. Nabokov asserted that the tracing of 'thematic designs' should be the 'true purpose of autobiography'. Indeed, *Speak, Memory* elevated autobiographical writing to the level of great literature, where image, metaphor, verbal playfulness and veracity of description take precedence over the traditional autobiography of chronology, turning-point and example. But Nabokov's concerns were not only aesthetic – *Speak, Memory* is also a vital investigation into the nature of self. 'The individual mystery remains to tantalize the memoirist,' Nabokov writes. 'Neither in environment nor in heredity can I find the exact instrument that fashioned me, the anonymous roller that pressed upon my life a certain intricate watermark whose unique design becomes visible when the lamp of art is made to shine through life's foolscap.'

From the 1960s onwards, autobiographical writers began to deal with many hitherto taboo subjects, both responding to a new climate of permissiveness and also helping to inform that climate. Writers in all genres started to tackle subjects that were formerly subject to censorship. The legalization of homosexuality in Britain in 1967 allowed for authors like Quentin Crisp and J.R. Ackerley to write candid memoirs that would have been punishable the year before – Crisp's *The Naked Civil Servant* and Ackerley's *My Father and Myself* both appeared in 1968. Although the genre of autobiography and memoir has always been remarkably open and democratic, the breaking down of class barriers and social prejudices in recent times has further widened the diversity.

Increasingly, autobiographers have explored and revealed the most intimate and difficult aspects of human experience, helping to erode the boundary between public and private lives that we so associate with modern culture. Memoirs about traumatic childhoods, of recovery from addiction, and of mental and physical illness have become immensely popular, creating genres within the genre. These sub-genres are often assumed to be a recent phenomenon, an indication of how deeply the language and techniques of therapy have pervaded the culture. In fact, most have their precedents. When the American author William Styron wrote *Darkness Visible* (1990) about his depression, he followed in the path of the 19th-century English poet William Cowper, who wrote one of the earliest accounts of mental illness: *Memoir of the Early Life of William Cowper Esq, written by himself* (1816). Dickens' description of his factory work as a boy prefigures a score of memoirs written by those who have suffered through impoverished childhoods. De Quincey's struggles with opium addiction came long before more recent tales of substance abuse. Courtesan memoirs by Harriette Wilson and others predate the modern kiss and tell.

Inevitably, in these times of fascination with celebrity and mass media, the memoirs of prominent figures – film stars, actors, politicians, musicians, activists and artists – have become fixtures on best-seller lists. Often authored with the help of a professional writer, the celebrity memoir has proved itself to be one of the only sure-fire ways to guarantee a best-seller in the unpredictable business of publishing. How authentic these accounts are varies from book to book. The journalist Alex Haley assured readers that the civil rights leader Malcolm X approved every single word of the co-written *The Autobiography of Malcolm X* (published immediately following Malcolm's assassinatin in 1965). The African-American jazz singer Billie Holiday, on the other hand, claimed never to have read her autobiography *Lady Sings the Blues* (1956), written with the journalist William Dufty. She never liked the title, pointing out to her publishers that she sang jazz, not blues. Certainly, the life stories of both Malcolm X and Billie Holiday follow a pattern that has become deeply embedded in popular culture – the sharing of private troubles in public. It seems that the more a famous person has struggled and suffered, and transcended his or her difficult beginnings, the more likely their story is to feel relevant to readers.

Just as the already famous have written their life stories, so there have been many instances of writers who have become famous *through* their memoirs. In the second volume of her autobiography, *Almost There: The Onward Journey of a Dublin Woman* (2003), the Irish journalist Nuala O'Faolain writes about this phenomenon, how her life changed in extraordinary ways after the publication of her first book, *Are You Somebody?: The Accidental Memoir of a Dublin Woman* (1998). By writing about her problematic childhood and youth, and about being a single and childless woman in her 50s, O'Faolain became a best-selling author of means. For O'Faolain, the act of putting words on the page, of making remembered experience become fixed and coherent – and then of having to read those words at book signings and radio appearances – brought her nearer to a reconciliation with her past and present circumstances than she feels would have been otherwise possible. The publication of an autobiography becomes a turning-point in a life, a point of transformation, bringing a new sense of usefulness, community and comfort. Salvation, it seems, can still be brought about through confession – a notion with which St Augustine would be familiar.

In many cases a certain knowing tone has entered the writings of modern-day autobiographers. Authors often feel it necessary to make their apologies before embarking on writing about themselves, sensing, possibly, the risk of appearing to be narcissistic – of speaking about personal matters that should probably better be kept to themselves. The charge of egotism can be justified and many writers prefer to anticipate it. Most recently, in the American writer Dave Eggers' *A Heartbreaking Work of Staggering Genius: A Memoir Based on a True Story* (2000), the author forewarned his readers that if they were perturbed by the fact he had written a memoir '… you are invited to do what the author should have done, and what authors and readers have been doing since the beginning of time: PRETEND IT'S FICTION.' Again, such ambivalence about how the reader will react is not a wholly recent phenomenon. As the Scottish philosopher David Hume pointed out in his deathbed memoir of 1776: 'It is difficult for a man to speak long of himself without vanity; therefore I shall be short.'

Modern authors' ambivalence about writing autobiography is mirrored, and perhaps exacerbated, by the fact that literary critics have mostly been wary of the form. When the author is also the subject of his narrative, both hero and narrator, will it be possible for a mind to accurately observe and be observed at the same time by the same person? How much of the remembered past is necessarily reinvented when it is written down? Aren't defining moments only made to seem momentous in retrospect? As the sole author of his or her story, there is nothing to stop an autobiographer recasting the events of a life in subjective fashion. Contemporary writers tend to be overtly conscious of charges of questionable authenticity. The South African novelist J.M. Coetzee, in two volumes of memoir, writes about himself in the third person, both to maintain a degree of objectivity as he writes and to remind readers that when an author describes himself, he creates a character as much as he would when writing a novel.

Inevitably, the writing of any autobiography is a subjective enterprise. The vast range of life's experience will always be necessarily reduced in any written work. Memory is unreliable. It is up to the autobiographer to create something that corresponds as closely as possible to a sense of 'reality', but he or she can never replicate the real in all its infinitesimal variety – a 'true story' can never be the whole story. Yet, as I hope this compendium proves, if a writer at least *seems* to be sincere, revealing to us their uncertainties and vulnerabilities, we easily forget to question the veracity of the narrative and quickly forgive any egotism as necessary to the project.

Now to the inevitable omissions in this compendium. It has been necessary to exclude any autobiographical material that can be found in other genres such as diaries, letters, travel writing, oral histories, ethnographic works, speeches, interviews and autobiographical poems. There are no biographies here, even if there are co-written life stories that have become such a staple of the genre. In the past 20 years, the study of 'life-writing' has gained in prominence in American and European universities. It is a subject that encompasses all kinds of personal writing, including diaries, letters, biographies and other categories mentioned above. All of these might have provided wonderful source material but are not included here, partly for the sake of concision, but also because they have been beautifully anthologized elsewhere. In the interests of coherence, there is also as little 'inadvertent' autobiography as possible, by which I mean I have focused on works that the author has consciously created or published as autobiography, either in full-length or essay form.

So as not to muddy the waters, there is no autobiographical fiction, however blurred the line separating fiction from non-fiction can be (I have gone on an author's word as to whether a book was a novel or a memoir). On the whole, memoirs dealing entirely with other people have been excluded, as this book is almost exclusively self-centred, focused on the individual's experience from the individual's perspective. As a result, although Nadezhda Mandelstam remains one of the pre-eminent memoirists of the 20th century, she is not included here as *Hope Against Hope* (1970) is devoted to the author's times, her husband and those she knew, but rarely to herself. I have, of course, made exceptions to my own rules. Sara Coleridge's memoir of her father Samuel Taylor, and his friends the Wordsworths, has been incorporated because it offered such an endearing child's-eye view of famous men. Claude Monet's life story was originally a newspaper interview; and Truman Capote has been allowed, even if his 'Self-Portrait' is in the form of an interview with himself.

Many other worthy authors are not excerpted here, not because they lack merit but often for the opposite reason. The most brilliant of memoirists often seemed to resist selection – Paula Fox, Edith Wharton and Frank Conroy spring to mind, although there are a host of others. With such gifted writers, the book is often the sum of all its parts and it seemed almost sacrilegious to remove only a small section – like shells brought home from the beach, they never look quite as shiny when you take them out of their context. Equally, there are memoirs written by non-writers that have tremendous overall impact, but where it was impossible to remove one piece from the whole and have it retain any effect – I am thinking of the many celebrity memoirs that have appeared in the last 50 years. In other cases, obtaining the rights to use a passage by a particularly well-known author turned out to be prohibitively expensive, and I would console myself with the thought that as Frank McCourt or Maya Angelou were so famous, I would not be depriving readers of someone they had not heard of or read before.

While seeking to select a few memorable moments from an author's many recollections, I know I have omitted vital junctures. Although I have tried to include a wide range of experiences, I am equally aware that various ages of life are missing and potentially a thousand types of crucial experiences. A book such as this could never hope to begin to be inclusive of every historical, political and social movement, for example. I have endeavoured to be global in scope, and while I have not managed to include a writer from every country in the world, I have incorporated at least one from each continent (with the exception of Antarctica).

Here, I must make my own confession. My reasons for including one writer, or piece of prose over another, were not always pre-conceived. The omissions listed above emerged from the process of compiling rather than the other way round. My decision to include someone had mostly to do with whether I was charmed, intrigued, or simply fell in love with the writing in question. Ultimately, the criteria for my selection of entries evolved from my own response to the calibre of writing and the impact of the experience it described; I also assumed from the start that my subjectivity would be a given. If I came upon a scene that seemed to speak directly to me of some aspect of my own experience or, conversely, was utterly unlike anything I had experienced but was fascinating to me, then I held on to it. If I chanced upon a passage that I remembered reading from before that had stayed with me, then I would earmark it. The excerpts needed to retain their impact when removed from their context and only a few sections of any given autobiography or memoir were able to do that, and so often making a choice was easy.

This book is also necessarily a reflection of the collection at the New York Public Library on Fifth Avenue, in the city where I live and where I did the bulk of the reading. Situated almost exactly in the middle of Manhattan Island, the library's collections are vast and deep, stretching a full block underneath the building and beyond the park behind it. It was a daily pleasure to go to its Rose Reading Room and graze for writers from so many centuries, continents and walks of life.

As the work of compiling this book progressed, the arrangement of the entries began to take on a life and a rhythm of its own. I began to envisage the book as one of those ideal dinner party scenarios – albeit on the scale of a grand banquet – with each guest taking turns to tell stories. In the childhood chapter, the Cuban writer Reinaldo Arenas talks about the freedom of his childhood, which is followed by a story from the Chinese writer Shen Fu about the games he played as a child; then Rousseau remembers how his father taught him to read, which, in turn, is followed by the scene described by Cellini where he recalls seeing a magical salamander in the fire, and so on and so on. These ideal raconteurs even began to make appearances in one another's stories. The English philosopher Bertrand Russell talks about his adolescence and then reappears to give advice to the boxer Muhammad Ali about his conscientious objection to the Vietnam War. The English novelist Rosamond

Lehmann describes the birth of her daughter Sally, who grows up to fall in love with the English poet and memoirist P.J. Kavanagh, who re-creates their meeting and marriage in excerpts included here. The African-American author James Baldwin writes about going to the movies as a child and later appears as a guest at the English actor Dirk Bogarde's 50th birthday party in France. Grandfather and granddaughter Charles Darwin and Gwen Raverat – who never met, as he died before she was born – are united here, both of them as authors of autobiographies and musing on old age.

This is, of course, the greatest virtue of good autobiographical- and memoir-writing, the sense that we are being spoken to by a recognizable human presence, leaning across the page, and sometimes across centuries and continents, to tell us about how they have viewed themselves and the world. A good autobiographer or memoirist could very well be sitting next to us towards the end of a dinner party, speaking confidentially and sharing the insights of a life that might seem at once unique and familiar, allowing us to feel in good company as we find our own way through the trials, turning-points and many phases of any given life.

EVE CLAXTON, 2005

PUBLISHER'S NOTE

1 SPELLINGS: In the main anthology sections, the selected extracts have been drawn from both UK and US editions. Our policy has been to adhere as closely as possible to the printed sources, so the reader will notice there is a mixture of British-English and American-English spellings. Archaic spellings from early editions have been left intact where appropriate.

To reduce inconsistency between entries, 'z' spellings (e.g. realize) have been used throughout this book.

2 TRANSLATIONS: A number of extracts by foreign writers (e.g. Jean-Jacques Rousseau) have been rendered into English as original translations by the editor Eve Claxton and her collaborator Christopher Durrance.

3 PUNCTUATION: Again, our policy has been to remain as faithful as possible to the printed source material, but to make archaic texts more accessible to the modern reader, certain obsolete grammatical marks have been omitted, and punctuation, overall, has been rendered in its standard British-English form.

Any minor abridgement in a given entry is indicated by '…'

4 DATES AND TITLES: For every book excerpted in the main body of this anthology, the editor has cited the first date of publication in book form, or, if that book was published posthumously, the date or range of dates when the work was produced. In the biographical section, she has indicated the date or range of dates during which a book was written *and* its first date of publication if these are substantially different. If a book was published in a number of volumes, the range of publication dates is given. If the book was substantially revised at any point, the date of the exact edition used is given. If the excerpt is in translation then the original date of publication rather than the date of translation is given. If the book has a different title in the US and the UK then both titles are given. If the excerpt is from an essay, or from a piece of writing originally included in a collection of works, the title is given in single quotation marks. In the credits and sources section at the back of the book, the editor has cited the dates and titles of

the actual editions from which she has selected her entries. (Titles, throughout, are taken directly from the editions used in each instance.)

∼ BEGINNINGS ∼

AGES 0–12

'My autobiography, however, is without any
artifice; nor is it intended to instruct anyone;
but, being merely a story, recounts my life,
not tumultuous events. Like the lives of Sulla,
of Caius Caesar, and even of Augustus, who,
there is no doubt, wrote accounts of their
careers and deeds, urged by the examples
of the ancients, so, in a manner by no means
new or originating with myself, do I set
forth my account.'

GIROLAMO CARDANO,
THE BOOK OF MY LIFE, 1576

ST AUGUSTINE

FOR AT THAT TIME I knew how to suck, to be satisfied when comfortable, and to cry when in pain – nothing beyond.

Afterwards I began to laugh – at first in sleep, then in waking. For this I have heard mentioned of myself, and I believe it (though I cannot remember it), for we see the same in other infants. And now little by little I realised where I was, and wished to tell my wishes to those who might satisfy them, but I could not! For my wants were within me, while they were without, and could not by any faculty of theirs enter into my soul. So I cast about limbs and voice, making the few and feeble signs I could, like, though indeed not much like, unto what I wished; and when I was not satisfied – either not being understood or because it would have been injurious to me – I grew indignant that my elders were not subject unto me, and that those on whom I had no claim did not wait on me, and avenged myself on them by tears. That infants are such I have been able to learn by watching them; and they, though unknowing, have better shown me that I was such a one than my nurses who knew it.

And, behold, my infancy died long ago, and I live.

THE CONFESSIONS OF ST AUGUSTINE, 397–400

ARIEL DORFMAN

I WAS A BABY; a pad upon which any stranger could scrawl a signature. A passive little bastard, shipwrecked, no ticket back, not even sure that a smile, a scream, my only weapons, could help me to the surface. And then Spanish slid to the rescue, in my mother's first cry, and soon in her murmurs and lullabies and in my father's deep voice of protection and in his jokes and in the hum of love that would soon envelop me from an extended family. Maybe that was my first exile: I had not asked to be born, had not chosen anything, not my face, not the face of my parents, not this extreme sensitivity that has always boiled out of me, not the early rash on my skin, not my remote asthma, not my nearby country, not my unpronounceable name. But Spanish was there at the beginning of my body or perhaps where my body ended and the world began, coaxing that body into life as only a lover can, convincing me slowly, sound by sound, that life was worth living, that together we could tame the fiends of the outer bounds and bend them to our will. That everything can be named and therefore, in theory, at least in desire, the world belongs to us. That if we cannot own the world, nobody can stop us from imagining everything in it, everything it can be, everything it ever was.

HEADING SOUTH, LOOKING NORTH: A BILINGUAL JOURNEY, 1998

HARRIET MARTINEAU

M Y FIRST RECOLLECTIONS are of some infantile impressions which were in abeyance for a long course of years, and then revived in an inexplicable way, as by a flash of lightning over a far horizon in the night. There is no doubt of the genuineness of the remembrance, as the facts could not have been told me by anyone else. I remember standing on the threshold of a cottage, holding fast by the doorpost, and putting my foot down, in repeated attempts to reach the ground. Having accomplished the step, I toddled (I remember the uncertain feeling) to a tree before the door, and tried to clasp and get around it; but the rough bark hurt my hands.

HARRIET MARTINEAU'S AUTOBIOGRAPHY, 1877

HANNAH LYNCH

T HE PICTURE IS CLEAR BEFORE ME of the day I first walked. My mother, a handsome, cold-eyed woman, who did not love me, had driven out from town to nurse's cottage. I shut my eyes, and I am back in the little parlour with its spindle chairs, an old-fashioned piano with green silk front, its pink-flowered wallpaper and the two wonderful black-and-white dogs on the mantelpiece ...

I do not remember my mother's coming or going. Memory begins to work from the moment nurse put me on a pair of unsteady legs. There were chairs placed for me to clutch, and I was coaxingly bidden to toddle along, 'over to mamma'. It was very exciting. First one chair had to be reached, then another fallen over, till a third tumbled me at my mother's feet. I burst into a passion of tears, not because of the fall, but from terror at finding myself so near my mother. Nurse gathered me into her arms and began to coo over me, and here the picture fades from my mind.

AUTOBIOGRAPHY OF A CHILD, 1899

THOMAS CARLYLE

M Y EARLIEST [MEMORY] OF ALL is a mad passion of rage at my elder Brother John (on a visit to us likely from his grandfather's); in which my father too figures though dimly, as a kind of cheerful comforter and soother. I had broken my little brown stool, by madly throwing it at my brother; and felt for perhaps the first time, the united pangs of Loss and of Remorse. I was perhaps hardly more than two years old; but can get no one to fix the date for me, though all is still quite legible for myself, with many of its [features] ... Backwards beyond all, are dim *ruddy* images, of deeper and deeper brown shade into the dark beginnings of being.

REMINISCENCES, 1881

HENRY JAMES

P ARTLY DOUBTLESS AS THE EFFECT of a life, now getting to be a tolerably long one, spent in the older world, I see the world of our childhood as very young indeed, young with its own juvenility as well as with ours; as if it wore the few and light garments and had gathered in but the scant properties and breakable toys of the tenderest age, or were at the most a very unformed young person, even a boisterous hobbledehoy. It exhaled at any rate a simple freshness, and I catch its pure breath, at our infantile Albany, as the very air of long summer afternoons – occasions tasting of ample leisure, still bookless, yet beginning to be bedless, or cribless; tasting of accessible garden peaches in a liberal backward territory that was still almost part of a country town, tasting of many-sized uncles, aunts, cousins, of strange legendary domestics, inveterately but archaically Irish, and whose familiar remarks and 'criticism of life' were handed down, as well as of dim family ramifications and local allusions — mystifications always – that flowered into anecdote as into small hard plums, tasting above all of a big much-shaded savoury house in which a softly-sighing widowed grandmother, Catherine Barber by birth, whose attitude was a resigned consciousness of complications and accretions, dispensed an hospitality seemingly as joyless as it was certainly boundless.

A SMALL BOY AND OTHERS, 1913

SHERWIN B. NULAND

MY FATHER DOES NOT actually appear in my earliest memory of him. But the threat of his furious anger looms over the series of moments even as they are recalled.

It is in the form of single still images that I remember him from those early years. Each picture is preserved as though a camera had caught a series of lifetime's memories in individual blinks of an eye. Sometimes, an image is followed by a brief cinematic flow of film, but rarely more. And always a distinct emotion or mood is brought back to my mind when the pictures appear.

It is mid-afternoon and I have just spied Daddy's pocket watch and chain on a small table alongside the living-room couch. The sight of the inexpensive silvery timepiece attached to a flat strand of worn and tarnished links is particularly attractive because its imperious owner has recently scolded me for daring to play with it. I pick up the entire clump of watch and chain. In the next remembered picture, I have made my way to the electric outlet on the nearest wall, and I am staring at it, as though trying to make a decision. Stabilizing myself on chubby knees, I stuff several links of the chain into one of the outlet's parallel slits.

With a sudden roaring wallop, a colossal burst of sparks and energy blasts up out of the wall as a paralyzing vibratory surge of electricity courses through every part of me and lifts my helpless body momentarily off the floor. Hearing my shrieking wail, terrified Momma flies out of some other room, screaming, no doubt certain that I have been killed. She gathers me up and I submerge myself into her softness. We are both weeping. She croons a gentle, familiar reassurance, but I am hysterical.

The pervasive feeling hovering over these horrifying images is not the sudden fright, but a sense of foreboding: something more is yet to come, and in its own way it will be as threatening as the terror I have just survived ...

The truth is not to be known. The only certainty is that the remembered sequence of images from that terrifying afternoon almost seventy years ago is inseparable from the dread of my father's coming rage; it is inseparable from the sense that Momma and I cowered in anticipation of its outburst just as we would cower in the torrential force of my father's wrath when it finally came.

Looking back on my earliest remembered years, I see my parents far less as a couple than as the sources of two quite disparate emotions — emotions of golden safety with one and sporadic danger with the other. They originated from Momma, who lived only for me, and Daddy, who never quite understood how to be my father.

LOST IN AMERICA: A JOURNEY WITH MY FATHER, 2003

CHARLES CHAPLIN

O NE OF MY EARLY RECOLLECTIONS was that each night before Mother went to the theater, Sydney and I were lovingly tucked up in a comfortable bed and left in the care of the housemaid. In my world of three and a half years, all things were possible; if Sydney, who was four years older than I, could perform *legerdemain* and swallow a coin and make it come out through the back of his head, I could do the same; so I swallowed a halfpenny and Mother was obliged to send for a doctor.

Every night, after she came home from the theater, it was her custom to leave delicacies on the table for Sydney and me to find in the morning – a slice of Neapolitan cake or candies – with the understanding that we were not to make a noise in the morning, as she usually slept late.

Mother was a soubrette on the variety stage, a *mignonne* in her late twenties, with fair complexion, violet-blue eyes and long light-brown hair that she could sit upon. Sydney and I adored our mother. Though she was not an exceptional beauty, we thought her divine-looking. Those who knew her told me in later years that she was dainty and attractive and had compelling charm. She took pride in dressing us up for Sunday excursions, Sydney in an Eton suit with long trousers and me in a blue velvet one with blue gloves to match. Such occasions were orgies of smugness, as we ambled along the Kennington Road.

London was sedate in those days. The tempo was sedate; even the horse-drawn tramcars along Westminster Bridge Road went at a sedate pace and turned sedately on a revolving table at the terminal near the bridge. In Mother's prosperous days we also lived in Westminster Bridge Road. Its atmosphere was gay and friendly with attractive shops, restaurants and music halls. The fruit shop on the corner facing the Bridge was a galaxy of color, with its neatly arranged pyramids of oranges, apples, pears and bananas outside, in contrast to the solemn gray Houses of Parliament directly across the river.

This was the London of my childhood, of my moods and awakenings: memories of Lambeth in the spring – of trivial incidents and things – of riding with Mother on the top of a horse-bus trying to touch passing lilac trees – of the many-colored bus tickets, orange, blue, pink and green, that bestrewed the pavement where the trams and buses stopped – of rubicund flower girls at the corner of Westminster Bridge, making gay *boutonnières*, their adroit fingers manipulating tinsel and quivering fern – of the humid odor of freshly watered roses that affected me with a vague sadness – of melancholy Sundays and pale-faced parents and their children escorting toy windmills and colored balloons over Westminster

Bridge – and the maternal penny steamers that softly lowered their funnels as they glided under it. From such trivia I believe my soul was born.

MY AUTOBIOGRAPHY, 1964

CZESLAW MILOSZ

M Y FIRST AWARENESS came with war. Peeping out from under my grandmother's cloak, I discovered horror: the bellow of cattle being driven off, the panic, the dust-laden air, the rumbling and flashing on a darkened horizon. The Germans were arriving in Lithuania and the Czarist army was retreating, accompanied by hordes of refugees.

A scene from that summer of 1914 is still very clear in my memory: bright sunshine, a lawn, myself sitting on a bench with a young Cossack whom I like a lot. He is slim-waisted and black-haired. On strips, crisscrossed over his chest, there are cartridges. He twists a bullet out and empties the powder grains onto the bench. Then a tragedy occurs. I was very attached to a little white lamb. Now the Cossacks are running him into the green grass, heading him off ... My desperate cry, the inability to bear irrevocable unhappiness, was my first protest against necessity.

NATIVE REALM: A SEARCH FOR SELF-DEFINITION, 1958

MRS SCOTT, JP

M Y FIRST CLEAR RECOLLECTION is of the time when I was about three years of age, when we lived near a hollow where a little girl had been maltreated and killed by a gang of youths. Mother told me I was not to go down to the hollow, because it was not safe for little girls. I remember getting something to drag behind me and asking one or two more children to venture with me, and going down to the hollow to see if anything really did happen to you. Although it is so long ago, I can still feel the thrill of marching down and seeing for myself. This I suppose was the beginning of my habit of testing things for myself and not taking facts and opinions ready-made.

'A FELT HAT WORKER', 1931

PAUL BOWLES

K NEELING ON A CHAIR and clutching the gilded top rung of its back, I stared at the objects on the shelves of the cabinet. To the left of the gold clock was an old pewter tankard. When I had looked at it for a while, I said the word 'mug' aloud. It looked like my own silver mug at home, from which I drank my milk. 'Mug,' I said again, and the word sounded so strange that I continued to say it, again and again, until I found myself losing touch with its meaning. This astonished me; it also gave me a vague feeling of unease. How could 'mug' not mean mug?

The room was very quiet. I was alone in that part of the house. Suddenly the gold clock chimed four times. As soon as the last stroke was stilled, I realised that something important was happening. I was four years old, the clock had struck four, and 'mug' meant mug. Therefore I was I, I was there, and it was that precise moment and no other. A satisfying new experience, to be able to say all this with certainty.

WITHOUT STOPPING, 1972

CHARLOTTE CHARKE

A S I HAVE PROMIS'D TO CONCEAL NOTHING that might raise a Laugh, I shall begin with a small Specimen of my former Madness, when I was but four Years of Age. Having, even then, a passionate Fondness for a Perriwig, I crawl'd out of Bed one Summer's Morning at Twickenham, where my Father had Part of a House and Gardens for the Season, and, taking it into my small Pate, that by Dint of a Wig and a Waistcoat, I should be the perfect

Representative of my Sire [my father], I crept softly into the Servants-Hall, where I had the Night before espied all Things in Order, to perpetrate the happy Design I had framed for the next Morning's Expedition. Accordingly I paddled down the Stairs, taking with me my Shoes, Stockings, and little Dimity Coat, which I artfully contrived to pin up, as well as I could, to supply the Want of a Pair of Breeches. By the Help of a long Broom, I took down a Waistcoat of my Brother's, and an enormous bushy Tie-wig of my Father's, which entirely enclos'd my Head and Body, with the Knots of the Ties thumping my little Heels as I march'd along, with slow and solemn Pace. The Covert of Hair in which I was conceal'd, with the Weight of a monstrous Belt and large Silver-hilted Sword, that I could scarce drag along, was a vast Impediment in my Procession: And, what still added to the other Inconveniences I labour'd under, was whelming myself under one of my Father's large Beaver-hats, laden with Lace, as thick and as broad as a Brickbat.

Being thus accoutred, I began to consider that 'twou'd be impossible for me to pass for Mr Cibber [my father] in Girl's Shoes, therefore took an Opportunity to slip out of Doors after the Gardener, who went to his Work, and roll'd myself into a dry Ditch, which was as deep as I was high; and in this Grotesque Pygmy-State, walk'd up and down the Ditch, bowing to all who came by me. But, behold, the Oddity of my Appearance soon assembled a Croud about me; which yielded me no small Joy, as I conceiv'd their Risibility on this Occasion to be Marks of Approbation, and walk'd myself into a Fever, in the happy Thought of being taken for the Squire.

When the family arose, 'till which Time I had employ'd myself in this regular March in my Ditch, I was the first Thing enquir'd after, and miss'd; 'till Mrs Heron, the Mother of the late celebrated Actress of that Name, happily espied me, and directly call'd forth the whole Family to be Witness of my State and Dignity.

The Drollery of my Figure render'd it impossible, assisted by the Fondness of both Father and Mother, to be angry with me; but, alas! I was borne off on the Footman's Shoulders, to my Shame and Disgrace, and forc'd into my proper Habiliments.

A NARRATIVE OF THE LIFE OF MRS CHARLOTTE CHARKE, 1755

VLADIMIR NABOKOV

I T WAS THE PRIMORDIAL CAVE (and not what Freudian mystics might suppose) that lay behind the games I played when I was four. A big cretonne-covered divan, white with black trefoils, in one of the drawing rooms at Vyra rises in my mind, like some massive product of a geological upheaval before the beginning of history. History begins (with the promise of fair Greece) not far from one end of this divan, where a large potted hydrangea shrub, with pale blue blossoms and some greenish ones, half conceals, in a corner of the room, the pedestal of a marble bust of Diana. On the wall against which the divan stands, another phase of history is marked by a gray engraving in an ebony frame – one of those Napoleonic-battle pictures in which the episodic and the allegoric are the real adversaries and where one sees, all grouped together on the same plane of vision, a wounded drummer, a dead horse, trophies, one soldier about to bayonet another, and the invulnerable emperor posing with his generals amid the frozen fray.

With the help of some grown-up person, who would use first both hands and then a powerful leg, the divan would be moved several inches away from the wall, so as to form a narrow passage which I would be further helped to roof snugly with the divan's bolsters and close up at the ends with a couple of its cushions. I then had the fantastic pleasure of creeping through that pitch-dark tunnel, where I lingered a little to listen to the singing in my ears – that lonesome vibration so familiar to small boys in dusty hiding places – and then, in a burst of delicious panic, on rapidly thudding hands and knees I would reach the tunnel's far end, push its cushion away, and be welcomed by a mesh of sunshine on the parquet under the canework of a Viennese chair and two gamesome flies settling by turns. A dreamier and more delicate sensation was provided by another cave game, when upon awakening in the early morning I made a tent of my bedclothes and let my imagination play in a thousand dim ways with shadowy snowslides of linen and with the faint light that seemed to penetrate my penumbral covert from some immense distance, where I fancied that strange, pale animals roamed in a landscape of lakes. The recollection of my crib, with its lateral nets of fluffy cotton cords, bring back, too, the pleasure of handling a certain beautiful, delightfully solid, garnet-dark crystal egg left over from some unremembered Easter; I used to chew a corner of the bedsheet until it was thoroughly soaked and then wrap the egg in it tightly, so as to admire and re-lick the warm, ruddy glitter of the snugly enveloped facets that came seeping through with a miraculous completeness of glow and color …

How small the cosmos (a kangaroo's pouch would hold it), how paltry and puny in comparison to human consciousness, to a single individual recollection, and its expression in words! I may be inordinately fond of my earliest impressions, but then I have reason to be grateful to them. They led the way to a veritable Eden of visual and tactile sensations. One night, during a trip abroad, in the fall of 1903, I recall kneeling on my (flattish) pillow at the window of a sleeping car (probably on the long-extinct Mediterranean Train de Luxe, the one whose six cars had the lower part of their body painted in umber and the panels in cream) and seeing with an inexplicable pang, a handful of fabulous lights that beckoned to me from a distant hillside, and then slipped into a pocket of black velvet: diamonds that I later gave away to my characters to alleviate the burden of my wealth. I had probably managed to undo and push up the tight tooled blind at the head of my berth, and my heels were cold, but I still kept kneeling and peering. Nothing is sweeter or stranger than to ponder those first thrills. They belong to the harmonious world of a perfect childhood and, as such, possess a naturally plastic form in one's memory, which can be set down with hardly any effort; it is only starting with the recollections of one's adolescence that Mnemosyne begins to get choosy and crabbed. I would moreover submit that, in regard to the power of hoarding up impressions, Russian children of my generation passed through a period of genius, as if destiny were loyally trying what it could for them by giving them more than their share, in view of the cataclysm that was to remove completely the world they had known. Genius disappeared when everything had been stored, just as it does with those other, more specialized child prodigies – pretty, curly-headed youngsters waving batons or taming enormous pianos, who eventually turn into second-rate musicians with sad eyes and obscure ailments and something vaguely misshapen about their eunuchoid hindquarters. But even so, the individual mystery remains to tantalize the memoirist. Neither in environment nor in heredity can I find the exact instrument that fashioned me, the anonymous roller that pressed upon my life a certain intricate watermark whose unique design becomes visible when the lamp of art is made to shine through life's foolscap.

SPEAK, MEMORY: AN AUTOBIOGRAPHY REVISITED, 1966

REINALDO ARENAS

I THINK THE SPLENDOR of my childhood was unique because it was absolute poverty but also absolute freedom; out in the open, surrounded by trees, animals, apparitions, and people who were indifferent toward me. My existence was not even justified, nobody cared. This gave me an incredible opportunity to escape it all without anyone worrying about where I was or when I would return. I used to climb trees, and everything seemed much more beautiful from up there. I could embrace the world in its completeness and feel a harmony that I could not experience down below, with the clamor of my aunts, the cursing of my grandfather, or the cackling of the hens … Trees have a secret life that is only revealed to those willing to climb them. To climb a tree is to slowly discover a unique world, rhythmic, magical, and harmonious, with its worms, insects, birds, and other living things, all apparently insignificant creatures, telling us their secrets.

BEFORE NIGHT FALLS: A MEMOIR, 1992

SHEN FU

WHEN I WAS SMALL I could stare directly at the sun with my eyes wide open. I could see the smallest things clearly and often took an almost mystic pleasure in making out the patterns on them.

During the summer, whenever I heard the sound of mosquitoes swarming, I would pretend they were a flock of cranes dancing across the open sky, and in my imagination they actually would become hundreds of cranes. I would look at them so long my neck became stiff. At night I would let mosquitoes inside my mosquito netting, blow smoke at them, and imagine that what I saw were white cranes flying soaring through blue clouds. It really did look like cranes flying among the clouds, and it was a sight that delighted me.

I would often squat down by unkempt grassy places in flower beds or by niches in walls, low enough so that my head was level with them, and concentrate so carefully that to me the grass became a forest and the insects became animals. Imagining that small mounds of earth were hills and that shallow holes were valleys, I let my spirit wander there in happiness and contentment.

Once while I was concentrating all my attention on two insects battling in the grass, a giant suddenly appeared, knocking down the mountains and pulling up the trees. It was nothing but a toad, but with one flick of his tongue he swallowed both the insects. I was small, and because I had been so caught up in the scene I could not help being frightened. When I had calmed down, I caught the toad, spanked it severely, and expelled it to a neighbour's yard.

SIX RECORDS OF A FLOATING LIFE, 1809

JEAN-JACQUES ROUSSEAU

I FELT BEFORE I THOUGHT; it is the common lot of humanity. I felt it more than anyone else. I do not know what I was, until I was five or six years old; I do not know how I learned to read; I only remember myself from when I first read and the effect of it on me; it is the time from which I date, without interruption, my awareness of myself. My mother had left some novels. We set about reading them after dinner, my father and I. In the beginning it was only a question of practising reading by way of amusing books; but soon my interest became so intense that we read, taking turns, without stopping, and passed nights at this occupation. We could only ever stop at the end of a volume. Sometimes my father, hearing the swallows in the morning, said, all ashamed, 'Let's go to bed; I'm more of a child than you.'

In little time I acquired, by this dangerous method, not only an extreme ease in reading and in comprehending myself, but a unique understanding, for my age, of the passions. I had no idea about things I came across, but all the feelings were already familiar to me. I had conceived nothing; I had felt everything. These confused emotions, that I experienced in rapid succession, did not in any way distort my ability to reason, as yet unformed; but they created within me one of another calibre and gave me bizarre and romantic notions about human existence, which experience and reflection have never been able to cure me of.

THE CONFESSIONS, 1782–1789

BENVENUTO CELLINI

WHEN I WAS AROUND five years old, my father, Giovanni, was in one of our small rooms – in which we had done the washing and lit a good fire made with little sticks of oak – playing his violin and singing alone around the fire. It was very cold: from time to time, looking into the fire, he could see a small animal like a lizard in the middle of the brightest flames, which was enjoying itself in the strongest blaze. Suddenly realizing what it was, he called my sister and me and pointed it out to us children, then he gave me such a hard smack that I burst into straight into tears. Then he gently consoled me, saying this: 'My dear little boy, I am not being mean to you because of what you have done, but only so that you remember that that lizard you saw in the fire is a salamander, which, so far as we know, has never been seen before by anyone else.' And then he kissed me and gave me some coins.

MY LIFE, 1558–1562

EDMUND GOSSE

MY FATHER AND MOTHER, in their serene discipline of me, never argued with one another, never even differed; their wills seemed absolutely one. My Mother always deferred to my Father, and in his absence spoke of him to me, as if he were all-wise. I confused him in some sense with God; at all events I believed that my Father knew everything and saw everything. One morning in my sixth year, my Mother and I were alone in the morning-room, when my Father came in and announced some fact to us. I was standing on the rug, gazing at him, and when he made this statement, I remember turning quickly, in embarrassment, and looking into the fire. The shock to me was as that of a thunderbolt, for what my Father had said 'was not true'. My Mother and I, who had been present at the trifling incident, were aware that it had not happened exactly as it had been reported to him. My Mother gently told him so, and he accepted the correction. Nothing could possibly have been more trifling to my parents, but to me it meant an epoch. Here was the appalling discovery, never suspected before, that my Father was not as God, and did not know everything. The shock was not caused by any suspicion that he was not telling the truth, as it appeared to him, but by the awful proof that he was not, as I had supposed, omniscient.

This experience was followed by another, which confirmed the first, but carried me a great deal further. In our little back-garden, my Father had built up a rockery for ferns and mosses and from the water-supply of the house he had drawn a leaden pipe so that it pierced upwards through the rockery and produced, when a tap was turned, a pretty silvery parasol of water. The pipe was exposed somewhere near the foot of the rockery. One day, two workmen, who were doing some repairs, left their tools during the dinner-hour in the back garden, and as I was marching about I suddenly thought that to see whether one of these tools could make a hole in the pipe would be attractive. It did make such a hole, quite easily, and then the matter escaped my mind. But a day or two afterwards, when my Father came in to dinner, he was very angry. He had turned the tap, and instead of the fountain arching at the summit, there had been a rush of water through a hole at the foot. The rockery was absolutely ruined.

Of course, I realized in a moment what I had done, and I sat frozen with alarm, waiting to be denounced. But my Mother remarked on the visit of the plumbers two or three days before, and my Father instantly took up the suggestion. No doubt that was it; the mischievous fellows had thought it amusing to stab the pipe and spoil the fountain. No suspicion fell on me; no question was asked of me. I sat there, turned to stone within, but outwardly sympathetic and with unchecked appetite …

In the first place, the theory that my Father was omniscient or infallible was now dead and buried. He probably knew very little; in this case he had not known a fact of such importance that if you did not know that, it could hardly matter what you knew. My Father, as a deity, as a natural force of immense prestige, fell in my eyes to a human level. In future, his statements about things in general need not be accepted implicitly. But of all the thoughts which rushed upon my savage and undeveloped little brain at this crisis, the most curious was that I had found a companion and a confidant in myself. There was a secret in this world and it belonged to me and to a somebody who lived in the same body with me. There were two of us, and we could talk with one another. It is difficult to define impressions so rudimentary, but it is certain that it was in this dual form that the sense of my individuality now suddenly descended upon me, and it is equally certain that it was a great solace to me to find a sympathizer in my own breast.

FATHER AND SON, 1907

PETER O'TOOLE

WHO WAS THE VILLAIN who assured me that there was no Father Christmas? There was most certainly a Father Christmas. Didn't he come down the bloody chimney, knock back the tumbler of whiskey provided by my father, fill up our stockings with oranges, nuts, gobstoppers, a new penny and a sheriff's star, and then piss off back up the chimney again? To be sure he did. I'll fling that villain's lies back in his teeth! I shall creep down from my bedroom, past the sleeping loyal McGilligan [the dog], sit unseen at the bottom of the stairs and watch our munificent, white-whiskered visitor from the North Pole tumble onto the hearth-rug and go about his merry old business.

Now, in the days before the modern architect decided that we had no practical use for the street and Christmas trees were small and put up only on the actual eve of the event, the ways of towns and cities were often lined with various shops selling goods to customers and putting the purchases into brown paper bags. If you puckered the opening of the bag between an encircling thumb and finger, blew deeply into it, squeezed the pucker tightly and then gave the inflated paper bag a fair old smack with the flat of your free hand, it would explode with a delightfully loud report.

I am sitting in my pyjamas at the bottom of the stairs, inspecting the dark living room through the crack left after I'd opened the door just a touch. Someone is coming into the room, all right, but not down the chimney. The door from the passageway has opened, letting in some figures and a little light, but now the door has been shut again and all is dark once more. Bumpings about I can hear and my mother's voice chuckling and giggling. Daddy's voice I can hear now, praying aloud to Jesus Christ and then gurgling out quietly my mother's pet name, 'Connie,' he wheezes, 'Connie.' The light snaps suddenly on and there is Daddy, sitting on the floor, his bowler hat tilted over one eye, cradling in his arms a Christmas tree. Mummy is standing with one hand on the light switch, her legs are crossed, she is shaking and crying with silent laughter, her arms are through the handles of carrier bags, there are other bags on the carpet and brown paper bags strewn all the way to where Daddy sits. The determined little sight of me seems to quiet and surprise them a bit, as it quite rightly should. When I firmly ask of them if Father Christmas is coming, they are, at first, silent but very shortly Daddy begins praying again while Mummy now bends double making hooting noises.

Marching up to my father I repeat: 'Is Father Christmas coming?' Daddy lays aside the Christmas tree, picks up a brown paper bag from the floor, unburdens it of its contents, slowly rises still holding the bag, walks in a curious way to the door, which he opens, and then exits the room, shutting the door behind him. There is a sort of silence for a second or two, a silence which is burst by a loud bang. The door opens and Daddy comes back into the room. He stands above me and looks solemnly down at me before pronouncing very clearly to me: 'Father Christmas has just shot himself.'

LOITERING WITH INTENT: THE CHILD, 1992

MARY KARR

S OMETIMES, WHEN MY PARENTS were raging at each other in the kitchen, Lecia [my sister] and I would talk about finding a shack on the beach to live in. We'd sit cross-legged under the blue cotton quilt with a flashlight, doing parodies of their fights. 'Reel Six, Tape Fifty-one. Let her roll,' Lecia would say. She would clap her arms together like a gator jaw as if what we were listening to was only one more take in a long movie we were shooting. She had a way of shining the flashlight under her chin and sucking in her cheeks, so her eyes became hooded and her cheekbones got as sharp as Mother's. She also had a knack for Mother's sometime Yankee accent, which only came out under stress or chemical influence. Think of a young Katharine Hepburn somehow infected with the syntax and inflections of an evangelist: *I wish that whatever God there might be had struck my car with lightning before I crossed the bridge into this goddamned East Texas Shithole.* Sometimes she'd just cry, and Lecia's imitation of that was cruelest: *There's no hope, there's no hope,* she'd say with a Gloria Swanson melodrama, her wrist flung back to her forehead like it had been stapled there.

I always did Daddy's part, which didn't require much in the way of thought, since he was either silent or his voice was too quiet to hear. The only thing he ever shouted clearly was *You kiss my ass!* He sometimes turned this invective into a line of advice aimed at whomever Mother found to rage about: *Tell them to kiss your ass,* he'd say. 'They' could be the IRS or a pack of Bible-thumpers knocking on our door to convert us. Tell them to kiss your ass was what you could expect him to suggest. (To this day I have some chute in my head from which 'kiss my ass' tumbles. It's truly amazing the number of times it seems applicable.)

Sometimes we'd hear a crash or the sound of a body hitting the linoleum, and then we'd go streaking in there in our pajamas to see who'd thrown what or who'd passed out. If they were still halfway conscious, they'd scare us back to bed. 'Git back to bed. This ain't nothing to do with you,' Daddy would say, or Mother would point at us and say, 'Don't talk to me like that in front of these kids!' Once I heard Daddy roar up out of sleep when Mother had apparently dumped a glass of vodka on him, after which she broke and ran for the back door. We got into the kitchen in time to see him dragging her back to the kitchen sink, where he systematically filled three glasses of water and emptied them on her head. That was one of the rare nights that ended with them laughing. In fact, it put them in such a good mood that they took us out to the drive-in to see *The Night of the Iguana* while they nuzzled in the front seat.

THE LIARS' CLUB, 1995

HELEN KELLER

M ANY INCIDENTS OF THOSE EARLY YEARS are fixed in my memory, isolated, but clear and distinct, making the sense of that silent, aimless, dayless life all the more intense.

One day I happened to spill water on my apron, and I spread it out to dry before the fire which was flickering on the sitting-room hearth. The apron did not dry quickly enough to suit me, so I drew nearer and threw it right over the hot ashes. The fire leaped into life; the flames encircled me so that in a moment my clothes were blazing. I made a terrified noise that brought Viny, my old nurse, to the rescue. Throwing a blanket over me, she almost suffocated me, but she put out the fire. Except for my hands and hair I was not badly burned.

About this time I found out the use of a key. One morning I locked my mother up in the pantry, where she was obliged to remain three hours, as the servants were in a detached part of the house. She kept pounding on the door, while I sat outside on the porch steps and laughed with glee as I felt the jar of the pounding. This most naughty prank of mine convinced my parents that I must be taught as soon as possible. After my teacher, Miss Sullivan, came to me, I sought an early opportunity to lock her in her room. I went upstairs with something which my mother made me understand I was to give to Miss Sullivan; but no sooner had I given it to her than I slammed the door to, locked it, and hid the key under the wardrobe in the hall. I could not be induced to tell where the key was. My father was obliged to get a ladder and take

Miss Sullivan out through the window – much to my delight. Months after I produced the key.

When I was about five years old we moved from the little vine-covered house to a large new one. The family consisted of my father and mother, two older half-brothers, and, afterward, a little sister, Mildred. My earliest distinct recollection of my father is making my way through great drifts of newspapers to his side and finding him alone, holding a sheet of paper before his face. I was greatly puzzled to know what he was doing. I imitated this action, even wearing his spectacles, thinking they might help solve the mystery. But I did not find out the secret for several years. Then I learned what those papers were, and that my father edited one of them.

THE STORY OF MY LIFE, 1903

WOLE SOYINKA

THERE WAS A BIRTHDAY PARTY for one of the Canon's children. Only the children of the parsonage were expected but I passed the secret to Osiki and he turned up at the party in his best *buba*. The entertainments had been set up out of doors in front of the house. I noticed that one of the benches was not properly placed, so that it acted like a see-saw when we sat on it close to the two ends. It was an obvious idea for a game, so, with the help of some of the other children, we carried it to an even more uneven ground, rested its middle leg on a low rock outcrop and turned it into a proper see-saw. We all took turns to ride on it.

For a long time it all went without mishap. Then Osiki got carried away. He was a bigger boy than I, so that I had to exert a lot of energy to raise him up, lifting myself on both hands and landing with all possible weight on my seat. Suddenly, while he was up in his turn, it entered his head to do the same. The result was that I was catapulted up very sharply while he landed with such force that the leg of the bench broke on his side. I was flung in the air, sailed over his head and saw, for one long moment, the Canon's square residence rushing out to meet me.

It was only after I had landed that I took much notice of what I had worn to the party. It was a yellow silk *dansiki*, and I now saw with some surprise that it had turned a bright crimson, though not yet entirely. But the remaining yellow was rapidly taking on the new colour. My hair on the left side was matted with blood and dirt and, just before the afternoon was shut out and I fell asleep, I wondered if it was going to be possible to squeeze the blood out of the *dansiki* and pump it back through the gash which I had located beneath my hair.

The house was still and quiet when I woke up. One moment there had been the noise, the shouts and laughter and the bumpy ride of the see-saw, now silence and semi-darkness and the familiar walls of my mother's bedroom. Despite mishaps, I reflected that there was something to be said for birthdays and began to look forward to mine. My only worry now was whether I would have recovered sufficiently to go to school and invite all my friends ... When I thought again of all the blood I had lost, it seemed to me that I might actually be bed-ridden for the rest of the year. Everything depended on whether or not the blood on my *dansiki* had been saved up and restored to my head. I raised it now and turned towards the mirror; it was difficult to tell because of the heavy bandage, but I felt quite certain that my head had not shrunk to any alarming degree.

The bedroom door opened and mother peeped in. Seeing me awake she entered, and was followed in by father ... I studied their faces intently as they asked me how I felt, if I had a headache or a fever and if I would like some tea. Neither would touch on the crucial question, so finally I decided to put an end to my suspense. I asked them what they had done with my *dansiki*.

'It's going to be washed,' mother said, and began to crush a half-tablet in a spoon for me to take.

'What did you do with the blood?'

She stopped; they looked at each other. Father frowned a little and reached forward to place his hand on my forehead. I shook my head anxiously, ignoring the throb of pain this provoked.

'Have you washed it away?' I persisted.

Again they looked at each other. Mother seemed about to speak but fell silent as my father raised his hand and sat on the bed, close to my head. Keeping his eyes on me he drew out a long, 'No-o-o-o.'

I sank back in relief. 'Because, you see, you mustn't. It wouldn't matter if I had merely cut my hand or stubbed my toe or something like that – not much blood comes out when that happens. But I saw this one, it was too much. And it comes from my head. So you must squeeze it out and pump it back into my head. That way I can go back to school at once.'

My father nodded agreement, smiling. 'How did you know that was the right thing to do?'

I looked at him in some surprise. 'But everybody knows.'

Then he wagged his finger at me, 'Ah-ha, but what you don't know is that we have already done it. It's all back in there, while you were asleep ...'

I was satisfied. 'I'll be ready for school tomorrow,' I announced.

I was kept home another three days. I resumed classes with my head still swathed in a bandage and proceeded to inform my favourite classmates that the next important event in the parsonage was going to be my birthday, still some months away.

AKÉ: THE YEARS OF CHILDHOOD, 1981

ALAN BENNETT

I WAS FIVE WHEN THE WAR STARTED, and Monday 4 September 1939 should have been my first day at school; but that was not to be. I wish I could record our family as gathered anxiously round the wireless, as most were at eleven o'clock that Sunday morning, but I already knew at the age of five that I belonged to a family that without being in the least bit remarkable or eccentric yet managed never to be quite like other families. If we had been, my brother and I would have been evacuated with all the other children the week before, but Mam and Dad hadn't been able to face it. So, not quite partaking in the national mood and, as ever, unbrushed by the wings of history, Mr Chamberlain's broadcast found us on a tram going down Tong Road into Leeds. Fearing the worst, my parents had told my brother and me that we were going out into the country that day and we were to have a picnic – something I had hitherto only come across in books. So on that fateful Sunday morning what was occupying my mind was the imminent conjunction of life with literature; that I should remember nothing of the most momentous event in the twentieth century because of the prospect of an experience found in books was, I see now, a melancholy portent.

Nor was the lesson that life was not going to live up to literature slow in coming, since the much-longed-for picnic wasn't eaten as picnics were in books, on a snowy tablecloth set in a field by a stream, but was taken on a form in the bus station at Vicar Lane, where we waited half that day for any bus that would take us out of the supposedly doomed city.

Early that afternoon a bus came, bound for Pateley Bridge, the other side of Harrogate. Somewhere along the way and quite at random the four of us got off and our small odyssey was ended. It was a village called Wilsill, in Nidderdale. There were a few houses, a shop, a school and a church and, though we were miles from any town, even here the stream had been dammed to make a static water tank in readiness for the firefighters and the expected bombs. Opposite the bus stop was a farm. My father was a shy man and, though I'm sure there were many larger acts of bravery being done elsewhere that day, to knock at the door of the farm and ask some unknown people to take us in still seems to me to be heroic. Their name was Weatherhead and they did take us in and without question, as people were being taken in all over England that first week of the war.

That night Dad took the bus back to Leeds, my mother weeping as if he were returning to the front, and there at Wilsill we stayed – but for how long? My brother, then aged eight, says it was three weeks; to me, three years younger, it seemed months; but, weeks or months, very happy it was until, once it became plain that nothing was going to happen for a while, we went back home, leaving Byril Farm (which is now, alas, not a farm and has carriage lamps) standing out in my mind as the one episode in my childhood that lived up to the story-books.

'THE TREACHERY OF BOOKS', 1994

JOHN MUIR

THE FIRST SCHOOLDAY was doubtless full of wonders, but I am not able to recall any of them. I remember the servant washing my face and getting soap in my eyes, and Mother hanging a little green bag with my first book in it around my neck so I would not lose it, and its blowing back in the sea-wind like a flag. But before I was sent to school, my grandfather, as I was told, had taught me my letters from shop signs across the street. I can remember distinctly how proud I was when I had spelled my way through the little first book into the second, which seemed large and important, and so on to the third. Going from one book to another formed a grand triumphal advancement, the memories of which still stand out in clear relief.

THE STORY OF MY BOYHOOD AND YOUTH, 1913

JANET FRAME

ONE MORNING, DURING MY FIRST WEEK AT SCHOOL, I sneaked into Mum and Dad's bedroom, opened the top drawer of the duchesse, where the coins 'brought back from the war' were kept, and helped myself to a handful. I then went to Dad's best trousers hanging behind the door, put my hand in the pocket (how cold and slippery the lining!), and took out two coins. Hearing someone coming, I hastily thrust the money under the duchesse and left the room, and later, when the coast was clear, I retrieved my hoard and on my way to school stopped at Heath's store to buy some chewing gum.

Mr Heath looked sternly at me. 'This money won't buy anything,' he said. 'It's Egyptian.'

'I know,' I lied. Then, handing him the money from Dad's pocket, I asked, 'Will this buy me some chewing gum?'

'That's better,' he said, returning yet another of the coins, a farthing.

Armed with a supply of chewing gum, I waited at the door of the Infant Room, a large room with a platform or stage at one end, and double doors opening on to Standard One, and as the children went into the room, I gave each a 'pillow' of chewing gum. Later, Miss

Botting, a woman in a blue costume the same color as the castor-oil bottle, suddenly stopped her teaching and asked, 'Billy Delamare, what are you eating?'

'Chewing gum, Miss Botting.'

'Where did you get it?'

'From Jean Frame, Miss Botting.' (I was known at school as Jean and at home as Nini.)

'Jean Frame, where did you get the chewing gum?'

'From Heath's, Miss Botting.'

'Where did you get the money?'

'My father gave it to me.'

Evidently Miss Botting did not believe me. Suddenly she was determined to get 'the truth' out of me. She repeated her question. 'Where did you get the money? I want the *truth*.'

I repeated my answer, substituting *dad* for *father*.

'Come out here.'

I came out in front of the class.

'Go up on the platform.'

I went up on to the platform.

'Now tell me where you got the money.'

Determinedly I repeated my answer.

Playtime came. The rest of the class went out to play while Miss Botting and I grimly faced each other.

'Tell me the truth,' she said.

I replied, 'Dad gave me the money.'

She sent for Myrtle and Bruddie, who informed her with piping innocence that Dad did not give me the money.

'Yes, he did,' I insisted. 'He called me back when you had both gone to school.'

'He didn't.'

'He did.'

All morning I stayed on the platform. The class continued their reading lessons. I stayed on the platform through lunchtime and into the afternoon, still refusing to confess. I was beginning to feel afraid, instead of defiant, as if I hadn't a friend in the world, and because I knew that Myrtle and Bruddie would 'tell' as soon as they got home, I felt that I never wanted to go home … I held out obstinately until mid-afternoon, when the light was growing thin with masses of dark tiredness showing behind it, and the schoolroom was filled with a nowhere dust, and a small voice answered from the scared me in answer to Miss Botting's repeated question. 'I took the money out of my father's pocket.'

While I'd been lying, I had somehow protected myself; I knew now that I had no protection. I'd been found out as a thief. I was so appalled by my future prospects that I don't remember if Miss Botting strapped me. I know she gave the news to the class, and it spread quickly around the school that I was a thief. Loitering at the school gate, wondering where to go and what to do, I saw Myrtle and Bruddie, carefree as ever, on their way home. I walked slowly along the cocksfoot-bordered road. I don't know when I had learned to read, but I had read and knew the stories in the primer books, and I thought of the story of the fox that sprang out from the side of the road and swallowed the child. No one knew what had happened or where the child had gone, until one day when the fox was walking by, a kind person heard, 'Let me out, let me out!' coming from the fox's belly, whereupon the kind person killed the fox, slit the belly open, and lo, the child emerged whole, unharmed, and was taken by the kind person to live in a wood in a cottage made of coconut ice with a licorice chimney ...

I finally arrived at our place. Myrtle was leaning over the gate. 'Dad knows,' she said, in a matter-of-fact voice. I went up the path. The front door was open and Dad was waiting with the strap in his hand. 'Come into the bedroom,' he said sternly. He administered his usual 'hiding', not excessive, as some children had, but sharp and full of anger that one of his children was a *thief. Thief, thief.* At home and at school I was now called thief.

TO THE IS-LAND, 1982

PATRICK CHAMOISEAU

THE FIRST LESSON WAS AN EXERCISE in ethics: the Teacher told them a story and asked questions. A poor peasant must feed his family, but his entire fortune consists of a single apple tree. This tree has dozens of apples. As luck would have it, however, the tree has grown crookedly. Most of the apples dangle gracefully over the street. The poor man picks this fruit regularly to sell at the market, thereby earning enough to buy milk for his children. It is thanks to these apples that his little ones do not starve. But on some spring days, when he goes to his tree, he finds nothing. Not one apple.

What has happened?

Dubitative silence in the classroom.

The Teacher waited awhile, then pointed to a luckless boy.

'You! What do you think happened?'

'Dunno, *mêssié* ...'

'Someone picked the apples, of course! Apples that did not belong to him. In picking these apples, has this perrson in your opinion, perrforrmed a good deed?'

'Ah nooo, *mêssié* ...'

'Correct. And this perrson – what should we call him?'

'He's a chicken t'ief, *mêssié* ...'

'*Th* ... ief, not t'ief! Apple thief, not chicken thief! A chicken thief steals chickens, an apple thief steals apples. Is it rright to steal?'

'Nooo!' (Unanimous cry from the audience, which thus managed to take a little breather.)

'Is it rright to pick from a trree that does not belong to us?'

'Nooo!'

Moral: *I will not pick apples that do not belong to me.*

And then he wrote it all out on the blackboard.

At the supper table that evening, the little boy recounted this business about the apple tree, but no one seemed impressed. The Papa merely wondered wherever did he think he could pick apples, since they all had to be imported to the island by boat in closed crates and arrived half rotten ... Unfazed by such incomprehension, the little boy topped off his drawings of their home by adding a bunch of apples, red with gigantic fruit, surrounded by policemen wielding huge truncheons.

He also drew tall, pointy castle towers and steeples rising sharply into skies striped with black clouds. He drew a wolf.

SCHOOL DAYS, 1994

LORNA SAGE

S O THE PLAYGROUND WAS HELL: Chinese burns, pinches, slaps and kicks, and horrible games. I can still hear the noise of a thick wet skipping rope slapping the ground. There'd be a big girl each end and you had to leap through without tripping. Joining in was only marginally less awful than being left out. It's said (truly) that most women forget the pain of childbirth; I think that we all forget the pain of being a child at school for the first time, the sheer ineptitude, as though you'll never learn to mark out your own space. It's doubly shaming – shaming to *remember* as well, to feel so sorry for your scabby little self back there in small people's purgatory.

My first days at school were punctuated by fierce contests in the yard, duels almost, complete with spectators, with one girl who might have been expected to be my friend. In fact, she did become my very best friend, years later, when we went round holding hands painfully fast and giggling together hysterically, but for now she was my sworn enemy. Gail (she even had a funny name, like me) had hair in ringlets, green-hazel eyes and pale, clear, slightly olive skin stretched tight and shiny over her muscles, and she was nearly a year older than I was. She'd have won our war in any case, though, since she was so physically confident, in charge of her body even when she was five. Was she already going to dancing lessons? I don't remember. In adult life she became a teacher of physical education and modern dance herself, and even in the days of our adolescent intimacy she would sometimes win an argument by twisting my wrist. I was convinced at the start, anyway, that she was simply better at inhabiting her body than I was – not only better at face-pulling, hair-pulling, pinching, scratching and every sort of violence, but wiry and graceful, so that she made me feel like an unstrung puppet.

Once she'd thoroughly trounced me in public, Gail ignored me and held court in her own corner every playtime.

BAD BLOOD, 2000

ANDREA ASHWORTH

S UMMER GAVE WAY TO RAIN, first spitting, then belting down. Our
mother kissed Laurie [my sister] and me goodbye at the school
gate and wheeled Sarah off in the pram. I spent the mornings
helping other children to read and to spell, since I was ahead of my
year in the Wide Range Reader stories. When I was three, my mother
had saved up to buy a set of Ladybird books and taught me to read
from them. My father had taken a photo of my mother grinning and
pointing at my head bowed over the pages.

When the bell rang for playtime, I would rush out to look for my
sister in the crowded playground. We touched hands for a second,
then ran off with separate groups of coloured faces. My eyes scooted
along the railings: sometimes, our mother would be standing there
on her way home from the shops, peering into the crowd for Laurie
and me.

One time, she stopped to give us some Opal Fruits before she
went home to sleep. We took the shiny yellow packets through the
railings and kissed her hand before she pushed off into the traffic
with Sarah's pram.

Laurie tore into hers. A flock of schoolmates swooped in, sticky
palms and begging smiles. I gave up a green sweet to a red-haired
girl who was taller than me. She was after a pink one, but I was
saving those. The freckles gathered over her eyes when she chewed.

'Why's your mum wear sunglasses all the time, then?' she asked
the playground as well as me. 'Even when it's raining.'

She took a pink sweet after all and sauntered back into the crowd,
her red plait swinging along her spine.

When I got home I tried not to stare at my mother while she
hoovered our trodden green carpet in her dark glasses. Rain tapped
at the windows. She put the kettle on. Auntie Livia came round to
show off the snaps of her new council house. In the photographs, my
mother stood out like a beetle: every shot caught her smiling in
sunglasses. My aunt and she giggled, but when my mother lifted the
shades, her face was puffy with green and purple bruises. Sarah's
dimpled fist reached for the colours; my mother winced.

Behind her teacup, Auntie Livia asked, 'He doesn't hit the girls
too, does he?'

'God, no!' My mother was adamant: 'He'd not lay a finger on them!'

I looked at my mother's swollen eyes. She knew nothing about the night my stepfather had knocked me out with the back of his hand.

Sarah had made a stinking mess in her nappy. My stepfather didn't know how to change it because my mother always made sure she had taken care of everything before she went to work. He pinched his hairy nostrils and rolled the dirty nappy into a ball. When he went to fasten the clean one he couldn't find the pin.

'Where the f—?' Biting his lip, he sent me upstairs to find it.

I couldn't find the pin anywhere. The nappy was loose, Sarah was screaming, but I couldn't find it anywhere. My stepfather came upstairs, spraying spittle.

'Where is it then?'

I couldn't say. My stepfather smacked me across the face, and I fell against the door jamb. My head hit the hinge.

When I woke up, Sarah had stopped screaming, and my stepfather was crouching over me, a chocolate bar in his fist. His black hair was dripping: he had gone out in the rain to buy it. Pressing the Milky Way into my hand, he murmured, 'You're not going to tell your mum, are you?'

My throat was tight, but I ate the chocolate to show that I was not going to tell. My stepfather watched me swallow before he stood up tall again. Then he took the bright blue Milky Way wrapper and buried it in the bin, underneath the potato peelings.

'Whichever you like, Andy, love.' My stepfather ruffled my hair in front of the man who owned the pet shop, smiling and urging me to pick out my favourite fish from the gurgling tanks. At home, in the alcove of our living-room, he had installed an aquarium; a second, living TV. Laurie and I spent hours gazing at it, hypnotized by the hum of the water pump and the sight of shiny backs skittering about: silver, gold, pink, electric blue. We kept our eyes on the black shark fish. They flared red when we tapped on the glass to distract them from nibbling the tiddlers that had hatched out of splurges of eggs. Laurie was fond of the yellow-and-black-striped ones we called bumblebees. Although they seemed stupid, the pink angels were my favourites: I watched their slow, O-shaped mouths kissing, while their pearly bodies shimmered, so pale you could see something pulsing inside.

'Do fish have hearts?' I asked my mother.

'Ask your dad,' she said.

I kept quiet. Presenting me with a tub of fish food, my stepfather had made it my job to sprinkle flakes on the water every morning and night: 'It's up to you to keep the blighters from goin' belly up.'

At first, I couldn't help grinning at the honour, which allowed me to lord it over my little sisters. But I soon found my heart doing dives every time I went near the aquarium. I had to kneel down and press my face close to the glass, willing every last fish to keep on swishing its tail and wafery fins.

ONCE IN A HOUSE ON FIRE, 1998

ABRAHAM COWLEY

As far as my memory can return back into my past life, before I knew, or was capable of guessing what the world, or glories, or business of it were, the natural affections of my soul gave me a secret bent of aversion from them, as some plants are said to turn away from others, by an antipathy imperceptible to themselves, and inscrutable to man's understanding. Even when I was a very young boy at school, instead of running about on holidays and playing with my fellows, I was wont to steal from them and walk into the fields, either alone with a book, or with some one companion, if I could find any of the same temper. I was then, too, so much an enemy to all constraint, that my masters could never prevail on me, by any persuasions or encouragements, to learn without book the common rules of grammar, in which they dispensed with me alone, because they found I made a shift to do the usual exercise out of my own reading and observation …

I was even then acquainted with the poets … and perhaps it was the immature and immoderate love of them which stamped first, or rather engraved, these characters in me. They were like letters cut into the bark of a young tree, which with the tree still grow proportionably. But how this love came to be produced in me so early is a hard question: I believe I can tell the particular little chance that filled my head first with such chimes of verse, as have never since left ringing there. For I remember when I began to read, and to take some pleasure in it, there was wont to lie in my mother's parlour (I know not by what accident, for she herself never in her life read any book but of devotion) but there was wont to lie Spenser's works; this I happened to fall upon, and was infinitely delighted with the stories of the knights, and giants, and monsters, and brave houses, which I found everywhere there (though my understanding had little to do with all this), and by degrees with the tinkling of the rhyme and dance of the numbers, so that I think I had read him all over before I was twelve years old, and was thus made a poet as irremediably as a child is made an eunuch.

'OF MYSELF', 1668

LYNNE TILLMAN

LIKE OTHER OBJECTS REMEMBERED FROM CHILDHOOD, a book is alive, absolute, vague and partial. Dreamlike, memory reassembles (and resembles) the past, a scene or a moment, and always in pieces: a sound, smell, color, shape. The script I write and cast as Memory is almost intangible and unfailingly incomplete. I turn and look at my bookshelves. There's a snapshot of my mother, my sister, and me, I'm the infant in the baby carriage. I keep a memory: I'm little, with my mother, walking over a footbridge; there's another woman and a baby carriage. Something disturbing happens. My mother doesn't remember the scene. She thinks I dreamed it. Is the picture what I remember?

When I was about five I read a seemingly simple tale that was impossible for me to grasp. A little girl has a blanket. The blanket gets a hole. The little girl wants to get rid of the hole so she cuts it out. The hole gets bigger, and she cuts that out. She cuts and cuts and finally the blanket disappears.

I read the story over and again, as if it might change, and at its new end explanation would erupt from its pages. But the story's dire conclusion – the blanket disappears – left me trying to understand why it made sense and didn't make sense. Why couldn't she cut out the hole? The mysterious effect of reading, the immense undecidability of meaning, all this was contained in a book whose title, author and illustrator I can't remember. And no one's ever heard of it. The book is like a memory whose status as an object is in question.

But I remember reading it on my bed, and on the floor of the bedroom I shared with one of my sisters, and sitting in a big chair, in a room whose walls were papered brown, with little blue and yellow flowers. I didn't like brown. Was the radio on? Was I aware of girls and holes? What am I making up?

Years later I wrote a novel in which a character reads the blanket story. By incorporating the lost book into 'my' book I found a way to restore it to some kind of existence outside, and yet within, 'me'. Now as I write about it again the blanket story gains significance and structure, becomes a private myth in my scripted childhood, overwhelming everything else, much as the hole consumed the blanket.

'HOLE STORY', 1992

ANNIE BESANT

A T FIVE YEARS OF AGE I must have read easily, for I remember being often unswathed from a delightful curtain, in which I used to roll myself with a book, and told to 'go and play', while I was still a five-year-old dot. And I had a habit of losing myself so completely in the book that my name might be called in the room where I was, and I never heard it, so that I used to be blamed for wilfully hiding myself, when I had simply been away in fairyland, or lying trembling beneath some friendly cabbage-leaf as a giant went by.

ANNIE BESANT: AN AUTOBIOGRAPHY, 1893

JOHN RUSKIN

M Y MOTHER'S GENERAL PRINCIPLES of first treatment were, to guard me with steady watchfulness from all avoidable pain or danger; and, for the rest, to let me amuse myself as I liked, provided I was neither fretful nor troublesome. But the law was, that I should find my own amusement. No toys of any kind were at first allowed; and the pity of my Croydon aunt for my monastic poverty in this respect was boundless. On one of my birthdays, thinking to overcome my mother's resolution by splendour of temptation, she bought the most radiant Punch and Judy she could find in all the Soho bazaar – as big as a real Punch and Judy, all dressed in scarlet and gold, and that would dance, tied to the leg of a chair. I must have been greatly impressed, for I remember well the look of the two figures, as my aunt herself exhibited their virtues. My mother was obliged to accept them; but afterwards quietly told me it was not right that I should have them; and I never saw them again.

Nor did I painfully wish, what I was never permitted for an instant to hope, or even imagine, the possession of such things as one saw in toy-shops. I had a bunch of keys to play with, as long as I was capable only of pleasure in what glittered and jingled; as I grew older, I had a cart, and a ball; and when I was five or six years old, two boxes of well-cut wooden bricks. With these modest, but, I still think, entirely sufficient possessions, and being always summarily whipped if I cried, did not do as I was bid, or tumbled on the stairs, I soon attained serene and secure methods of life and motion; and could pass my days contentedly in tracing the squares and comparing the colours of my carpet; examining the knots in the wood of the floor, or counting the bricks in the opposite houses; with rapturous intervals of excitement during the filling of the water-cart, through its leathern pipe, from the dripping iron post at the pavement edge; or the still more admirable proceedings of the turncock, when he turned and turned till a fountain sprang up in the middle of the street.

PRAETERITA: OUTLINES OF SCENES AND THOUGHTS PERHAPS WORTHY OF MEMORY IN MY PAST LIFE, 1885–1889

MARLON BRANDO

WHEN I WAS VERY SMALL, I remember carrying a tiny pillow around everywhere, a talisman of childhood. Hugging it, I went to sleep at odd times and odd places, and as I grew older, I even carried it when I started climbing trees and laying claim to empty lots in our neighborhood as my own private kingdom.

It's hard – probably impossible – to sort out the extent to which our experiences as children shape our outlook, behavior and personalities as adults, as opposed to the extent to which genetics are responsible. One has to be a genius to give a simple or absolute answer to anything in this world, and I don't know any tougher question than this one, although I suspect it's a subtle mixture of both. From my mother, I imagine I inherited my instinctual traits, which are fairly highly developed, as well as an affection for music. From my father, I probably acquired my strength of endurance, for he was truly a tough monkey. In later years, he reminded me of a British officer in the Bengal Lancers, perhaps a Victor McLaglen with more refinement. He was a traveling salesman who spent most of his time on the road selling calcium carbonate products – materials from the fossilized remains of ancient marine animals used in building, manufacturing and farming. It was an era when a traveling salesman slipped $5 to a bellboy, who would return with a pint of whiskey and a hooker. Then the house detective got a dollar so that the woman could stay in his room. My pop was such a man.

BRANDO: SONGS MY MOTHER TAUGHT ME, 1994

MARCUS AURELIUS ANTONINUS

1. FROM MY GRANDFATHER VERUS [I learned] good morals and the government of my temper.
2. From the reputation and remembrance of my father, modesty and a manly character.
3. From my mother, piety and beneficence, and abstinence, not only from evil deeds, but even from evil thoughts; and further

simplicity in my way of living, far removed from the habits of the rich.

4. From my great-grandfather, not to have frequented public schools, and to have had good teachers at home, and to know that on such things a man should spend liberally.

THE MEDITATIONS, 167

EUDORA WELTY

LEARNING STAMPS YOU WITH ITS MOMENTS. Childhood's learning is made up of moments. It isn't steady. It's a pulse.

In a children's art class, we sat in a ring on kindergarten chairs and drew three daffodils that had just been picked out of the yard; and while I was drawing, my sharpened yellow pencil and the cup of the yellow daffodil gave off whiffs just alike. That the pencil doing the drawing should give off the same smell as the flower it drew seemed part of the art lesson – as shouldn't it be? Children, like animals, use all their senses to discover the world. Then artists come along and discover it the same way, all over again. Here and there, it's the same world. Or now and then we'll hear from an artist who's never lost it.

In my sensory education I include my physical awareness of the *word*. Of a certain word, that is; the connection it has with what it stands for. At around age six, perhaps, I was standing by myself in our front yard waiting for supper, just at that hour in a late summer day when the sun is already below the horizon and the risen full moon in the visible sky stops being chalky and begins to take on light. There comes the moment, and I saw it then, when the moon goes from flat to round. For the first time it met my eyes as a globe. The word 'moon' came into my mouth as though fed to me out of a silver spoon. Held in my mouth the moon became a word. It had the roundness of a Concord grape Grandpa took off his vine and gave me to suck out of its skin and swallow whole, in Ohio.

ONE WRITER'S BEGINNINGS, 1984

P.T. BARNUM

BEFORE I WAS FIVE YEARS OF AGE I began to accumulate pennies and sixpennies. At the age of six years my grandfather informed me that all my little pieces of coin amounted to one dollar, and if I would go with him and take my money, he would show me something worth having. Placing all my wealth in a pocket handkerchief which was closely wound up and firmly grasped, I started with my grandfather. He took me to the village tavern, then kept by Mr Stiles Wakelee, and approaching the landlord, he said, 'Here, Mr Wakelee, is the richest boy in this part of the country. He has a dollar in cash. I wish you to take his change and give him a silver dollar for it.'

The complaisant landlord took my deposits and presently handed me a silver dollar.

Never have I seen the time (nor shall I ever again) when I felt so rich, so absolutely independent of all the world, as I did when I looked at that monstrous big silver dollar, and felt that it was all my own. Talk of 'cart wheels', there was never one half so large as that silver dollar looked to me. I believed, without the slightest reservation, that this entire earth and all its contents could be purchased by that wonderful piece of bullion, and that it would be a bad bargain at that.

THE LIFE OF P.T. BARNUM, WRITTEN BY HIMSELF, 1855

WILLIAM COWPER

AT SIX YEARS OLD I WAS TAKEN from the nursery, and from the immediate care of a most indulgent mother, and sent to a considerable school in Bedfordshire. Here I had hardships of different kinds to conflict with, which I felt more sensibly, in proportion to the tenderness with which I had been treated at home. But my chief affliction consisted in my being singled out from all the other boys, by a lad about fifteen years of age, as a proper object upon whom he might let loose the cruelty of his temper. I choose to forbear a particular recital of the many acts of barbarity, with which he made it his business continually to persecute me: it will be sufficient to say, that he had, by his savage treatment of me, impressed such a dread of his figure upon my mind, that I well remember being afraid to lift up my eyes upon him, higher than his knees; and that I knew him by his shoe-buckles, better than any other part of his dress. May the Lord pardon him, and may we meet in glory!

One day as I was sitting alone on a bench in the school, melancholy, and almost ready to weep at the recollection of what I had already suffered, and expecting at the same time my tormentor every moment, these words of the Psalmist came into my mind, 'I will not be afraid of what man can do unto me.' I applied this to my own case, with a degree of trust and confidence in God, that would have been no disgrace to a more experienced Christian. Instantly I perceived in myself a briskness of spirits, and a cheerfulness, which I had never before experienced; and took several paces up and down the room with joyful alacrity – *his* gift in whom I trusted. Happy had it been for me, if this early effort towards a dependance on the blessed God, had been frequently repeated by me. But, alas! it was the first and last instance of the kind, between infancy and manhood. The cruelty of this boy, which he had long practised in so secret a manner that no creature suspected it, was at length discovered. He was expelled from the school and I was taken from it.

MEMOIR OF THE EARLY LIFE OF WILLIAM COWPER ESQ, WRITTEN BY HIMSELF, 1767

SARA COLERIDGE

MY YOUNG LIFE IS ALMOST a blank in memory ... till the time of my visit to Allan Bank, when I was six years old. That journey to Grasmere gleams before me as the shadow of a shade. Some goings on of my stay there I remember more clearly. Allan Bank is a large house on a hill overlooking Easedale on one side, and Grasmere on the other. Dorothy, Mr Wordsworth's only daughter, was at this time very picturesque in her appearance, with her long, thick, yellow locks, which were never cut, but curled with papers, a thing which seems much out of keeping with the poetic simplicity of the household. I remember being asked by my father and Miss Wordsworth, the poet's sister, if I did not think her very pretty. 'No,' said I, bluntly; for which I met a rebuff which made me feel as if I was a culprit.

My father's wish it was to have me for a month with him at Grasmere, where he was domesticated with the Wordsworths. He insisted upon it that I became rosier and hardier during my absence from Mama. She did not much like to part with me, and I think my father's motive, at bottom, must have been a wish to fasten my affections on him. I slept with him, and he would tell me fairy stories when he came to bed at twelve and one o'clock. I remember his telling me a wild tale, too, in his study, and my trying to repeat it to the maids afterwards.

I have no doubt there was much enjoyment in my young life at that time, but some of my recollections are tinged with pain. I think my dear father was anxious that I should learn to love him and the Wordsworths and their children, and not cling so exclusively to my mother, and all around me at home. He was therefore much annoyed when, on my mother's coming to Allan Bank, I flew to her, and wished not to be separated from her any more. I remember his shewing displeasure to me, and accusing me of want of affection. I could not understand why. The young Wordsworths came in and caressed him. I sate benumbed; for truly nothing does so freeze affection as the breath of jealousy. The sense that you have done very wrong, or at least given great offence, you know not how or why – that you are dunned for some payment of love or feeling which you know not how to produce or to demonstrate on a sudden, chills the heart, and fills it with perplexity and bitterness. My father reproached me, and contrasted my coldness with the childish caresses of the little Wordsworths. I slunk away, and hid myself in the wood behind the house, and there my friend John, whom at that time I called my future husband, came to seek me.

It was during this stay at Allan Bank that I used to see my father and Mr De Quincey pace up and down the room in conversation. I understood not, nor listened to a word they said, but used to note the handkerchief hanging out of the pocket behind, and long to clutch it. Mr Wordsworth, too, must have been one of the room walkers. How gravely and earnestly used Samuel Taylor Coleridge and William Wordsworth and my uncle Southey also to discuss the affairs of the nation, as if it all came home to their business and bosoms, as if it were their private concern! Men do not canvass these matters now-a-days, I think, quite in the same tone. Domestic concerns absorb their deeper feelings, national ones are treated more as things aloof, the speculative rather than the practical.

My father used to talk to me with much admiration and affection of Sara Hutchinson, Mrs Wordsworth's sister, who resided partly with the Wordsworths, partly with her own brothers. At this time she used to act as my father's amanuensis. She wrote out a great part of the 'Friend' to his dictation. She had fine, long, light brown hair, I think her only beauty, except a fair skin, for her features were plain and contracted, her figure dumpy, and devoid of grace and dignity. She was a plump woman, of little more than five feet. I remember my father talking to me admiringly of her long light locks, and saying how mildly she bore it when the baby pulled them hard in play.

Miss Wordsworth, Mr Wordsworth's sister, of most poetic eye and temper, took a great part with the children. She told us once a pretty story of a primrose, I think, which she spied by the way-side when she went to see me soon after my birth, though that was at Christmas, and how this same primrose was still blooming when she went back to Grasmere.

… My father had particular feelings and fancies about dress, as had my uncle Southey and Mr Wordsworth also. He could not abide the scarlet socks which Edith and I wore at one time. I remember going to him when Mama had just dressed me in a new stuff frock. He took me up, and set me down again without a caress. I thought he disliked the dress; perhaps he was in an uneasy mood. He much liked everything feminine and domestic, pretty and becoming, but not fine-ladyish. My uncle Southey was all for gay, bright, cheerful colours, and even declared he had a taste for the *grand*, in half jest.

Mr Wordsworth loved all that was rich and picturesque, light and free in clothing. A deep Prussian blue or purple was one of his favourite colours for a silk dress. He wished that white dresses were banished, and that our peasantry wore blue and scarlet and other warm colours, instead of sombre, dingy black, which converts a crowd that might be ornamental in the landscape into a swarm of magnified ants. I remember his saying how much better young girls looked of an evening in bare arms, even if the arms themselves were not very lovely, it gave such a lightness to their general air. I think he was looking at Dora when he said this. White dresses he thought cold, a blot and disharmony in any picture, in door or out of door. My father admired white clothing because he looked at it in reference to woman, as expressive of her delicacy and purity, not merely as a component part of a general picture.

My father liked my wearing a cap. He thought it looked girlish and domestic. Dora and I must have been a curious contrast – she with her wild eyes, impetuous movements, and fine, long, floating yellow hair – I with my timid, large blue eyes, slender form, and little fair delicate face, muffled up in lace border and muslin.

'MEMOIR', 1873

NAGUIB MAHFOUZ

I WAS LESS THAN SEVEN YEARS OLD when I said a prayer for the revolution.

One morning I went to my primary school, escorted by the maid. I walked like someone being led off to prison. In my hand was a copybook, in my eyes a look of dejection, in my heart a longing for anarchy. The cold air stung my half-naked legs below my shorts. We found the school closed, with the janitor saying in a stentorian voice, 'Because of the demonstrations there will again be no school today.'

A wave of joy flowed over me and swept me to the shores of happiness.

From the depths of my heart I prayed to God that the revolution might last forever.

ECHOES OF AN AUTOBIOGRAPHY, 1994

SALVADOR DALI

A T THE AGE OF SIX I WANTED TO BE A COOK. At seven I wanted to be Napoleon. And my ambition has been growing steadily ever since.

Stendhal somewhere quotes the remark of an Italian princess who was eating ice-cream with enormous relish one hot evening. 'Isn't it too bad this is not a sin!' she exclaimed. When I was six, it was a sin for me to eat food of any kind in the kitchen. Going into this part of the house was one of the few things categorically forbidden me by my parents. I would stand around for hours, my mouth watering, till I saw my chance to sneak into that place of enchantment; and while the maids stood by and screamed with delight I would snatch a piece of raw meat or a broiled mushroom on which I would nearly choke but which, to me, had the marvelous flavor, the intoxicating quality, that only fear and guilt can impart.

Aside from being forbidden the kitchen I was allowed to do anything I pleased. I wet my bed till I was eight for the sheer fun of it. I was the absolute monarch of the house. Nothing was good enough for me. My father and mother worshipped me. On the day of the Feast of Kings I received among innumerable gifts a dazzling king's costume – a gold crown studded with great topazes and an ermine cape; from that time on I lived almost continually disguised in this costume. When I was chased out of the kitchen by the bustling maids, how often would I stand in the dark hallway glued to one spot – dressed in my kingly robes, my scepter in one hand, and in the other a leather-thonged mattress beater – trembling with rage and possessed by an overwhelming desire to give the maids a good beating.

THE SECRET LIFE OF SALVADOR DALI, 1942

JAMES HOGG

I AM THE SECOND OF FOUR SONS by the same father and mother; namely Robert Hogg and Margaret Laidlaw, and was born on the 25th of January, 1772. My progenitors were all shepherds of this country. My father, like myself, was bred to the occupation of a shepherd, and served in that capacity until his marriage with my mother; about which time, having saved a considerable sum of money, for those days, he took a lease of the farms of Ettrick House and Ettrick Hall. He then commenced dealing in sheep – bought up great numbers, and drove them both to the English and Scottish markets; but, at length, owing to a great fall in the price of sheep, and the absconding of his principal debtor, he was ruined, became bankrupt, every thing was sold by auction, and my parents were turned out of doors without a farthing in the world. I was then in the sixth year of my age, and remember well the distressed and destitute condition we were in. At length the late worthy Mr Brydon, of Crosslee, took compassion upon us; and, taking a short lease of the farm of Ettrick House, placed my father there as his shepherd, and thus afforded him the means of supporting us for a time. This gentleman continued to interest himself in our welfare until the day of his untimely death, when we lost the best friend that we had in the world.

At such an age, it cannot be expected that I should have made great progress in learning. The school-house, however, being almost at our door, I had attended it for a short time, and had the honour of standing at the head of a juvenile class, who read the *Shorter Catechism* and the *Proverbs of Solomon*. At the next Whitsunday after our expulsion from the farm I was obliged to go to service; and being only seven years of age, was hired by a farmer in the neighbourhood to herd a few cows; my wages for the half year being a ewe lamb and a pair of new shoes. Even at that early age my fancy seems to have been a hard neighbour for both judgment and memory. I was wont to strip off my clothes, and run races against time, or rather against myself; and, in the course of these exploits, which I accomplished much to my own admiration, I first lost my plaid, then my bonnet, then my coat, and finally, my hosen; for, as for shoes, I had none. In that naked state did I herd for several days, till a shepherd and a maid-servant were sent to the hills to look for them, and found them all. Next year my parents took me home during the winter quarter, and put me to school with a lad named Ker, who was teaching the children of a neighbouring farmer. Here I advanced so far as to get into the class who read in the Bible. I had likewise, for some time before my quarter was out, tried writing; and had horribly defiled several sheets of paper with copy-lines, every letter of which was nearly an inch in length.

Thus terminated my education. After this I was never another day at any school whatever. In all I had spent about half a year at it. It is true, my former master denied this; and when I was only twenty years of age, said, if he was called on to make oath, he would swear I was never at his school. However, I know I was at it for two or three months, and I do not choose to be deprived of the honour of having attended the school of my native parish; nor yet that old John Beattie should lose the honour of such a scholar. I was again, that very spring, sent away to my old occupation of herding cows. This employment, the worst and lowest known in our country, I was engaged in for several years under sundry masters, till at length I got into the more honourable one of keeping sheep.

'MEMOIR OF THE AUTHOR'S LIFE', 1832

MARY DARBY ROBINSON

As soon as I had learned to read, my great delight was that of learning epitaphs and monumental inscriptions. A story of melancholy import never failed to excite my attention; and before I was seven years old I could correctly repeat Pope's 'Lines to the Memory of an Unfortunate Lady'; Mason's 'Elegy on the Death of the Beautiful Countess of Coventry', and many smaller poems on similar subjects. I had then been attended two years by various masters. Mr Edmund Broadrip taught me music, my father having presented me with one of Kirkman's finest harpsichords, as an incitement to emulation. Even there my natural bent of mind evinced itself. The only melody which pleased me was that of the mournful and touching kind. Two of my earliest favourites were the celebrated ballad by Gay, beginning, 'Twas when the sea was roaring', and the simple pathetic stanzas of 'The Heavy Hours', by the poet Lord Lyttelton. These, though nature had given me but little voice, I could at seven years of age sing so pathetically that my mother, to the latest hour of her life, never could bear to hear the latter of them repeated. They reminded her of sorrows in which I have since painfully learned to sympathize.

The early hours of boarding-school study I passed under the tuition of the Misses More, sisters to the lady of that name ... The education of their young pupils was undertaken by the five sisters. 'In my mind's eye', I see them now before me; while every circumstance of those early days is minutely and indelibly impressed upon my memory.

I remember the first time I ever was present at a dramatic representation: it was the benefit of that great actor [Mr Powel] who was proceeding rapidly toward the highest paths of fame, when death dropped the oblivious curtain, and closed the scene for ever. The part which he performed was King Lear; his wife, afterward Mrs Fisher, played Cordelia, but not with sufficient *éclat* to render the profession an object for her future exertions. The whole school attended, Mr Powel's two daughters being then pupils of the Misses More. Mrs John Kemble, then Miss P. Hopkins, was also one of my schoolfellows, as was the daughter of Mrs Palmer, formerly Miss Pritchard, and afterward Mrs Lloyd. I mention these circumstances merely to prove that memory does not deceive me.

MEMOIRS OF THE LATE MRS ROBINSON, WRITTEN BY HERSELF, 1801

FREDERICK DOUGLASS

MY MOTHER WAS NAMED HARRIET BAILEY. She was the daughter of Isaac and Betsey Bailey, both colored, and quite dark. My mother was of a darker complexion than either my grandmother or grandfather. My father was a white man. He was admitted to be such by all I ever heard speak of my parentage. The opinion was also whispered that my master was my father; but of the correctness of this opinion, I know nothing; the means of knowing was withheld from me. My mother and I were separated when I was but an infant – before I knew her as my mother. It is a common custom, in the part of Maryland from which I ran away, to part children from their mothers at a very early age. Frequently, before the child has reached its twelfth month, its mother is taken from it, and hired out on some farm a considerable distance off, and the child is placed under the care of an old woman, too old for field labour. For what this separation is done, I do not know, unless it be to hinder the development of the child's affection toward its mother, and to blunt and destroy the natural affection of the mother for the child. This is the inevitable result.

I never saw my mother, to know her as such, more than four or five times in my life; and each of these times was very short in duration, and at night. She was hired by a Mr Stewart, who lived about twelve miles from my home. She made her journeys to see me in the night, traveling the whole distance on foot, after the performance of her day's work. She was a field hand, and a whipping is the penalty of not being in the field at sunrise, unless a slave has special permission from his or her master to the contrary – a permission which they seldom get, and one that gives to him that gives it the proud name of being a kind master. I do not recollect of ever seeing my mother by the light of day. She was with me in the night. She would lie down with me, and get me to sleep, but long before I waked she was gone. Very little communication ever took place between us. Death soon ended what little we could have while she lived, and with it her hardships and suffering. She died when I was about seven years old, on one of my master's farms, near Lee's Mill. I was not allowed to be present during her illness, at her death, or burial. She was gone long before I knew any thing about it. Never having enjoyed, to any considerable extent, her soothing presence, her tender and watchful care, I received the tidings of her death with much the same emotions I should have probably felt at the death of a stranger.

Called thus suddenly away, she left me without the slightest intimation of who my father was. The whisper that my master was my father, may or may not be true; and, true or false, it is of but little consequence to my purpose whilst the fact remains, in all its glaring odiousness, that slaveholders have ordained, and by law established, that the children of slave women shall in all cases follow the condition of their mothers; and this is done too obviously to administer to their own lusts, and make a gratification of their wicked desires profitable as well as pleasurable; for by this cunning arrangement, the slaveholder, in cases not a few, sustains to his slaves the double relation of master and father.

I know of such cases; and it is worthy of remark that such slaves invariably suffer greater hardships, and have more to contend with, than others. They are, in the first place, a constant offence to their mistress. She is ever disposed to find fault with them; they can seldom do any thing to please her; she is never better pleased than when she sees them under the lash, especially when she suspects her husband of showing to his mulatto children favors which he withholds from his black slaves. The master is frequently compelled to sell this class of his slaves, out of deference to the feelings of his white wife; and, cruel as the deed may strike any one to be, for a man to sell his own children to human flesh-mongers, it is often the dictate of humanity for him to do so; for, unless he does this, he must not only whip them himself, but must stand by and see one white son tie up his brother, of but few shades darker complexion than himself, and ply the gory lash to his naked back; and if he lisp one word of disapproval, it is set down to his parental partiality, and only makes a bad matter worse, both for himself and the slave whom he would protect and defend.

Every year brings with it multitudes of this class of slaves. It was doubtless in consequence of a knowledge of this fact, that one great statesman of the south predicted the downfall of slavery by the inevitable laws of population. Whether this prophecy is ever fulfilled or not, it is nevertheless plain that a very different-looking class of people are springing up at the south, and are now held in slavery, from those originally brought to this country from Africa; and if their increase do no other good, it will do away the force of the argument, that God cursed Ham, and therefore American slavery is right. If the lineal descendants of Ham are alone to be scripturally enslaved, it is certain that slavery at the south must soon become unscriptural; for thousands are ushered into the world, annually, who, like myself, owe their existence to white fathers, and those fathers most frequently their own masters.

NARRATIVE OF THE LIFE OF FREDERICK DOUGLASS, AN AMERICAN SLAVE, 1845

ANTHONY TROLLOPE

M Y TWO ELDER BROTHERS HAD BEEN SENT as day boarders to
Harrow School from the bigger house, and may probably
have been received among the aristocratic crowd, not on equal
terms, because a day boarder at Harrow in those days was never so
received, but at any rate as other day boarders. I don't suppose that
they were well treated, but I doubt whether they were subjected to
the ignominy which I endured. I was only seven, and I think that
boys at seven are now spared among their more considerate seniors.
I was never spared – and was not even allowed to run to and fro
between our house and the school without a daily purgatory. No
doubt my appearance was against me. I remember well, when I was
still the junior boy in the school, Dr Butler, the headmaster, stopping
me in the street, and asking me with all the clouds of Jove upon his
brow, and all the thunder in his voice, whether it was possible that
the Harrow School was disgraced by so disreputably dirty a little
boy as I! Oh what I felt at that moment! But I could not look my
feelings. I do not doubt that I was dirty – but I think that he was
cruel. He must have known me, had he seen me as he was wont to
see me, for he was in the habit of flogging me constantly. Perhaps he
did not recognize me by my face.

At this time I was three years at Harrow; and as far as I can
remember, I was the junior boy in the school when I left it.

AN AUTOBIOGRAPHY, 1883

MICHEL DE MONTAIGNE

T HE FIRST TASTE I HAD FOR BOOKS came from pleasure I took in
the fables of Ovid's *Metamorphoses*. For when I was about
seven or eight years old, I would steal away from all other
pleasures to read them since this was my mother tongue and since
it was the easiest book that I knew and the best suited by its
content to my tender age. For as for the Lancelots of the Lake, the
Amadises, the Huons of Bordeaux, and such trashy books on
which children waste their time, I did not know even their names,

nor do I yet know their substance, so exact was my discipline. This made me more careless in the study of my other prescribed lessons. Here I happened very opportunely to have to do with an understanding tutor who knew enough to connive cleverly at this escapade of mine and others of the same nature. For by this means I ran straight through Virgil's *Aeneid*, and then Terence, and then Plautus, and some Italian comedies, allured always by the pleasantness of the subject. Had he been so foolish as to break up this activity, I believe I should have brought nothing away from school but a hatred of books, as almost all our noblemen do. He handled himself cleverly in that business. Pretending to see nothing, he whetted my appetite, allowing me to devour these books only on the sly and holding me gently at my job on the regular studies. For the chief qualities my father sought in those whom he put in charge of me were affability of manners and good humor. For my own character had no other vice but listlessness and laziness. The danger was not that I should do ill, but that I should do nothing. Nobody predicted that I should be wicked, but only useless; they foresaw idleness, but no viciousness.

'OF THE EDUCATION OF CHILDREN', 1580

GERTRUDE SIMMONS BONNIN

ALWAYS AFTER THESE CONFINING LESSONS I was wild with surplus spirits, and found joyous relief in running loose in the open again. Many a summer afternoon, a party of four or five of my playmates roamed over the hills with me. We each carried a light sharpened rod about four feet long, with which we pried up certain sweet roots. When we had eaten all the choice roots we chanced upon, we shouldered our rods and strayed off into patches of a stalky plant under whose yellow blossoms we found little crystal drops of gum. Drop by drop we gathered this nature's rockcandy, until each of us could boast of a lump the size of a small bird's egg. Soon satiated with its woody flavor, we tossed away our gum to return again to the sweet roots.

I remember well how we used to exchange our necklaces,

beaded belts, and sometimes even our moccasins. We pretended to offer them as gifts to one another. We delighted in impersonating our own mothers. We talked of things we had heard them say in their conversations. We imitated their various manners, even to the inflection of their voices. In the lap of the prairie we seated ourselves upon our feet; and leaning our painted cheeks in the palms of our hands, we rested our elbows on our knees, and bent forward as old women were most accustomed to do.

While one of us was telling of some heroic deed recently done by a near relative, the rest of us listened attentively, and exclaimed in undertones, 'Han! Han!' (Yes! Yes!) whenever the speaker paused for breath, or sometimes for our sympathy. As the discourse became more thrilling, according to our ideas, we raised our voices in these interjections. In these impersonations our parents were led to say only those things that were in common favor.

No matter how exciting a tale we might be rehearsing, the mere shifting of a cloud shadow in the landscape nearby was sufficient to change our impulses; and soon we were all chasing the great shadows that played among the hills. We shouted and whooped in the chase; laughing and calling to one another, we were like little sportive nymphs on that Dakota sea of rolling green.

On one occasion, I forgot the cloud shadow in a strange notion to catch up with my own shadow. Standing straight and still, I began to glide after it, putting out one foot cautiously. When, with the greatest care, I set my foot in advance of myself, my shadow crept onward too. Then again I tried it; this time with the other foot. Still again my shadow escaped me. I began to run; and away flew my shadow, always just a step beyond me. Faster and faster I ran, setting my teeth and clenching my fists, determined to overtake my own fleet shadow. But ever swifter it glided before me, while I was growing breathless and hot. Slackening my speed, I was greatly vexed that my shadow should check its pace also. Daring it to the utmost, as I thought, I sat down upon a rock imbedded in the hillside.

So! My shadow had the impudence to sit down beside me!

Now my comrades caught up with me, and began to ask why I was running away so fast.

'Oh, I was chasing my shadow! Didn't you ever do that?' I inquired, surprised that they should not understand.

They planted their moccasined feet firmly upon my shadow to stay it, and I arose. Again my shadow slipped away, and moved as often as I did. Then we gave up trying to catch my shadow.

Before this peculiar experience I have no distinct memory of having recognised any vital bond between myself and my own shadow. I never gave it an afterthought.

Returning our borrowed belts and trinkets, we rambled homeward. That evening, as on other evenings, I went to sleep over my legends.

IMPRESSIONS OF AN INDIAN CHILDHOOD, 1900

ANDREW CARNEGIE

IN AN INCAUTIOUS MOMENT my parents had promised that I should never be sent to school until I asked leave to go. This promise I afterward learned began to give them considerable uneasiness because as I grew up I showed no disposition to ask. The schoolmaster, Mr Robert Martin, was applied to and induced to take some notice of me. He took me upon an excursion one day with some of my companions who attended school, and great relief was experienced by my parents when one day soon afterward I came and asked for permission to go to Mr Martin's school. I need not say the permission was duly granted. I had then entered upon my eighth year, which subsequent experience leads me to say is quite early enough for any child to begin attending school.

The school was a perfect delight to me, and if anything occurred which prevented my attendance I was unhappy. This happened every now and then because my morning duty was to bring water from the well at the head of Moodie Street. The supply was scanty and irregular. Sometimes it was not allowed to run until late in the morning and a score of old wives were sitting around, the turn of each having been previously secured through the night by placing a worthless can in the line. This, as might be expected, led to numerous contentions in which I would not be put down even by these venerable old dames. I earned the reputation of being 'an awfu' laddie'. In this way I probably developed the strain of argumentativeness, or perhaps combativeness, which has always remained with me.

In the performance of these duties I was often late for school, but the master, knowing the cause, forgave the lapses. In the same connection I may mention that I had often the shop errands to run after school, so that in looking back upon my life I have the satisfaction of feeling that I became useful to my parents even at the early age of ten. Soon after that the accounts of the various people who dealt with the shop were entrusted to my keeping so that I became acquainted, in a small way, with business affairs even in childhood.

One cause of misery there was, however, in my school experience. The boys nicknamed me 'Martin's pet', and sometimes called out that dreadful epithet to me as I passed along the street. I did not know all that it meant, but it seemed to me a term of the utmost opprobrium, and I know that it kept me from responding as freely as I should otherwise have done to that excellent teacher, my only schoolmaster, to whom I owe a debt of gratitude which I regret I never had opportunity to do more than acknowledge before he died.

AUTOBIOGRAPHY OF ANDREW CARNEGIE, 1920

INGMAR BERGMAN

THE WEEKS BEFORE CHRISTMAS. The immensely rich Aunt Anna's uniformed Mr Jansson had already delivered a quantity of presents. As usual, they were placed in the Christmas present basket in the cupboard under the stairs. One parcel in particular aroused my excited curiosity. It was brown and angular with 'Forsners' on the wrapping paper. Forsners was a photographic store in Hamngatan which sold not only cameras but real cinematographs.

More than anything else, I longed for a cinematograph. The year before I had been to the cinema for the first time and seen a film about a horse. I think it was called *Black Beauty* and was based on a famous book. The film was on at the Sture cinema and we sat in the front row of the circle. To me, it was the beginning. I was overcome with a fever that has never left me. The silent shadows turned their pale faces towards me and spoke in audible voices to my most secret feelings. Sixty years have gone by and nothing has changed; the fever is the same.

Later that autumn, I went to see a school friend who had a cinematograph and a few films, and he put on a dutiful performance for [my friend] Tippan and me. I was allowed to wind the machine while our host necked with Tippan.

Christmas was an explosion of amusements. Mother directed it all with a firm hand, and there must have been considerable organization behind this orgy of hospitality, meals, visiting relatives, Christmas presents and church arrangements.

At home, Christmas Eve was a fairly quiet affair which began with Christmas prayers in church at five o'clock, then a happy but restrained meal, the lighting of the candles on the tree, the reading of the Christmas story and early bed. (We had to be up for early mass the next day, in those days really early.) No presents were handed out, but the evening was joyful, an exciting prelude to the festivities of Christmas Day. After early church service with lighted candles and trumpets came Christmas breakfast. By then Father had carried out his professional duties and had exchanged his cassock for his smoking jacket. He was in his most merry mood and made an improvised speech in verse to our guests, sang a song composed for the occasion, toasted everyone in schnapps, gave imitations of his colleagues and made everyone laugh. I sometimes think about his cheerful light-heartedness, his kindness, friendliness and extravagance, everything that had been concealed behind darkness, severity, brutality and remoteness. I think that in memory I have often done my father an injustice.

After breakfast, everyone went to bed for a few hours. The internal domestic routine must have gone on working, for at two o'clock, just as dusk was falling, afternoon coffee was served. We had open house for anyone who cared to come and wish the parsonage a happy Christmas. Several friends were practising musicians and part of the afternoon festivities was usually an improvised concert. Then the sumptuous culmination of Christmas Day approached: the evening meal. This was held in our spacious kitchen, where the social hierarchy was temporarily set aside. All the food was laid out on a serving table and covered working surfaces, and the distribution of Christmas gifts took place at the dining-room table. The baskets were carried in, Father officiated with a cigar and glass of sweet liqueur, the presents were handed out, verses were read aloud, applauded and commented on; no presents without verses.

That was when the cinematograph affair occurred. My brother was the one who got it.

At once I began to howl. I was ticked off and disappeared under the table, where I raged on and was told to be quiet immediately. I rushed off to the nursery, swearing and cursing, considered running away, then finally fell asleep exhausted by grief.

The party went on.

Later in the evening I woke up. Gertrud was singing a folk song downstairs and the nightlight was glowing. A transparency of the Nativity scene and the shepherds at prayer was glimmering faintly on the tall chest-of-drawers. Among my brother's other Christmas presents on the white gate-legged table was the cinematograph, with its crooked chimney, its beautifully shaped brass lens and its rack for the film loops.

I made a swift decision. I woke my brother and proposed a deal. I offered him my hundred tin soldiers in exchange for the cinematograph. As Dag possessed a huge army and was always involved in war games with his friends, an agreement was made to the satisfaction of both parties.

The cinematograph was mine.

It was not a complicated machine. The source of light was a paraffin lamp and the crank was attached with a cogwheel and a Maltese cross. At the back of the metal box was a simple reflecting mirror, behind the lens a slot for coloured lantern slides. The apparatus also included a square purple box which contained some glass slides and a sepia-coloured film strip (35mm). This was about three metres long and glued into a loop. Information on the lid stated that the film was called *Mrs Holle*. Who this Mrs Holle was no one knew, but later it turned out that she was the popular equivalent of the Goddess of Love in Mediterranean countries.

The next morning I retreated into the spacious wardrobe in the nursery, placed the cinematograph on a sugar crate, lit the paraffin lamp and directed the beam of light on to the whitewashed wall. Then I loaded the film.

A picture of a meadow appeared on the wall. Asleep in the meadow was a young woman apparently wearing national costume. *Then I turned the handle!* It is impossible to describe this. I can't find words to express my excitement. But at any time I can recall the smell of the hot metal, the scent of mothballs and dust in the wardrobe, the feel of the crank against my hand. I can see the trembling rectangle on the wall.

I turned the handle and the girl woke up, sat up, slowly got up, stretched her arms out, swung round and disappeared to the right. If I went on turning, she would again lie there, then make exactly the same movements all over again.

She was moving.

THE MAGIC LANTERN, 1987

JAMES BALDWIN

J OAN CRAWFORD'S STRAIGHT, NARROW, AND LONELY BACK. We are following her through the corridors of a moving train. She is looking for someone, or she is trying to escape from someone. She is eventually intercepted by, I think, Clark Gable.

I am fascinated by the movement on, and of, the screen, that movement which is something like the heaving and swelling of the sea (though I have not yet been to the sea): and which is also something like the light which moves on, and especially beneath, the water.

I am about seven. I am with my mother, or my aunt. The movie is *Dance, Fools, Dance.*

I don't remember the film. A child is far too self-centered to relate to any dilemma which does not, somehow, relate to him – to his own evolving dilemma. The child escapes into what he would like his situation to be, and I certainly did not wish to be a fleeing fugitive on a moving train; and, also, with quite another part of my mind, I was aware that Joan Crawford was a white lady. Yet, I remember being sent to the store sometime later, and a colored woman, who, to me, looked exactly like Joan Crawford, was buying something. She was so incredibly beautiful – she seemed to be wearing the sunlight, rearranging it around her from time to time, with a movement of one hand, with a movement of her head, and with her smile – that when she paid the man and started out of the store, I started out behind her. The storekeeper, who knew me, and others in the store who knew my mother's little boy (and who also knew my Miss Crawford!) laughed and called me back. Miss Crawford also laughed and looked down at me with so beautiful a smile that I was not even embarrassed. Which was rare for me.

'THE DEVIL FINDS WORK', 1976

ISADORA DUNCAN

A S MY MOTHER HAD DIVORCED my father when I was a baby in arms, I had never seen him. Once, when I asked one of my aunts whether I had ever had a father, she replied, 'Your father was a demon who ruined your mother's life.' After that I always imagined him as a demon in a picture book, with horns and a tail, and when other children at school spoke of their fathers, I kept silent.

When I was seven years old, we were living in two very bare rooms on the third floor, and one day I heard the front door bell ring and, on going out into the hall to answer it, I saw a very good-looking gentleman in a top hat who said:

'Can you direct me to Mrs Duncan's apartment?'

'I am Mrs Duncan's little girl,' I replied.

'Is this my Princess Pug?' said the strange gentleman. (That had been his name for me when I was a baby.)

And suddenly he took me in his arms and covered me with tears and kisses. I was very much astonished at this proceeding and asked him who he was. To which he replied with tears, 'I am your father.'

I was delighted at this piece of news and rushed in to tell the family.

'There is a man out there who says he is my father.'

My mother rose, very white and agitated, and, going into the next room, locked the door behind her. One of my brothers hid under the bed and the other retired to a cupboard, while my sister had a violent fit of hysterics.

'Tell him to go away, tell him to go away,' they cried.

I was much amazed, but being a very polite little girl, I went into the hall and said:

'The family are rather indisposed, and cannot receive today,' at which the stranger took me by the hand and asked me to come for a walk with him.

We descended the stairs into the street, I trotting by his side in a state of bewildered enchantment to think that this handsome gentleman was my father, and that he had not got horns and a tail, as I had always pictured him.

He took me to an ice-cream parlour and stuffed me with ice-cream and cakes. I returned to the family in a state of the wildest excitement and found them in a terribly depressed condition.

'He is a perfectly charming man and he is coming tomorrow to give me more ice-cream,' I told them.

But the family refused to see him, and after a time he returned to his other family in Los Angeles.

MY LIFE, 1927

EDMUND GOSSE

THE LIFE OF A CHILD IS SO BRIEF, its impressions are so illusory and fugitive, that it is as difficult to record its history as it would be to design a morning cloud sailing before the wind. It is short, as we count shortness in after years, when the drag of lead pulls down to earth the foot that used to flutter with a winged impetuosity, and to float with the pulse of Hermes. But in memory, my childhood was long, long with interminable hours, hours with the pale cheek pressed against the windowpane, hours of mechanical and repeated lonely 'games', which had lost their savour, and were kept going by sheer inertness. Not unhappy, not fretful, but long – long, long. It seems to me, as I look back to the life in the motherless Islington house, as I resumed it in that slow eighth year of my life, that time had ceased to move. There was a whole age between one tick of the eight-day clock in the hall, and the next tick. When the milkman went his rounds in our grey street, with his eldritch scream over the top of each set of area railings, it seemed as though he would never disappear again. There was no past and no future for me, and the present felt as though it were sealed up in a Leyden jar. Even my dreams were interminable, and hung stationary from the nightly sky.

At this time, the street was my theatre, and I spent long periods, as I have said, leaning against the window. I feel now that coldness of the pane, and the feverish heat that was produced, by contrast, in the orbit round the eye. Now and then amusing things happened.

FATHER AND SON, 1907

GIACOMO CASANOVA

At THE BEGINNING OF AUGUST in the year 1733, the organ of my memory developed. I was eight years and four months old then. I remember nothing of what might have happened to me before that time. Here is the event.

I was standing in the corner of a room, bent towards the wall, holding my head, and staring intently at the blood that was streaming copiously out of my nose onto the floor. Marzia, my grandmother, whose favourite I was, came to me, washed my face with cool water, and without anyone else in the house knowing about it, made me climb into a gondola with her and took me to Murano. This is a very populated island half an hour away from Venice.

Stepping out of the gondola, we went inside a run-down shack where we found an old woman sitting on a pallet bed, holding a black cat in her arms, with five or six more surrounding her. She was a sorceress. The two old women had a long conversation about me. At the end of their chat – in the local dialect spoken in Friuli – the sorceress, having received from my grandmother a ducat of silver, opened a chest, took me in her arms, put me inside and shut me in, telling me not to be scared. It would have been the best way to terrify me if I'd had a bit of spirit; but I was stunned into silence. I stayed still, holding my handkerchief to my nose because I was still bleeding, indifferent to the racket that I heard outside. I heard, by turns, laughter, crying, shouting, singing and banging on the chest. It was all the same to me. Finally, I was pulled out, my bleeding stopped. This extraordinary woman, having caressed me a hundred times, undressed me, put me on the bed, cooked up some drugs, collected the smoke thye gave off in a sheet, wrapped me up in it, recited some spells over me, unwrapped me afterwards, and gave me five lozenges to eat that were very delicious. Suddenly, she rubbed my temples and my skull with a sweet-smelling ointment, and she put my clothes back on. She told me that my bleeding would always subside, provided that I did not tell anyone what she had done to cure me, and she suggested to me that on the contrary I would lose all my blood and die, if I dared to reveal her mysteries to anyone. Having instructed me in this, she told me that a charming lady, upon whom my happiness depended, would come and visit me the coming night, if I had the strength not to tell anyone that I had received this visit. We left and returned home.

I had hardly gone to bed before I fell asleep, without even remembering the lovely visit that I was meant to receive; but having woken up some hours later, I saw, or thought I saw, a stunning woman in a *panier* dress coming down the chimney; she was dressed in superb fabrics and wearing on her head a crown studded with precious stones on her head that seemed to sparkle with fire. With slow steps and a majestic and soft air, she came to sit on my bed. She took from her pocket some small boxes, which she emptied over my head while murmuring some words. Having spoken to me for a long time, in words I could not understand at all, and having kissed me, she left the way she came; and I fell asleep again.

The next day, before she came to my bed to dress me, my grandmother made me stay silent. She intimated that I would die if I dared relate what must have happened to me in the night. This sentence, uttered by the only woman who had the absolute upper hand over me, and who had made me accustomed to obeying her every order blindly, was the reason I remembered the vision, and by sealing it, I placed it in the most secret corner of my nascent memory. Anyway, I did not feel tempted to recount this event to anyone. I didn't know others might find it interesting or whom to tell. My illness made me dreary, and not at all fun; everyone felt sorry for me and left me alone; they thought my time on earth would be short. My father and my mother never spoke to me.

After the trip to Murano and the nocturnal visit by the fairy, I still bled, but less and less; and my memory developed little by little; in less than a month I learned to read. It would be ridiculous to attribute my cure to these two extravagances, but it would also be wrong to say that they could not have contributed to it. As far as the apparition of the beautiful queen is concerned, I have always thought it was a dream, unless someone staged this masquerade for me on purpose; even so, the remedies for the most serious illnesses cannot always be found in the pharmacy. Every day some phenomenon demonstrates to us our ignorance. I believe that it is for this reason that nothing is so rare as a wise man with a mind completely free of superstition.

STORY OF MY LIFE, 1789–1792

GEORGE ORWELL

S OON AFTER I ARRIVED AT CROSSGATES (not immediately, but after a week or two, just when I seemed to be settling into the routine of school life) I began wetting my bed. I was now aged eight, so that this was a reversion to a habit which I must have grown out of at least four years earlier.

Nowadays, I believe, bed-wetting in such circumstances is taken for granted. It is a normal reaction in children who have been removed from their homes to a strange place. In those days, however, it was looked on as a disgusting crime which the child committed on purpose and for which the proper cure was a beating. For my part I did not need to be told it was a crime. Night after night I prayed, with a fervour never previously attained in my prayers, 'Please God, do not let me wet my bed! Oh, please God, do not let me wet my bed!' but it made remarkably little difference. Some nights the thing happened, others not. There was no volition about it, no consciousness. You did not properly speaking *do* the deed: you merely woke up in the morning and found that the sheets were wringing wet.

After the second or third offence I was warned that I should be beaten next time, but I received the warning in a curiously roundabout way. One afternoon, as we were filing out from tea, Mrs Simpson, the headmaster's wife, was sitting at the head of one of the tables, chatting with a lady of whom I know nothing, except that she was on an afternoon's visit to the school. She was an intimidating, masculine-looking person wearing a riding habit, or something that I took to be a riding habit. I was just leaving the room when Mrs Simpson called me back, as though to introduce me to the visitor.

Mrs Simpson was nicknamed Bingo, and I shall call her by that name for I seldom think of her by any other. (Officially, however, she was addressed as Mum, probably a corruption of the 'Ma'am' used by public school boys to their housemasters' wives.) She was a stocky square-built woman with hard red cheeks, a flat top to her head, prominent brows and deepset, suspicious eyes. Although a great deal of the time she was full of false heartiness, jollying one along with mannish slang ('*Buck* up, old chap!' and so forth), and even using one's Christian name, her eyes never lost their anxious, accusing look. It was very difficult to look her in the face without feeling guilty, even at moments when one was not guilty of anything in particular.

'Here is a little boy,' said Bingo, indicating me to the strange lady, 'who wets his bed every night. Do you know what I am going to do if you wet your bed again?' she added, turning to me. 'I am going to get the Sixth Form to beat you.'

The strange lady put on an air of being inexpressibly shocked, and exclaimed 'I-should-think-so!' And here occurred one of those wild, almost lunatic misunderstandings which are part of the daily experience of childhood. The Sixth Form was a group of older boys who were selected as having 'character' and were empowered to beat smaller boys. I had not yet learned of their existence, and I misheard the phrase 'the Sixth Form' as 'Mrs Form'. I took it as referring to the strange lady – I thought, that is, that her name was Mrs Form. It was an improbable name, but a child has no judgement in such matters. I imagined, therefore, that it was she who was to be deputed to beat me. It did not strike me as strange that this job should be turned over to a casual visitor in no way connected with the school. I merely assumed that 'Mrs Form' was a stern disciplinarian who enjoyed beating people (somehow her appearance seemed to bear this out) and I had an immediate terrifying vision of her arriving for the occasion in full riding kit and armed with a hunting whip. To this day I can feel myself almost swooning with shame as I stood, a very small, round-faced boy in short corduroy knickers, before the two women. I could not speak. I felt that I should die if 'Mrs Form' were to beat me. But my dominant feeling was not fear or even resentment: it was simply shame because one more person, and that a woman, had been told of my disgusting offence.

A little later, I forget how, I learned that it was not after all 'Mrs Form' who would do the beating. I cannot remember whether it was that very night that I wetted my bed again, but at any rate I did wet it again quite soon. Oh, the despair, the feeling of cruel injustice, after all my prayers and resolutions, at once again waking between the clammy sheets! There was no chance of hiding what I had done. The grim statuesque matron, Daphne by name, arrived in the dormitory specially to inspect my bed. She pulled back the clothes, then drew herself up, and the dreaded words seemed to come rolling out of her like a peal of thunder:

'REPORT YOURSELF to the headmaster after breakfast!'

I do not know how many times I heard that phrase during my early years at Crossgates. It was only very rarely that it did not mean a beating. The words always had a portentous sound in my ears, like muffled drums or the words of the death sentence.

When I arrived to report myself, Bingo was doing something or other at the long shiny table in the ante-room to the study. Her uneasy eyes searched me as I went past. In the study Mr Simpson, nicknamed Sim, was waiting. Sim was a round-shouldered curiously oafish-looking man, not large but shambling in gait, with a chubby face which was like that of an overgrown baby, and which was capable of good humour. He knew, of course, why I had been sent to him, and had already taken a bone-handled riding crop out of the cupboard, but it was part of the punishment of reporting yourself that you had to proclaim your offence with your own lips. When I had said my say, he read me a short but pompous lecture, then seized me by the scruff of the neck, twisted me over and began beating me with the riding crop. He had a habit of continuing his lecture while he flogged you, and I remember the words 'you dir-ty lit-tle boy' keeping time with the blows. The beating did not hurt (perhaps as it was the first time, he was not hitting me very hard), and I walked out feeling very much better. The fact that the beating had not hurt was a sort of victory and partially wiped out the shame of the bed-wetting. I was even incautious enough to wear a grin on my face. Some small boys were hanging about in the passage outside the door of the ante-room.

'D'you get the cane?'

'It didn't hurt,' I said proudly.

Bingo had heard everything. Instantly her voice came screaming after me:

'Come here! Come here this instant! What was that you just said?'

'I said it didn't hurt,' I faltered out.

'How dare you say a thing like that? Do you think that is a proper thing to say? Go in and REPORT YOURSELF AGAIN!'

This time Sim laid on in real earnest. He continued for a length of time that frightened and astonished me – about five minutes, it seemed – ending up by breaking the riding crop. The bone handle went flying across the room.

'Look what you've made me do!' he said furiously, holding up the broken crop.

I had fallen into a chair, weakly snivelling. I remember that this was the only time throughout my boyhood when a beating actually reduced me to tears, and curiously enough I was not even now crying because of the pain. The second beating had not hurt very much either. Fright and shame seemed to have anaesthetized me. I was crying partly because I felt that this was expected of me, partly from genuine repentance, but partly also because of a deeper grief which is peculiar to childhood and not easy to convey: a sense of desolate loneliness and helplessness, of being locked up not only in a hostile world but in a world of good and evil where the rules were such that it was actually not possible for me to keep them.

I knew that bed-wetting was (a) wicked and (b) outside my control. The second fact I was personally aware of, and the first I did not question. It was possible, therefore, to commit a sin without knowing that you committed it, without wanting to commit it, and without being able to avoid it. Sin was not necessarily something that you did: it might be something that happened to you. I do not want to claim that this idea flashed into my mind as a complete novelty at this very moment, under the blows of Sim's cane: I must have had glimpses of it even before I left home, for my early childhood had not been altogether happy. But at any rate this was the great, abiding lesson of my boyhood: that I was in a world where it was *not possible* for me to be good. And the double beating was a turning-point, for it brought home to me for the first time the harshness of the environment into which I had been flung. Life was more terrible, and I was more wicked, than I had imagined. At any rate, as I sat on the edge of a chair in Sim's study, with not even the self-possession to stand up while he stormed at me, I had a conviction of sin and folly and weakness, such as I do not remember to have felt before.

In general, one's memories of any period must necessarily weaken as one moves away from it. One is constantly learning new facts, and old ones have to drop out to make way for them. At twenty I could have written the history of my schooldays with an accuracy which would be quite impossible now. But it can also happen that one's memories grow sharper after a long lapse of time, because one is looking at the past with fresh eyes and can isolate and, as it were, notice facts which previously existed undifferentiated among a mass of others. Here are two things which in a sense I remembered, but which did not strike me as strange or interesting until quite recently. One is that the second beating seemed to me a just and reasonable punishment. To get one beating, and then to get another and far fiercer one on top of it, for being so unwise as to show that the first had not hurt – that was quite natural. The gods are jealous, and when you have good fortune you should conceal it. The other is that I accepted the broken riding crop as my own crime. I can still recall my feeling as I saw the handle lying on the carpet – the feeling of having done an ill-bred clumsy thing, and ruined an expensive object. *I* had broken it: so Sim told me, and so I believed. This acceptance of guilt lay unnoticed in my memory for twenty or thirty years.

So much for the episode of the bed-wetting. But there is one more thing to be remarked. This is that I did not wet my bed again – at least, I did wet it once again, and received another beating, after which the trouble stopped. So perhaps this barbarous remedy does work, though at a heavy price, I have no doubt.

'SUCH, SUCH WERE THE JOYS...', 1952

HARRIET MARTINEAU

W HEN I WAS EIGHT OR NINE, an aunt died whom I had been in the constant habit of seeing. She was old-fashioned in her dress, and peculiar in her manners. Her lean arms were visible between the elbow-ruffles and the long mitts she wore; and she usually had an apron on, and a muslin handkerchief crossed on her bosom. She fell into absent-fits which puzzled and awed us children: but we heard her so highly praised (as she richly deserved) that she was a very impressive personage to us. One morning when I came down, I found the servants at breakfast unusually early: they looked very gloomy; bade me make no noise; but would not explain what it was all about. The shutters were half-closed; and when my mother came down, she looked so altered by her weeping that I hardly knew whether it was she. She called us to her, and told us that Aunt Martineau had died very suddenly, of a disease of the heart. The whispers which were not meant for us somehow reached our ears all that week. We heard how my father and mother had been sent for in the middle of the night by the terrified servants, and how they had heard our poor uncle's voice of mourning before they had reached the house; and how she looked in her coffin, and all about the funeral: and we were old enough to be moved by the sermon in her praise at chapel, and especially by the anthem composed for the occasion, with the words from *Job*, 'When the ear heard her then it blessed her,' &c. My uncle's gloomy face and unpowdered hair were awful to us; and, during the single year of his widowhood, he occasionally took us children with him in the carriage, when he went to visit country patients. These drives came to an end with the year of widowhood; but he gave us something infinitely better than any other gift or pleasure in his second wife, whose only child was destined to fill a large space in our hearts and our lives. Soon after that funeral, I somehow learned that our globe swims in space, and that there is sky all round it. I told this to James; and we made a grand scheme which we never for a moment doubted about executing. We had each a little garden, under the north wall of our garden. The soil was less than two feet deep; and below it was a mass of rubbish – broken bricks, flints, pottery, &c. We did not know this; and our plan was to dig completely through the globe, till we came out at the other side. I fully expected to do this, and had an idea of an extremely deep hole, the darkness of which at the bottom would be lighted up by the passage of stars, slowly traversing the hole. When we found our little spades would not dig through the globe, nor even through the brickbats, we altered our scheme. We lengthened the hole to our own length, having an extreme desire to know what dying was like. We lay down alternately in this grave, and shut our eyes, and fancied ourselves dead, and told one another our feelings when we came out again. As far as I can remember, we fully believed that we now knew all about it.

HARRIET MARTINEAU'S AUTOBIOGRAPHY, 1877

ROALD DAHL

ON THE WAY TO SCHOOL and on the way back we always passed the sweet-shop. No we didn't, we never passed it. We always stopped. We lingered outside its rather small window gazing in at the big glass jars full of Bull's-eyes and Old Fashioned Humbugs and Strawberry Bonbons and Glacier Mints and Acid Drops and Pear Drops and Lemon Drops and all the rest of them. Each of us received sixpence a week for pocket-money, and whenever there was any money in our pockets, we would all troop in together to buy a pennyworth of this or that. My own favourites were Sherbet Suckers and Liquorice Bootlaces.

One of the other boys, whose name was Thwaites, told me I should never eat Liquorice Bootlaces. Thwaites's father, who was a doctor, had said that they were made from rats' blood. The father had given his young son a lecture about Liquorice Bootlaces when he had caught him eating one in bed. 'Every rat-catcher in the country,' the father had said, 'takes his rats to the Liquorice Bootlace Factory, and the manager pays tuppence for each rat. Many a rat-catcher has become a millionaire by selling his dead rats to the Factory.'

'But how do they turn the rats into liquorice?' the young Thwaites had asked his father.

'They wait until they've got ten thousand rats,' the father had answered, 'then they dump them all into a huge shiny steel cauldron and boil them up for several hours. Two men stir the bubbling cauldron with long poles and in the end they have a thick steaming rat-stew. After that, a cruncher is lowered into the cauldron to crunch the bones, and what's left is a pulpy substance called rat-mash.'

'Yes, but how do they turn that into Liquorice Bootlaces, Daddy?' the young Thwaites had asked, and this question, according to Thwaites, had caused his father to pause and think for a few moments before he answered it. At last he had said, 'The two men who were doing the stirring with the long poles now put on their wellington boots and climb into the cauldron and shovel the hot rat-mash out on to a concrete floor. Then they run a steam-roller over it several times to flatten it out. What is left looks rather like a gigantic black pancake, and all they have to do after that is to wait for it to cool and to harden so they can cut it into strips to make the Bootlaces. Don't ever eat them,' the father had said. 'If you do, you'll get ratitis.'

'What is ratitis, Daddy?' young Thwaites had asked.

'All the rats that the rat-catchers catch are poisoned with rat-poison,' the father had said. 'It's the rat poison that gives you ratitis.'

'Yes, but what happens to you when you catch it?' young Thwaites had asked.

'Your teeth become very sharp and pointed,' the father had answered. 'And a short stumpy tail grows out of your back just above your bottom. There is no cure for ratitis. I ought to know. I'm a doctor.'

We all enjoyed Thwaites's story and we made him tell it to us many times on our walks to and from school. But it didn't stop any of us except Thwaites buying Liquorice Bootlaces. At two for a penny they were the best value in the shop. A Bootlace, in case you haven't had the pleasure of handling one, is not round. It's like a flat black tape about half an inch wide. You buy it rolled up in a coil, and in those days it used to be so long that when you unrolled it and held one end at arm's length above your head, the other end touched the ground.

Sherbet Suckers were also two a penny. Each Sucker consisted of a yellow cardboard tube filled with sherbet powder, and there was a hollow liquorice straw sticking out of it. (Rat's blood again, young Thwaites would warn us, pointing at the liquorice straw.) You sucked the sherbet up through the straw and when it was finished you ate the liquorice. They were delicious, those Sherbet Suckers. The sherbet fizzed in your mouth, and if you knew how to do it, you could make white froth come out of your nostrils and pretend you were throwing a fit.

Gobstoppers, costing a penny each, were enormous hard round balls the size of small tomatoes. One Gobstopper would provide about an hour's worth of non-stop sucking and if you took it out of your mouth and inspected it every five minutes or so, you would find it had changed colour. There was something fascinating about the way it went from pink to blue to green to yellow. We used to wonder how in the world the Gobstopper Factory managed to achieve this magic. 'How *does* it happen?' we would ask each other. 'How *can* they make it keep changing colour?'

'It's your spit that does it,' young Thwaites proclaimed. As the son of a doctor, he considered himself to be an authority on all things that had to do with the body. He could tell us about scabs and when they were ready to be picked off. He knew why a black eye was blue and why blood was red.

'It's your spit that makes a Gobstopper change colour,' he kept insisting. When we asked him to elaborate on this theory, he answered, 'You wouldn't understand it if I did tell you.'

Pear Drops were exciting because they had a dangerous taste. They smelled of nail-varnish and they froze the back of your throat. All of us were warned against eating them, and the result was that we ate them more than ever.

Then there was a hard brown lozenge called the Tonsil Tickler. The Tonsil Tickler tasted and smelled very strongly of chloroform. We had not the slightest doubt that these things were saturated in the dreaded anaesthetic which, as Thwaites had many times pointed out to us, could put you to sleep for hours at a stretch. 'If my father has to saw off somebody's leg,' he said, 'he pours chloroform on to a pad and the person sniffs it and goes to sleep and my father saws his leg off without him even feeling it.'

'But why do they put it into sweets and sell them to us?' we asked him.

You might think a question like this would have baffled Thwaites. But Thwaites was never baffled. 'My father says Tonsil Ticklers were invented for dangerous prisoners in jail,' he said. 'They give them one with each meal and the chloroform makes them sleepy and stops them rioting.'

'Yes,' we said, 'but why sell them to children?'

'It's a plot,' Thwaites said. 'A grown-up plot to keep us quiet.'

The sweet-shop in Llandaff in the year 1923 was the very centre of our lives. To us, it was what a bar is to a drunk or a church is to a bishop. Without it, there would have been little to live for.

BOY: TALES OF CHILDHOOD, 1984

P.J. KAVANAGH

I WAS BORN DURING THE SLUMP, when the family fortunes were at their most pinched. By the time I was old enough to care, it was wartime and everybody was pinched.

There was some rather splendid bombing in Bristol. We went down every night to the cellar-smell until one dawn a tin-hatted warden stuck his head through the grating and shrieked at us to 'evacuate'. Then we walked through the blazing city – even the barrage balloons were on fire in the sky – and I noted with satisfaction that my school was also burning. A young couple whom I liked used to read the *Daily Worker* in the cellar, and I remember my father pointing this out to my mother in a way that made me realize they were 'odd'. A sign, I suppose, that my father was moving to the Right with age, a remarkable and almost invariable phenomenon. Gladstone is the only notable exception I can think of, and then only on certain topics: Ireland, for instance. Robert Frost once said that he was never a radical in his youth in case he became a Tory in his old age.

I also remember the house next door being on fire and hoses being played against the outside of our walls to stop them cracking, while my father sat writing. I don't know whether I admired him for this or copied the admiration of my mother ...

To my mother I owe a special debt of gratitude. For twelve years she tirelessly made me feel the centre of the Universe. When I felt the centre slipping at all I got her to walk behind me, as I strutted before in my beloved overcoat, and call out over and again: Who is that *handsome* little boy? Who is that *interesting* little boy? until I felt better. At twelve she let me go my own way, with scarcely a struggle; this seems to me perfect; or, at least, uncomplicated.

All the spoiling I had was luck, a kind of preliminary bonus; it wasn't for being a good little boy. In fact I must have been horrible. I managed to knock out several of my mother's teeth with my head, on purpose, and tried the same trick on my brother, splitting his lip. The only thing I remember with pride is announcing that I didn't believe in God. This took courage because I'm sure I'd never heard of anybody who didn't, and it made me a minority of one. Of course I *did* believe in God, possessively, secretly. I suppose I didn't want my God confused with theirs.

At some stage during the bombing of Bristol I began to ponder the chances of Eternal Punishment and became very frightened indeed. My father was listening with his head cocked to the sound of the explosions which were only a few yards away. It seemed like a good moment to confide my fears – that I hadn't been to Confession, wasn't in a State of Grace – which was all that mattered at such a moment I'd been told. Usually so gentle, he turned on me with a contorted face: 'Don't be so bloody silly!' he said.

I pondered his reaction and it rather cheered me up.

THE PERFECT STRANGER, 1966

MRS WRIGLEY

SOME OF THE HAPPIEST DAYS OF MY CHILDHOOD were when my mother packed us off with food for the day with other children, and to take the clothes to wash. Then, by the River Dee, we would take a bucket full of coal and get a few boulder stones and make a fire to boil the clothes in the bucket, and rinse them in the river, for there was plenty of water and we hadn't to carry it. Then, while the clothes was drying we had a good romp. We would take the babies with us as well, for there was plenty fields for them to pick the little daisies, and the older ones looked after the little ones. Some of our parents would come down to see if we was all right, and then we would fold the clothes and go home singing and rejoicing that we had had a good washing day and a good play.

All this was when I was about eight years old. When I was about nine, the Vicar of the Church asked if I would go to be with his children and take them out. There was another servant, but I did not stay long, for we were rationed with our food and everything was locked up. My mother was glad for me to go out for food alone.

I had been at home a few days when the doctor's wife came to our house and said a lady and gentleman wanted a little nurse for their child, to go back with them to Hazel Grove, near Stockport. My little bundle of clothes was packed up and I went in full of glee with them. Instead of being a nurse I had to be a servant-of-all-work, having to get up at six in the morning, turn a room out and get it ready for breakfast. My biggest trouble was I could not light the fire, and my master was very cross and would tell me to stand away, and give me a good box on my ears. That was my first experience of service life. I fretted very much for my home. Not able to read or write, I could not let my parents know, until a kind old lady in the village wrote to my parents to fetch me home from the hardships I endured. I had no wages at this place, only a few clothes.

My next situation was on a farm where they kept 150 milking cows, near to Oswestry. It was where I learnt to milk and make cheese and butter. I was very happy there looking after the calves, ducks, hens and chickens, and gathering the eggs. My wage was 2/6 per month. I stayed there until I was twelve years old.

'A PLATE-LAYER'S WIFE', 1931

COLLEY CIBBER

In THE YEAR 1682, at little more than Ten Years of Age, I was sent to the Free-School of *Grantham* in *Lincolnshire*, where I staid till I got through it, from the lowest Form to the uppermost. And such Learning as that School could give me is the most I pretend to (which, tho' I have not utterly forgot, I cannot say I have much improv'd by Study) but even there I remember I was the same inconsistent Creature I have been ever since! Always in full Spirits, in some small Capacity to do right, but in a more frequent Alacrity to do wrong; and consequently often under a worse Character than I wholly deserv'd: A giddy Negligence always possess'd me, and so much, that I remember I was once whipped for my *Theme*, tho' my Master told me, at the same time, what was good of it was better than any Boy's in the Form. And (whatever Shame it may be to own it) I have observ'd the same odd Fate has frequently attended the course of my later Conduct in Life. The unskilful openness, or in plain Terms, the Indiscretion I have always acted with from my Youth, has drawn more ill-will towards me, than Men of worse Morals and more Wit might have met with. My Ignorance and want of Jealousy of Mankind has been so strong, that it is with Reluctance I even yet believe any Person I am acquainted with can be capable of Envy, Malice, or Ingratitude: And to shew you what a Mortification it was to me, in my very boyish Days, to find myself mistaken, give me leave to tell you a School Story.

A great Boy, near the Head taller than myself, in some wrangle at Play had insulted me; upon which I was fool-hardy enough to give him a Box on the Ear; the Blow was soon return'd with another that brought me under him and at his Mercy. Another Lad, whom I really lov'd and thought a good-natur'd one, cry'd out with some warmth to my Antagonist (while I was down) Beat him, beat him soundly! This so amaz'd me that I lost all my Spirits to resist and burst into Tears! When the Fray was over I took my Friend aside, and ask'd him, How he came to be so earnestly against me? To which, with some glouting sullen confusion, he reply'd, 'Because you are always jeering and making a Jest of me to every Boy in the school.' Many a Mischief have I brought upon myself by the same Folly in riper Life. Whatever Reason I had to reproach my Companion's declaring against me, I had none to wonder at it while I was so often hurting him: Thus I deserv'd his Enmity by my not having Sense enough to know I *had* hurt him; and he hated me because he had not Sense enough to know that I never *intended* to hurt him.

As this is the first remarkable Error of my Life I can recollect, I cannot pass it by without throwing out some further Reflections upon it; whether flat or spirited, new or common, false or true, right or wrong, they will be still my own, and consequently like me; I will therefore boldly go on; for I am only oblig'd to give you my *own*, and not a *good* Picture, to shew as well the Weakness as the Strength of my Understanding. It is not on what I write, but on my Reader's Curiosity I relie to be read through: At worst, tho' the Impartial may be tir'd, the Ill-natur'd (no small number) I know will see the bottom of me.

What I observ'd then, upon my having undesignedly provok'd my School-Friend into an Enemy is a common Case in Society; Errors of this kind often sour the Blood of Acquaintance into an inconceivable Aversion, where it is little suspected. It is not enough to say of your Raillery that you intended no Offence; if the Person you offer it to has either a wrong Head, or wants a Capacity to make that distinction, it may have the same Effect as the Intention of the grossest Injury: And in reality, if you know his Parts are too slow to return it in kind, it is a vain and idle Inhumanity, and sometimes draws the Aggressor into difficulties not easily got out of ...

AN APOLOGY FOR THE LIFE OF MR COLLEY CIBBER, WRITTEN BY HIMSELF, 1740

JEAN-PAUL SARTRE

WHEN I WAS TEN, I was not yet aware of my manias and repetitions, and doubt never crossed my mind: trotting along, chattering, fascinated by what was going on in the street, I never stopped renewing my skin and I could hear the old skins falling one on top of the other. When I went back up the Rue Soufflot, I felt at each step, as the dazzling rows of shop windows went by, the movement of my life, its law and the noble mandate of being unfaithful to everything. I was taking my whole self along with me. My grandmother wanted to match her dinner service; I went with her into a glass and china shop; she pointed to a soup tureen, with a red apple on top of its lid, and to some flowered plates. It was not quite what she wanted: there were flowers on the plates, of course, but also some brown insects climbing up the stems. It was the shopkeeper's turn to brighten: she knew exactly what the customer wanted, she used to have it, but they stopped making it three years ago; this was a more recent model, better value, and then, with or without insects, flowers were still flowers, weren't they, no one was going to look for the little creature, you must admit. My grandmother did not agree; she kept on: couldn't they have a look in the stockroom? Ah, yes, of course, in the stockroom. But that would take time and the shopkeeper was on her own: her assistant had just left her. I had been consigned to a corner, with a warning to touch nothing. I was forgotten, terrified by the fragile objects around me with their dusty sheen, Pascal's death mask and a chamber-pot decorated with the head of President Fallières. Now, in spite of appearances, I was a bogus supporting player. In the same way, some authors push small part players to the front of the stage and present their hero receding off stage.

But the reader is not deceived: he has run through the last chapter to see if the novel has a happy ending, and he knows that the pale young man, against the fireplace, has three hundred and fifty pages in the womb. Three hundred and fifty pages of love and adventure. I had at least five hundred. I was the hero of a long story with a happy ending. I had stopped telling myself this story: what was the use? I felt romantic, that was all. Time was dragging backwards the puzzled old ladies, the china flowers and the whole shop; the black shirts were fading; the voices were getting woolly; I felt sorry for my grandmother; she would certainly not be appearing in the second part. But I was the beginning, the middle and the end all rolled into one small boy, already old, already dead, *here*, in the shadows, between the stacks of plates higher than himself, and *outside*, very far away, in the vast and gloomy sunshine of glory. I was the particle at the beginning of its trajectory and the series of waves which flows back on it after it has struck the terminal buffer. Reassembled and compressed, one hand on my tomb and the other on my cradle, I felt brief and splendid, a flash of lightning swallowed up in darkness.

THE WORDS, 1964

CHARLES DICKENS

'THE BLACKING-WAREHOUSE was the last house on the left-hand side of the way, at old Hungerford Stairs. It was a crazy, tumble-down old house, abutting of course on the river, and literally overrun with rats. Its wainscotted rooms and its rotten floors and staircase, and the old grey rats swarming down in the cellars, and the sound of their squeaking and scuffling coming up the stairs at all times, and the dirt and decay of the place, rise up visibly before me, as if I were there again. The counting-house was on the first floor, looking over the coal-barges and the river. There was a recess in it, in which I was to sit and work. My work was to cover the pots of paste-blacking; first with a piece of oil-paper, and then with a piece of blue paper; to tie them round with a string; and then to clip the paper close and neat, all round, until it looked as smart as a pot of ointment from an apothecary's shop. When a certain number of grosses of pots had attained this pitch of perfection, I was to paste on each a printed label; and then go on again with more pots. Two or three other boys were kept at similar duty downstairs on similar wages. One of them came up, in a ragged apron and a paper cap, on the first Monday morning, to show me the trick of using the string and tying the knot. His name was Bob Fagin; and I took the liberty of using his name long afterwards, in *Oliver Twist*.

'Our relative had kindly arranged to teach me something in the dinner-hour; from twelve to one, I think it was; every day. But an arrangement so incompatible with counting-house business soon died away, from no fault of his or mine; and for the same reason, my small work-table and my grosses of pots, my papers, string, scissors, paste-pot and labels, by little and little, vanished out of the recess in the counting-house, and kept company with the other small work-tables, grosses of pots, papers, string, scissors, and paste-pots downstairs. It was not long before Bob Fagin and I, and another boy whose name was Paul Green, but who was currently believed to have been christened Poll (a belief which I transferred, long afterwards again, to Mr Sweedlepipe, in *Martin Chuzzlewit*), worked generally, side by side. Bob Fagin was an orphan, and lived with his brother-in-law, a waterman. Poll Green's father had the additional distinction of being a fireman, and was employed at Drury Lane theatre; where another relation of Poll's, I think his little sister, did imps in the pantomimes.

'No words can express the secret agony of my soul as I sunk into this companionship; compared these everyday associates with those of my happier childhood; and felt my early hopes of growing up to be a learned and distinguished man, crushed in my breast. The deep remembrance of the sense I had of being utterly neglected and hopeless; of the shame I felt in my position; of the misery it was to my young heart to believe that, day by day, what I had learned, and thought, and delighted in, and raised my fancy and my emulation up by, was passing away from me, never to be brought back any more; cannot be written. My whole nature was so penetrated with the grief and humiliation of such considerations, that even now, famous and caressed and happy, I often forget in my dreams that I have a dear wife and children; even that I am a man; and wander desolately back to that time of my life.

'My mother and my brothers and sisters (excepting Fanny in the Royal Academy of Music) were still encamped, with a young servant-girl from Chatham Workhouse, in the two parlours in the emptied house in Gower Street North. It was a long way to go and return within the dinner-hour, and, usually, I either carried my dinner with me, or went and bought it at some neighbouring shop. In the latter case, it was commonly a saveloy and a penny loaf; sometimes, a fourpenny plate of beef from a cook's shop; sometimes, a plate of bread and cheese, and a glass of beer, from a miserable old public-house over the way: the Swan, if I remember right, or the Swan and something else that I have forgotten. Once, I remember tucking my own bread (which I had brought from home in the morning) under my arm, wrapped up in a piece of paper like a book, and going into the best dining-room in Johnson's alamode beef-house in Clare Court, Drury Lane, and magnificently ordering a small plate of alamode beef to eat with it. What the waiter thought of such a strange little apparition, coming in all alone, I don't know; but I can see him now, staring at me as I ate my dinner, and bringing up the other waiter to look. I gave him a halfpenny, and I wish, now, that he hadn't taken it.'

I lose here for a little while the fragment of direct narrative, but

I perfectly recollect that he used to describe Saturday night as his great treat. It was a grand thing to walk home with six shillings in his pocket, and to look in at the shop windows, and think what it would buy. Hunt's roasted corn, as a British and patriotic substitute for coffee, was in great vogue just then; and the little fellow used to buy it, and roast it on the Sunday. There was a cheap periodical of selected pieces called the *Portfolio,* which he had also a great fancy for taking home with him. The new proposed 'deed', meanwhile, had failed to propitiate his father's creditors; all hope of arrangement passed away; and the end was that his mother and her encampment in Gower Street North broke up and went to live in the Marshalsea. I am able at this point to resume his own account.

'The key of the house was sent back to the landlord, who was very glad to get it; and I (small Cain that I was, except that I had never done harm to any one) was handed over as a lodger to a reduced old lady, long known to our family, in Little College Street, Camden Town, who took children in to board, and had once done so at Brighton; and who, with a few alterations and embellishments, unconsciously began to sit for Mrs Pipchin in *Dombey* when she took me in.

'She had a little brother and sister under her care then; somebody's natural children, who were very irregularly paid for; and a widow's little son. The two boys and I slept in the same room. My own exclusive breakfast, of a penny cottage loaf and a pennyworth of milk, I provided for myself. I kept another small loaf, and a quarter of a pound of cheese, on a particular shelf of a particular cupboard; to make my supper on when I came back at night. They made a hole in the six or seven shillings, I know well; and I was out at the blacking-warehouse all day, and had to support myself upon that money all the week. I suppose my lodging was paid for, by my father. I certainly did not pay it myself; and I certainly had no other assistance whatever (the making of my clothes, I think, excepted), from Monday morning until Saturday night. No advice, no counsel, no encouragement, no consolation, no support, from any one that I can call to mind, so help me God.

"Sundays, Fanny and I passed in the prison. I was at the academy in Tenterden Street, Hanover Square, at nine o'clock in the morning, to fetch her; and we walked back there together, at night.

'I was so young and childish, and so little qualified – how could it be otherwise? – to undertake the whole charge of my own existence that, in going to Hungerford Stairs of a morning, I could not resist the stale pastry put out at half-price on trays at the confectioners' doors in Tottenham Court Road; and I often spent in that, the money I should have kept for my dinner. Then I went without my dinner, or bought a roll, or a slice of pudding. There were two pudding shops between which I was divided, according to my finances. One was in a court close to St Martin's Church (at the back of the church) which is now removed altogether. The pudding at that shop was made with currants, and was rather a special pudding, but was dear: two penn'orth not being larger than a penn'orth of more ordinary pudding. A good shop for the latter was in the Strand, somewhere near where Lowther Arcade is now. It was a stout, hale pudding, heavy and flabby; with great raisins in it, stuck in whole, at great distances apart. It came up hot, at about noon every day; and many and many a day did I dine off it.

'We had half-an-hour I think, for tea. When I had money enough, I used to go to a coffee-shop and have half-a-pint of coffee, and a slice of bread and butter. When I had no money, I took a turn in Covent Garden Market, and stared at the pineapples. The coffee-shops to which I most resorted were, one in Maiden Lane; one in a court (non-existent now) close to Hungerford Market; and one in St Martin's Lane, of which I only recollect that it stood near the church, and that in the door there was an oval glass-plate, with COFFEE-ROOM painted on it, addressed towards the street. If I ever find myself in a very different kind of coffee-room now, but where there is such an inscription on glass, and read it backward on the wrong side MOOR-EEFFOC (as I often used to do then, in a dismal reverie), a shock goes through my blood.

'I know I do not exaggerate, unconsciously and unintentionally, the scantiness of my resources and the difficulties of my life. I know that if a shilling or so were given me by any one, I spent it in a dinner or a tea. I know that I worked, from morning to night, with common men and boys, a shabby child. I know that I tried, but ineffectually, not to anticipate my money, and to make it last the week through; by putting it away in a drawer I had in the counting-house, wrapped into six little parcels, each parcel containing the same amount, and labelled with a different day. I know that I have lounged about the streets, insufficiently and unsatisfactorily fed. I know that, but for the mercy of God, I might easily have been, for any care that was taken of me, a little robber or a little vagabond.'

'AUTOBIOGRAPHICAL FRAGMENT', 1847

CHARLES DARWIN

JULY (10 & ½ YEARS OLD). Went to sea at Plas Edwards & staid there three weeks, which now appears to me like three months. I remember a certain shady green road (where I saw a snake) & a waterfall with a degree of pleasure, which must be connected with the pleasure from scenery, though not directly recognized as such. The sandy plain before the house has left a strong impression, which is obscurely connected with indistinct remembrance of curious insects – probably a Cimex mottled with red – the Zygena. I was at that time very passionate (when I swore like a trooper) & quarrelsome – the former passion has I think nearly wholly, but slowly died away. When journeying there by stage coach I remember a recruiting officer (I think I should know his face to this day) at tea time, asking the maid servant for *toasted* bread butter. I was convulsed with laughter, & thought it the quaintest & wittiest speech that ever passed from the mouth of man. Such is wit at 10 & ½ years old.

The memory now flashes across me, of the pleasure I had in the evening or on [a] blowy day walking along the beach by myself, & seeing the gulls & cormorants wending their way home in a wild & irregular course. Such poetic pleasures, felt so keenly in after years, I should not have expected so early in life.

1820 July. Went riding tour (on old Dobbin) with Erasmus to Pistol Rhyadwr – of this I recollect little – an indistinct picture of the fall – but I well remember my astonishment on hearing that fishes could jump up it.

'AN AUTOBIOGRAPHICAL FRAGMENT', 1838

GERALD DURRELL

I GREW VERY FOND OF THESE SCORPIONS. I found them to be pleasant, unassuming creatures with, on the whole, the most charming habits. Provided you did nothing silly or clumsy (like putting your hand on one) the scorpions treated you with respect, their one desire being to get away and hide as quickly as possible. They must have found me rather a trial, for I was always ripping sections of the plaster away [on the wall] so that I could watch them, or capturing them and making them walk about in jam jars so that I could see the way their feet moved. By means of my sudden and unexpected assaults on the wall I discovered quite a bit about the scorpions. I found that they would eat bluebottles (though how they caught them was a mystery I never solved), grasshoppers, moths, and lacewing flies. Several times I found one of them eating another, a habit I found most distressing in a creature otherwise so impeccable.

By crouching under the wall at night with a torch, I managed to catch some brief glimpses of the scorpions' wonderful courtship dances. I saw them standing, claws clasped, their bodies raised to the skies, their tails lovingly entwined; I saw them waltzing slowly in circles among the moss cushions, claw in claw. But my view of these performances was all too short, for almost as soon as I switched on the torch the partners would stop, pause for a moment, and then, seeing that I was not going to extinguish the light, would turn round and walk firmly away, claw in claw, side by side. They were definitely beasts that believed in keeping themselves *to* themselves. If I could have kept a colony in captivity I would probably have been able to see the whole of the courtship, but the family had forbidden scorpions in the house, despite my arguments in favour of them.

Then one day I found a fat female scorpion in the wall, wearing what at first glance appeared to be a pale fawn fur coat. Closer inspection proved that this strange garment was made up of a mass of tiny babies clinging to the mother's back. I was enraptured by this family, and I made up my mind to smuggle them into the house and up to my bedroom so that I might keep them and watch them grow up. With infinite care I manoeuvred the mother and family into a matchbox, and then hurried to the villa. It was rather unfortunate that just as I entered the door lunch should be served; however, I placed the matchbox carefully on the mantelpiece in the drawing-room, so that the scorpions should get plenty of air, and made my way to the dining-room and joined the family for the meal. Dawdling over my food, feeding Roger [the dog] surreptitiously under the table and listening to the family arguing, I completely forgot about my exciting new captures. At last Larry, having finished, fetched the cigarettes from the drawing-room, and lying back in his chair he put one in his mouth and picked up the matchbox he had brought. Oblivious of my impending doom I watched him interestedly as, still talking glibly, he opened the matchbox.

Now I maintain to this day that the female scorpion meant no harm. She was agitated and a trifle annoyed at being shut up in a matchbox for so long, and so she seized the first opportunity to escape. She hoisted herself out of the box with great rapidity, her babies clinging on desperately, and scuttled onto the back of Larry's hand. There, not quite certain what to do next, she paused, her sting curved up at the ready. Larry, feeling the movement of her claws, glanced down to see what it was, and from that moment things got increasingly confused.

He uttered a roar of fright that made Lugaretzia drop a plate and brought Roger out from beneath the table, barking wildly. With a flick of his hand he sent the unfortunate scorpion flying down the table, and she landed midway between Margo and Leslie, scattering babies like confetti as she thumped onto the cloth. Thoroughly enraged at this treatment, the creature sped towards Leslie, her sting quivering with emotion. Leslie leaped to his feet, overturning his chair, and flicked out desperately with his napkin, sending the scorpion rolling across the cloth towards Margo, who promptly let out a scream that any railway engine would have been proud to produce. Mother, completely bewildered by this sudden and rapid change from peace to chaos, put on her glasses and peered down the table to see what was causing the pandemonium, and at that moment Margo, in a vain attempt to stop the scorpion's advance, hurled a glass of water at it. The shower missed the animal completely, but successfully drenched Mother, who, not being able to stand cold water, promptly lost her breath and sat gasping at the end of the table, unable even to protest. The scorpion had now gone to ground under Leslie's plate, while her babies swarmed wildly all over the table. Roger, mystified by the panic, but determined to do his share, ran round and round the room, barking hysterically.

'It's that bloody boy again ... ' bellowed Larry.

'Look out! Look out! They're coming!' screamed Margo.

'All we need is a book,' roared Leslie; 'don't panic, hit 'em with a book.'

'What on earth's the *matter* with you all?' Mother kept imploring, mopping her glasses.

'It's that bloody boy ... he'll kill the lot of us ... Look at the table ... knee-deep in scorpions ...'

'Quick ... quick ... do something ... Look out, look out!'

'Stop screeching and get a book, for God's sake ... You're worse than the dog ... Shut *up*, Roger...'

'By the grace of God I wasn't bitten ...'

'Look out ... there's another one ... Quick ... quick ...'

'Oh, shut up and get me a book or something ...'

'But how did the scorpions get on the table, dear?'

'That bloody boy ... Every matchbox in the house is a deathtrap ...'

'Look out, it's coming towards me ... Quick, quick, do something ...'

'Hit it with your knife ... *your knife* ... Go on, hit it ...'

Since no one had bothered to explain things to him, Roger was under the mistaken impression that the family were being attacked, and that it was his duty to defend them. As Lugaretzia was the only stranger in the room, he came to the logical conclusion that she must be the responsible party, so he bit her in the ankle. This did not help matters very much.

By the time a certain amount of order had been restored, all the baby scorpions had hidden themselves under various plates and bits of cutlery. Eventually, after impassioned pleas on my part, backed up by Mother, Leslie's suggestion that the whole lot be slaughtered was quashed. While the family, still simmering with rage and fright, retired to the drawing-room, I spent half an hour rounding up the babies, picking them up in a teaspoon, and returning them to their mother's back. Then I carried them outside on a saucer and, with the utmost reluctance, released them on the garden wall. Roger and I went and spent the afternoon on the hillside, for I felt it would be prudent to allow the family to have a siesta before seeing them again.

MY FAMILY AND OTHER ANIMALS, 1956

ROY HATTERSLEY

GOING TO SEE A REAL FOOTBALL MATCH seemed to me as grown-up and as daring as smoking or wearing long trousers – neither of which adult habit I had acquired. Indeed, as a result of that first visit to the Hillsborough ground of Sheffield Wednesday Football Club, I have still to experience what I assume to be the repulsive taste of a first cigarette. For from the moment that my father and I took our seat in the wooden 'Old Stand', I knew that God had called me to play left-half for 'the Owls' and when other little boys puffed away surreptitiously behind scout huts and in school lavatories, I never risked my health and respiration. I kept myself pure for Sheffield Wednesday.

Inevitably the first game I saw was against Nottingham Forest. Indeed, I suspect the decision that I was old enough and big enough to be jostled by the crowd was partly influenced by my father's desire to take me to see his team. It was concern for my safety that prompted the extravagance of tickets and seats. In later years, we always stood on Spion Kop, exposed to the weather and the pressure of the thousand tightly packed football supporters. But on the first day I was in comfort and under cover, only in danger as we were swept in and out of the ground at the start and after the end of the game. My father guided me through the crush with his arm over my shoulders in a way which was supposed to protect me but caused something approaching strangulation. I knew he was trying to be helpful and felt unable to beg him to release the pressure on my windpipe.

I was enchanted by the game. It ended in a goalless draw and was, so my father later assured me, unexceptional in every way. But I think that I recognized what J.B. Priestley called the combination of 'conflict and art'. It was the beginning of a lifetime of eager anticipation of winter Saturday afternoons, climaxing in the hour after four forty-five being filled by the triumph of victory, the despair of defeat, or the cold consolation of a draw and a single point. I know that I should have grown out of such infantile passion. But becoming a prejudiced football partisan, was, for me, part of the onset of age, wisdom and maturity – the discovery of one of the wonders of the world.

A YORKSHIRE BOYHOOD, 1983

WALT WHITMAN

INSIDE THE OUTER BARS OR BEACH this south bay is everywhere comparatively shallow; of cold winters all thick ice on the surface. As a boy I often went forth with a chum or two, on those frozen fields, with hand-sled, axe and eel-spear, after messes of eels. We would cut holes in the ice, sometimes striking quite an eel-bonanza, and filling our baskets with great, fat, sweet, white-meated fellows. The scenes, the ice, drawing the hand-sled, cutting holes, spearing the eels, &c., were of course just such fun as is dearest to boyhood. The shores of this bay, winter and summer, and my doings there in early life, are woven all through L. of G. [*Leaves of Grass*]. One sport I was very fond of was to go on a bay-party in summer to gather sea-gulls' eggs. (The gulls lay two or three eggs, more than half the size of hens' eggs, right on the sand, and leave the sun's heat to hatch them.)

The eastern end of Long Island, the Peconic bay region, I knew quite well too – sail'd more than once around Shelter Island, and down to Montauk – spent many an hour on Turtle Hill by the old lighthouse, on the extreme point, looking out over the ceaseless roll of the Atlantic. I used to like to go down there and fraternize with the blue-fishers, or the annual squads of sea-bass takers. Sometimes, along Montauk peninsula (it is some 15 miles long, and good grazing), met the strange, unkempt, half-barbarous herdsmen, at that time living there entirely aloof from society or civilization, in charge, on those rich pasturages, of vast droves of horses, kine or sheep, own'd by farmers of the eastern towns.

Sometimes, too, the few remaining Indians, or half-breeds, at that period left on Montauk peninsula, but now I believe altogether extinct.

More in the middle of the island were the spreading Hempstead plains, then (1830–40) quite prairie-like, open, uninhabited, rather sterile, cover'd with kill-calf and huckleberry bushes, yet plenty of fair pasture for the cattle, mostly milch-cows, who fed there by hundreds, even thousands, and at evening (the plains too were own'd by the towns, and this was the use of them in common) might be seen taking their way home, branching off regularly in the right places. I have often been out on the edges of these plains toward sundown, and can yet recall in fancy the interminable cow-processions, and hear the music of the tin or copper bells clanking far or near, and breathe the cool of the sweet and slightly aromatic evening air, and note the sunset.

Through the same region of the island, but further east, extended wide central tracts of pine and scrub-oak (charcoal was largely made here), monotonous and sterile. But many a good day or half-day did I have, wandering through those solitary cross-roads, inhaling the peculiar and wild aroma. Here, and all along the island and its shores, I spent intervals many years, all seasons, sometimes riding, sometimes boating, but generally afoot (I was always then a good walker), absorbing fields, shores, marine incidents, characters, the bay-men, farmers, pilots – always had a plentiful acquaintance with the latter, and with fishermen – went every summer on sailing trips – always liked the bare sea-beach, south side, and have some of my happiest hours on it to this day.

As I write, the whole experience comes back to me after the lapse of forty and more years – the soothing rustle of the waves, and the saline smell – boyhood's times, the clam-digging, barefoot, and with trowsers roll'd up – hauling down the creek – the perfume of the sedge-meadows – the hay-boat, and the chowder and fishing excursions; or, of later years, little voyages down and out New York bay, in the pilot boats. Those same later years, also, while living in Brooklyn (1836–50), I went regularly every week in the mild seasons down to Coney Island, at that time a long, bare unfrequented shore, which I had all to myself, and where I loved, after bathing, to race up and down the hard sand,

and declaim Homer or Shakspere [sic] to the surf and sea-gulls by the hour. But I am getting ahead too rapidly, and must keep more in my traces.

'SPECIMEN DAYS', 1882

DYLAN THOMAS

AUGUST BANK HOLIDAY – a tune on an ice-cream cornet. A slap of sea and a tickle of sand. A fanfare of sunshades opening. A wince and whinny of bathers dancing into deceptive water. A tuck of dresses. A rolling of trousers. A compromise of paddlers. A sunburn of girls and a lark of boys. A silent hullabaloo of balloons.

I remember the sea telling lies in a shell held to my ear for a whole harmonious, hollow minute by a small, wet girl in an enormous bathing suit marked Corporation Property.

I remember sharing the last of my moist buns with a boy and a lion. Tawny and savage, with cruel nails and capacious mouth, the little boy tore and devoured. Wild as seedcake, ferocious as a hearthrug, the depressed and verminous lion nibbled like a mouse at his half a bun and hiccupped in the sad dusk of his cage.

I remember a man like an alderman or a bailiff, bowlered and collarless, with a bag of monkeynuts in his hand, crying 'Ride 'em, cowboy!' time and again as he whirled in his chairaplane giddily above the upturned laughing faces of the town girls bold as brass and the boys with padded shoulders and shoes sharp as knives; and the monkeynuts flew through the air like salty hail.

Children all day capered or squealed by the glazed or bashing sea, and the steam-organ wheezed its waltzes in the threadbare playground and the waste lot, where the dodgems dodged, behind the pickle factory.

And mothers loudly warned their proud pink daughters or sons to put that jellyfish down; and fathers spread newspapers over their faces; and sandfleas hopped on the picnic lettuce; and someone had forgotten the salt.

In those always radiant, rainless, lazily rowdy and skyblue summers departed, I remember August Monday from the rising of the sun over the stained and royal town to the husky hushing of the roundabout music and the dowsing of the naptha jets in the seaside fair: from bubble-and-squeak to the last of the sandy sandwiches.

'HOLIDAY MEMORY', 1954

BENJAMIN FRANKLIN

AT TEN YEARS OLD, I WAS TAKEN HOME to assist my Father in his Business, which was that of a Tallow-Chandler and Sope-Boiler. A business he was not bred to, but had assumed on his Arrival in New England, & on finding his Dying Trade would not maintain his Family, being in little Request. Accordingly I was employed in cutting Wick for the Candles, filling the Dipping Mold & the Molds for Cast Candles, attending the Shop, going of Errands, &c.

I dislik'd the Trade, and had a strong Inclination for the Sea, but my father declar'd against it; however, living near the Water, I was much in and about it, learnt early to swim well, & to manage Boats; and when in a Boat or Canoe with other Boys, I was commonly allow'd to govern, especially in any case of Difficulty; and upon other Occasions I was generally a Leader among the Boys, and sometimes led them into Scrapes, of which I will mention one Instance, as it shows an early projecting public Spirit, tho' not then justly conducted.

There was a salt marsh that bounded part of the mill pond, on the Edge of which, at Highwater, we used to stand to fish for Minews [minnows]. By much trampling, we had made it a mere Quagmire. My Proposal was to build a Wharf there fit for us to stand upon, and I show'd my Comrades a large Heap of Stones, which were intended for a new House near the Marsh, and which would very well suit our Purpose. Accordingly in the evening when the Workmen were gone, I assembled a Number of my Playfellows, and working with them diligently like so many Emmets, sometimes two or three to a Stone, we brought them all away and built our little Wharf. The Next morning the Workmen were surpriz'd at missing the Stones, which were found in our Wharf. Enquiry was made after the Removers; we were discovered & complain'd of; several of us were corrected by our Fathers; and tho' I pleaded the Usefulness of the Work, mine convinc'd me that nothing was useful which was not honest.

I think you may like to know something of his Person & Character. He had an excellent Constitution of Body, was of middle Stature, but well set and very strong. He was ingenious, could draw prettily, was skill'd a little in Music, and had a clear pleasing Voice, so that when he play'd Psalm Tunes on his Violin & sung withal, as he sometimes did in an Evening after the Business of the Day was over, it was extremely agreeable to hear. He had a mechanical Genius too, and on occasion, was very handy in the Use of other Tradesmen's Tools. But his great Excellence lay in a sound understanding and solid Judgment in prudential Matters, both in private & publick affairs. In the latter indeed he was never employed, the numerous Family he had to educate & the Straitness of his Circumstances keeping him close to his Trade; but I remember well his being frequently visited by leading People, who consulted him for his Opinion on Affairs of the Town or of the Church he belong'd to, and show'd a good deal of Respect for his Judgment and Advice. He was also much consulted by private Persons about their Affairs when any Difficulty occur'd, and frequently chosen an Arbitrator between contending Parties.

At his Table he lik'd to have, as often as he could, some sensible Friend or neighbour to converse with, and always took care to start some ingenious or useful Topic for Discourse, which might tend to improve the Minds of his Children. By this means he turn'd our attention to what was good, just & prudent in the Conduct of Life; and little or no Notice was ever taken of what related to the Victuals on the table, whether it was well or ill drest, in or out of season, of good or bad flavour, preferable or inferior to this or that other thing of the kind; so that I was bro't up in such a perfect Inattention to those Matters as to be quite Indifferent what kind of Food was set before me, and so unobservant of it, that to this Day if I am ask'd I can scarce tell a few Hours after Dinner what I din'd upon. This has been a Convenience to me in travelling, where my Companions have been sometimes very unhappy for want of a suitable gratification of their more delicate, because better instructed, Tastes and Appetites.

THE AUTOBIOGRAPHY, 1771–1788

MAXIM GORKY

I N MY OPINION OUR LIFE WASN'T BAD. The independent life in the streets was very much to my liking. I liked my friends as well and they inspired in me a feeling of restlessness, of always wanting to do them some good.

Things became difficult for me at school again and the boys laughed at me, calling me a rag-and-bone man, a tramp, and once, after a quarrel, they told the teacher I smelt of sewers and that it was impossible to sit next to me. I remember how deeply this hurt me and how hard it was to go to school after that. They invented the complaint just to spite me: every morning I used to wash myself thoroughly and never went to school in the clothes I wore for collecting rags.

But at last I passed into the third class and won some prizes: a *New Testament*, a bound Krilov's *Fables* and another book without a binding, with the mysterious title of *Fata Morgana*. I also got a good report. When I brought my prizes home Grandfather was very pleased and deeply touched, and announced that the books must be carefully put away in his own trunk. Grandmother had been ill for some days, and now had no money, and Grandfather moaned and roared at her: 'You'll eat and drink me out of house and home ... you lot ...'

I took the books to a shop and sold them for fifty-five kopeks, and gave the money to Grandmother. I scrawled all over the testimonial and gave it to Grandfather. He hid it away carefully without unrolling it or seeing that I'd ruined it.

I said farewell to school and settled down once more to street life, which now was more enjoyable. Spring was in full bloom, there was more money to be earned, and on Sundays we would all go out to the country, the fields and pine groves, and didn't return until late in the evening, pleasantly exhausted and firmer friends than ever.

But this kind of existence was short-lived: my stepfather got the sack and vanished again and Mother took my little brother Nikolai and went to live with Grandfather. As Grandmother had gone to live in the house of a rich merchant for whom she was embroidering a cover depicting the Body of Christ, I had to be nursemaid.

My mother, silent and wasted away, could barely move her legs, and looked at everything with terrifying eyes. My brother had *scrofula*, ulcers on his ankles, and was so weak he could only raise a feeble cry and moaned pitifully if he was hungry. When he'd been fed he would doze off and sigh strangely in his sleep, quietly purring like a kitten.

Grandfather felt him carefully all over and said:

'He needs proper food, but how can I feed all of you?'

Mother, who was sitting on the bed in a corner of the room, sighed hoarsely: 'He doesn't need much ...'

'A little is often a lot for others ...' Grandfather waved his arm and turned to me:

'He needs to be free, out in the sun, on the sands ...'

I dragged home a sack of clean dry sand, heaped it in a sunny place by the window and buried my brother up to the neck, according to Grandfather's instructions. The baby liked sitting in the sand, sweetly blinking and looking at me with his strange shining eyes; they had no whites, only blue irises surrounded by a bright ring.

At once I became strongly attached to my brother. He seemed to understand everything I was thinking as I lay beside him in the sand by the window, through which would come Grandfather's squeaky voice:

'You don't have to be clever to die, but it's time you knew how to live.'

Mother would then have a long fit of coughing.

My brother would free his little arms and stretch out towards me, shaking his small white head; his thin hair was shot with grey and his face old and wise.

If a hen or a cat came near him, Nikolai would take a long close look, then turn to me with a faint smile, which disturbed me and made me think perhaps my brother sensed I was bored sitting there with him and really wanted to leave him and go out to play in the street.

We had a small yard crammed full with rubbish. Next to the gates were some ramshackle sheds, storehouses all made from odd bits of timber. These stretched away down to the bath house. The roofs were covered all over with bits of wood from boats, logs, planks, damp shavings, all fished out of the Oka during the spring floods. Ugly piles of wood cluttered up the yard, most of it still wet from the river, and lay there rotting in the sun, giving off a smell of decay.

Next door was a slaughterhouse for small livestock. Almost every morning we could hear the calves lowing and sheep bleating, and there was such a strong smell of blood that at times it seemed to hang in the air like a transparent purple net.

Whenever the animals bellowed, stunned by a blow with the back of an axe between the horns, Kolya, my brother, would screw up his eyes and puff out his cheeks in an effort, no doubt, to imitate them, but only succeeded in puffing out air: 'Phooooh.'

At midday Grandfather would stick his head out of the window and shout: 'Dinner!'

He fed the baby himself, holding him on his knees and chewing up bits of potato and bread, poking them into Nikolai's little mouth with his crooked finger, and getting the food all over his thin lips and little chin.

After he'd fed him for a while, Grandfather would lift the child's vest, poke its swollen belly and say out loud:

'Do you think he's had enough? Should I give him some more?'

Mother's voice would come from the dim corner near the door:

'Can't you see he's reaching for the bread!'

'But babies are stupid! How can he know when he's had enough?'

And he continued shoving chewed-up food into Nikolai's mouth. It was intolerable and I felt a nauseating, stifling sensation down in my throat.

'That's enough now,' Grandfather said at last. 'Take him to his mother.'

When I lifted him up he would moan and reach out towards the table. Tall and thin like a fir stripped of its branches, Mother would force herself on to her feet and come to take the baby from me, stretching out her thin arms which hardly had any flesh on them.

It was as if she had been struck dumb. Whenever she spoke, which was very rarely, it was in a voice seething with emotion. And she stayed in her corner the whole day, just dying. I could feel that, and Grandfather was always talking about death, obsessively, particularly in the evenings when it grew dark outside and the warm smell of decay crept through the window, warm and stuffy, like a sheepskin.

Grandfather's bed stood in the front of the room, almost under the icons and he slept with his head towards them and the window. He would lie there muttering to himself for hours in the darkness.

'Now it's time for me to die. And how shall I look before my Maker? What shall I say? ... My whole life's been spent running around after nothing. And what for? What does it all add up to?'

I slept on the floor between the stove and the window. This didn't leave much room for my legs, so I stretched them out under the stove, where I could feel the cockroaches tickling my toes. From this corner I could witness many events which filled me with malicious pleasure. When Grandfather was cooking he always managed to knock some of the windowpanes out with the end of the poker or oven fork. So strange and funny, that a clever man like him never thought of cutting down the handles.

Once, when something boiled over in one of the pots, he tugged so furiously at the oven fork that he smashed the window-frame and both panes of glass, upset the pot over the fireplace and broke it into the bargain. This incensed him so much that he sat on the floor and cried:

'My God, my God!'

During the day, when he'd gone, I took a bread knife and shortened the oven-fork handle by about three quarters. But when Grandfather saw my work he started cursing:

'Damn and blast you! You should have used a saw, a s-a-w! We could have made some rolling pins from the offcuts and got good money for them, you little devil!'

Waving his arms, he ran into the hall. Mother said: 'You shouldn't interfere ...'

She died in August, on a Sunday, about midday. My stepfather had just returned from his travels and had got another job somewhere in the town. Grandmother had taken Nikolai with her and gone to live in a clean little flat near the station; Mother was eventually going to join them there.

The morning of the day she died she'd said to me softly, but in a clearer, more carefree voice than usual:

'Go to Yevgeny Vassilyevich and tell him to come here!'

She lifted herself up on the bed, propping her hand against the wall, and sat up. 'Quick as you can!'

I thought she was smiling, and there was a new shining light in her eyes. My stepfather was at mass, and Grandmother sent me off to a Jewess (the wife of a policeman), who sold tobacco, for some snuff. She didn't have any ready and I had to wait while she rubbed the flakes.

When I got back to Grandfather's, Mother was sitting at the table, dressed in a clean, lilac-coloured dress. Her hair was beautifully combed and she looked commanding, just like she used to.

'Feel any better?' I asked, somewhat timidly.

She gave me a pained look and said: 'Come here! Where have you been all this time, eh?' I'd hardly time to answer when she seized me by the hair, took a long, supple knife made from a saw in her other hand and hit me several times with the flat side, lifting her hand high above her head. The knife flew out of her hand.

'Pick it up. Give it to me.'

I picked it up, threw it on the table and Mother pushed me away. I sat in front of the stove, terribly frightened, and watched every movement she made. She got up from the table and slowly made her way back to her corner, lay down on her bed and started wiping the sweat off her face with a handkerchief. Her hand shook, and twice dropped down to the pillow, which she wiped instead of her face.

'Bring me some water.'

I scooped a cupful from the bucket and she raised her head with difficulty, took a small sip, and a cold hand pushed mine away. She sighed deeply, looked at the corner where the icons were, then looked at me again.

What I thought was a smile flickered on her quivering lips. Gradually she lowered her eyelashes. Keeping her elbows pressed tightly against her side she moved her finger weakly while her hands crept slowly across the breast towards her throat. A shadow ran over her face, seemed to penetrate it, tightening her yellow skin and sharpening her nose. Her mouth opened as if in surprise, but I couldn't hear her breathe.

For what seemed an eternity I stood there with the cup in my hand and watched her face turn stiff, cold and grey.

When Grandfather came in I said:

'Mother's dead.'

He looked at the bed, 'Lying again, are you?'

He went over to the stove and made a deafening noise with the griddle and oven door as he drew out a pie. I looked at him, knowing full well Mother had died and wondering when it would sink in.

My stepfather arrived in a linen jacket and white cap. Without any noise he took a chair and carried it to Mother's bed, suddenly let it fall heavily on the floor and made a loud bellowing noise, like a trumpet:

'Yes, she's dead … look.'

Grandfather, with staring eyes, quietly shuffled away from the stove like a blind man, still carrying the griddle.

MY CHILDHOOD, 1913

EMMELINE PANKHURST

I HAVE NOT PERSONALLY SUFFERED from the deprivations, the bitterness and sorrow which bring so many men and women to a realization of social injustice. My childhood was protected by love and a comfortable home. Yet, while still a very young child, I began instinctively to feel that there was something lacking, even in my own home, some false conception of family relations, some incomplete ideal.

This vague feeling of mine began to shape itself into conviction about the time my brothers and I were sent to school. The education of the English boy, then as now, was considered a much more serious matter than the education of an English boy's sister. My parents, especially my father, discussed the question of my brothers' education as a matter of real importance. My education and that of my sister were scarcely discussed at all. Of course we went to a carefully selected girls' school, but beyond the facts that the headmistress was a gentlewoman and that all the pupils were girls of my own class, nobody seemed concerned. A girl's education at that time seemed to have for its prime object the art of 'making home attractive' – presumably to migratory male relatives. It used to puzzle me to understand why I was under such a particular obligation to make home attractive to my brothers. We were on excellent terms of friendship, but it was never suggested to them as a duty that they make home attractive to me. Why not? Nobody seemed to know.

The answer to these puzzling questions came to me unexpectedly one night when I lay in my little bed waiting for sleep to overtake me. It was a custom of my father and mother to make the round of our bedrooms every night before going themselves to bed. When they entered my room that night I was still awake, but for some reason I chose to feign slumber. My father bent over me, shielding the candle flame with his big hand. I cannot know exactly what thought was in his mind as he gazed down at me, but I heard him say, somewhat sadly, 'What a pity she wasn't born a lad.'

My first hot impulse was to sit up in bed and protest that I didn't want to be a boy, but I lay still and heard my parents' footsteps pass on toward the next child's bed. I thought about my father's remark for many days afterward, but I think I never decided that I regretted my sex. However, it was made quite clear that men considered themselves superior to women, and that women apparently acquiesced in that belief.

I found this view of things difficult to reconcile with the fact that both my father and my mother were advocates of equal suffrage. I was very young when the Reform Act of 1867 was passed, but I very well remember the agitation caused by certain circumstances attending it. This Reform Act, known as the Household Franchise Bill, marked the first popular extension of the ballot in England since 1832. Under its terms, householders paying a minimum of ten pounds a year rental were given the Parliamentary vote. While it was still under discussion in the House of Commons, John Stuart Mill moved an amendment to the bill to include women householders as well as men. The amendment was defeated, but in the act as passed the word 'man' instead of the usual 'male person' was used. Now, under another act of Parliament it had been decided that the word 'man' always included 'woman' unless otherwise specifically stated. For example, in certain acts containing rate-paying clauses, the masculine noun and pronoun are used throughout, but the provisions apply to women rate-payers as well as to men. So when the Reform Bill with the word 'man' in it became law, many women believed that the right of suffrage had actually been bestowed upon them. A tremendous amount of discussion ensued, and the matter was finally tested by a large number of women seeking to have their names placed upon the register as voters. In my city of Manchester 3,924 women, out of a total of 4,215 possible women voters, claimed their votes, and their claim was defended in the law courts by eminent lawyers, including my future husband, Dr Pankhurst. Of course the women's claim was settled adversely in the courts, but the agitation resulted in a strengthening of the women's-suffrage agitation all over the country.

I was too young to understand the precise nature of the affair, but I shared in the general excitement. From reading newspapers aloud to my father I had developed a genuine interest in politics, and the Reform Bill presented itself to my young intelligence as something that was going to do the most wonderful good to the country. The first election after the bill became law was naturally a memorable occasion. It is chiefly memorable to me because it was the first one in which I ever participated. My sister and I had just been presented with new winter frocks, green in colour, and made alike, after the custom of proper British families. Every girl child in those days wore a red flannel petticoat, and when we first put on our new frocks I was struck with the fact that we were wearing red and green – the colours of the Liberal Party. Since our father was a Liberal, of course the Liberal Party ought to carry the election, and I conceived a brilliant scheme for helping its progress. With my small sister trotting after me, I walked the better part of a mile to the nearest polling-booth. It happened to be in a rather rough factory district, but we did not notice that. Arrived there, we two children picked up our green skirts to show our scarlet petticoats, and brimful of importance, walked up and down before the assembled crowds to encourage the Liberal vote. From this eminence we were shortly snatched by outraged authority in the form of a nursery-maid. I believe we were sent to bed into the bargain, but I am not entirely clear on this point.

MY OWN STORY, 1914

OLAUDAH EQUIANO

As I was the youngest of the sons, I became, of course, the greatest favourite with my mother, and was always with her; and she used to take particular pains to form my mind. I was trained up from my earliest years in the art of war; my daily exercise was shooting and throwing javelins; and my mother adorned me with emblems, after the manner of our greatest warriors. In this way I grew up till I was turned the age of eleven, when an end was put to my happiness in the following manner.

Generally when the grown people in the neighbourhood were gone far in the fields to labour, the children assembled together in some of the neighbours' premises to play; and commonly some of us used to get up a tree to look out for any assailant, or kidnapper, that might come upon us; for they sometimes took those opportunities of our parents' absence to attack and carry off as many as they could seize. One day, as I was watching at the top of a tree in our yard, I saw one of those people come into the yard of our next neighbour but one, to kidnap, there being many stout young people in it. Immediately on this I gave the alarm of the rogue, and he was surrounded by the stoutest of them, who entangled him with cords, so that he could not escape till some of the grown people came and secured him. But alas! ere long it was my fate to be thus attacked, and to be carried off, when none of the grown people were nigh. One day, when all our people were gone out to their works as usual, and only I and my dear sister were left to mind the house, two men and a woman got over our walls, and in a moment seized us both, and, without giving us time to cry out, or make resistance, they stopped our mouths, and ran off with us into the nearest wood. Here they tied our hands, and continued to carry us as far as they could, till night came on, when we reached a small house where the robbers halted for refreshment, and spent the night. We were then unbound, but were unable to take any food; and, being quite overpowered by fatigue and grief, our only relief was some sleep, which allayed our misfortune for a short time. The next morning we left the house, and continued travelling all the day. For a long time we had kept to the woods, but at last we came into a road which I believed I knew. I had now some hopes of being delivered; for we had advanced but a little way before I discovered some people at a distance, on which I began to cry out for their assistance: but my cries had no other effect than to make them tie me faster and stop my mouth, and then they put me into a large sack. They also stopped my sister's mouth, and tied her hands; and in this manner we proceeded till we were out of the sight of these people. When we went to rest the following night they offered us some victuals; but we refused it; and the only comfort we had was in being in one another's arms all that night, and bathing each other with our tears. But alas! we were soon deprived of even the small comfort of weeping together.

The next day proved a day of greater sorrow than I had yet experienced; for my sister and I were then separated, while we lay clasped in each other's arms. It was in vain that we besought them not to part us; she was torn from me, and immediately carried away, while I was left in a state of distraction not to be described. I cried and grieved continually; and for several days I did not eat anything but what they forced into my mouth. At length, after many days travelling, during which I had often changed masters, I got into the hands of a chieftain, in a very pleasant country. This man had two wives and some children, and they all used me extremely well, and did all they could to comfort me; particularly the first wife, who was something like my mother. Although I was a great many days journey from my father's house, yet these people spoke exactly the same language with us. This first master of mine, as I may call him, was a smith, and my principal employment was working his bellows, which were the same kind as I had seen in my vicinity.

THE INTERESTING NARRATIVE OF THE LIFE OF OLAUDAH EQUIANO, OR GUSTAVUS VASSA, THE AFRICAN, WRITTEN BY HIMSELF, 1789

ALBERT EINSTEIN

WHEN I WAS A FAIRLY PRECOCIOUS YOUNG MAN I became thoroughly impressed with the futility of the hopes and strivings that chase most men relentlessly through life. Moreover, I soon discovered the cruelty of that chase, which in those years was much more carefully covered up by hypocrisy and glittering words than is the case today. By the mere existence of his stomach everyone was condemned to participate in that chase. The stomach might well be satisfied by such participation, but not man insofar as he is a thinking and feeling being. As the first way out there was religion, which is implanted into every child by way of the traditional education-machine. Thus I came – though the child of entirely irreligious (Jewish) parents – to a deep religiousness, which, however, reached an abrupt end at the age of twelve. Through the reading of popular scientific books I soon reached the conviction that much in the stories of the Bible could not be true. The consequence was a positively [fanatic orgy] of freethinking coupled with the impression that youth is intentionally being deceived by the state through lies; it was a crushing impression. Mistrust of every kind of authority grew out of this experience, a sceptical attitude toward the convictions that were alive in any specific social environment – an attitude that has never again left me, even though, later on, it has been tempered by a better insight into the causal connections.

It is quite clear to me that the religious paradise of youth, which was thus lost, was a first attempt to free myself from the chains of the 'merely personal', from an existence dominated by wishes, hopes, and primitive feelings. Out yonder there was this huge world, which exists independently of us human beings and which stands before us like a great, eternal riddle, at least partially accessible to our inspection and thinking. The contemplation of this world beckoned as a liberation, and I soon noticed that many a man whom I had learned to esteem and to admire had found inner freedom and security in its pursuit. The mental grasp of this extra-personal world within the frame of our capabilities presented itself to my mind, half consciously, half unconsciously, as a supreme goal. Similarly motivated men of the present and of the past, as well as the insights they had achieved, were the friends who could not be lost. The road to this paradise was not as comfortable and alluring as the road to the religious paradise; but it has shown itself reliable, and I have never regretted having chosen it.

What I have said here is true only in a certain sense, just as a drawing consisting of a few strokes can do justice to a complicated object, full of perplexing details, only in a very limited sense. If an individual enjoys well-ordered thoughts, it is quite possible that this side of his nature may grow more pronounced at the cost of the other sides and thus may determine his mentality in increasing degree. In this case it may well be that such an individual sees in retrospect a uniformly systematic development, whereas the actual experience takes place in kaleidoscopic particular situations. The great variety of the external situations and the narrowness of the momentary content of consciousness bring about a sort of atomizing of the life of every human being. In a man of my type, the turning point of the development lies in the fact that gradually the major interest disengages itself to a far-reaching degree from the momentary and the merely personal and turns toward the striving for a conceptual grasp of things. Looked at from this point of view, the above schematic remarks contain as much truth as can be stated with such brevity.

AUTOBIOGRAPHICAL NOTES, 1949

MUHAMMAD ALI

THE STORY THAT MY BOXING CAREER BEGAN because my bike was stolen is a true one, as far as it goes. But that was only a part of it. I was twelve years old, and me and Johnny Willis, my closest buddy, had been out riding around on our bikes until the rain got too heavy. We were looking for something else to do when Johnny suddenly remembered seeing an ad for a black business exhibition at Columbia Auditorium on 4th and York. The auditorium is a big recreational center, with a boxing gym and a bowling alley. Every year the black people in the city hold a big bazaar, the Louisville Home Show, at the Columbia Gym.

At first I didn't want to go to the Home Show very much, but when we read the leaflet we saw that there would be free popcorn, free hot dogs and free candy. Besides, my father had bought me a new bike for Christmas, a Schwinn with red lights and chrome trim, a spotlight in the front, whitewall tires and chrome spokes and rims, and I wanted to show it off.

At the show we focused in on the food, and we hung around eating until seven o'clock, when everybody was leaving.

The rain was still coming down heavy as we left, so it took a while for us to notice that my bicycle was gone. Angry and frightened of what my father would do, we ran up and down the streets, asking about the bike. Someone told us to go downstairs to the Columbia Gym. 'There's a policeman, Joe Elsby Martin, down there in the recreation center. Go and see him.'

I ran downstairs, crying, but the sights and sounds and the smell of the boxing gym excited me so much that I almost forgot about the bike.

There were about ten boxers in the gym, some hitting the speed bag, some in the ring, sparring, some jumping rope. I stood there, smelling the sweat and rubbing alcohol, and a feeling of awe came over me. One slim boy shadowboxing in the ring was throwing punches almost too fast for my eyes to follow.

'You'll have to give me a report,' Martin said calmly, and wrote down what I told him. Then, as I was about to go, he tapped me on the shoulder. 'By the way, we got boxing every night, Monday through Friday, from six to eight. Here's an application in case you want to join the gym.'

I was about 112 pounds, skinny, and I'd never had on a pair of boxing gloves. I folded up the paper and stuck it in my pocket, thinking it was a poor thing to take home instead of a bike. That night my father bawled me out for being so careless. And for once I was in total agreement with him. I told him I was sorry, and I meant it.

That Saturday I was home looking at a TV show called *Tomorrow's Champions*, an amateur boxing show, and there was the face of Joe Martin, working in the corner with one of his boys.

I nudged my mother. 'Bird, that's the man I told about the bicycle. He wants me to come and box. Where's that application?'

She had taken the paper out of my pocket when she washed my clothes, but now she went and got it. 'You want to be a boxer?' She was serious.

'I want to be a boxer,' I said.

'How you going to get down there? It's a long way off. Your bike is gone. There's no car fare for that.'

'Oh, I'll borrow somebody's bike,' I said. 'And I don't have nothin' else to do.'

I remember my father looked uncertain. Then someone outside opened the door and yelled, 'Johnny Willis's out here waiting for Cassius.'

That decided it. 'Well, boxing is better than running around with Willis and that gang,' my father said. 'Anything will beat that. Let him go.'

When I got to the gym, I was so eager I jumped into the ring with some older boxer and began throwing wild punches. In a minute my nose started bleeding. My mouth was hurt. My head was dizzy. Finally someone pulled me out of the ring.

At that moment I was thinking I would be better off in the streets, but a slim welterweight came up and put his arms around my shoulders saying, 'You'll be all right. Just don't box those older fellows first. Box the fellows who are new, like you. Get someone to teach you how to do it.'

But there was hardly anybody to teach me anything. Martin knew a little. He could show me how to place my feet and how to throw a right cross, but he knew very little else. I was fighting like a girl, throwing wild, loopy punches. But something was driving me and I kept fighting and I kept training. And although I still roamed the streets with the gang, I kept coming back to the gym.

THE GREATEST: MY OWN STORY, 1975

～ YOUTH ～

AGES 13–20

'I had arrived at that difficult and
unattractive age of adolescence, conforming
to the teenage pattern. I was a worshipper of
the foolhardy and the melodramatic, a
dreamer and a moper, raging at life and
loving it, a mind in a chrysalis yet erupting
with sudden bursts of maturity.'

CHARLES CHAPLIN,
MY AUTOBIOGRAPHY, 1964

VIRGINIA WOOLF

M ANY BRIGHT COLOURS; MANY DISTINCT SOUNDS; some human beings, caricatures; comic; several violent moments of being, always including a circle of the scene which they cut out: and all surrounded by a vast space – that is a rough visual description of childhood. This is how I shape it; and how I see myself as a child, roaming about, in that space of time which lasted from 1882 to 1895. A great hall I could liken it to; with windows letting in strange lights; and murmurs and spaces of deep silence. But somehow into that picture must be brought, too, the sense of movement and change. Nothing remained stable long. One must get the feeling of everything approaching and then disappearing, getting large, getting small, passing at different rates of speed past the little creature; one must get the feeling that made her press on, the little creature driven on as she was by growth of her legs and arms, driven without her being able to stop it, or to change it, driven as a plant is driven up out of the earth, up until the stalk grows, the leaf grows, buds swell. That is what is indescribable, that is what makes all images too static, for no sooner has one said this was so, than it was past and altered. How immense must be the force of life which turns a baby, who can just distinguish a great blot of blue and purple on a black background, into the child who thirteen years later can feel all that I felt on May 5th 1895 – now almost exactly to a day, forty-four years ago – when my mother died.

'A SKETCH OF THE PAST', 1940

EVA HOFFMAN

I T IS APRIL 1959, I'm standing at the railing of the *Batory*'s upper deck, and I feel that my life is ending. I'm looking out at the crowd that has gathered on the shore to see the ship's departure from Gdynia

– a crowd that, all of a sudden, is irrevocably on the other side – and I want to break out, run back, run toward the familiar excitement, the waving hands, the exclamations. We can't be leaving all this behind – but we are. I am thirteen years old, and we are emigrating. It's a notion of such crushing, definitive finality that to me it might as well mean the end of the world.

My sister, four years younger than I, is clutching my hand wordlessly; she hardly understands where we are, or what is happening to us. My parents are highly agitated; they had just been put through a body search by the customs police, probably as the farewell gesture of anti-Jewish harassment. Still, the officials weren't clever enough, or suspicious enough, to check my sister and me – lucky for us, since we are both carrying some silverware we were not allowed to take out of Poland in large pockets sewn onto our skirts especially for this purpose, and hidden under capacious sweaters.

When the brass band on the shore strikes up the jaunty mazurka rhythms of the Polish anthem, I am pierced by a youthful sorrow so powerful that I suddenly stop crying and try to hold still against the pain. I desperately want time to stop, to hold the ship still with the force of my will. I am suffering my first, severe attack of nostalgia, or *tęsknota* – a word that adds to nostalgia the tonalities of sadness and longing. It is a feeling whose shades and degrees I'm destined to know intimately, but at this hovering moment, it comes upon me like a visitation from a whole new geography of emotions, an annunciation of how much an absence can hurt. Or a premonition of absence, because at this divide, I'm filled to the brim with what I'm about to lose – images of Cracow, which I loved as one loves a person, of the sun-baked villages where we had taken summer vacations, of the hours I spent poring over passages of music with my piano teacher, of conversations and escapades with friends. Looking ahead, I come across an enormous, cold blankness – a darkening, an erasure, of the imagination, as if a camera eye has snapped shut, or as if a heavy curtain has been pulled over the future. Of the place where we're going – Canada – I know nothing. There are vague outlines of half a continent, a sense of vast spaces and little habitation. When my parents were hiding in a branch-covered forest bunker during the war, my father had a book with him called *Canada Fragrant with Resin* which, in his horrible confinement, spoke to him of majestic wilderness, of animals roaming without being pursued, of freedom. That is partly why we are going there, rather than to Israel, where most of our Jewish friends have gone. But to me the word 'Canada' has ominous echoes of the 'Sahara'. No, my mind rejects the idea of being taken there, I don't want to be pried out of my childhood, my pleasures, my safety, my hopes for becoming a pianist. The *Batory* pulls away, the foghorn emits its lowing, shofar sound, but my being is engaged in a stubborn refusal to move. My parents put their hands on my shoulders consolingly; for a moment, they allow themselves to acknowledge that there's pain in this departure, much as they wanted it.

Many years later, at a stylish party in New York, I met a woman who told me that she had had an enchanted childhood. Her father was a highly positioned diplomat in an Asian country, and she had lived surrounded by sumptuous elegance, the courtesy of servants, and the delicate advances of older men. No wonder, she said, that when this part of her life came to an end, at age thirteen, she felt she had been exiled from paradise, and had been searching for it ever since.

No wonder. But the wonder is what you can make a paradise out of. I told her I grew up in a lumpen apartment in Cracow, squeezed into three rudimentary rooms with four other people, surrounded by squabbles, dark political rumblings, memories of wartime suffering, and daily struggle for existence. And yet, when it came time to leave, I, too, felt I was being pushed out of the happy, safe enclosures of Eden.

Lost in Translation: A life in a New Language, 1989

JANET FRAME

WHERE IN MY EARLIER YEARS time had been horizontal, progressive, day after day, year after year, with memories being a true personal history known by dates and specific years, or vertical, with events stacked one upon the other, 'sacks on the mill and more on still', the adolescent time now became a whirlpool, and so the memories do not arrange themselves to be observed and written about, they whirl, propelled by a force beneath, with different memories rising to the surface at different times and thus denying the existence of a 'pure' autobiography and confirming, for each moment, a separate story accumulating to a million stories, all different and with some memories forever staying beneath the surface. I sit here at my desk, peering into the depths of the dance, for the movement is dance with its own pattern, neither good nor bad, but individual in its own right – a dance of dust or sunbeams or bacteria or notes of sounds or colors or liquids or ideas that the writer, trying to write an autobiography, clings to in one moment only.

TO THE IS-LAND, 1982

BERTRAND RUSSELL

M Y CHILDHOOD WAS, on the whole, happy and straightforward, and I felt affection for most of the grown-ups with whom I was brought in contact. I remember a very definite change when I reached what in modern child psychology is called the 'latency period'. At this stage, I began to enjoy using slang, pretending to have no feelings, and being generally 'manly'. I began to despise my people, chiefly because of their extreme horror of slang and their absurd notion that it was dangerous to climb trees. So many things were forbidden me that I acquired the habit of deceit, in which I persisted up to the age of twenty-one. It became second nature to me to think whatever I was doing had better be kept to myself, and I have never quite overcome the impulse to concealment which was thus generated. I still have an impulse to hide what I am reading when anybody comes into the room, and to hold my tongue generally as to where I have been, and what I have done. It is only with a certain effort of will that I can overcome this impulse, which was generated by the years during which I had to find my way among a set of foolish prohibitions.

The years of adolescence were to me very lonely and very unhappy. Both in the life of the emotions and in the life of the intellect, I was obliged to preserve an impenetrable secrecy towards my people. My interests were divided between sex, religion, and mathematics. I find the recollection of my sexual preoccupation in adolescence unpleasant. I do not like to remember how I felt in those years, but I will do my best to relate things as they were and not as I could wish them to have been. The facts of sex first became known to me when I was twelve years old, through a boy named Ernest Logan who had been one of my kindergarten companions at an earlier age. He and I slept in the same room one night, and he explained the nature of copulation and its part in the generation of children, illustrating his remarks by funny stories. I found what he said extremely interesting, although I had as yet no physical response.

The Autobiography of Bertrand Russell, 1967–1969

ROBERT GRAVES

FROM THE MOMENT I ARRIVED AT THE SCHOOL I suffered an oppression of spirit that I hesitate now to recall in its full intensity. It was something like being in that chilly cellar at Laufzorn among the potatoes, but being a potato out of a different bag from the rest. The school consisted of about six hundred boys. The chief interests were games and romantic friendships. School-work was despised by every one; the scholars, of whom there were about fifty in the school at any given time, were not concentrated in a single dormitory-house as at Winchester, but divided among ten. They were known as 'pro's' and unless they were good at games and willing to pretend that they hated work as much or more than the non-scholars, and ready whenever called on to help these with their work, they usually had a bad time. I was a scholar and really liked work, and I was surprised and disappointed at the apathy of the class-rooms. My first term I was left alone more or less, it being a school convention that new boys should be neither encouraged nor baited. The other boys seldom spoke to them except to send them on errands, or to inform them of breaches of school convention. But my second term the trouble began. There were a number of things that naturally made for my unpopularity. Besides being a scholar and not outstandingly good at games, I was always short of pocket-money. I could not conform to the social custom of treating my contemporaries to food at the school shop, and because I could not treat them I could not accept their treating. My clothes were all wrong; they conformed outwardly to the school pattern, but they were ready-made and not of the best quality cloth that the other boys all wore. Even so, I had not been taught how to make the best of them. Neither my mother nor my father had any regard for the niceties of modern dress, and my elder brothers were abroad by this time. The other boys in my house, except for five scholars, were nearly all the sons of business men; it was a class of whose interests and prejudices I knew nothing, having hitherto only met boys of the professional class. And I talked too much for their liking. A further disability was that I was as prudishly innocent as my mother had planned I should be. I knew nothing about simple sex, let alone the many refinements of sex constantly referred to in school conversation. My immediate reaction was one of disgust. I wanted to run away.

The most unfortunate disability of all was that my name appeared on the school list as 'R. von R. Graves'. I had only known hitherto that my second name was Ranke; the 'von', discovered on my birth certificate, was disconcerting. Carthusians were secretive about their second names; if these were fancy ones they usually managed to conceal them. Ranke, without the 'von' I could no doubt have passed off as monosyllabic and English, but 'von Ranke' was glaring. The business class to which most of the boys belonged was strongly feeling at this time the threat and even the necessity of a trade war; 'German' meant 'dirty German'. It meant 'cheap, shoddy goods competing with our sterling industries', and it also meant military menace, Prussianism, sabre-rattling. There was another boy in my house with a German name, but English by birth and upbringing. He was treated much as I was. On the other hand a French boy in the house was very popular, though he was not much good at games; King Edward VII had done his *entente* work very thoroughly. There was also considerable anti-Jewish feeling (the business prejudice again) and the legend was put about that I was not only a German but a German Jew.

Of course I always maintained that I was Irish. This claim was resented by an Irish boy who had been in the house about a year and a half longer than myself. He went out of his way to hurt me, not only by physical acts of spite, like throwing ink over my school-books, hiding my games-clothes, setting on me suddenly from behind corners, pouring water over me at night, but by continually forcing his bawdy humour on my prudishness and inviting everybody to laugh at my disgust; he also built up a sort of humorous legend of my hypocrisy and concealed depravity. I came near a nervous breakdown. School morality prevented me from informing the house-master of my troubles. The house-monitors were supposed to keep order and preserve the moral tone of the house, but at this time they were not the sort to interfere in any case of bullying among the juniors. I tried violent resistance, but as the odds were always heavily against me this merely encouraged the ragging. Complete passive resistance would probably have been better. I only got accustomed to bawdy-talk in my last two years at Charterhouse, and it was not until I had been some time in the army that I got hardened to it and could reply in kind to insults.

A former headmaster of Charterhouse, an innocent man, is reported to have said at a Headmasters' Conference: 'My boys are amorous but seldom erotic.' Few cases of eroticism indeed ever came to his notice; there were not more than five or six big rows all the time I was at Charterhouse and expulsions were rare. But the house-masters knew little about what went on in their houses; their living quarters were removed from the boys'. There was a true distinction between 'amorousness', by which the headmaster meant a sentimental falling in love with younger boys, and eroticism, which was adolescent lust. The intimacy, as the newspapers call it, that frequently took place was practically never between an elder boy and the object of his affection, for that would have spoilt the romantic illusion, which was heterosexually cast. It was between boys of the same age who were not in love, but used each other coldly as convenient sex-instruments. So the atmosphere was always heavy with romance of a very conventional early-Victorian type, yet complicated by cynicism and foulness.

GOOD-BYE TO ALL THAT, 1929

HARPO MARX

S CHOOL WAS ALL WRONG. It didn't teach anybody how to exist from day to day, which was how the poor had to live. School prepared you for Life – that thing in the far-off future – but not for the World, the thing you had to face today, tonight, and when you woke up in the morning with no idea of what the new day would bring.

When I was a kid there really was no Future. Struggling through one twenty-four-hour span was rough enough without brooding about the next one. You could laugh about the Past, because you'd been lucky enough to survive it. But mainly there was only a Present to worry about.

Another complaint I had was that school taught you about holidays you could never afford to celebrate, like Thanksgiving and Christmas. It didn't teach you about the real holidays like St Patrick's Day, when you could watch a parade for free, or Election Day, when you could make a giant bonfire in the middle of the street and the cops wouldn't stop you. School didn't teach you what to do when you were stopped by an enemy gang – when to run, when to stand your ground. School didn't teach you how to collect tennis balls, build a scooter, ride the El trains and trolleys, hitch onto delivery wagons, own a dog, go for a swim, get a chunk of ice or a piece of fruit – all without paying a cent.

School didn't teach you which hockshops would give you dough without asking where you got your merchandise, or how to shoot pool or bet on a poker hand or where to sell junk or how to find sleeping room in a bed with four other brothers.

School simply didn't teach you how to be poor and live from day to day. This I had to learn for myself, the best way I could. In the streets I was, according to present-day standards, a juvenile delinquent. But by the East Side standards of 1902, I was an honors student.

HARPO SPEAKS, 1961

MAHATMA GANDHI

A RELATIVE AND I BECAME FOND OF SMOKING. Not that we saw any good in smoking, or were enamoured of the smell of a cigarette. We simply imagined a sort of pleasure in emitting clouds of smoke from our mouths. My uncle had the habit, and when we saw him smoking, we thought we should copy his example. But we had no money. So we began pilfering stumps of cigarettes thrown away by my uncle.

The stumps, however, were not always available, and could not emit much smoke either. So we began to steal coppers from the servant's pocket money in order to purchase Indian cigarettes. But the question was where to keep them. We could not of course smoke in the presence of elders. We managed somehow for a few weeks on these stolen coppers. In the meantime we heard that the stalks of a certain plant were porous and could be smoked like cigarettes. We got them and began this kind of smoking.

But we were far from being satisfied with such things as these. Our want of independence began to smart. It was unbearable that we should be unable to do anything without the elders' permission. At last, in sheer disgust, we decided to commit suicide!

But how were we to do it? From where were we to get the poison? We heard that *Dhatura* seeds were an effective poison. Off we went to the jungle in search of these seeds, and got them. Evening was thought to be the auspicious hour ... But our courage failed us. Supposing we were not instantly killed? And what was the good of killing ourselves? Why not rather put up with the lack of independence? But we swallowed two or three seeds nevertheless. We dared not take more ...

I realized that it was not as easy to commit suicide as to contemplate it. And since then, whenever I have heard of someone threatening to commit suicide, it has had little or no effect on me.

The thought of suicide ultimately resulted in both of us bidding goodbye to the habit of smoking stumps of cigarettes and of stealing the servant's coppers for the purpose of smoking.

Ever since I have been grown up, I have never desired to smoke and have always regarded the habit of smoking as barbarous, dirty and harmful. I have never understood why there is such a rage for smoking throughout the world. I cannot bear to travel in a compartment full of people smoking. I become choked.

AN AUTOBIOGRAPHY: THE STORY OF MY EXPERIMENTS WITH TRUTH, 1927–1929

MAXIM GORKY

ALL THE SAME I DID RUN AWAY in the spring. One morning I was sent to buy some sugar and tea. The shopkeeper, who was having a row with his wife at the time, did not take any notice of me when I entered and he hit her over the head with a weight from a pair of scales. She ran out into the street and collapsed. A crowd gathered immediately and the woman was taken to hospital in a four-wheeled cab. I ran after the driver and before I knew where I was I found myself on the banks of the Volga – with a twenty-kopek piece in my hand. The spring day was bright and radiant, and the Volga was in full flood. Everything around me was animated, spacious – and it seemed that up to then I had been living like a mouse in a cellar. So I decided not to go back to my master and mistress, nor to Grandmother at Kunavino ....

For two or three days I wandered around the quays, scrounging food from kind-hearted porters with whom I spent the nights. After not very long one of them said:

'You're wasting your time round here! Go to the steamship *Dobry*, they need a washer-up.'

So I went. A tall, bearded steward in a black silk peakless cap peered at me through his spectacles with dull eyes and said softly:

'The pay's two roubles a month. Where's your passport?'

I said that I did not have one so the steward thought for a moment and said:

'Fetch your mother.'

I rushed back to Grandmother who approved of my trying to get a job and persuaded Grandfather to go down to the labour exchange and get me a passport while she accompanied me back to the ship.

'Fine,' the steward said as he looked us over. 'Let's go.'

He took me astern where an enormous cook in a white jacket and hat was sitting at a table sipping tea and puffing away at a thick cigarette. The steward pushed me over to him and announced:

'The new dish-washer.'

Then he immediately left us.

The cook snorted, his black whiskers bristled and he shouted after the steward:

'You'd take on any street urchin, as long as it's cheap labour.'

He angrily shook his head with its short black hair, opened his eyes wide, stiffened up, puffed himself out and shouted in a loud voice:

'And who are you?'

I took a great dislike to that man. Although he was dressed in white, to me he seemed filthy. A kind of wool grew on his fingers and hair stuck out of his big ears.

'I'm hungry,' I said.

He winked and suddenly his fierce expression changed into a broad smile. His chubby, flushed-looking cheeks rippled in waves down to his ears, revealing large, horsy teeth, and his whiskers gently drooped. He looked just like a fat, kindly old peasant woman. He threw what was left of his tea overboard and poured a fresh cup. Then he pushed a whole French roll and a large slice of sausage over to me.

'Tuck in! Got a mother and a father? Know how to steal? Well, don't worry, we're all thieves here, so we'll teach you!'

He sounded just like a dog barking. His enormous face, which was shaved until it was blue, had thick networks of red veins around the puffy, purple nose which drooped down over his whiskers. His lower lip hung heavily, as if in disgust, and a lighted cigarette stuck to the corner of his mouth. Obviously he had just had a bath, as he smelled of birch branches, and pepper brandy, and heavy beads of sweat glistened on his temples and neck.

When I had drunk my tea he shoved over a one-rouble note.

'Go and buy yourself two aprons with stomachers. No, wait, I'll go and get them myself.'

He straightened his cap and went off, swaying heavily to and fro, feeling the deck with his feet – just like a bear.

It was night-time now. The moon shone brightly, sailing away from the port side of the ship into the meadows. The old reddish steamboat which had a white stripe on its funnel moved slowly and slapped its paddles unevenly in the silvery water. Dark banks seemed to be gently swimming towards it and threw shadows over the river. Along their ridges I could make out the red lights of cottage windows. In one of the villages they were singing, girls were dancing, and the refrain *ai lyuli* sounded like 'hallelujah' to me.

Our ship was towing a barge, which was painted dirty red as well, and it moved behind us at the end of a long cable. Its deck was covered by an iron cage full of convicts sentenced to penal colonies or hard labour. A sentry's bayonet shone on the bows like a candle, and the tiny stars in the blue sky glinted like candles as well. No noise came from the barge and it was brightly illuminated by the moon. Behind metal bars I could see dim, round grey figures – these were convicts looking at the Volga. The water sobbed and seemed to be crying, and then quietly laughing. Everything around me reminded me of a church; there was that same strong smell of burning oil.

As I looked at the barge I recalled my early childhood, that journey from Astrakhan to Nizhny-Novgorod, Mother's expressionless face, and Grandmother, who had brought me out into the world of people, which was full of fascination despite its harshness. But particularly when I recalled Grandmother, everything nasty and offensive vanished, and changed into something more interesting and pleasant, and everyone became better and kinder.

The beauty of the night brought me near to tears, and that barge made a deep impression on me. In the brooding silence of that warm night it looked like a coffin and seemed completely out of place in that broad expanse of water in full flood. The uneven line of the bank always rising and falling had a pleasant, stimulating effect on me, and made me want to be kind to people and to feel needed by them.

There was nothing special about the passengers however – young and old, men and women, they all looked exactly the same. The ship moved very slowly (businessmen used to travel then by mailboat) and the people round me were gentle and easy-going. From morning until night they ate and drank and made all the crockery, all the knives and forks dirty; it was my job to wash and polish then, and this kept me busy from six in the morning right up to midnight.

MY APPRENTICESHIP, 1916

SHEN FU

WHEN I WAS THIRTEEN, my mother took me along on a visit to her relatives. That was the first time I met my cousin Yün, and we two children got on well together. I had a chance to see her poems that day, and though I sighed at her brilliance I privately feared she was too sensitive to be completely happy in life. Still, I could not forget her, and I remember saying to my mother, 'If you are going to choose a wife for me, I will marry no other than Yün.'

Mother also loved her gentleness, so she was quick to arrange our engagement, sealing the match by giving Yün a gold ring from her own finger. This was in the 39th year of the reign of the Emperor Chien Lung, on the 16th day of the seventh month.

That winter mother took me to their home once again, for the marriage of Yün's cousin. Yün and I were born in the same year, but because she was ten months older than I, I had always called her 'elder sister', while she called me 'younger brother'. We continued to call one another by these names even after we were engaged.

At her cousin's wedding the room was full of beautifully dressed people. Yün alone wore a plain dress; only her shoes were new. I noticed they were skilfully embroidered, and when she told me she had done them herself I began to appreciate that her cleverness lay not only in her writing.

Yün had delicate shoulders and a stately neck, and her figure was slim. Her brows arched over beautiful, lively eyes. Her only blemish was two slightly protruding front teeth, the sign of a lack of good fortune. But her manner was altogether charming, and she captivated all who saw her.

I asked to see more of her poems that day, and found some had only one line, others three or four, and most were unfinished. I asked her why.

'I have done them without a teacher,' she replied, laughing. 'I hope you, my best friend, can be my teacher now and help me finish them.' Then as a joke I wrote on her book, 'The Embroidered Bag of Beautiful Verses'.

Six Records of a Floating Life, 1809

STEPHEN FRY

THE BEGINNING OF MY SECOND YEAR at Uppingham saw me no more clued up about this whole business of sex than I ever had been: I probably had a clearer idea of the terms and their meanings: cunnilingus, urinobibe, Fallopian tubes, epididymis, snatch, pussy, tit, jizz and clit, I knew the words all right. But then I knew what a diminished seventh was, but it didn't mean I could play or sing. I knew what a googly was and I still couldn't bowl a cricket ball without causing twenty-one boys to collapse in a heap of laughter. Knowledge is not always power.

The erotic in life did not occupy me or engage my attention much because I was still neither physically developed nor sexually aware enough to have that need to 'get my bloody rocks off' that seemed so to exercise the other boys, passing their *Penthouses*, sniggers, phwors and Kleenex boxes from study to study. Games and how to avoid them, that was still what mattered most to me. Sweets and where to get them from, that too. Sex, that could take a powder.

And then ...

And then I saw *him* and nothing was ever the same again.

The sky was never the same colour, the moon never the same shape: the air never smelt the same, food never tasted the same. Every word I knew changed its meaning, everything that once was stable and firm became as insubstantial as a puff of wind, and every puff of wind became a solid thing I could feel and touch.

This is where language is so far beyond music. The chord that Max Steiner brings in when Bogart catches sight of Bergman in his bar in *Casablanca*, how can I bring that into a book of black ink marks on white paper? The swell and surge of the *Liebestod* from Tristan, Liszt's Sonata in B minor – even Alfred Brendel can't conjure that up from *this* keyboard, this alphanumeric piano beneath my fingers. Maybe, because sometimes pop music can hit the mark as well as anything else, I could write you out a playlist. We would start with The Monkees:

And then I saw her face, and now I'm a believer

Naaah ... it's no use.

There's nothing for it but old words and cold print. Besides, you've been there yourself. You've been in love. Why am I getting so hysterical? Just about every film, every book, every poem, every song is a love story. This is not a genre with which you are unfamiliar even if by some fluke (whether a cursed fluke or a blessed one I would be the last able to decide) you have never been there yourself.

MOAB IS MY WASHPOT: AN AUTOBIOGRAPHY, 1997

ELIZABETH ASHBRIDGE

THUS MY YOUNG YEARS WERE ATTENDED with such like tender desires, tho' I was sometimes guilty of those things incident to children, but then I always found something in me that made me sorry for what I did amiss. Till I arrived at the age of fourteen years, I was as innocent as most children, about which time my sorrows began, and have continued most part of my life, through my giving way to a foolish passion, in setting my affections on a young man, who became a suitor to me, without my parents' consent, till I suffered myself (I may say with sorrow of heart) to be carried off in the night, and to be married before my parents found me; altho' as soon as they missed me all possible search was made after me, but all in vain, till too late to recover me.

This precipitate act plunged me into a vast scene of sorrow, for I was soon smote with remorse for thus leaving my parents, who had a right to have disposed of me, or at least their approbation ought to have been consulted in the affair, for I was soon chastised for my disobedience. Divine Providence let me see my error, and in five months I was stripped of the darling of my soul, and left a young and disconsolate widow.

I had then no home to fly to. My father was so displeased that he would do nothing for me, but my dear mother had some compassion towards me, and kept me amongst the neighbours for some time, till by her advice I went to Dublin, to a relation of hers, in hopes that absence would help to regain my father's affection. But he continued inflexible and would not send for me, and I dared not to return without his permission. This relation with whom I lived was one of the people called Quakers. His conduct was so different from the manner of my education, which was in the way of the Church of England, that it made my situation disagreeable, for tho' ... I had a religious education, yet I was allowed to sing and dance, which my cousins were against, and I having a great vivacity in my natural disposition could not bear to give way to the gloomy scene of sorrow, and conviction gave it the wrong effect, and made me more wild and airy than before, for which I was often reproved. But I then thought, as a great many do now, that it was the effect of singularity and therefore would not be subject to it.

I having at that time a distant relation in the west of Ireland, I left Dublin, and went there, where I was entertained, and what rendered me disagreeable in the former place was quite pleasing to the latter. Between these two relations I spent 3 years and 2 months. While I was in Ireland I contracted an intimacy with a widow and her daughter, who were Papists, with whom I used to discourse about religion, they in defence of their faith, and I of mine; and altho' I was then very wild, it made me very thoughtful.

SOME ACCOUNT OF THE FORE-PART OF THE LIFE OF ELIZABETH ASHBRIDGE, 1774

EDMUND GOSSE

IT WAS IN MY FIFTEENTH YEAR that I became again, this time intelligently, acquainted with Shakespeare. I got hold of a single play, *The Tempest*, in a school edition, prepared, I suppose, for one of the university examinations which were then being instituted in the provinces. This I read through and through, not disdaining the help of the notes, and revelling in the glossary. I studied *The Tempest* as I had hitherto studied no classic work, and it filled my whole being with music and romance. This book was my own hoarded possession; the rest of Shakespeare's works were beyond my hopes. But gradually I contrived to borrow a volume here and a volume there. I completed *The Merchant of Venice*, read *Cymbeline*, *Julius Caesar* and *Much Ado*; most of the others, I think, remained closed to me for a long time. But these were enough to steep my horizon with all the colours of sunrise. It was due, no doubt, to my bringing up, that the plays never appealed to me as bounded by the exigencies of a stage or played by actors. The images they raised in my mind were of real people moving in the open air, and uttering, in the natural play of life, sentiments that were clothed in the most lovely, and yet, as it seemed to me, the most obvious and the most inevitable language.

FATHER AND SON, 1907

MARY MCCARTHY

I N MY FIRST YEAR AT ANNIE WRIGHT SEMINARY, I lost my virginity. I am not sure whether this was an 'educational' experience or not. The act did not lead to anything and was not repeated for two years. But at least it dampened my curiosity about sex and so left my mind free to think about other things. Since in that way it was formative, I had better tell about it.

It took place in a Marmon roadster, in the front seat – roadsters had no back seats, though there was often a rumble, outside, in the rear, where the trunk is now. That day the car was parked off a lonely Seattle boulevard; it was a dark winter afternoon, probably during Thanksgiving vacation, since I was home from school. In my memory, it feels like a Saturday. 'His' name was Forrest Crosby; he was a Phi Delt, I understood, and twenty-three years old, a year or so out of the university and working for his family's business – the Crosby Lines, which went back and forth across Puget Sound to points like Everett and Bremerton. He was medium short, sophisticated, with bright blue eyes and crisp close-cut ash-blond curly hair, smart gray flannels, navy-blue jacket, and a pipe. He had a friend, Windy Kaufman, who was half-Jewish and rode a motorcycle.

He believed I was seventeen, or, rather, that was what I had told him. Afterwards I had reason to think that while I was adding three years to my age, he was subtracting three from his. So in reality he was an old man of twenty-six. Probably we were both scared by what we were doing, he for prudential reasons and I because of my ignorance, which I could not own up to while pretending to be older. My main aim in life, outside of school (where I could not hide the truth), was to pass for at least sixteen ...

Of the actual penetration, I remember nothing; it was as if I had been given chloroform. How long it lasted, whether or not we were kissing – everything but the bare fact is gone. It must have hurt, but I have no memory of that or of any other sensations, perhaps a slight sense of being stuffed. Yes, there is also a faint recollection of his instructing me to move, keep step as in dancing, but I am not sure of that. What I *am* sure of is a single dreadful, dazed moment having to do with the condom. No, Reader, it did not break.

HOW I GREW, 1987

ST TERESA OF AVILA

I BEGAN TO WEAR FINERY, and to wish to charm by my appearance. I took great care of my hands and my hair, using perfumes and all the vanities I could obtain – and I obtained plenty of them, for I was very persistent. I had no bad intentions, for I should never have wished anyone to sin against God because of me. This excessive care for my appearance, together with other practices which I did not think wicked, lasted for many years, and now I see how wrong they must have been. I had some cousins, who were the only people allowed to enter my father's house. He was very careful about this, and would to God he had been careful about them too. For I now see the danger of conversation, at an age when the virtues should be beginning to grow, with those who do not recognise the vanity of the world, but encourage one to give oneself up to it. They were about my own age, or a little older. We always went about together, and they were very fond of me. I kept conversing with them about everything that pleased them, and I heard their accounts of their affections and follies, which were anything but edifying. What was worse, my soul became exposed to what has been the cause of all its troubles.

If parents were to ask me for advice, I would tell them to take great care what people their children consort with at this age. For great harm comes of bad company, since we are inclined by nature to follow the worse rather than the better. So it was with me. I had a sister many years older than I, from whose modesty and goodness – of which she had plenty – I learnt nothing, whereas from a relative who often visited us I learnt every kind of evil. Her conversation was so frivolous that my mother had tried her hardest to prevent her coming to the house. She seems to have realized what harm this person might do me. But there were so many pretexts for these visits that my mother was powerless. I loved the company of this person. I often talked and gossiped with her, for she helped me to get all the amusements I was so fond of, and even introduced me to some others. She also told me about her friends and own pastimes. Until I knew her, and I was then a little more than fourteen – I mean until we became friends and she took me into her confidence – I do not believe that I had ever turned away from God in mortal sin, or lost my fear of Him.

The Life of St Teresa of Avila by herself, 1562–1565

JEAN-JACQUES ROUSSEAU

Thus I reached my sixteenth year, anxious, unhappy with everything and with myself, with no taste for my work, without pleasure common to my age, devoured by desire for which I did not know the object, crying for no reason, sighing without knowing why; finally, caressing my illusions tenderly, for want of seeing anything around me that might be as valuable.

The Confessions, 1782

CLAUDE MONET

I was unruly from birth; they could never bend me to a rule, even when I was a tiny baby. It was at home that I learned the little that I know. School always had the effect of a prison on me, and I could never convince myself to stay there, even for four hours a day, when the sun was inviting, the sea was so beautiful and it felt so good to run along the cliffs in the fresh air, or to paddle in the water.

Until I was fourteen or fifteen, I lived, to the great despair of my father, this rather irregular but very healthy life. In the meantime, I had learned (as best I could) my four rules of arithmetic, with a touch of spelling. My studies were limited to this. They weren't too tiresome, because they were interspersed with distractions. I doodled in the margins of my books, I decorated the blue paper of my exercise books with ultra-fantastic ornaments, and I depicted there, in the most disrespectful way, the face or profile of my teachers, deformed as much as possible.

I quickly became very good at this game. At fifteen, I was known through the whole of Le Havre as a caricaturist. My reputation was so well established that people everywhere would entreat me for a caricature. The sheer number of orders – also the meagre amount of pocket money that my mother in her generosity provided me with – caused me to make a bold resolution, one that of course scandalized my family: I had people pay me for my portraits. According to the look of a person, I would charge them ten or twenty francs per job, and the scheme succeeded marvellously. In a month my clientele doubled. I could set the standard price at twenty francs without slowing down the orders in any way. If I had continued, I would be a millionaire today.

Thanks to the attention I received, I soon became a well-known figure in the town. In the storefront of the only frame shop doing business in Le Havre, my caricatures were sprawled five or six in a row, insolently, in gold frames, under glass, like works of high art, and when I would see curious onlookers pointing their fingers and gathering in admiration in front of them, crying out – That's so and so! – I would burst with pride.

'AN INTERVIEW', 1900

HARRIETTE WILSON

I SHALL NOT SAY WHY AND HOW I BECAME, at the age of fifteen, the mistress of the Earl of Craven. Whether it was love, or the severity of my father, the depravity of my own heart, or the winning arts of the noble Lord, which induced me to leave my paternal roof and place myself under his protection, does not now much signify: or if it does, I am not in the humour to gratify curiosity in this matter.

I resided on the Marine Parade, at Brighton; and I remember that

Lord Craven used to draw cocoa trees, and his fellows, as he called them, on the best vellum paper, for my amusement. Here stood the enemy, he would say; and here, my love, are my fellows: there the cocoa trees, etc. It was, in fact, a dead bore. All these cocoa trees and fellows, at past eleven o'clock at night, could have no peculiar interest for a child like myself, so lately in the habit of retiring early to rest. One night, I recollect, I fell asleep; and, as I often dream, I said, yawning, and half awake, 'Oh, Lord! oh, Lord! Craven has got me into the West Indies again.' In short, I soon found that I had made a bad speculation by going from my father to Lord Craven. I was even more afraid of the latter than I had been of the former; not that there was any particular harm in the man, beyond his cocoa trees; but we never suited nor understood each other.

I was not depraved enough to determine immediately on a new choice, and yet I often thought about it. How, indeed, could I do otherwise, when the Honourable Frederick Lamb was my constant visitor, and talked to me of nothing else? However, in justice to myself, I must declare that the idea of the possibility of deceiving Lord Craven, while I was under his roof, never once entered into my head. Frederick was then very handsome; and certainly tried, with all his soul and with all his strength, to convince me that constancy to Lord Craven was the greatest nonsense in the world. I firmly believe that Frederick Lamb sincerely loved me, and deeply regretted that he had no fortune to invite me to share with him.

Lord Melbourne, his father, was a good man. Not one of your stiff-laced, moralizing fathers, who preach chastity and forbearance to their children. Quite the contrary; he congratulated his son on the lucky circumstance of his friend Craven having such a fine girl with him. 'No such thing,' answered Frederick Lamb; 'I am unsuccessful there. Harriette will have nothing to do with me.' 'Nonsense!' rejoined Melbourne, in great surprise; 'I never heard anything half so ridiculous in all my life. The girl must be mad! She looks mad: I thought so the other day, when I met her galloping about, with her feathers blowing and her thick dark hair about her ears.'

'I'll speak to Harriette for you,' added his Lordship, after a long pause; and then continued repeating to himself, in an undertone, 'Not have my son, indeed! six feet high! a fine, straight, handsome, noble young fellow! I wonder what she would have!'

In truth, I scarcely knew myself; but something I determined on: so miserably tired was I of Craven, and his cocoa trees, and his sailing boats, and his ugly cotton nightcap. Surely, I would say, all men do not wear those shocking cotton nightcaps; else all women's illusions had been destroyed on the first night of the marriage!

I wonder, thought I, what sort of a nightcap the Prince of Wales wears? Then I went on to wonder whether the Prince of Wales would think me so beautiful as Frederick Lamb did? Next I reflected that Frederick Lamb was younger than the Prince; but then, again, a Prince of Wales!!!

I was undecided: my heart began to soften. I thought of my dear mother, and wished I had never left her. It was too late, however, now. My father would not suffer me to return; and as to passing my life, or any more of it, with Craven, cotton nightcap and all, it was death! He never once made me laugh nor said anything to please me.

Thus, musing, I listlessly turned over my writing-book, half in the humour to address the Prince of Wales. A sheet of paper, covered with Lord Craven's cocoa trees, decided me; and I wrote the following letter, which I addressed to the Prince.

BRIGHTON

I am told that I am very beautiful, so, perhaps, you would like to see me; and I wish that, since so many are disposed to love me, one, for in the humility of my heart I should be quite satisfied with one, would be at the pains to make me love him. In the mean time, this is all very dull work, Sir, and worse even than being at home with my father: so, if you pity me, and believe you could make me in love with you, write to me, and direct to the post-office here.

By return of post, I received an answer nearly to this effect: I believe, from Colonel Thomas.

Miss Wilson's letter has been received by the noble individual to whom it was addressed. If Miss Wilson will come to town, she may have an interview, by directing her letter as before.

I answered this note directly, addressing my letter to the Prince of Wales.

SIR

To travel fifty-two miles, this bad weather, merely to see a man, with only the given number of legs, arms, fingers, etc., would, you must admit, be madness, in a girl like myself, surrounded by humble admirers, who are ever ready to travel any distance for the honour of kissing the tip of her little finger; but if you can prove to me that you are one bit better than any man who may be ready to attend my bidding, I'll e'en start for London directly. So, if you can do anything better, in the way of pleasing a lady, than ordinary men, write directly: if not, adieu, Monsieur le Prince.

HARRIETTE WILSON'S MEMOIRS, 1825

NASDIJJ

ADULTS WHO TRIED TO FIGURE US OUT SOON GAVE UP. Going to the moon would have been a smoother ride.

It was spring, and Bad Nell, Frankie Descheene, and I were fifteen. Fifteen and freaks of nature. Nothing had ever been invented that was more weird than the three of us. Frankie and I were awkward, gawky. We thought our ruffian image might disguise us but it never did. It just made authority look at us all that much harder. We were like huge birds that flap and squawk about. At least Bad Nell had tits and this could define her as a woman. She could lead us around (there were no rings in our noses) with her bracelets and her magical amulets.

She knew the tarot cards, too. We were freaks.

We did not fit in with the nice children. Children who lived in nice houses, had telephones in their rooms, cars in their garages, got good grades on their report cards, took the SAT, and at some point could sit back and let the world come to them.

No one we knew took us seriously. No one believed the things that had been done to us. We were a parenthesis of some yet unseen direction and not unlike the dandelions we sat among.

We could sit anywhere until twilight. Even in the snow.

Adults would ask us where we had been and what we'd been doing. We would attempt to answer this – losing ourselves in the crevice of our words – until whatever adult had inquired as to our whereabouts simply shook his head and walked away. We were a place that lived within.

Adults could not have been more baffled than we were with our demon misfit selves. Onerous with such self-assured cut-throat gristle.

Our communication skills were negligible except as they got expressed among us three and we were forgiving.

We didn't stumble all over our words and our feet when it was just the three of us. We were the demon misfits born near the boxcar tracks. We were hypnotized with hunger, with the emptiness itself, and weary as the outer members of the herd that finally turn around to face the other way, gazing with our thirst into the eyes of growling wolves. Creatures of the ditch bitches. We had not been born so much as spit out like the defiance we still wore as afterbirth. Somehow we always managed to find the edges of the herd. We were the stragglers. It would not have been possible for a nice white person to be our friend. I'm not sure that having grown up makes it much different.

We weren't like anyone we knew.

We didn't talk like anyone we knew.

We didn't dress like anyone we knew.

We didn't want the things other children wanted. Mainly what we wanted was to be left alone.

THE BLOOD RUNS LIKE A RIVER THROUGH MY DREAMS: A MEMOIR, 2000

ELIE WIESEL

LIFE IN THE CATTLE CARS was the death of my adolescence. How quickly I aged. As I child I loved the unexpected: a visitor from afar, an unforeseen event, a marriage, a storm, even a disaster. Anything was preferable to routine. Now it was just the opposite. Anything was preferable to change. We clung to the present, we dreaded the future.

Hunger, thirst, and heat, the fetid stench, the hysterical howling of a woman gone mad – we were ready to endure it all, to suffer it all. So much so that a 'normal', structured social life soon took shape in the car. Families stayed together, sharing whatever came their way: hard-boiled eggs, dried cakes, or fruit, respecting strict rules about drinking water, allowing each member a turn near the barred openings or at the waste pail shielded by blankets. People adjusted with disconcerting rapidity. Morning and evening we said our prayers together. I had brought some precious books along in my pack: a commentary by Rabbi Haim David Azoulai (the Hida), the K'dushat Levi of the Berdichever Rebbe. I opened them and tried hard to concentrate. A phrase of the Zohar, a major work of the Kabala, haunted me: 'When the people of Israel set out into exile, God went with them.' And now? I wondered. How far would God follow us now?

On the last day, when the train stopped near the Auschwitz station, our premonitions resurfaced. A few 'neighbors' devoured more than their rations, as though sensing their days were numbered. My mother kept entreating us: Stay together at all costs. Someone, I can't remember who, asked, 'What if we can't? What if they separate us?' My mother's answer: 'Then we'll meet again at home as soon as the war is over.'

Certain images of the days and nights spent on that train invade my dreams even now: anticipation of danger, fear of the dark; the screams of poor Mrs Schechter, who, in her delirium, saw flames in the distance; the efforts to make her stop; the terror in her little boy's eyes. I recall every hour, every second. How could I forget? They were the last hours I spent with my family: the murmured prayers of my grandmother, whose eyes saw beyond this world; my mother's gestures, which had never been more tender; the troubled face of my little sister, who refused to show her fear. Yes, my memory gathered it all in, retained it all.

There was sudden trepidation that gripped us when, toward midnight, the train lurched forward again after stopping for several hours. I can still hear the whistle. Elsewhere I have told of what happened next – or rather, I have tried to tell it. But it feels like yesterday. It feels like now. Through the cracks in the boards I see barbed wire stretching to infinity. A thought occurs to me: the Kabala is right, infinity exists.

I see myself sitting there, haggard and disoriented, a shadow among shadows. I hear my little sister's fitful breathing. I try to conjure up my mother's features, and my father's. I need someone to reassure me. My heart thunders in deafening beats. Then there is silence, heavy and complete. Something was about to happen, we could feel it. Fate would at last reveal a truth reserved exclusively for us, a primordial truth, an ultimate postulate that would annihilate or overshadow all received ideas. There was a burst of noise and the night was shattered into a thousand pieces. I felt myself shaken, pulled to my feet, pushed toward the door, toward strange shouting beings and barking dogs, a swelling throng that would cover the earth.

ALL RIVERS RUN TO THE SEA: MEMOIRS, 1994

LEO TOLSTOY

THE [RELIGIOUS] BELIEF INSTILLED FROM CHILDHOOD in me, as in so many others, gradually disappeared, but with this difference, that as from fifteen years of age I had begun to read philosophical works, I was conscious of my own disbelief. From the age of sixteen I ceased to pray, and ceased, from conviction, to attend the services of the church and to fast. I no longer accepted the faith of my childhood, but I had a vague belief in something, though I do not think I could exactly explain in what. I believed in a God, or rather, I did not deny the existence of God, but anything relating to the nature of that godhead I could not have described; I denied neither Christ nor His teaching, but in what that teaching consisted I could not have said.

Now, when I think over that time, I see clearly that the faith I had, the only belief which, apart from mere animal instinct, swayed my life, was a belief in a possibility of perfection, though what it was in itself, or what would be its results, I was unable to say. I endeavoured to reach perfection in intellectual attainments: my studies were extended in every direction of which my life afforded me a chance; I strove to strengthen my will, forming for myself rules which I forced myself to follow; I did my best to develop my physical powers by every exercise calculated to give

strength and agility, and by way of accustoming myself to patient
endurance, I subjected myself to many voluntary hardships and
trials of privation. All this I looked upon as necessary to obtain the
perfection at which I aimed. At first, of course, moral perfection
seemed to me the main end, but I soon found myself contemplating
in its stead an ideal of general perfectibility; in other words, I
wished to be better, not in my own eyes nor in those of God, but in
the sight of other men. This feeling again soon ended in another –
the desire to have more power than others, to secure for myself a
greater share of fame, of social distinction, and of wealth.

'MY CONFESSION', 1884

ST AUGUSTINE

I WILL NOW CALL TO MIND MY PAST FOULNESS, and the carnal
corruptions of my soul, not because I love them, but that I
may love Thee, O my God. For love of Thy love do I it, recalling, in
the very bitterness of my remembrance, my most vicious ways, that
Thou mayest grow sweet to me – Thou sweetness without deception!
Thou sweetness happy and assured! – and re-collecting myself out of
that my dissipation, in which I was torn to pieces, while, turned away
from Thee the One, I lost myself among many vanities. For I even
longed in my youth formerly to be satisfied with worldly things, and
I dared to grow wild again with various and shadowy loves; my form
consumed away, and I became corrupt in Thine eyes, pleasing myself,
and eager to please in the eyes of men.

But what was it that I delighted in save to love and to be beloved?
But I held it not in moderation, mind to mind, the bright path of
friendship, but out of the dark concupiscence of the flesh and the
effervescence of youth exhalations came forth which obscured and
overcast my heart, so that I was unable to discern pure affection from
unholy desire. Both boiled confusedly within me, and dragged away
my unstable youth into the rough places of unchaste desires, and
plunged me into a gulf of infamy. Thy anger had overshadowed me,
and I knew it not. I was become deaf by the rattling of the chains of
my mortality, the punishment for my soul's pride; and I wandered

farther from Thee, and Thou didst 'suffer' me; and I was tossed to and fro, and wasted, and poured out, and boiled over in my fornications, and Thou didst hold Thy peace, O Thou my tardy joy! Thou then didst hold Thy peace, and I wandered still farther from Thee, into more and more barren seed-plots of sorrows, with proud dejection and restless lassitude.

Oh for one to have regulated my disorder, and turned to my profit the fleeting beauties of the things around me, and fixed a bound to their sweetness, so that the tides of my youth might have spent themselves upon the conjugal shore, if so be they could not be tranquillized and satisfied within the object of a family, as Thy law appoints, O Lord – who thus formest the offspring of our death, being able also with a tender hand to blunt the thorns which were excluded from Thy paradise! For Thy omnipotency is not far from us even when we are far from Thee, else in truth ought I more vigilantly to have given heed to the voice from the clouds: 'Nevertheless, such shall have trouble in the flesh, but I spare you;' and, 'It is good for a man not to touch a woman;' and, 'He that is unmarried careth for the things that belong to the Lord, how he may please the Lord; but he that is married careth for the things that are of the world, how he may please his wife.' I should, therefore, have listened more attentively to these words, and, being severed 'for the kingdom of heaven's sake', I would with greater happiness have expected Thy embraces.

But I, poor fool, seethed as does the sea, and, forsaking Thee, followed the violent course of my own stream, and exceeded all Thy limitations; nor did I escape Thy scourges. For what mortal can do so? But Thou wert always by me, mercifully angry, and dashing with the bitterest vexations all my illicit pleasures, in order that I might seek pleasures free from vexation. But where I could meet with such except in Thee, O Lord, I could not find – except in Thee, who teachest by sorrow, and woundest us to heal us, and killest us that we may not die from Thee. Where was I, and how far was I exiled from the delights of Thy house, in that sixteenth year of the age of my flesh, when the madness of lust – to the which human shamelessness granteth full freedom, although forbidden by Thy laws – held complete sway over me, and I resigned myself entirely to it?

THE CONFESSIONS OF ST AUGUSTINE, 397–400

P.T. BARNUM

M Y FATHER WAS BROUGHT TO HIS BED with a severe attack of fever in March, and departed this life, I trust for a better world, on the 7th of September, 1825, aged 48 years.

I was then fifteen years of age. I stood by his bedside. The world looked dark indeed, when I realized that I was forever deprived of my paternal protector! I felt that I was a poor inexperienced boy, thrown out on the wide world to shift for myself, and a sense of forlornness completely overcame me. My mother was left with five children. I was the oldest, and the youngest was only seven years of age. We followed the remains of husband and parent to their resting-place, and returned to our desolate home, feeling that we were forsaken by the world, and that but little hope existed for us this side of the grave.

Administrators to the estate were appointed, and the fact was soon apparent that my father had not succeeded in providing any of this world's goods for the support of his family. The estate was declared *insolvent*, and it did not pay fifty cents upon a dollar. My mother, like many widows before her, was driven to many straits to support her little family, but being industrious, economical and persevering, she succeeded in a few years in redeeming the homestead and becoming its sole possessor. The few dollars which I had accumulated, I had loaned to my father, and held his note therefor, but it was decided that the property of a minor belonged to the father, and my claim was ruled out. I was subsequently compelled to earn as clerk in a store the money to pay for the pair of shoes that were purchased for me to wear at my father's funeral. I can truly say, therefore, that I began the world with nothing, and was barefooted at that.

THE LIFE OF P.T. BARNUM, WRITTEN BY HIMSELF, 1855

JEAN DANIEL

I WAS SIXTEEN YEARS OLD and I will let anyone say that it is the most wonderful age in life. Each dawn would bring me its harvest of glories. I felt protected and I was eagerly reaping all forms of the sensuality of existence and every ambition, too. I dreamed that later on I would dance like Fred Astaire, would play tennis like Borotra, would sing like Charles Trenet, play the piano like Artur Rubinstein, and, of course, write like Tolstoy or Malraux. When my mother was sick, I would immediately become the most famous physician in the world. Until the day when Paulette, our Spanish servant, gnarled, haughty, and dressed in black, came to the house to say, 'My son Vincent, Jean's friend, has died in Spain. He signed up without telling me. So you will not see me anymore. Not you, not anyone.' That was how, one day, in the full bliss of my sixteen years, tragedy and history entered my life like black suns.

'DWELLING ON IMAGES', 1997

BENJAMIN FRANKLIN

WHEN ABOUT 16 YEARS OF AGE I happen'd to meet with a Book, written by one Tryon, recommending a Vegetable Diet. I determined to go into it. My Brother, being yet unmarried, did not keep House, but boarded himself & his Apprentices in another Family. My refusing to eat Flesh occasioned an Inconveniency, and I was frequently chid for my singularity. I made myself acquainted with Tryon's Manner of preparing some of his Dishes, such as Boiling Potatoes, or Rice, making Hasty Pudding, & a few others, and then propos'd to my Brother, that if he would give me Weekly half the Money he paid for my Board, I would board myself. He instantly agreed to it, and I presently found that I could save half what he paid me. This was an additional Fund for buying Books. But I had another Advantage in it. My Brother and the rest going from the Printing House to their Meals, I remain'd there alone, and, dispatching presently my light Repast (which often was no more than a Bisket or a Slice of Bread, a Handful of Raisins or a Tart from the Pastry Cook's, and a Glass of Water) had the rest of the Time till their Return for Study, in which I made the greater Progress, from that greater Clearness of Head & quicker Apprehension which usually attend Temperance in Eating & Drinking.

THE AUTOBIOGRAPHY, 1771–1778

SALVADOR DALI

I WAS SIXTEEN. It was at the Marist Brothers' School in Figueras. From our classrooms we went out into the recreation yard by a nearly vertical stone stairway. One evening, for no reason at all, I got the idea of flinging myself down from the top of the stairs. I was all set to do this, when at the last moment fear held me back. I was haunted by the idea, however, secretly nursing the plan to do it the following day. And the next day I could in fact no longer hold back, and at the moment of going down with all my classmates I made a fantastic leap into the void, landed on the stairs, and bounced all the way to the bottom. I was violently bumped and bruised all over, but an intense and inexplicable joy made the pain entirely secondary. The effect produced upon the other boys and the superiors who came running to my aid was enormous. Wet handkerchiefs were applied to my head.

I was at this time extremely timid, and the slightest attention made me blush to the ears; I spent my life hiding, and remained solitary. This flocking of people around me caused in me a strange emotion. Four days later I re-enacted the same scene, but this time I threw myself from the top of the stairway during the second recreation period, at the moment when the animation in the yard was at its height. I even waited until the Brother Superior was also outdoors. The effect of my fall was even greater than the first time: before flinging myself down I uttered a shrill scream so that everyone would look at me. My joy was indescribable and the pain from the fall insignificant. This was a definite encouragement to continue, and from time to time I repeated my fall. Each time I was about to go down the stairs there was great expectation. Will he throw himself off, or will he not? What was the pleasure of going down quietly and normally when I realized a hundred pairs of eyes were eagerly devouring me?

I shall always remember a certain rainy October evening. I was about to start down the stairs. The yard exhaled a strong odor of damp earth mingled with the odor of roses; the sky, on fire from the setting sun, was massed with sublime clouds in the form of rampant leopards, Napoleons and caravels, all dishevelled; my upturned face was illuminated by the thousand lights of apotheosis. I descended the stairway step by step, with a slow deliberation of blind ecstasy so moving that suddenly a great silence fell upon the shouting whirlwind in the play-yard. I would not at that moment have changed places with a god.

The Secret Life of Salvador Dali, 1942

HENRY ADAMS

I F SCHOOL HELPED, IT WAS ONLY BY REACTION. The dislike of school was so strong as to be a positive gain. The passionate hatred of school methods was almost a method in itself. Yet the day-school of that time was respectable, and the boy had nothing to complain of. In fact, he never complained. He hated it because he was herded with a crowd of other boys and compelled to learn by memory a quantity of things that did not amuse him. His memory was slow, and the effort painful. For him to conceive that his memory could compete for school-prizes with machines of two or three times its power, was to prove himself wanting not only in memory, but flagrantly in mind. He thought his mind a good enough machine, if it were given time to act, but it acted wrong if hurried. Schoolmasters never gave time.

In any and all its forms, the boy detested school, and the prejudice became deeper with years. He always reckoned his school-days, from ten to sixteen years old, as time thrown away. Perhaps his needs turned out to be exceptional, but his existence was exceptional. Between 1850 and 1900 nearly everyone's existence was exceptional. For success in the life imposed on him he needed, as afterwards appeared, the facile use of only four tools: mathematics; French; German, and Spanish. With these, he could master in very short time any special branch of inquiry, and feel at home in any society. Latin and Greek, he could, with the help of the modern languages, learn more completely by the intelligent work of six weeks than in the six years he spent on them at school. These four tools were necessary to his success in life, but he never controlled any one of them.

Thus, at the outset, he was condemned to failure more or less complete in the life awaiting him, but not more so than his companions. Indeed, had his father kept the boy at home, and given him half an hour's direction every day, he would have done more for him than school ever could do for them. Of course, school-taught men and boys looked down on home-bred boys, and rather prided themselves on their own ignorance, but the man of sixty can generally see what he needed in life, and in Henry Adams's opinion it was not school.

Most school experience was bad. Boy associations at fifteen were worse than none. Boston at that time offered few healthy resources for boys or men. The bar-room and billiard-room were more familiar than parents knew. As a rule boys could skate and swim and were sent to dancing-school; they played a rudimentary game of baseball, football and hockey; a few could sail a boat; still fewer had been out with a gun to shoot yellow-legs or a stray wild duck; one or two may have learned something of natural history if they came from the neighborhood of Concord; none could ride across country, or knew what shooting with dogs meant. Sport as a pursuit was unknown. Boat-racing came after 1850. For horse-racing, only the trotting-course existed. Of all pleasures, winter-sleighing was still the gayest and most popular. From none of these amusements could the boy learn anything likely to be of use to him in the world. Books remained as in the eighteenth century, the source of life, and as they came out – Thackeray, Dickens, Bulwer, Tennyson, Macaulay, Carlyle and the rest – they were devoured; but as far as happiness went, the happiest hours of the boy's education were passed in summer lying on a musty heap of Congressional Documents in the old farmhouse at Quincy, reading *Quentin Durward*, *Ivanhoe* and *The Talisman*, and raiding the garden at intervals for peaches and pears. On the whole he learned most then.

THE EDUCATION OF HENRY ADAMS, 1907

HIS HOLINESS THE DALAI LAMA OF TIBET

A LL IN ALL, it was not an unhappy childhood. The kindness of my teachers will always remain with me as a memory I shall cherish. They gave me the religious knowledge which has always been and will always be my greatest comfort and inspiration, and they did their best to satisfy what they regarded as a healthy curiosity in other matters. But I know that I grew up with hardly any knowledge of wordly affairs, and it was in that state, when I was sixteen, that I was called upon to lead my country against the invasion of Communist China.

MY LAND AND MY PEOPLE, 1962

MARGARET OLIPHANT

W HEN I WAS SIXTEEN I BEGAN TO HAVE – what shall I say? – not lovers exactly, except in the singular – but one or two people about who revealed to me the fact that I too was like the girls in the poets. I recollect distinctly the first compliment, though not a compliment in the ordinary sense of the word, which gave me that bewildering happy sense of being able to touch somebody else's heart – which was half fun and infinitely amusing, yet something more. The speaker was a young Irishman, one of the young ministers that came to our little church, at that time 'vacant'. He had joined Frank [my brother] and me on a walk, and when we were passing and looking at a very pretty cottage on the slope of the hill at Everton, embowered in gardens and shrubberies, he suddenly looked at me and said, 'It would be Elysium.' I laughed till I cried at this speech afterwards, though at the moment demure and startled. But the little incident remains to me, as so many scenes in my early life do, like a picture suffused with a soft delightful light: the glow in the young man's eyes; the lowered tone and little speech aside; the soft thrill of meaning which was nothing and yet much. Perhaps if I were not a novelist addicted to describing such scenes, I might not remember it after – how long? Forty-one years. What a long time! I could not have been sixteen. Then came the episode of J.Y., which was very serious indeed. We were engaged on the eve of his going away. He was to go to America for three years and then return for me. He was a good, simple, pious, domestic, kind-hearted fellow, fair-haired, not good-looking, not ideal at all. He cannot have been at all clever, and I was rather. When he went away our correspondence for some time was very full; then I began to find his letters silly, and I suppose said as much. Then there were quarrels, quarrels with the Atlantic between, then explanations, and then dreadful silence. It is amusing to look back upon, but it was not at all amusing to me then. My poor little heart was broken. I remember another scene without being able to explain it: my mother and myself walking home from somewhere – I don't know where – after it was certain that there was no letter, and that all was over. I think it was a winter night and rainy, and I was leaning on her arm, and the blank of the silence, and the dark and the separation, and the cutting off of all the dreams that had grown about his name, came over me and seemed to stop my very life. My poor little heart was broken. I was a little over seventeen, I think.

These were the only breaks in my early life. We lived in the most singularly secluded way. I never was at a dance till after my marriage, never went out, never saw anybody at home. Our pleasures were books of all and every kind, newspapers and magazines, which formed the staple of our conversation, as well as all our amusement. In the time of my depression and sadness my mother had a bad illness, and I was her nurse, or at least attendant. I had to sit for hours by the bedside and keep quiet. I had no liking then for needlework, a taste which developed afterwards, so I took to writing. There was no particular purpose in my beginning except this, to secure some amusement and occupation for myself while I sat by my mother's bedside. I wrote a little book in which the chief character was an angelic elder sister, unmarried, who had the charge of a family of motherless brothers and sisters, and who had a shrine of sorrow in her life in the shape of the portrait and memory of her lover who had died young. It was all very innocent and guileless, and my audience – to wit, my mother and brother Frank – were highly pleased with it … Afterwards I wrote another very much concerned with the Church business, in which the heroine, I recollect, was a girl, who in the beginning of the story was a sort of half-witted undeveloped creature, but who ended by being one of those lofty poetical beings whom girls love. She was called, I recollect, Ibby, but why, I cannot explain. I had the satisfaction afterwards, when I came to my full growth, of burning the

manuscript, which was a three-volume business. I don't think any
effort was ever made to get a publisher for it.

THE AUTOBIOGRAPHY OF MARGARET OLIPHANT, 1864–1894

LORNA SAGE

I RECALL A FLATTENED PATCH in the long grass going to seed on
the bank of the towpath along the Shropshire Union Canal. It's a
hot, bright afternoon in summer ... and Vic and I are semi-hidden
from the surrounding fields, not from walkers on the towpath or
canal boats, although they're very few and far between. It's not safe
to undress, we'd be more secure in the dark, but what we're doing
isn't part of the timetable for lovemaking, it doesn't count. We're
trying to get inside each other's skins, but without taking our clothes
off, and the parts that touch are swaddled in stringy rucked-up
shirts, jeans, pants. There are no leisurely caresses, no long looks, it's
a bruising kind of bliss mostly made of aches. Motes of pollen seethe
around us, along with a myriad of tiny moths and flies whose patch
this was. We're dissolving, eyes half shut, holding each other's
hands at arm's length, crucified on each other, butting and
squirming. Our kisses are like mouth-to-mouth resuscitation – you'd
think we were dying it's so urgent, this childish mathematics of two
into one won't go.

Spots of time. One day when my parents are out we're lying on
the edge of the old tennis lawn at Sunnyside, in the weeds, and
there's a rapping on the window. Grandma peers out, too short-
sighted to register details, but she can see that I'm horizontal and
hugging a boy, that's enough. Rat-tat-tat, wake up. I opened my eyes
wide and looked at us, and saw that my breasts and his chest were
covered in little worms of dirt rolled out of sweat and dust by our
friction. That particular day sticks in my memory.

Most days in the summer holidays merge into each other, though.
Every morning I sat in the kitchen, in a fireside chair lined with old
newspapers (because it was where my father sat in his filthy overalls
to take off his boots when he came in from work) and I translated
two or three hundred lines of Virgil's *Aeneid*, without using a

dictionary, guessing at words I didn't know. Latin was still my favourite subject; despite *Lady C.* and Mrs Davies, it was almost a kind of licensed laziness to sit there scribbling out Rome's epic with old *Daily Mails* crackling under me. In the afternoons I played tennis on Whitchurch courts with Gail, or we wandered from Edward's to coffee bar to milk bar, or listened to records, or I went for a walk down the canal with Vic to make a nest in the grass. One day Gail told me that Vic had told a friend who'd told his girlfriend, who'd told her, that we'd gone all the way and that he had a trophy, a smear or spatter of blood on his washed-out jeans, to prove it. She was shocked that something so momentous had happened and I hadn't confided in her. But it hadn't, I protested, truly, or I would have – and he and I had an angry and reproachful conversation about loyalty, betrayal and boasting, because after all, we *hadn't*, had we?

It was so unthinkable that when I felt ill, bloated, headachy, nauseous and, oh yes, my period hadn't come, I stayed in bed till we called out our new doctor, a pale, prim man in his thirties, Dr Clayton. After taking my temperature, asking about bowel movements and looking at my tongue, he looked out of the window at the copper beech tree, cleared his throat and asked could I be – um – pregnant? No, I said, feeling hot suddenly. No. He recommended a urine test anyway. Meanwhile I took aspirins for my aches, but they didn't go away and, although school had started and I'd finished Virgil, I spent days at home. On one of them Dr Clayton turned up again, embarrassed and puzzled. How old was I? Sixteen. He'd heard I was a clever girl, doing well at school, didn't we ever have biology lessons? I must have known what I was up to … From his first words and his tone, which had weariness and contempt in it, I knew it was true, just as absolutely as until that moment I knew it couldn't be.

I'd been caught out, I would have to pay. I was in trouble, I'd have no secrets any longer, I'd be exposed as a fraud, my fate wasn't my own, my treacherous body had somehow delivered me into other people's hands. Dr Clayton asked if he should tell my mother, but he wasn't really asking. I sat there in my new Sunnyside bedroom, everything falling into place in my aching head, thud, thud, thud. My mother came upstairs and opened the door, her face red and puffed up with outrage, her eyes blazing with tears. She'll tell, this time, no question. For a minute she says nothing and then it come out in a wail, *What have you done to me?* Over and over again, I've spoiled everything, now this house will be a shameful place like the vicarage. I've soiled and insulted her with my promiscuity, my sly, grubby lusts … I've done it now, I've made my mother pregnant.

BAD BLOOD, A MEMOIR, 2000

MARY DARBY ROBINSON

SHE WAS THE MOST BEAUTIFUL OF INFANTS! I thought myself the happiest of mothers; her first smile appeared like something celestial – something ordained to irradiate my dark and dreary prospect of existence …

I seldom quitted my apartment, and never till the evening, when for air and exercise I walked on the racket-ground with my husband.

It was during one of these night walks that my little daughter first blessed my ears with the articulation of words. The circumstance made a forcible and indelible impression on my mind. It was a clear moonlight evening; the infant was in the arms of her nursery maid; she was dancing her up and down, and was playing with her; her eyes were fixed on the moon, to which she pointed with her small forefinger. On a sudden a cloud passed over it, and the child, with a slow falling of her hand, articulately sighed, 'All gone!' This had been a customary expression with her maid, whenever the infant wanted anything which it was deemed prudent to withhold or to hide from her. These little nothings will appear insignificant to the common reader, but to the parent whose heart is ennobled by sensibility they will become matters of important interest. I can only add, that I walked till near midnight, watching every cloud that passed over the moon, and as often, with a rapturous sensation, hearing my little prattler repeat her observation.

Having much leisure and many melancholy hours, I again turned my thoughts towards the muses. I chose 'Captivity' for the subject of my pen, and soon composed a quarto poem of some length; it was superior to my former productions; but it was full of defects, replete with weak or laboured lines. I never now read my early compositions without a suffusion on my cheek, which marks my humble opinion of them.

MEMOIRS OF THE LATE MRS ROBINSON, WRITTEN BY HERSELF, 1801

W.B. YEATS

THE GREAT EVENT OF A BOY'S LIFE is the awakening of sex. He will bathe many times a day, or get up at dawn and having stripped leap to and fro over a stick laid upon two chairs and hardly know, and never admit, that he has begun to take pleasure in his own nakedness, nor will he understand the change until some dream discovers it. He may never understand at all the greater change in his mind.

It all came upon me when I was close upon seventeen like the bursting of a shell. Somnambulistic country girls, when it is upon them, throw plates about or pull them with long hairs in simulation of the poltergeist, or become mediums for some genuine spirit-mischief, surrendering to their desire of the marvellous. As I look backward, I seem to discover that my passions, my loves and my despairs, instead of being my enemies, a disturbance and an attack, became so beautiful that I had to be constantly alone to give them my whole attention. I notice that now, for the first time, what I saw when alone is more vivid in my memory than what I did or saw in company.

A herd had shown me a cave some hundred and fifty feet below the cliff path and a couple of hundred above the sea, and told me that an evicted tenant called Macrom, dead some fifteen years, had lived there many years, and shown me a rusty nail in the rock which had served perhaps to hold up some wooden protection from wind and weather. Here I stored a tin of cocoa and some biscuits, and instead of going to my bed, would slip out on warm nights and sleep in the cave on the excuse of catching moths. One had to pass over a rocky ledge, safe enough for anyone with a fair head, yet seeming, if looked at from above, narrow and sloping; and a remonstrance from a stranger who had seen me climbing along it doubled my delight in the adventure. When, however, upon a bank holiday, I found lovers in my cave, I was not content with it again till I heard that the ghost of Macrom had been seen a little before dawn, stooping over his fire in the cave-mouth. I had been trying to cook eggs, as I had read in some book, by burying them in the earth under a fire of sticks.

At other times, I would sleep among the rhododendrons and rocks in the wilder part of the grounds of Howth Castle. After a while my father said I must stay indoors half the night, meaning that I should get some sleep in my bed; but I, knowing that I would be too sleepy and comfortable to get up again, used to sit over the kitchen fire till half the night was gone. Exaggerated accounts spread through the school, and sometimes when I did not know a lesson some master would banter me about the way my nights were spent.

'REVERIES OVER CHILDHOOD AND YOUTH', 1915

WALT WHITMAN

I DEVELOP'D (1833–4–5) into a healthy, strong youth (grew too fast, though, was nearly big as a man at 15 or 16). Our family at this period moved back to the country, my dear mother very ill for a long time, but recover'd. All these years I was down Long Island more or less every summer, now east, now west, sometimes months at a stretch. At 16, 17, and so on, was fond of debating societies, and had an active membership with them, off and on, in Brooklyn and one or two country towns on the island. A most omnivorous novel-reader, these and later years, devour'd everything I could get. Fond of the theatre, also, in New York, went whenever I could – sometimes witnessing fine performances.

1836–7, work'd as compositor in printing offices in New York city. Then, when little more than eighteen, and for a while afterwards, went to teaching country schools down in Queens and Suffolk counties, Long Island, and 'boarded round'. (This latter I consider one of my best experiences and deepest lessons in human nature behind the scenes, and in the masses.) In '39 and '40, I started and publish'd a weekly paper in my native town, Huntington. Then returning to New York city and Brooklyn, work'd on as a printer and writer, mostly prose, but an occasional shy at 'poetry'.

'SPECIMEN DAYS', 1882

CHRISTY BROWN

I WANTED DESPERATELY TO SAY SOMETHING, not merely to my family, not merely to my friends, but rather to everyone, to the world as a whole. There was something in me, some inner urge to speak, and I wanted to get it out of me, to communicate it to others and make them understand it. I felt I had found something, something I had been looking for ever since I began to think and feel about myself. It had taken years to find, but now I was positive that I had discovered it at last, and suddenly I wanted to fling it to the four winds and let it go round the world, bearing its message into everyone's heart.

It wasn't just something about myself, but about all who had a life similar to my own, a life bounded and shut in on all sides by the high walls of a narrow, suppressed life. I felt that I had at last found a way of scaling those walls and breaking loose from the shadow of them, a way of taking my place in the sun and of playing my part in the world along with the able-bodied.

But – how could I express what I wanted to say, what I wanted everyone to know? My hands were of no use to me at all; they were still twisted and unruly, still powerless to grasp or hold anything. Nor could my lips utter the thoughts which were whirling around in my mind like swarms of impatient bees, because I still wasn't able to speak any sort of intelligible language outside the family circle, so that in general I was still tongue-tied, still doomed to a brooding silence ...

It seemed I had reached a dead-end; everywhere I turned the way was blocked. I felt the way anyone would feel with their hands and feet tied and a gag in their mouth.

Then suddenly I had an idea, an inspiration. I was sitting in the kitchen one afternoon thinking about how I could find a way of putting down all I wanted to say on paper when I noticed one of my brothers sitting over a copy book at the table with a pen in his hand, writing something into it. This was Eamonn, just twelve years of age at the time, and he was doing his homework – an English composition, which I could see, by the scowl on his face, he wasn't enjoying very much. The idea of him sitting there writing and not yet knowing what to write about, and me sitting there by the window, my brain teeming with ideas and yet not able to hold a pen in my hand, almost made me want to jump up from the chair and run amok!

Instead I leaned forward and asked him what he was doing.

'Trying to write a composition for school,' answered Eamonn with a sigh. 'I'll get biffed if I don't do it right.'

I saw my chance. I told him I'd help him – on condition that he'd do something for me in return.

'Sure I will,' he said confidently. 'What do you want me to do?'

'Write for me,' I told him briefly.

His face fell. 'But I can't even do my own writing!' he protested, 'I wouldn't know what to say!'

'Fool,' I replied. 'You'll just hold the pen and I'll tell you what to put down.'

My brother was doubtful about this idea; it sounded too complicated to him and he felt there was something 'fishy' at the back of it. But at the same time he wanted to get that composition right, so in the end he agreed to my condition and I did his homework for him.

When we were done we went out to my study at the back of the house, got a nine-penny jotter out of the drawer, sat down at the table and looked at each other.

'What d'ye want me to write for you?' asked my brother innocently, the pen poised in his hand.

I looked out the window at the branches of the trees waving against the bright spring sky, thought a bit, then turned back to look at my younger brother's inquiring face.

'My life-story,' I told him.

Poor Eamonn let his pen clatter down on the table.

'Your ... what?' he asked.

I told him again, and this time he was quite silent.

In the end I got him to agree to write for me for 'an indefinite period'. We started that very afternoon, without any sort of preparation whatever.

I was eighteen when I began that first attempt to write my autobiography. It was a ponderous piece of work, a veritable forest of seven- and eight-syllabled words. My only reading experience up to this had been Dickens, and in my inexperience I imagined it my duty to try and imitate his style of writing – with the result that the English I used was fifty years out of date! I used words and phrases that would have tied up anybody's tongue in a matter of seconds. So long were the words that I had to spell them letter by letter, before my brother could write them down on to the page. I am still wondering why neither of us had a nervous breakdown during the writing of that tremendous first attempt. It must have amounted to tens of thousands of words before I became discouraged. It dragged on and on sluggishly like a stream of molten lead. My poor brother often got writer's cramp. He had written almost four hundred pages of manuscript before I saw that if I went on like this the book would go on for ever.

My Left Foot, 1954

GRAHAM GREENE

I CAN REMEMBER VERY CLEARLY the afternoon I found the revolver in the brown deal corner-cupboard in a bedroom which I shared with my elder brother. It was the early autumn of 1923. The revolver was a small ladylike object with six chambers like a tiny egg-stand, and there was a cardboard box full of bullets. I never mentioned the discovery to my brother because I had realized the moment I saw the revolver the use I intended to make of it. (I don't to this day know why he possessed it; certainly he had no licence, and he was only three years older than myself. A large family is as departmental as a Ministry.)

My brother was away – probably climbing in the Lake District

– and until he returned the revolver was to all intents my own. I knew what to do with it because I had been reading a book (I think Ossendowski was the author) which described how the White Russian officers, condemned to inaction in southern Russia at the tail-end of the counter-revolutionary war, used to invent hazards with which to escape boredom. One man would slip a charge into a revolver and turn the chambers at random, and his companion would put the revolver to his head and pull the trigger. The chance, of course, was five to one in favour of life.

One forgets emotions easily. If I were dealing with an imaginary character, I might feel it necessary for verisimilitude to make him hesitate, put the revolver back into the cupboard, return to it again after an interval, reluctantly and fearfully, when the burden of boredom and despair became too great. But in fact there was no hesitation at all: I slipped the revolver into my pocket, and the next I can remember is crossing Berkhamsted Common towards the Ashridge beeches. Perhaps before I had opened the corner-cupboard, boredom had reached an intolerable depth. The boredom was as deep as the love and more enduring – indeed it descends on me too often today. For years, after my analysis, I could take no aesthetic interest in any visual thing: staring at a sight that others assured me was beautiful I felt nothing. I was fixed, like a negative in a chemical bath. Rilke wrote, 'Psychoanalysis is too fundamental a help for me, it helps you once and for all, it clears you up, and to find myself finally cleared up one day might be even more helpless than this chaos.'

Now with the revolver in my pocket I thought I had stumbled on the perfect cure. I was going to escape in one way or another, and perhaps because escape was inseparably connected with the Common in my mind, it was there that I went.

Beyond the Common lay a wide grass ride known for some reason as Cold Harbour to which I would occasionally take a horse, and beyond again stretched Ashridge Park, the smooth olive skin of beech trees and last year's quagmire of leaves, dark like old pennies. Deliberately I chose my ground, I believe without real fear – perhaps because so many semi-suicidal acts which my elders would have regarded as neurotic, but which I still consider to have been under the circumstances highly reasonable, lay in the background of this more dangerous venture. They removed the sense of strangeness as I slipped a bullet into a chamber and, holding the revolver behind my back, spun the chambers round.

Had I romantic thoughts about my love? I must have had, but I think, at the most, they simply eased the medicine down. Unhappy love, I suppose, has sometimes driven boys to suicide, but this was not suicide, whatever a coroner's jury might have said: it was a gamble with five chances to one against an inquest. The discovery that it was possible to enjoy again the visible world by risking its total loss was one I was bound to make sooner or later.

I put the muzzle of the revolver into my right ear and pulled the trigger. There was a minute click, and looking down at the chamber I could see that the charge had moved into the firing position. I was out by one. I remember an extraordinary sense of jubilation, as if carnival lights had been switched on in a drab street. My heart knocked in its cage, and life contained an infinite number of possibilities. It was like a young man's first successful experience of sex – as if among the Ashridge beeches I had passed the test of manhood. I went home and put the revolver back in the corner-cupboard.

This experience I repeated a number of times. At fairly long intervals I found myself craving for the adrenalin drug, and I took the revolver with me when I returned to Oxford. There I would walk out from Headington towards Elsfield down what is now a wide arterial road, smooth and shiny like the walls of a public lavatory. Then it was a sodden unfrequented country lane. The revolver would be whipped behind my back, the chamber twisted, the muzzle quickly and surreptitiously inserted in my ear beneath the black winter trees, the trigger pulled.

Slowly the effect of the drug wore off – I lost the sense of jubilation, I began to receive from the experience only the crude kick of excitement. It was the difference between love and lust. And as the quality of the experience deteriorated, so my sense of responsibility grew and worried me. I wrote a bad piece of free verse (free because it was easier in that way to express my meaning clearly without literary equivocation) describing how, in order to give myself a fictitious sense of danger, I would 'press the trigger of a revolver I already know to be empty'. This verse I would leave permanently on my desk, so that if I lost the gamble, it would provide incontrovertible evidence of an accident, and my parents, I thought, would be less troubled by a fatal play-acting than by a suicide – or the rather bizarre truth. (Only after I had given up the game did I write other verses which told the true facts.)

It was back in Berkhamsted during the Christmas of 1923 that I paid a permanent farewell to the drug. As I inserted my fifth dose, which corresponded in my mind to the odds against death, it occurred to me that I wasn't even excited: I was beginning to pull the trigger as casually as I might take an aspirin tablet. I decided to give the revolver – since it was six-chambered – a sixth and last chance. I twirled the chambers round and put the muzzle to my ear for a second time, then heard the familiar empty click as the chambers shifted. I was through with the drug, and walking back over the Common, down the new road by the ruined castle, past the private entrance to the gritty old railway station reserved for the use of Lord Brownlow, my mind was already busy on other plans. One campaign was over, but the war against boredom had got to go on.

A Sort of Life, 1971

SIGMUND FREUD

I WAS BORN ON MAY 6TH, 1856, at Freiberg in Moravia, a small town in what is now Czecho-Slovakia. My parents were Jews, and I have remained a Jew myself. I have reason to believe that my father's family were settled for a long time on the Rhine (at Cologne), that, as a result of a persecution of the Jews during the fourteenth or fifteenth century, they fled eastwards, and that, in the course of the nineteenth century, they migrated back from Lithuania through Galicia into German Austria. When I was a child of four I came to Vienna, and I went through the whole of my education there. At the 'Gymnasium' I was at the top of my class for seven years; I enjoyed special privileges there, and was required to pass scarcely any examinations. Although we lived in very limited circumstances, my father insisted that, in my choice of a profession, I should follow my own inclinations. Neither at that time, nor indeed in my later life, did I feel any particular predilection for a career of a physician. I was moved, rather, by a sort of curiosity, which was, however, directed more towards human concerns than towards natural objects; nor had I grasped the importance of observation as one of the best means of gratifying it. My early familiarity with the Bible story (at a time almost before I had learnt the art of reading) had, as I recognized much later, an enduring effect upon the direction of my interest. Under the powerful influence of a school friendship with a boy rather my senior who grew up to be a well-known politician I developed a wish to study law like him and to engage in social activities. At the same time, the theories of Darwin, which were then of topical interest, strongly attracted me, for they held out hopes of an extraordinary advance in our understanding of the world; and it was hearing Goethe's beautiful essay on Nature read aloud at a popular lecture by Professor Carl Brühl just before I left school that decided me to become a medical student.

When, in 1873, I first joined the university, I experienced some appreciable disappointments. Above all, I found that I was expected to feel myself inferior and an alien because I was a Jew. I refused absolutely to do the first of these things. I have never been able to see why I should feel ashamed of my descent or, as people were beginning to say, of my race. I put up, without much regret, with my non-acceptance into the community; for it seemed to me that in spite of this exclusion an active fellow-worker could not fail to find some nook or cranny in the framework of humanity. These first impressions at the university, however, had one consequence which was afterwards to prove important; for at an early age I was made familiar with the fate of being in the Opposition and of being put under the ban of the 'compact majority'. The foundations were thus laid for a certain degree of independence of judgment.

AN AUTOBIOGRAPHICAL STUDY, 1925

WINSTON CHURCHILL

I T TOOK ME THREE TRIES to pass into Sandhurst [military academy]. There were five subjects, of which Mathematics, Latin and English were obligatory, and I chose in addition French and Chemistry. In this hand I held only a pair of Kings – English and Chemistry. Nothing less than three would open the jackpot. I had to find another useful card. Latin I could not learn. I had a rooted prejudice which seemed to close my mind against it. Two thousand marks were given for Latin. I might perhaps get 400! French was interesting but rather tricky, and difficult to learn in England. So there remained only Mathematics. After the first Examination was over, when one surveyed the battlefield, it was evident that the war could not be won without another army being brought into the line. Mathematics was the only resource available. I turned to them – I turned on them – in desperation. All my life from time to time I have had to get up disagreeable subjects at short notice, but I consider my triumph, moral and technical, was learning Mathematics in six months. At the first of these three ordeals I got no more than 500 marks out of 2,500 for Mathematics. At the second I got nearly 2,000. I owe this achievement not only to my own 'back-to-the-wall' resolution – for which no credit is too great; but to the very kindly interest taken in my case by a very much respected Harrow master, Mr C.H.P. Mayo. He convinced me that Mathematics was not a hopeless bog of nonsense, and that there were meanings and rhythms beyond the comical hieroglyphics; and that I was not incapable of catching glimpses of some of these.

Of course what I call Mathematics is only what the Civil Service Commissioners expected you to know to pass a very rudimentary examination. I suppose that to those who enjoy this peculiar gift, Senior Wranglers and the like, the waters in which I swam must seem only a duck-puddle compared to the Atlantic Ocean. Nevertheless, when I plunged in, I was soon out of my depth. When I look back upon those care-laden months, their prominent features rise from the abyss of memory. Of course I had progressed far beyond Vulgar Fractions and the Decimal System. We were arrived in an 'Alice-in-Wonderland' world, at the portals of which stood 'A Quadratic Equation'. This with a strange grimace pointed the way to the Theory of Indices, which again handed on the intruder to the full rigours of the Binomial Theorem. Futher dim chambers lighted by sullen, sulphurous fires were reputed to contain a dragon called the 'Differential Calculus'. But this monster was beyond the bounds appointed by the Civil Service Commissioners who regulated this stage of Pilgrim's heavy journey. We turned aside, not indeed to the uplands of the Delectable Mountains, but into a strange corridor of things like anagrams and acrostics called Sines, Cosines and Tangents. Apparently they were very important, especially when multiplied by each other, or by themselves! They had also this merit – you could learn many of their evolutions off by heart. There was a question in my third and last Examination about these Cosines and Tangents in a highly square-rooted condition which must have been decisive upon the whole of my after life. It was a problem. But luckily I had seen its ugly face only a few days before and recognized it at first sight.

I have never met any of these creatures since. With my third and successful Examination they passed away like the phantasmagoria of a fevered dream. I am assured that they are most helpful in engineering, astronomy and things like that. It is very important to build bridges and canals and to comprehend all the stresses and potentialities of matter, to say nothing of counting all the stars and even universes and measuring how far off they are, and foretelling eclipses, the arrival of comets and such like. I am very glad there are quite a number of people born with a gift and liking for all of this; like great chess-players who play sixteen games at once blindfold and die quite soon of epilepsy. Serve them right! I hope the Mathematicians, however, are well rewarded. I promise never to blackleg their profession nor take the bread out of their mouths.

I had a feeling once about Mathematics, that I saw it all – depth beyond depth was revealed to me – the Byss and the Abyss. I saw, as one might see the transit of Venus – or even the Lord Mayor's Show, a quantity passing through infinity and changing its sign from plus to minus. I saw exactly how it happened and why the tergiversation was inevitable: and how the one step involved all the others. It was like politics. But it was after dinner and I let it go!

The practical point is that if this aged, weary-souled Civil Servant Commissioner had not asked this particular question about these Cosines or Tangents in their squared or even cubed condition, which I happened to have learned scarcely a week before, not one of the subsequent chapters of this book would ever have been written. I might have gone into the Church and preached orthodox sermons in a spirit of audacious contradiction to the age. I might have gone into the City and made a fortune. I might have resorted to the Colonies, or 'Dominions' as they are now called, in the hopes of pleasing, or at least placating them; and thus had, *à la* Lindsay Gordon or Cecil Rhodes, a lurid career. I might even have gravitated to the Bar, and persons might have been hanged through my defence who now nurse their guilty secrets with complacency. Anyhow the whole of my life would have been altered, and that I suppose would have altered a great many other lives, which, in their turn, and so on ...

MY EARLY LIFE / A ROVING COMMISSION, 1930

PABLO NERUDA

AFTER MANY YEARS OF SCHOOL, and the struggle through the math exam each December, I was outwardly prepared to face the university in Santiago. I say outwardly because my head was filled with books, dreams, and poems buzzing around like bees.

Carrying a metal trunk, wearing the requisite black suit of the poet, all skin and bones, thin-featured as a knife, I boarded the third-class section of a night train that took an interminable day and night to reach Santiago.

This long train crossed different zones and climates; I took it so many times and it still holds a strange fascination for me. Peasants with wet ponchos and baskets filled with chickens, uncommunicative Indians – an entire life unfolded in the third-class coach. Quite a number of people traveled without paying, under the seats. Whenever the ticket collector came around, a metamorphosis took place. Many disappeared, and others might hide under a poncho on which two passengers immediately pretended to play a game of cards, to keep the conductor from noticing the improvised table.

Meanwhile, the train passed from the countryside covered with oaks and araucaria trees and frame houses with sodden walls to the poplars and dusty adobe buildings of central Chile. I made the round trip between the capital and the provinces many times, but I always felt myself stifling as soon as I left the great forests, the timberland that drew me back like a mother. To me, the adobe houses, the cities with a past, seemed to be filled with cobwebs and silence. Even now I am still a poet of the great outdoors, of the cold forest that was lost to me after that.

I brought my references to the rooming house at 513 Maruri Street. Nothing can make me forget this number. I forget all kinds of dates, even years, but the number 513 is still in my mind, where I engraved it so many years ago, fearing I would never find that rooming house and would lose my way in the strange, awe-inspiring city. On the street just mentioned I used to sit out on the balcony and watch the dying afternoon, the sky with its green and crimson banners, the desolation of the rooftops on the edge of town threatened by the burning sky.

MEMOIRS, 1974

THOMAS DE QUINCEY

IT IS VERY LONG SINCE I FIRST TOOK OPIUM; *so* long, that if it had been a trifling incident in my life, I might have forgotten its date; but cardinal events are not to be forgotten; and, from circumstances connected with it, I remember that this inauguration into the use of opium must be referred to the spring or to the autumn of 1804; during which seasons I was in London, having come thither for the first time since my entrance at Oxford. And this event arose in the following way: from an early age I had been accustomed to wash my head in cold water at least once a day; being suddenly seized with toothache, I attributed it to some relaxation caused by a casual intermission of that practice; jumped out of bed; plunged my head into a basin of cold water, and with hair thus wetted went to sleep. The next morning, as I need hardly say, I awoke with excruciating rheumatic pains of the head and face, from which I had hardly any respite for about twenty days. On the twenty-first day I think it was, and on a Sunday, that I went out into the streets; rather to run away, if possible, from my torments, than with any distinct purpose of relief. By accident, I met a college acquaintance, who recommended opium. Opium! dread agent of unimaginable pleasure and pain! I had heard of it as I had of manna or of ambrosia, but no further. How unmeaning a sound was opium at that time! what solemn chords does it now strike upon my heart! what heart-quaking vibrations of sad and happy remembrances! Reverting for a moment to these, I feel a mystic importance attached to the minutest circumstances connected with the place, and the time, and the man (if man he was), that first laid open to me the paradise of opium-eaters. It was a Sunday afternoon, wet and cheerless; and a duller spectacle this earth of ours has not to show than a rainy Sunday in London. My road homewards lay through Oxford Street; and near 'the *stately* Pantheon' (as Mr Wordsworth has obligingly called it) I saw a druggist's shop. The druggist (unconscious minister of celestial pleasures!), as if in sympathy with the rainy Sunday, looked dull and stupid, just as any mortal druggist might be expected to look on a rainy London Sunday; and when I asked for the tincture of opium, he gave it to me as any other man might do; and, furthermore, out of my shilling returned me what seemed to be real copper halfpence, taken out of a real wooden drawer. Nevertheless, and not withstanding all such indications of humanity, he has ever since figured in my mind as a beatific vision of an immortal druggist, sent down to earth on a special mission to myself. And it confirms me in this way of considering him that, when I next came up to London, I sought him near the stately Pantheon, and found him not; and thus to me, who knew not his name (if, indeed, he had one), he seemed rather to have vanished from Oxford Street than to have flitted into any other locality, or (which some abominable man suggested) to have absconded from the rent. The reader may choose to think of him as, possibly, no more than a sublunary druggist; it may be so, but my faith is better. I believe him to have evanesced. So unwillingly would I connect any mortal remembrances with that hour, and place, and creature, that first brought me acquainted with the celestial drug.

Arrived at my lodgings, it may be supposed that I lost not a moment in taking the quantity prescribed. I was necessarily ignorant of the whole art and mystery of opium-taking; and what I took, I took under every disadvantage. But I took it; and in an hour, O heavens! what a revulsion! what a resurrection, from its lowest depths of the inner spirit! what an apocalypse of the world within me! That my pains had vanished was now a trifle in my eyes; this negative effect was swallowed up in the immensity of those positive effects which had opened before me, in the abyss of divine enjoyment thus suddenly revealed. Here was a panacea, a *pharmakon nepenthez*, for all human woes; here was the secret of happiness, about which philosophers had disputed for so many ages, at once discovered; happiness might now be bought for a penny, and carried in the waistcoat pocket; portable ecstasies might be had corked up in a pint-bottle; and peace of mind could be sent down by the mail.

CONFESSIONS OF AN ENGLISH OPIUM-EATER, 1856

ANTHONY TROLLOPE

LOOKING BACK NOW I think I can see with accuracy what was then the condition of my own mind and intelligence. Of things to be learned by the lessons I knew almost less than could be supposed possible after the amount of schooling I had received. I could read neither French, Latin, nor Greek. I could speak no foreign language – and I may as well say here as elsewhere that I never acquired the power of really talking French. I have been able to order my dinner and take a railway ticket, but never got much beyond that. Of the merest rudiments of the sciences I was completely ignorant. My handwriting was in truth wretched. My spelling was imperfect. There was no subject as to which examination would have been possible on which I could have gone through an examination otherwise than disgracefully. And yet, I think, I knew more than the average of young men of the same rank who had begun life at nineteen. I could have given a fuller list of the names of the poets of all countries, with their subjects and periods – and probably of historians – than many others; and had, perhaps, a more accurate idea of the manner in which my own country was governed. I knew the names of all the bishops, all the judges, all the heads of colleges and all the cabinet ministers – not a very useful knowledge, indeed, but one that had not been acquired without other matter which was more useful. I had read Shakespeare and Byron and Scott and could talk about them. The music of the Miltonic line was familiar to me. I had already made up my mind that *Pride and Prejudice* was the best novel in the English language – a palm which I only partially withdrew after a second reading of *Ivanhoe* and did not completely bestow elsewhere till *Esmond* was written. And though I would occasionally break down in my spelling, I could write a letter. If I had a thing to say I could so say it in written words that the reader should know what I meant – a power which is by no means at the command of all those who come out from these competitive examinations with triumph. Early in life, at the age of fifteen, I had commenced the dangerous habit of keeping a journal, and this I maintained for ten years. The volumes remained in my possession unregarded – never looked at – till 1870, when I examined them and with many blushes destroyed them. They convicted me of folly, ignorance, indiscretion, idleness, extravagance, and conceit, but they had habituated me to the rapid use of pen and ink and taught me how to express myself with facility.

I will mention here another habit which had grown upon me from still earlier years – which I myself often regarded with dismay when I thought of the hours devoted to it, but which I suppose must have tended to make me what I have been. As a boy, even as a child, I was thrown much upon myself. I have explained, when speaking of my school-days, how it came to pass that other boys would not play with me. I was therefore alone and had to form my plays within myself. Play of some kind was necessary to me then, as it has always been. Study was not my bent, and I could not please myself by being all idle. Thus it came to pass that I was always going about with some castle in the air firmly built within my mind. Nor were these efforts in architecture spasmodic, or subject to constant change from day to day. For weeks, for months, if I remember rightly, from year to year I would carry on the same tale, binding myself down to certain laws, to certain proportions and proprieties and unities. Nothing impossible was ever introduced – nor even anything which from outward circumstances would seem to be violently improbable. I myself was of course my own hero. Such is a necessity of castle-building. But I never became a king, or a duke – much less, when my height and personal appearance were fixed, would I be an Antinous, or six feet high. I never was a learned man, nor even a philosopher. But I was a very clever person, and beautiful young women used to be fond of me. And I strove to be kind of heart and open of hand and noble in thought, despising mean things; and altogether I was a very much better fellow than I have ever succeeded in being since. This had been the occupation of my life for six or seven years before I went to the Post Office, and was by no means abandoned when I commenced my work. There can, I imagine, hardly be a more dangerous mental practice; but I have often doubted whether, had it not been my practice, I should ever have written a novel. I learned in this way to maintain an interest in a fictitious story, to dwell on a work created by my own imagination, and to live in a world altogether outside the world of my own material life. In after years I have done the same – with this difference, that I have discarded the hero of my early dreams, and have been able to lay my own identity aside.

An Autobiography, 1883

ROBERT GRAVES

I HAD NOW BEEN IN THE TRENCHES for five months and was getting past my prime. For the first three weeks an officer was not much good in the trenches; he did not know his way about, had not learned the rules of health and safety, and was not yet accustomed to recognizing degrees of danger. Between three weeks and four months he was at his best, unless he happened to have any particular bad shock or sequence of shocks. Then he began gradually to decline in usefulness as neurasthenia developed in him. At six months he was still more or less all right; but by nine or ten months, unless he had been given a few weeks' rest on a technical course or in hospital, he began to be a drag on the other members of the company. After a year or fifteen months he was often worse than useless. Officers had a less laborious but a more nervous time than the men. There were proportionately twice as many neurasthenic cases among officers as among men, though the average life of a man before getting killed or wounded was twice as long as an officer's. Officers between the ages of twenty-three and thirty-three had a longer useful life than those older or younger. I was too young. Men over forty, though they did not suffer from the want of sleep as much as those under twenty, had less resistance to the sudden alarms and shocks. Dr W.H.R. Rivers told me later that the action of one of the ductless glands – I think the thyroid – accounted for this decline in military usefulness. It pumped its chemical into the blood as a sedative for tortured nerves; this process went on until the condition of the blood was permanently affected and a man went about his tasks in a stupid and doped way, cheated into further endurance. It has taken some ten years for my blood to run at all clean. The unfortunates were the officers who had two years' or more continuous trench service. In many cases they became dipsomaniacs. I knew three or four who had worked up to the point of two bottles of whisky a day before they were lucky enough to get wounded or sent home in some other way. A two-bottle company commander of one of our line battalions still happens to be alive who, in three shows running, got his company needlessly destroyed because he was no longer capable of taking clear decisions.

GOOD-BYE TO ALL THAT, 1929

LAURIE LEE

THE STOOPING FIGURE OF MY MOTHER, waist-deep in the grass and caught there like a piece of sheep's wool, was the last I saw of my country home as I left it to discover the world. She stood old and bent at the top of the bank, silently watching me go, one gnarled red hand raised in farewell and blessing, not questioning why I went. At the bend of the road I looked back again and saw the gold light die behind her; then I turned the corner, passed the village school, and closed that part of my life for ever.

It was a bright Sunday morning in early June, the right time to be leaving home. My three sisters and a brother had already gone before me; two other brothers had yet to make up their minds. They were still sleeping that morning, but my mother had got up early and cooked me a heavy breakfast, had stood wordlessly while I ate it, her hand on my chair, and had then helped me pack up my few belongings. There had been no fuss, no appeals, no attempts at advice or persuasion, only a long and searching look. Then, with my bags on my back, I'd gone out into the early sunshine and climbed through the long wet grass to the road.

It was 1934. I was nineteen years old, still soft at the edges, but with a confident belief in good fortune. I carried a small rolled-up tent, a violin in a blanket, a change of clothes, a tin of treacle biscuits, and some cheese. I was excited, vain-glorious, knowing I had far to go; but not, as yet, how far. As I left home that morning and walked away from the sleeping village, it never occurred to me that others had done this before me.

I was propelled, of course, by the traditional forces that had sent many generations along this road – by the small tight valley closing in around one, stifling the breath with its mossy mouth, the cottage walls narrowing like the arms of an iron maiden, the local girls whispering, 'Marry, and settle down.' Months of restless unease, leading to this inevitable moment, had been spent wandering about the hills, mournfully whistling, and watching the high open fields stepping away eastwards under gigantic clouds.

And now I was on my journey, in a pair of thick boots and with a hazel stick in my hand. Naturally, I was going to London, which lay a hundred miles to the east; and it seemed equally obvious that I should go on foot. But first, as I'd never yet seen the sea, I thought I'd walk to the coast and find it. This would add another hundred miles to my journey, going by way of Southampton. But I had all the summer and all time to spend.

That first day alone – and now I was really alone at last – steadily declined in excitement and vigour. As I tramped through the dust towards the Wiltshire Downs a growing reluctance weighed me down. White elder-blossom and dog-roses hung in the hedges, blank as unwritten paper, and the hot empty road – there were few motor cars then – reflected Sunday's waste and indifference. High sulky summer sucked me towards it, and I offered no resistance at all. Through the solitary morning and afternoon I found myself longing for some opposition or rescue, for the sound of hurrying footsteps coming after me and family voices calling me back.

None came. I was free. I was affronted by freedom. The day's silence said, Go where you will. It's all yours. You asked for it. It's up to you now. You're on your own, and nobody's going to stop you. As I walked, I was taunted by echoes of home, by the tinkling sounds of the kitchen, shafts of sun from the windows falling across the familiar furniture, across the bedroom and the bed I had left.

When I judged it to be tea-time I sat on an old stone wall and opened my tin of treacle biscuits. As I ate them I could hear mother banging the kettle on the hob and my brothers rattling their teacups. The biscuits tasted sweetly of the honeyed squalor of home – still only a dozen miles away.

I might have turned back then if it hadn't been for my brothers, but I couldn't have borne the look on their faces. So I got off the wall and went on my way. The long evening shadows pointed to folded villages, homing cows, and after-church walkers. I tramped the edge of the road, watching my dusty feet, not stopping again for a couple of hours.

When darkness came, full of moths and beetles, I was too weary to put up the tent. So I lay myself down in the middle of a field and stared up at the brilliant stars. I was oppressed by the velvety emptiness of the world and the swathes of soft grass I lay on. Then the fumes of the night finally put me to sleep – my first night without a roof or bed.

I was woken soon after midnight by drizzling rain on my face, the sky black and the stars all gone. Two cows stood over me, windily sighing, and the wretchedness of that moment haunts me still. I crawled into a ditch and lay awake till dawn, soaking alone in that nameless field. But when the sun rose in the morning the feeling of desolation was over. Birds sang, and the grass steamed warmly. I got up and shook myself, ate a piece of cheese, and turned again to the south.

As I Walked Out One Midsummer Morning, 1969

MRS F.H. SMITH

I AM NOT MUCH OF A SCHOLAR as I had to leave school at an early age owing to my father not being in regular employment. I am a native of Cardiff and went to service up the Rhondda where I had a brother working, and it was there I met my husband, who was a miner. I was nineteen when I married in 1903. As a town-bred girl I found the life very different from what I had been used to. I was very shocked that we had no convenience for our husbands to bath in. We had to bring a tub or tin bath, whichever we had, into the same room that we lived in, and heat the water over our living-room fire in a bucket or iron boiler, whichever we possessed. So you can imagine the life of a miner's wife is no bed of roses. We have also to do our weekly wash in the same room, so our one room was not much to look at. By the time we had done our daily clean, it was looking all right, until Hubby came home. Then after he had bathed and his clothes put to dry, and turned from time to time, there is a nice film of coal dust all over the room, and it means you want the duster in your hand continually. Well, time went on and eleven months after my marriage my first daughter was born, and as she grew older it was very trying, as no matter how you try to keep your baby nice and clean it is practically impossible.

When she was just a year old I was lucky enough to rent a house under the Colliery Company for which my husband worked, and we had hardly settled down before we had the terrible experience of a pit explosion. My husband was down the pit at the same time, but was working in what they call the New Pit, and the explosion was in the Old Pit. But it will always live in my memory the terrible scenes I witnessed among the men and boys and neighbours from around me. One poor woman opposite me lost her husband, two sons and an adopted son in that terrible blast – lost all her breadwinners. There was only one survivor and 122 killed.

Well, as I said, it was very close quarters in two rooms – one living-room and one bedroom. It was much better to have a house, though it meant more furniture to fill the six rooms now, or partially. As my husband was a steady, sober man we had a chance to get on a bit in that way. In the course of time my family increased until I had nine children ...

'IN A MINING VILLAGE', 1931

ANNIE BESANT

BEFORE LEAVING THE HARBOURAGE of girlhood to set sail on the troublous sea of life, there is an occurrence of which I must make mention, as it marks my first awakening of interest in the outer world of political struggle. In the autumn of 1867 my mother and I were staying with some dear friends of ours, the Robertses, at Pendleton, near Manchester. Mr Roberts was 'the poor man's lawyer', in the affectionate phrase used of him by many a hundred men. He was a close friend of Ernest Jones, and was always ready to fight a poor man's battle without fee. He worked hard in the agitation which saved women from working in the mines, and I have heard him tell how he had seen them toiling, naked to the waist, with short petticoats barely reaching to their knees, rough, foul-tongued, brutalized out of all womanly decency and grace; how he had seen little children working there too, babies of three and four set to watch a door and falling asleep at their work to be roused by curse and kick to the unfair toil. The old man's eye would begin to flash and his voice to rise as he told of these horrors, and then his face would soften as he added that, after it was all over and the slavery was put an end to, as he went through a coal district the women standing at their doors would lift up their children to see 'Lawyer Roberts' go by, and would bid 'God bless him' for what he had done. This dear old man was my first tutor in Radicalism, and I was an apt pupil. I had taken no interest in politics, but had unconsciously reflected more or less the decorous Whiggism which had always surrounded me. I regarded 'the poor' as folk to be educated, looked after, charitably dealt with, and always treated with perfect courtesy, the courtesy being due from me, as a lady, to all equally, whether they were rich or poor. But to Mr Roberts 'the poor' were the working-bees, the wealth producers, with a right to self-rule, not to looking after, with a right to justice, not to charity, and he preached his doctrines to me in season and out of season. I was a pet of his, and used often to drive him to his office in the morning, glorying much in the fact that my skill was trusted in guiding a horse through the crowded Manchester streets. During these drives, and on all other available occasions, Mr Roberts would preach to me the cause of the people.

ANNIE BESANT: AN AUTOBIOGRAPHY, 1893

JOYCE MAYNARD

To MY FRIEND HANNA, at five, I am a grown-up. I do not feel like one – at nineteen, I'm at the midway point between the kindergartner and her mother, and I belong to neither generation – but I can vote, and drink in New York, and marry without parental consent in Mississippi, and get a life sentence, not reform school, if I shoot someone premeditatedly. Walking with Hanna in New York, and keeping to the inside, as the guidebooks tell me, so that doorway muggers lunging out will get not her but me, I'm suddenly aware that, of the two of us, I am the adult, the one whose life means less, because I've lived more of it already; I've moved from my position as protected child to child protector; I am the holder of a smaller hand, where, just ten years ago, *my* hand was held through streets whose dangers lay not in the alleys but in the roads themselves, the speeding cars, roaring motorcycles. I have left childhood, and though I longed to leave it, when being young meant finishing your milk and missing *Twilight Zone* on TV because it came on too late, now that it's gone I'm uneasy. Not fear of death yet (I'm still young enough to feel immortal) or worry over wrinkles or gray hair, but a sense that the fun is over before it began, that I'm old before my time – why isn't someone holding *my* hand still, protecting *me* from the dangers of the city, guiding me home?

I remember kneeling on the seat of a subway car, never bothering to count the stops or peer through all those shopping bags and knees to read the signs, because *she* would know when to get off, she'd take my hand; I remember looking out the window to see the sparks fly, underpants exposed to all the rush-hour travelers and never worrying that they could see, while all around me, mothers had to cross their legs or keep their knees together. And later, driving home, leaning against my mother's shoulder while her back tensed on the seat and her eyes stared out at the yellow lines, it was so nice to know I was responsible for nothing more than brushing my teeth when we got home, and not even that, if we got home late enough.

Hanna doesn't look where we're going, never bothers to make sure she can find her way home again, because she knows I will take care of those things, and though I feel I am too young to be so old in anybody's eyes, it's just a feeling, not a fact. When it rains, she gets the plastic rain hat, and when the ball of ice cream on her cone falls off, I give her mine. But if Hanna uses my ice cream and my hat, my knowledge of the subways and my hand, well, I use Hanna too; she's my excuse to ride the Ferris wheel, to shop for dolls. And when the circus comes to town – Ringling Brothers, no less – and I take her, everything evens up. Walking to Madison Square Garden, stepping over sidewalk lines and dodging muggers, she is my escort more than I am hers.

LOOKING BACK: A CHRONICLE OF GROWING UP OLD IN THE SIXTIES, 1973

JOHN STUART MILL

IT WAS IN THE AUTUMN OF 1826. I was in a dull state of nerves, such as everybody is occasionally liable to; unsusceptible to enjoyment or pleasurable excitement; one of those moods when what is pleasure at other times, becomes insipid or indifferent; the state, I should think, in which converts to Methodism usually are, when smitten by their first 'conviction of sin'. In this frame of mind it occurred to me to put the question directly to myself, 'Suppose that all your objects in life were realized; that all the changes in institutions and opinions which you are looking forward to, could be completely effected at this very instant: would this be a great joy and happiness to you?' And an irrepressible self-consciousness distinctly answered, 'No!' At this my heart sank within me: the whole foundation on which my life was constructed fell down. All my happiness was to have been found in the continual pursuit of this end. The end had ceased to charm, and how could there ever again be any interest in the means? I seemed to have nothing left to live for.

At first I hoped that the cloud would pass away of itself; but it did not. A night's sleep, the sovereign remedy for the smaller vexations of life, had no effect on it. I awoke to a renewed consciousness of the woeful fact. I carried it with me into all companies, into all occupations. Hardly anything had power to cause me even a few minutes' oblivion of it. For some months the cloud seemed to grow thicker and thicker. The lines in Coleridge's 'Dejection' – I was not then acquainted with them – exactly describe my case:

> A grief without a pang, void, dark and drear,
> A drowsy, stifled, unimpassioned grief,
> Which finds no natural outlet or relief
> In word, or sigh, or tear.

In vain I sought relief from my favourite books; those memorials of past nobleness and greatness, from which I had always hitherto drawn strength and animation. I read them now without feeling, or with the accustomed feeling *minus* all its charm; and I became persuaded, that my love of mankind, and of excellence for its own sake, had worn itself out. I sought no comfort by speaking to others of what I felt. If I had loved any one sufficiently to make confiding my griefs a necessity, I should not have been in the condition I was. I felt, too, that mine was not an interesting, or in any way respectable distress. There was nothing in it to attract sympathy. Advice, if I had known where to seek it, would have been most precious.

AUTOBIOGRAPHY, 1873

AMBROSE BIERCE

F OR US THERE WAS NO REST. Foot by foot we moved through the dusky fields, we knew not whither. There were men all about us, but no camp fires; to have made a blaze would have been madness. The men were of strange regiments; they mentioned the names of unknown generals. They gathered in groups by the wayside, asking eagerly our numbers. They recounted the depressing incidents of the day. A thoughtful officer shut their mouths with a sharp word as he passed; a wise one coming after encouraged them to repeat their doleful tale all along the line.

Hidden in hollows and behind clumps of rank brambles were large tents, dimly lighted with candles, but looking comfortable. The kind of comfort they supplied was indicated by pairs of men entering and reappearing, bearing litters; by low moans from within and by long rows of dead with covered faces outside. These tents were constantly receiving the wounded, yet were never full; they were continually ejecting the dead, yet were never empty. It was as if the helpless had been carried in and murdered, that they might not hamper those whose business it was to fall tomorrow.

The night was now black-dark; as is usual after a battle, it had begun to rain. Still we moved; we were being put into position by somebody. Inch by inch we crept along, treading on one another's heels by way of keeping together. Commands were passed along the line in whispers; more commonly none were given. When the men had pressed so closely together that they could advance no farther, they stood stock-still, sheltering the locks of their rifles with their ponchos. In this position many fell asleep. When those in front suddenly stepped away those in the rear, roused by the tramping, hastened after with such zeal that the line was soon choked again. Evidently the head of the division was being piloted at a snail's pace by some one who did not feel sure of his ground. Very often we struck our feet against the dead; more frequently against those who still had spirit enough to resent it with a moan. These were lifted carefully to one side and abandoned. Some had sense enough to ask in their weak way for water. Absurd! Their clothes were soaked, their hair dank; their white faces, dimly discernible, were clammy and cold. Besides, none of us had any water. There was plenty coming, though, for before midnight a thunderstorm broke upon us with great violence. The rain, which had for hours been a dull drizzle, fell with a copiousness that stifled us; we moved in running water up to our ankles. Happily, we were in a forest of great trees heavily 'decorated' with Spanish moss, or with an enemy standing to his guns the disclosures of the lightning might have been inconvenient. As it was, the incessant blaze enabled us to consult our watches and encouraged us by displaying our numbers; our black, sinuous line, creeping like a giant serpent beneath the trees, was apparently interminable. I am almost ashamed to say how sweet I found the companionship of those coarse men.

So the long night wore away, and as the glimmer of morning crept in through the forest we found ourselves in a more open country. But where? Not a sign of battle was here. The trees were neither splintered nor scarred, the underbrush was unmown, the ground had no footprints but our own. It was as if we had broken into glades sacred to eternal silence. I should not have been surprised to see sleek leopards come fawning about our feet, and milk-white deer confront us with human eyes.

A few inaudible commands from an invisible leader had placed us in order of battle. But where was the enemy? Where, too, were the riddled regiments that we had come to save? Had our other divisions arrived during the night and passed the river to assist us? Or were we to oppose our paltry five thousand breasts to an army flushed with victory? What protected our right? Who lay upon our left? Was there really anything in our front?

There came, borne to us on the raw morning air, the long weird note of a bugle. It was directly before us. It rose with a low clear, deliberate warble, and seemed to float in the gray sky like the note of a lark. The bugle calls of the Federal and Confederate armies were the same; it was the 'assembly'! As it died away I observed that the atmosphere had suffered a change; despite the equilibrium established by the storm, it was electric. Wings were growing on blistered feet. Bruised muscles and jolted bones, shoulders pounded by the cruel knapsack, eyelids leaden from lack of sleep – all were pervaded by the subtle fluid, all were unconscious of their clay. The men thrust forward their heads, expanded their eyes and clenched their teeth. They breathed hard, as if throttled by tugging at the leash. If you had laid your hand in the beard or hair of one of these men it would have crackled and shot sparks.

'WHAT I SAW OF SHILOH', 1881

JONATHAN EDWARDS

WHILE I WAS THERE AT NEW YORK, I sometimes was much affected with reflections on my past life, considering how late it was, before I began to be truly religious; and how wickedly I had lived 'til then; and once so as to weep abundantly, and for a considerable time together.

On January 12, 1722–3 I made a solemn dedication of myself to God, and wrote it down; giving up myself, and all that I had to God; to be for the future in no respect my own; to act as one that had no right to himself, in any respect. And solemnly vowed to take God for my whole portion and felicity, looking on nothing else as any part of my happiness, nor acting as if it were; and His law for the constant rule of my obedience, engaging to fight with all my might against the world, the flesh and the devil, to the end of my life. But have reason to be infinitely humbled, when I consider, how much I have failed of answering my obligation.

I had then abundance of sweet religious conversation in the family where I lived, with Mr John Smith, and his pious mother. My heart was knit in affection to those in whom were appearances of true piety, and I could bear the thoughts of no other companions but such as were holy, and the disciples of the blessed Jesus.

I had great longings for the advancement of Christ's kingdom in the world. My secret prayer used to be in great part taken up in praying for it. If I heard the least hint of anything that happened in any part of the world that appeared to me, in some respect or other, to have a favorable aspect on the interest of Christ's kingdom, my soul eagerly catched at it; and it would much animate and refresh me. I used to be earnest to read public newsletters, mainly for that end, to see if I could not find some news favorable to the interest of religion in the world.

I very frequently used to retire into a solitary place, on the banks of Hudson's river, at some distance from the city, for contemplation on divine things and secret converse with God, and had many sweet hours there. Sometimes Mr Smith and I walked there together to converse of the things of God, and our conversation used much to turn on the advancement of Christ's kingdom in the world, and the glorious things that God would accomplish for His church in the latter days.

I had then, and at other times, the greatest delight in the holy Scriptures, of any book whatsoever. Oftentimes in reading it, every word seemed to touch my heart. I felt an harmony between something in my heart, and those sweet and powerful words. I seemed often to see so much light exhibited by every sentence, and such a refreshing ravishing food communicated, that I could not get along in reading. Used oftentimes to dwell long on one sentence, to see the wonders contained in it; and yet almost every sentence seemed to be full of wonders.

'PERSONAL NARRATIVE', 1765

MARGERY KEMPE

WHEN THIS CREATURE WAS twenty years of age, or some deal more, she was married to a worshipful burgess (of Lynne) and was with child within a short time, as nature would. And after she had conceived, she was belaboured with great accesses till the child was born and then, what with the labour she had in childing, and the sickness going before, she despaired of her life, weening she might not live. And then she sent for her ghostly father, for she had a thing on her conscience which she had never shewn before that time in all her life. For she was ever hindered by her enemy, the devil, evermore saying to her that whilst she was in good health she needed no confession, but to do penance by herself alone and all should be forgiven, for God is merciful enough. And therefore this creature oftentimes did great penance in fasting on bread and water, and other deeds of alms with devout prayers, save she would not shew that in confession.

And when she was at any time sick or dis-eased, the devil said in her mind that she should be damned because she was not shriven of that default. Wherefore after her child was born, she, not trusting to live, sent for her ghostly father, as is said before, in full will to be shriven of all her lifetime, as near as she could. And when she came to the point for to say that thing which she had so long concealed, her confessor was a little too hasty and began sharply to reprove her, before she had fully said her intent, and so she would no more say for aught he might do. Anon, for the dread she had of damnation on the one side, and his sharp reproving of her on the other side, this creature went out of her mind and was wondrously vexed and laboured with spirits for half a year, eight weeks and odd days.

And in this time she saw, as she thought, devils opening their mouths all inflamed with burning waves of fire, as if they would have swallowed her in, sometimes ramping at her, sometimes threatening her, pulling her and hauling her, night and day during the aforesaid time. Also the devils cried upon her with great threatenings, and bade her that she should forsake Christendom, her faith, and deny her God, His Mother and all the Saints in Heaven, her good works and all good virtues, her father, her mother and all her friends. And so she did. She slandered her husband, her friends and her own self. She said many a wicked word, and many a cruel word; she knew no virtue nor goodness; she desired all wickedness; like as the spirits tempted her to say and do, so she said and did. She would have destroyed herself many a time at their stirrings and have been damned with them in Hell, and in witness thereof, she bit her own hand so violently, that the mark was seen all her life after.

And also she rived the skin on her body against her heart with her nails spitefully, for she had no other instruments, and worse she would have done, but that she was bound and kept with strength day and night so that she might not have her will. And when she had long been laboured in these and many other temptations, so that men weened she should never have escaped or lived, then on a time as she lay alone and her keepers were from her, Our Merciful Lord Jesus Christ, ever to be trusted, worshiped be His Name, never forsaking His servant in time of need, appeared to His creature who had forsaken Him, in the likeness of a man, most seemly, most beauteous and most amiable that ever might be seen with man's eye, clad in a mantle of purple silk, sitting upon her bedside, looking upon her with so blessed a face that she was strengthened in all her spirit, and said to her these words:

'Daughter, why hast thou forsaken Me, and I forsook never thee?'

And anon, as He said these words, she saw verily how the air opened as bright as any lightning. And He rose up into the air, not right hastily and quickly, but fair and easily, so that she might well behold Him in the air till it was closed again.

And anon this creature became calmed in her wits and reason, as well as ever she was before, and prayed her husband as soon as he came to her, that she might have the keys of the buttery to take her meat and drink as she had done before. Her maidens and her keepers counselled him that he should deliver her no keys, as they said she would but give away such goods as there were, for she knew not what she said, as they weened.

Nevertheless, her husband ever having tenderness and compassion for her, commanded that they should deliver to her the keys; and she took her meat and drink as her bodily strength would serve her, and knew her friends and her household and all others that came to see how Our Lord Jesus Christ had wrought His grace in her, so blessed may He be, Who ever is near in tribulation. When men think He is far from them, He is full near by His grace. Afterwards, this creature did all other occupations as fell to her to do, wisely and soberly enough, save she knew not verily the call of Our Lord.

THE BOOK OF MARGERY KEMPE, 1436–1438

CHARLES DARWIN

ALTHOUGH AS WE SHALL PRESENTLY SEE there were some redeeming features in my life at Cambridge, my time was sadly wasted there and worse than wasted. From my passion for shooting and for hunting and when this failed for riding across country I got into a sporting set, including some dissipated low-minded young men. We used often to dine together in the evening, though these dinners often included men of a higher stamp, and we sometimes drank too much, with jolly singing and playing at cards afterwards. I know that I ought to feel ashamed of days and evenings thus spent, but as some of my friends were very pleasant and we were all in the highest spirits, I cannot help looking back to these times with much pleasure.

But I am glad to think that I had many other friends of a widely different nature. I was very intimate with Whitley, who was afterwards Senior Wrangler, and we used continually to take long walks together. He inoculated me with a taste for pictures and good engravings, of which I bought some. I frequently went to the Fitzwilliam Gallery, and my taste must have been fairly good, for I certainly admired the best pictures, which I discussed with the old curator. I read also with much interest Sir J. Reynolds' book. This taste, though not natural to me, lasted for several years and many of the pictures in the National Gallery in London gave me much pleasure; that of Sebastian del Piombo exciting in me a sense of sublimity.

I also got into a musical set, I believe by means of my warm-hearted friend Herbert, who took a high wrangler's degree. From associating with these men and hearing them play, I acquired a strong taste for music, and used very often to time my walks so as to hear on week days the anthem in King's College Chapel. This gave me intense pleasure, so that my backbone would sometimes shiver. I am sure that there was no affectation or mere imitation in this taste, for I used generally to go by myself to King's College, and I sometimes hired the chorister boys to sing in my rooms. Nevertheless, I am so utterly destitute of an ear, that I cannot perceive a discord, or keep time and hum a tune correctly; and it is a mystery how I could possibly have derived pleasure from music.

My musical friends soon perceived my state, and sometimes amused themselves by making me pass an examination, which consisted in ascertaining how many tunes I could recognize, when they were played rather more quickly or slowly than usual. 'God Save the King' when thus played was a sore puzzle. There was another man with almost as bad an ear as I had, and strange to say he played a little on the flute. Once I had the triumph of beating him in one of our musical examinations.

But no pursuit at Cambridge was followed with nearly so much eagerness or gave me so much pleasure as collecting beetles. It was the mere passion for collecting, for I did not dissect them and rarely compared their external characters with published descriptions, but got them named anyhow. I will give proof of my zeal: one day, on tearing off some old bark, I saw two rare beetles and seized one in each hand; then I saw a third and new kind, which I could not bear to lose, so that I popped the one which I held in my right hand into my mouth. Alas it ejected some intensely acrid fluid, which burnt my tongue so that I was forced to spit the beetle out, which was lost, as well as the third one.

'RECOLLECTIONS OF THE DEVELOPMENT OF MY MIND AND CHARACTER', 1876

JUNG CHANG

I BENEFITED ENORMOUSLY from my ability to read English, as although the university library had been looted during the Cultural Revolution, most of the books it had lost had been in Chinese. Its extensive English-language collection had been turned upside down, but was still largely intact.

The librarians were delighted that these books were being read, especially by a student, and were extremely helpful. The index system had been thrown into chaos, and they dug through piles of books to find the ones I wanted. It was through the efforts of these kind young men and women that I laid my hands on some English classics. Louisa May Alcott's *Little Women* was the first novel I read in English. I found women writers like her, Jane Austen, and the Brontë sisters much easier to read than male authors like Dickens, and I also felt more empathy with their characters. I read a brief history of European and American literature, and was enormously impressed by the Greek tradition of democracy, Renaissance humanism, and the Enlightenment's questioning of everything. When I read in *Gulliver's Travels* about the emperor who 'published an Edict, commanding all his Subjects, upon great Penalties, to break the smaller End of their Eggs', I wondered if Swift had been to China. My joy at the sensation of my mind opening up and expanding was beyond description.

Being alone in the library was heaven for me. My heart would leap as I approached it, usually at dusk, anticipating the pleasure of solitude with my books, the outside world ceasing to exist. As I hurried up the flight of stairs, into the pastiche classical-style building, the smell of old books long stored in airless rooms would give me

THE BOOK OF LIFE

tremors of excitement, and I would hate the stairs for being too long.

With the help of dictionaries which some professors lent me, I became acquainted with Longfellow, Walt Whitman, and American history. I memorized the whole of the Declaration of Independence, and my heart swelled at the words, 'We hold these truths to be self-evident, that all men are created equal,' and those about men's 'unalienable Rights', among them 'Liberty and the pursuit of Happiness'. These concepts were unheard of in China, and opened up a marvelous new world for me. My notebooks, which I kept with me at all times, were full of passages like these, passionately and tearfully copied out.

WILD SWANS: THREE DAUGHTERS OF CHINA, 1991

KATHARINE HEPBURN

BEFORE MY SENIOR YEAR ENDED, I had made friends with a man named Jack Clarke, who lived in a house next door to the college campus. His best friend was Ludlow Ogden Smith.

Jack had several friends in the theatre and he happened to know Edwin Knopf, who ran a theatre company – a very good one, with big stars – in Baltimore. Mary Boland, Kenneth MacKenna, Eliot Cabot. I got him to give me a letter to Knopf, and one weekend Lib Rhett and I drove over to Baltimore. My mother's sister Edith Houghton Hooker lived there. I went to see Knopf and he said, 'Well, write me a note when you finish college.'

I finished college.

Dad always said if you want to get something, don't write. Don't telephone. Be there yourself. In person. Harder to turn down a living presence.

So I did. My aunt and her family had left Baltimore and gone to Maine for the summer, so I stayed at the Bryn Mawr Club. It, too, was half closed, but they let me stay in their cheaper room, in a hall bedroom. On an air shaft. High ceilings, very dark and scary. Not too far from theatre. I was too shy to go into a restaurant. I'd hardly ever been in a restaurant, in fact. And certainly not alone. My great friend Bob McKnight, who had a car (you see how wise I was in picking friends), had come with me. He was on his way to Rome to study sculpture. He'd won a Prix de Rome. He lived there with me. And we'd get food from a delicatessen. It was all very innocent. We were both wildly ambitious and thrilled with life and its possibilities. We weren't wasting our strength rolling around. It was all or nothing for *me me me*. With each of us. Don't get sidetracked. We protected each other.

I went to see Eddy Knopf. I found my way in from the front. I didn't even know there was such a thing as a stage door. I heard voices. It sounded like a rehearsal. I opened a door so that I could see the stage. It was a rehearsal. I crept in and sat in a back row like a mouse. An hour passed. I needed to go to the bathroom. Finally I *had* to go to the bathroom. The whole theatre away from the stage area was as black as pitch. I felt my way around the lobby – down a stairway into another lobby. And finally a john. Then I found my way out and went back to my spot. Another hour. Even a third. Then all of a sudden it was over. They were finishing. The lights in the auditorium came on.

Eddie Knopf saw me. He walked up the aisle. Stopped by me and said, 'Oh – you – yes, report for rehearsal Monday – eleven o'clock.'

And he was gone.

My God! I had a job! He gave me a job! He knew me! He gave me a job!

That Monday I walked into his office at ten forty-five.

'I'm here for rehearsal.'

'You're in the wrong place.'

It was thus I learned about the stage door.

ME: STORIES OF MY LIFE, 1991

JEAN-JACQUES ROUSSEAU

THESE LONG DETAILS of my early youth will have seemed really rather childish and I am annoyed about it: though born a man in certain respects, I was a child for a long time and I still am in many others. I have not promised to offer the public a great personality; I have promised to portray myself as I am; and, to know me in my advanced age, you must know me well in my youth. As, in general, objects make less of an impression on me than does their memory, and as all my ideas are in the form of images, the first traces that engraved themselves in my mind have stayed there, and those that imprinted themselves later on have rather combined themselves more than erased them. There has been a certain succession of affections and ideas that modify those that follow them, and that you must know to judge me properly. I devote myself to developing those first causes thoroughly in every instance so that the chain of effects can be felt. I wanted to be able to make my soul transparent to the eyes of the reader in some way, and for that purpose I am trying to show it to him from every point of view, in every light, by writing in such a way that no movement might happen without him noticing, and being able to judge for himself the principle that produces them.

If I took responsibility for the result and I told him, 'Such was my nature', he might believe that I was misleading him, or at least that I was deceiving myself. But in detailing for him in simple terms everything that happened to me, everything I have done, everything I thought, everything I felt, I cannot lead him astray, unless I want to; and even when I want to, I would not easily manage to. It is up to him to assemble these elements and to determine the being that they compose: the result should be his work; if he is wrong, then the error will be entirely his doing. Thus, it is not sufficient for this end that my tales be faithful, they must also be exact. It is not for me to judge the importance of the fact, I have to relate them all, and leave to him the trouble of choosing. It is to this that I have applied myself up to this point with all my courage, and I will not let up from now on. But the memories of my middle age are always less vivid than those of my earliest youth. I have begun by drawing the best part possible from them. If the other memories return to me with the same force, impatient readers may perhaps get bored, but I will not be unhappy with my work. I have only one thing to fear in this enterprise: it is not that I might say too much or tell lies, but that I might not say everything and keep truths quiet.

THE CONFESSIONS, 1782–1789

~ THE MIDDLE ~

AGES 21–59

'A hundred more suchlike modest memories
breathe upon me, each with its own dim little
plea, as I turn to face them, but my idea is to
deal somehow more conveniently with the
whole gathered mass of my subsequent
impressions in this order, a fruitage that I feel
to have been only too abundantly stored.
Half a dozen of those of a larger and more
immediate dignity, incidents more
particularly of the rather invidiously so-
called social contact, pull my sleeve as I pass;
but the long, backward-drawn train of the
later life drags them along with it, lost and
smothered in its spread ...'

HENRY JAMES,
THE MIDDLE YEARS, 1916

GIACOMO CASANOVA

AFTER AN EDUCATION designed to lead me to an honourable position appropriate to a young man with a good grounding in literature and with the happy qualities of spirit and accidents of person, that always and everywhere make an impression, here I was despite this, at the age of twenty, evolved into the lowly agent of a sublime art, in which those who excel are admired and those who are mediocre are rightly despised. I became a player in a theatre orchestra, where I could demand neither esteem nor consideration and where I even had to expect to be the laughing-stock of those who had known me as a doctor, then clergyman, then military man, and had seen me welcomed and feted at fine and noble gatherings.

I understood all this; but the scorn, to which I could not have remained indifferent, was not immediately apparent. I defied it, because I knew it was due only to cowardice, and I could not reproach myself for that in any way. As far as esteem was concerned, I was letting my ambition rest a while. Happy to belong to no one, I was going about my business without becoming worried about the future. Forced to join the clergy, and powerless to succeed without becoming a hypocrite, I would have despised myself had I stayed the course; and pursuing my career in the military would have required a patience that I knew I did not have. It seemed to me that the position I engaged in should provide me with enough of a living, and the compensation I would have received, for serving with the troops of the Republic, would not have been enough; because my needs were, thanks to my education, greater than those of another. By playing the violin I earned enough to take care of myself without depending on anyone else. *Happy are they who take pride in their self-sufficiency.* My work was not noble, but I did not care. In treating everything with prejudice, I took on all the habits of my lowly comrades in no time. After the performance, I went to the tavern with them, and we would leave drunk to spend the night in houses of ill repute. When we found them occupied, we threw out the occupants and we denied the unfortunate creatures that we had subjected to our brutality the small recompense that the law accords them. For this violence we often exposed ourselves to the most obvious risks.

We often spent the night strolling around the various neighbourhoods of the town inventing and executing every imaginable prank. We amused ourselves by untying the gondolas from the moorings of particular houses, and then would let them drift with the current from one side to the other of the Grand Canal, delighting in the curses uttered by the gondoliers in the morning when they could not find their gondolas where they had tethered them.

We often went to wake up the midwives, making them dress and come down to help women give birth who, on their arrival, called them mad. We did the same with the most famous doctors, disturbing them from rest to make them visit lords whom we announced had been struck down with apoplexy; and we made priests get up out of bed to go and pray for the souls of people who were quite healthy, and whom we had said were dying.

On every street we went down we would pitilessly cut the ropes to the doorbells which hang by the doors to the houses; and when by chance we found a door open because someone had forgotten to close it, we climbed the stairs quietly and we surprised the people who slept inside, warning them that their front door was open. Afterwards we left quickly, leaving the doors open exactly as we had found them.

One very dark night we decided to destroy a large slab of marble that was a sort of monument. This slab of marble was located almost in the middle of the Campo Sant' Angelo. It was said that during the war which the Republic waged against the League of Cambrai, the commissioners had paid the recruits who signed up to serve St Mark from this table.

When we could get into the bell towers, we took great pleasure in scaring the wits out of the whole parish by ringing the bell used to warn of fires, or else to cut through the bell ropes. When we crossed over to the other side of the canal, instead of all going in one gondola, each one of us took one and when we got to the other side, we would all run off to make the unpaid oarsmen follow us.

The whole town complained about these night-time pranks and we didn't care about the investigations made to track down the people who were disturbing of the public peace.

STORY OF MY LIFE, 1789–1792

GEORGE SAND

WE WERE MARRIED IN SEPTEMBER 1822, and after the exchanges of wedding visits, and after a break of several days at our friends the du Plessises, we left with my brother for Nohant, where the good Deschartres [my former tutor] welcomed us joyfully.

I spent the winter of 1822–23 at Nohant, fairly ill but absorbed in the feeling of motherly love that revealed itself to me in the most delicate dreams and the most vivid longings. The transformation that takes place at that moment in our lives and in women's thoughts is, in general, complete and sudden. It was like that for me, as it is for the vast number of us. The needs of intelligence, of anxiety of thinking, the curiosity of study, as those of observation, all these disappeared in me as soon as the gentle burden began to make itself felt and even before its first stirrings had shown their existence. Providence ensures that the physical life and the life of feeling predominate in this phase of waiting and hope. Also, my usual waking, reading, day-dreaming – in a word, my intellectual life – was naturally suppressed, and without the slightest advantage or the slightest regret.

Winter was long and harsh; a deep snow covered the ground, already hardened by sharp frosts, for a long time. My husband also loved the countryside, though in a different way to me, and, liking to hunt, he left me for long, leisurely periods that I filled with work on making baby clothes. I had never sewn in my life. While always saying that I should know how, my grandmother never pushed me to and I thought I was most clumsy at it. But when its goal was to dress the little being that I saw in all my dreams, I threw myself into it with a sort of passion. My good Ursula came and gave me the basic skills of *surjet* and *rabattu*. I was totally surprised to see how easy it was; but, at the same time, I understood that in sewing, as in everything, there could be inventiveness and mastery in the scissor stroke ...

[In June of 1823] we left for Paris where, after several days in the Plessis with our good friends, I rented a small, decorated flat, in the Hotel de Florence, a townhouse on Rue Neuve-des-Mathurins, owned by a former chef of the emperor ...

It was in this building that they had furnished that I found – at the back of a second courtyard planted with a garden – a small pavilion where my son Maurice came into this world, on the 30 June 1823, without any trouble and full of life. It was the most beautiful moment of my life when – after an hour of deep sleep following the terrible pains of his birth – I saw upon waking this little one asleep on my pillow. I had dreamed so much about him beforehand, and I was so weak that I was not sure that I was not still dreaming. I was worried about stirring and the vision flying off, as it had flown away before.

I was kept in bed much longer than necessary. It is the custom in Paris to take more precautions over women in this situation than in the countryside. When I became a mother for the second time, I got up on the second day and was perfectly fine.

I breast-fed my son, as I later did his sister. My mother was his godmother and my father-in-law his godfather.

STORY OF MY LIFE, 1854–1855

SIMONE DE BEAUVOIR

THE MOST INTOXICATING ASPECT of my return to Paris in September, 1929, was the freedom I now possessed. I had dreamed of it since childhood, when I played with my sister at being a 'grown-up' girl. I have recorded elsewhere my passionate longing for it as a student. Now, suddenly, it was mine. I was astonished to find an effortless buoyancy in all my movements. From the moment I opened my eyes every morning I was lost in a transport of delight. When I was about twelve I had suffered through not having a private retreat of my own at home. Leafing through Mon Journal I had found a story about an

English schoolgirl, and gazed enviously at the coloured illustration portraying her room. There was a desk, and a divan, and shelves filled with books. Here, within these gaily painted walls, she read and worked and drank tea, with no one watching her – how envious I felt! For the first time ever I had glimpsed a more fortunate way of life than my own. And now, at long last, I too had a room to myself. My grandmother had stripped her drawing room of all its armchairs, occasional tables, and knickknacks. I had bought some unpainted furniture, and my sister had helped me to give it a coat of brown varnish. I had a table, two chairs, a large chest which served both as a seat and as a hold-all, shelves for my books. I papered the walls orange, and got a divan to match. From my fifth-floor balcony I looked out over the Lion of Belfort and the plane trees on the Rue Denfert-Rochereau. I kept myself warm with an evil-smelling kerosene stove. Somehow its stink seemed to protect my solitude, and I loved it. It was wonderful to be able to shut my door and keep my daily life free of other people's inquisitiveness. For a long time I remained indifferent to the décor of my surroundings. Possibly because of that picture in *Mon Journal* I preferred rooms that offered me a divan and bookshelves, but I was prepared to put up with any sort of retreat in a pinch. To have a door that I could shut was still the height of bliss for me.

The Prime of Life, 1960

WILLIAM COWPER

AT THE EXPIRATION OF THIS TERM, I became, in a manner, complete master of myself; and took possession of a complete set of chambers in the Temple, at the age of twenty-one. This being a critical season of my life, and one upon which much depended, it pleased my all-merciful Father in Christ Jesus, to give a check to my rash and ruinous career of wickedness at the very outset.

I was struck, not long after my settlement in the Temple, with such a dejection of spirits, as none but they who have felt the same, can have the least conception of. Day and night I was upon the rack, lying down in horror, and rising up in despair. I presently lost all relish for those studies, to which I had before been closely attached;

the classics had no longer any charms for me; I had need of something more salutary than amusement, but I had no one to direct me where to find it.

At length I met with Herbert's Poems; and, gothic and uncouth as they are, I yet found in them a strain of piety which I could not but admire. This was the only author I had any delight in reading. I pored over him, all day long; and though I found not in them what I might have found – a cure for my malady – yet it never seemed so much alleviated as while I was reading him. At length, I was advised by a very near and dear relative, to lay him aside; for he thought such an author more likely to nourish my disorder, than to remove it.

In this state of mind I continued near a twelvemonth; when, having experienced the inefficacy of all human means, I at length betook myself to God in prayer. Such is the rank our Redeemer holds in our esteem, that we never resort to him but in the last instance, when all creatures have failed to succour us! My hard heart was at length softened, and my stubborn knees brought to bow. I composed a set of prayers, and made frequent use of them. Weak as my faith was, the Almighty, who will not break the bruised reed, nor quench the smoking flax, was graciously pleased to hear me.

A change of scene was recommended to me; and I embraced an opportunity of going with some friends to Southampton, where I spent several months. Soon after our arrival we walked to a place called Freemantle, about a mile from the town; the morning was clear and calm; the sun shone bright upon the sea; and the country on the borders of it was the most beautiful I had ever seen. We sat down upon an eminence, at the end of that arm of the sea, which runs between Southampton and the New Forest. Here it was, that on a sudden, as if another sun had been kindled that instant in the heavens, on purpose to dispel sorrow and vexation of spirit, I felt the weight of all my misery taken off; my heart became light and joyful in a moment; I could have wept with transport had I been alone. I must needs believe that nothing less than the Almighty fiat have filled me with such inexpressible delight; not by a gradual dawning of peace, but, as it were, with a flash of his life-giving countenance. I think I remember something like a glow of gratitude to the Father of mercies, for this unexpected blessing, and that I ascribed it to His gracious acceptance of my prayers. But Satan, and my own wicked heart, quickly persuaded me that I was indebted, for my deliverance, to nothing but a change of scene, and the amusing varieties of the place. By this means he turned the blessing into a poison; teaching me to conclude, that nothing but a continued circle of diversion, and indulgence of appetite, could secure me from a relapse.

Upon this hellish principle, as soon as I returned to London, I burnt my prayers, and away went all thoughts of devotion and of dependence upon God my Saviour. Surely it was of his mercy that I was not consumed. Glory be to his grace!

Memoir of the Early Life of William Cowper Esq, written by himself, 1767

QUESTIN CRISP

MY OUTLOOK WAS SO LIMITED that I assumed that all deviates were openly despised and rejected. Their grief and their fear drew my melancholy nature strongly. At first I wanted only to wallow in their misery, but, as time went by, I longed to reach its very essence. Finally I desired to represent it. By this process I managed to shift homosexuality from being a burden to being a cause. The weight lifted and some of the guilt evaporated.

It seemed to me that there were few homosexuals in the world. I felt that the entire strength of the club must be prepared to show its membership card at any time, and, to a nature as dramatic as mine, not to deny rapidly became to protest. By the time I was twenty-three I had made myself into a test case. I realized that it did no good to be seen to be homosexual in the West End where sin reigned supreme or in Soho which was inhabited exclusively by other outcasts of various kinds, but the rest of England was straightforward missionary country. It was densely populated by aborigines who had never heard of homosexuality and who, when first they did, became frightened and angry. I went to work on them.

The message I wished to propagate was that effeminacy existed in people who were in all other respects just like home. I went about the routine of daily living looking undeniably like a homosexual person. I had had a lot of practice at school in being the one against the many but, even so, I was not prepared for the effect my appearance had on the great British public. I had to begin cautiously.

I was from birth an object of mild ridicule because of my movements – especially the perpetual flutter of my hands – and my voice. Like the voices of a number of homosexuals, this is an insinuating blend of eagerness and caution in which even such words as 'hello' and 'goodbye' seem not so much uttered as divulged. But these natural outward and visible signs of inward and spiritual disgrace were not enough. People could say that I was ignorant of them or was trying without success to hide them. I wanted it to be known that I was not ashamed and therefore had to display symptoms that could not be thought to be accidental.

I began to wear make-up. For a while I still went on as before at home and never mentioned to my mother anything about the life I lived in the outer world. She once protested that I never brought home any of my friends. I explained, quite truthfully, that she would hate them if I did. She never mentioned the matter again, which I took to be a sign that the protest was formal and that secretly she would be glad to hear no more on that subject.

Once outside the flat, I hurried like a wrong hushed-up to the nearest public lavatory and put on my war paint. Then I proceeded calmly wherever I was going. If I wasn't going anywhere, I tried to look as though I was. It became harder and harder to think of places to go and things to do as it slowly dawned on me that sex was definitely out – a realization that usually leaves people with a lot of spare time. If I was to become Miss Arc's only rival, it wouldn't do to allow myself to be picked up by strange men. This would give people the opportunity to say that I had only adopted an effeminate appearance for this purpose. Actually, from the moment I began to look really startling, men ceased to make propositions to me. They found it too risky or too distasteful. But even the idea that this might be my intention must be eliminated. I began to walk faster and learned never to look strangers in the eye. Frequently in the street I swept past people I knew quite well. I once did this to my brother.

This was just as well. He was with a girl who said, 'Did you see that?' to which he replied, 'Yes. Matter of fact, I've seen it before.'

Without knowing it, I was acquiring that haughty bearing which is characteristic of so many eccentrics. What other expression would you expect to find on the face of anyone who knows that if he turns his head too quickly, he will see on the faces of others glares of stark terror, or grimaces of hatred? Aloofness is the posture of self-defence, but even people who quite liked me said that I felt superior to the rest of the world. I felt scared and before long I was to have good cause.

By constantly complaining that the Battersea flat was sunless, my mother induced my father to buy a house outside High Wycombe. I could not do otherwise than go with them. My sister was by this time married; one of my brothers was abroad and the other was soon to go. Abroad was thought in those days to have some special advantages for men of the middle classes and in this connection the word 'scope' was on everybody's lips. As in childhood I had evinced so much distaste for even going outside the front door, my parents made little attempt to send me overseas. In this they were very wise, I don't hold with abroad and think that foreigners speak English when our backs are turned.

Even High Wycombe to me was like a desert at the edge of civilization. As I roamed the fields adjacent to the house, forced by my mother to take her chow for a walk, between the hedges my starved eyes would see mirages of the London Pavilion or the Marble Arch and I would stumble toward them with little cries. My great fear was that here I might live and die and not matter. Just how distasteful my life was at this time cannot have been apparent to others. A friend of my sister, rushing in where even devils would have feared to tread, remarked, 'I wonder what you'd have been like if you'd been a woman. I suppose you'd have lived in the country and kept a dog and played bridge.' I was too choked with fury to be able to defend myself against this charge. Among other objections to this image of me was the fact that I hated animals. I still do. I have enough dumb friends without them.

In childhood I had longed to be taught dancing but nothing ever came of this. In a characteristic fit of indulgence my mother went so far as to buy me a pair of blocked ballet shoes (she did not know or care that no male dancer, except Mr Dolin in *Train Bleu*, had ever worn such things), but she never dared to mention to my father the idea of my becoming a dancer. It would have made him difficult to deal with for days. After the failure of journalism, she hammered away at commercial art as the last door through which it might be possible to push me into the outer world. I was sent to an art school in High Wycombe.

I had already done one term at Battersea Polytechnic before we left London and there had drawn a frog that the principal had thought was a piece of drapery. I don't think that I was taught anything. The only good that came of my attendance at this school was my meeting there with a girl who was to remain my friend for more than twenty years. She had been crippled by polio and wore a metal splint on one leg. At every step the whole side of her body had to be swung forward by a great effort from the shoulder. Despite this she was determined not to be left out of things. Her willpower was formidable. Because of her handicap, she was sympathetic to all deformity and was especially drawn to anyone she felt to be worse off than she. I came into this category.

The school at High Wycombe was, naturally, further out of touch with reality than the one in Battersea. Furniture design was well taught there because the town was the home of that industry which many years later formulated the 'G' plan. All other subjects were thought to be rather beside the point. None of the three or four men who comprised the staff had ever worked in an advertising agency or made freelance commercial art into a paying profession. They would have been secretly ashamed to do so. Advertising was considered in those days a disgraceful trade. As no one felt confident to teach or even control me, I did more or less as I liked.

'What are you going to do this morning?'

'Oh, I don't know. A poster.'

'What of?'

'Coty's Ashes of Roses.' All my posters were exotic.

I very much doubt if, at the end of such a piece of dialogue as this, I was shown any advertising that Mr Coty had recently put out, or, if I was, that I was warned that I must follow closely the existing line. I was encouraged to be original with some very far-fetched results. As I was now twenty-one and in a class full of girls in gym slips, I seemed by comparison a genius and behaved like one. I went to school, as one might say, in mufti, but my hair and fingernails were long enough to cause comment from strangers on the way there and back.

THE NAKED CIVIL SERVANT, 1968

ELIZABETH ASHBRIDGE

I WAS ACCOUNTED A FINE SINGER and dancer, in which I took great delight, and once falling in company with some of the stage players, then at New York, they took a great fancy to me, as they said, and persuaded me to become an actress amongst them, and they would find means to get me from my servitude, and that I should live like a lady. The proposal took with me, and I used much pains to qualify myself for the stage, by reading plays, even when I should have slept, but after all this I found a stop in my mind, when I came to consider what my father would think when he heard of it, who had not only forgiven my disobedience in marriage, but had sent for me home, tho' my proud heart would not suffer me to return in so mean a condition I was then in, but rather chose bondage.

When I had served three years I bought the remainder of my time, and got a genteel maintenance by my needle, but alas! I was not sufficiently punished by my former servitude but got into another, and that for life; for a few months after this, I married a young man, who fell in love with me for my dancing – a poor motive for a man to choose a wife, or a woman to choose a husband.

As to my part I fell in love for nothing I saw in him, and it seems unaccountable, that I, who had refused several offers, both in this country and in Ireland, should at last marry a man I had no value for.

In a week after we were married, my husband, who was a schoolmaster, removed from New York, and took me along with him to New England, and settled at a place called Westerley, in Rhode Island government. With respect to religion, he was much like myself, without any; for when he was in drink he would use the worst of oaths. I don't mention this to expose my husband, but to show the effect it had upon me, for I now saw myself ruined, as I thought, being joined to a man I had no love for, and who was a pattern of no good to me. I therefore began to think we were like two joining hands and going to destruction, which made me conclude that if I was not forsaken of God, to alter my course of life. But to love the Divine Being, and not to love my husband, I saw was an inconfidency, and seemed impossible; therefore I requested, with tears, that my affections might increase towards my husband, and I can say in truth that my love was sincere to him. I now resolved to do my duty towards God, and expecting that I must come to the knowledge of it by reading the Scriptures, I read them with a strong resolution of following their directions, but the more I read the more uneasy I grew, especially about baptism, for altho' I had reason to believe I was sprinkled in my infancy, because at the age of fourteen I passed under the bishop's hand for confirmation, as it is called, yet I could not find any precedent for that practice, and upon reading where it is said, he that believes and is baptized, etc., I observed that belief went before baptism, which I was not capable of when I was sprinkled, at which I grew very uneasy, and living in a neighborhood that were mostly Seventh Day Baptists, I conversed with them, and at length thinking it to be really my duty, I was baptized by one of their teachers, but did not join strictly with them, tho' I began to think the seventh-day the true sabbath, and for some time kept it as such. My husband did not yet oppose me, for he saw I grew more affectionate to him, but I did not yet leave off singing and dancing so much, but I could divert him whenever he desired it.

Soon after this my husband and I concluded to go for England, and for that purpose went to Boston, where we found a ship bound for Liverpool, and agreed for our passage, expecting to sail in two weeks. But my time was not yet come, for there came one called a gentleman, who hired the ship to carry him and his attendants to Philadelphia, and to take no other passengers. There being no other ship near sailing, we for that time gave it over.

We stayed several weeks at Boston, and I remained still dissatisfied as to religion, tho' I had reformed my conduct so as to be accounted by those that knew me a sober woman. But that was not sufficient; for even then I expected to find the sweets of such a change, and though several thought me religious, I dared not think myself so, and what to do to be so, I seemed still an utter stranger to. I used to converse with people of all societies, as opportunity offered, and, like many others, had got a deal of head knowledge, and several societies thought me of their opinion, but I joined strictly none, resolving never to leave searching till I found the TRUTH. This was in the 22nd year of my age.

SOME ACCOUNT OF THE FORE-PART OF THE LIFE OF ELIZABETH ASHBRIDGE, 1774

DAVID SEDARIS

THE DAY AFTER GRADUATING from college, I found fifty dollars in the foyer of my Chicago apartment building. The single bill had been folded into eighths and was packed with cocaine. It occurred to me then that if I played my cards right, I might never have to find a job. People lost things all the time. They left class rings on the sinks of public bathrooms and dropped gem-studded earrings at the doors of the opera house. My job was to keep my eyes open and find these things. I didn't want to become one of those coots who combed the beaches of Lake Michigan with a metal detector, but if I paid attention and used my head, I might never have to work again.

The following afternoon, hung over from cocaine, I found twelve cents and an unopened tin of breath mints. Figuring in my previous fifty dollars, that amounted to an average of twenty-five dollars and six cents per day, which was still a decent wage.

The next morning I discovered two pennies and a comb matted with short curly hairs. The day after that I found a peanut. It was then that I started to worry.

'SOMETHING FOR EVERYONE', 1997

SEI SHŌNAGON

ONE WRITES A LETTER, taking particular trouble to get it up as prettily as possible; then waits for the answer, making sure every moment that it cannot be much longer before something comes. At last, frightfully late, is brought in – one's own note, still folded or tied exactly as one sent it, but so finger-marked and smudged that even the address is barely legible. 'The family is not in residence,' the messenger says, giving one back the note. Or 'It is his day of observance and they said they could not take any letters in.' Such experiences are dismally depressing.

One has been expecting someone, and rather late at night there is a stealthy tapping at the door. One sends a maid to see who it is, and lies waiting, with some slight flutter of the breast. But the name one hears when she returns is that of someone completely different, who does not concern one at all. Of all depressing experiences, this is by far the worst.

Someone comes, with whom one has decided not to have further dealings. One pretends to be fast asleep, but some servant or person connected with one comes to wake one up, and pulls one about, with a face as much as to say 'What a sleep-hog!' This is always exceedingly irritating.

If someone with whom one is having an affair keeps on mentioning some woman whom he knew in the past, however long ago it is since they separated, one is always irritated.

It is very tiresome when a lover who is leaving one at dawn says that he must look for a fan or pocket-book that he has left somewhere about the room last night. As it is still too dark to see anything, he goes fumbling about all over the place, knocking into everything and muttering to himself, 'How very odd!' When at last he finds the pocket-book he crams it into his dress with a great rustling of the pages; or if it is a fan he has lost, he swishes it open and begins flapping it about, so that when he finally takes his departure, instead of experiencing the feelings of regret proper to such an occasion, one merely feels irritated at his clumsiness ...

It is important that a lover should know how to make his departure. To begin with, he ought not to be too ready to get up, but should require a little coaxing: 'Come, it is past daybreak. You don't want to be found here ...' and so on. One likes him, too, to behave in such a way that one is sure he is unhappy at going and would stay longer if he possibly could. He should not pull on his trousers the moment he is up, but should first of all come close to one's ear and in a whisper finish off whatever was left half-said in the course of the night. But though he may in reality at these moments be doing nothing at all, it will not be amiss that he should appear to be buckling his belt. Then he should raise the shutters, and both lovers should go out together at the double doors, while he tells her how much he dreads the day that is before him and longs for the approach of night. Then, after he has slipped away, she can stand gazing after him, with charming recollections of those last moments. Indeed, the success of a lover depends greatly on his method of departure. If he springs to his feet with a jerk and at once begins fussing round, tightening the waistband of his breeches, or adjusting the sleeves of his court robe, hunting jacket, or what not, collecting a thousand odds and ends, and thrusting them into the folds of his dress, or pulling in his overbelt – one begins to hate him.

THE PILLOW BOOK OF SEI SHŌNAGON, C.990–C.1000

P.J. KAVANAGH

I WAS IN DIGS NOW, LOCKED AWAY, but the other lodgers had streams of visitors up and down the stairs past my door. None of these disturbed me except one girl who went 'Pom pom POM' as she ran up to the room above. It was a sound of extraordinary sweetness, musical, soft, unselfconscious and happy. I began to listen out for it, jump up from my table, throw the door open to catch a glimpse of her as she passed, but I was always too late. I asked the people upstairs who she was, described the beautiful sound she made. They became rather guarded and exchanged glances and hesitatingly admitted it just might be Sally. I gathered she was someone special, not to be discussed in the ordinary way, and became vaguely curious to meet her. But the last thing I wanted at that stage was to get involved with anybody. I'd just come to the end of a satisfactorily painful affair with a professional dons' girl (one met dons' girls at Oxford just as one met officers' girls in the Army). This one collected threats of suicide and broken marriages from the younger tutors like Girl Guides collect badges – she wore them on her sleeve. She was also great fun. It had been tempestuous and poignant in a way that was satisfactory to both of us and I considered myself to have suffered. Now, I had work to do.

One day I came face to face with a girl on the landing. It was certainly her, whoever made the noise had to look as she did. We stood and stared at each other too long for comfort. I broke the moment and, excusing myself, moved past her because it was too like the movies, or so I thought to myself of that long, silent stare, and laughed. She was tall and proud-looking with a slight round-shouldered stoop that made me breathless, I didn't know why.

It is difficult to describe someone who is surrounded by a special nimbus, perceived at once. But as this girl had the same effect, in one way or another, on many others, I must try. She had soft yellow hair, greeny-blue eyes, lovely eyebrows below a broad, quiet forehead and the most perfect mouth I have ever seen; underneath her skin there were golden lights. I am not a good physiognomist, I find it distorts a face to see it in detail, and I imagine the peculiar, extraordinary charm of her face lay in its proportions and in its expression. When I first saw the friezes in the museum on the Acropolis I couldn't believe it, most of the girls are portraits of her. Her face, and above all her expression, belonged to the same ideal, golden time. But beautiful girls are, in a sense, two a penny. There was something even more arresting, something unique in her face. She had the simplicity of a young girl (she was nineteen) who found life good; but it was a simplicity that had somehow been earned, was, as it were, on the second time round. This second simplicity has the directness and potency of a natural force. She had the kind of beauty that can change but not diminish – it depended for so much of its power on the kind of person she was that it could only end when she did. One trembled for her (it was too good to survive) and was humbled at the same time, by a face that was more strongly alive than anyone else's, which contained an indestructible, fearless happiness. She shone.

A few days later we met at a small party and I stood at her side. We didn't speak much. I told her of the noise she made as she passed my door. And often on the days that followed when I got back to my room I found the words 'Poop, poop poop' written on a piece of paper lying on my table – her phonetic spelling of the noise I hadn't been there to hear. One night we made part of a party that went to the theatre together. This entailed her staying the night out of her college and I found her a room in the house where I was living. After saying goodnight I went upstairs back to my desk, I had an essay to write. After a few lines I felt I had to be sure she had everything she needed and went downstairs. She had, and I went back to my work. Another few lines and I knew it was no use. I went down again and she seemed to be waiting for me, her face luminous and amused. I did what I should have done days before, I took her in my arms and kissed her; every experience, however simple, has its maximum brilliance. This happens only once, and is so startlingly different from anything less than itself that it seems to contain indications of a strength and a joy far beyond it, a hint that we live only on the edges of a possibility.

I fought and struggled and kicked. I wasn't ready, not for this, not now. I gathered she came from the *haute bourgeoisie* – her mother Rosamond Lehmann, the novelist – her father's father a lord. I had no money, my father had no money, and I hadn't the slightest intention of trying to earn any. I wanted to wander some more and find myself, I didn't want to get mixed up with people like that. Also I had no intention of being caught up in all the flummeries of love, about which I'd read so much that was always suspiciously vague and religiose. I wanted to use my mind, not be trapped in a gust of unspecific dismays and exaltations by a blonde princess I couldn't take my eyes off. I had fighting to do.

I had to admit she had none of the mannerisms or presuppositions of her class – in fact, she was less of a snob than I was myself. Nor was this the protected beauty's ignorance of how the world was made. Her incredulous hatred of injustice was far more immediately practical than my own – when she could she acted, without hesitation – her father was a Communist, and as she once said, she wasn't his daughter for nothing. Nor was she rich, she had the same amount of money as I had. Nevertheless ... I spent hours in my room explaining to her in so many words, as darkness slowly fell outside, that it was all impossible, without ever defining quite what. And then I'd realize with a spasm of relief that watching me attentively as I strode about she wasn't listening to a word I said but hearing all she wanted to hear revealed in the tone of my voice.

A crust was falling from my surface; the layer of muscles under the skin seemed to be losing their tensions – like waking from a deep sleep they were fresh and elastic and eager for use. I saw her face as it really was. For the first time I was looking at a person outside myself. It was as though my arms, instead of being locked protectively across my chest, were opening out, exposing what I was and what I wanted to be. If I was a dancer I could dance that feeling.

I continued to work, with new energy in fact. Far from coming in between, her face lent further colour and meaning to what I had just been beginning to understand. I began to write, and for the first time finish, poems. There was some point in finishing them now – I had her to show them to.

THE PERFECT STRANGER, 1966

ST AUGUSTINE

IN THOSE YEARS, WHEN I FIRST BEGAN to teach rhetoric in my native town, I had acquired a very dear friend, from association in our studies, of mine own age, and, like myself, just rising up into the flower of youth. He had grown up with me from childhood, and we had been both school-fellows and play-fellows. But he was not then my friend, nor, indeed, afterwards, as true friendship is; for true it is not but in such as Thou bindest together, cleaving unto Thee by that love which is shed abroad in our hearts by the Holy Ghost, which is given unto us. But yet it was too sweet, being ripened by the fervour of similar studies. For, from the true faith (which he, as a youth, had not soundly and thoroughly become master of), I had turned him aside towards those superstitious and pernicious fables which my mother mourned in me. With me this man's mind now erred, nor could my soul exist without him. But behold, Thou wert close behind Thy fugitives – at once God of vengeance and Fountain of mercies, who turnest us to Thyself by wondrous means. Thou removedst that man from this life when he had scarce completed one whole year of my friendship, sweet to me above all the sweetness of that my life.

'Who can show forth all Thy praise' which he hath experienced in himself alone? What was it that Thou didst then, O my God, and how unsearchable are the depths of Thy judgments! For when, sore sick of a fever, he long lay unconscious in a death-sweat, and all despaired of his recovery, he was baptized without his knowledge; myself meanwhile little caring, presuming that his soul would retain rather what it had imbibed from me, than what was done to his unconscious body. Far different, however, was it, for he was revived and restored. Straightaway, as soon as I could talk to him (which I could as soon as he was able, for I never left him, and we hung too much upon each other), I attempted to jest with him, as if he also would jest with me at that baptism which he had received when mind and senses were in abeyance, but had now learnt that he had received. But he shuddered at me, as if I were his enemy; and, with a remarkable and unexpected freedom, admonished me, if I desired to continue his friend, to desist from speaking in such a way. I, confounded and confused, concealed all my emotions, till he should get well, and his health be strong enough to allow me to deal with him as I wished. But he was withdrawn from my frenzy, that with Thee he might be preserved for my comfort. A few days after, during my absence, he had a return of the fever, and died.

At this sorrow my heart was utterly darkened, and whatever I looked upon was death. My native country was a torture to me, and my father's house a wondrous unhappiness; and whatsoever I had participated in with him, wanting him, turned into a frightful torture. Mine eyes sought him everywhere, but he was not granted them; and I hated all places because he was not in them; nor could they now say to me, 'Behold, he is coming,' as they did when he was alive and absent. I became a great puzzle to myself, and asked my soul why she was so sad, and why she so exceedingly disquieted me; but she knew not what to answer me. And if I said, 'Hope thou in God,' she very properly obeyed me not; because that most dear friend whom she had lost was, being man, both truer and better than that phantasm she was bid to hope in. Naught but tears were sweet to me, and they succeeded my friend in the dearest of my affections.

And now, O Lord, these things are passed away, and time hath healed my wound.

THE CONFESSIONS OF ST AUGUSTINE, 397–400

TOBIAS WOLFF

WHEN THE ASSAULT, the so-called Tet Offensive, first began we didn't know what was going on.

The firing woke us up. It was about three-thirty, four in the morning, January 31, 1968, which I think of now as a kind of birthday; the first day in the rest of my life, for sure. Sergeant Benet and I hustled outside and saw flares going up all over the town. Soldiers from the battalion were running past us, carbines in hand, heading for the perimeter. I said I didn't like this. I could hear myself say it: 'I don't like this.'

We got dressed and walked over to Major Chau's headquarters. His staff officers were carrying out tables and chairs, map cases, radios. One of them told the major we were there. He came to the door and said, 'Later. You come back later.' When I asked him for a situation report, he said, 'Later. Now is too busy, yes,' and went back inside.

Sergeant Benet and I spent the morning cleaning our weapons and listening to the radio. In this way we learned that My Tho was in enemy hands and most of our division under attack. We also found out that the same thing was happening everywhere else. All the towns of the Delta – My Tho, Ben Tre, Soc Trang, Can Tho, Ca Mau, Vinh Long, all of them – were full of VC. Every town and city in the country was under siege. Every airfield had been hit. Every road cut. They were in the streets of Saigon, in the American embassy. All in one night. The whole country.

I could barely take in what I was hearing. To make sense of it was especially hard because nothing could be put to use, or translated into hope. Even the official optimism of the Armed Forces Radio announcers couldn't patch over the magnitude of the facts they were reporting, and when we tuned in the regular military frequencies we heard nothing but shock and frenzied pleas for support. Nobody was getting any support because the supporting units needed support themselves. That meant we couldn't get relief from anyone, which was sorry news for us. The battalion was undermanned to begin with, and a lot of our troops had gone home for Tet. We would have to defend this ridiculously exposed piece of land with a skeleton crew and without a prayer of help from the air or the ground. We were completely on our own.

Sergeant Benet and I listened to the radio and said little. He was lying on the couch, gazing up at the ceiling, which was a kindness. I didn't want him to see how I was taking this because I didn't really know how I was taking it. I felt as if I were looking on from a great distance. As the morning passed I got hungry and made a sandwich, still listening. I became aware of my hands and what they were doing. How strange it is to spread mayonnaise. It can be the strangest thing you've ever done. I ate a few bites and had to stop, my mouth was so dry.

Major Chau sent for us. He was in the bunker where he'd set up his command post. 'This is too bad,' he said. 'You can get air support, yes?'

'No. Nothing.'

'Yes! Come. Look.' He showed me the map, tapping with his pointer, trying to make me see the difficulty of our position. When he finally understood that I couldn't call down jets if we were attacked, he made a hissing noise and bared his teeth. He laid the pointer on the map and fumbled out a Marlboro but couldn't fit it into the holder he used. He looked down at the cigarette and the holder, then turned and walked outside. A few minutes later he came back and acted as if nothing had happened. Sergeant Benet and I leaned over the map with him and his staff officers, trying to imagine a plan of some kind, but none of us had anything much to say.

I felt hollow, loopy. I was dull and slow-tongued, the others as well. What we did was stand around and wait for something to happen.

All this time we could hear the sound of the shooting in My Tho.

A shell exploded somewhere outside. We hit the deck, our mouths twisted in dire grins. Two more went off almost together. They weren't very close, but I felt the shock in my chest. We waited for the next one. Then we stood up again, very, very slowly. I was wide-awake ...

The process by which we helped lay waste to My Tho seemed not of our making and at all times necessary and right. As the battalions in town came under more and more pressure, we began to drop shells on the buildings around them. We bombarded the old square surrounding General Ngoc's headquarters, where he and the province chief were holed up with their staff officers. There were pockets of terrified government officialdom and soldiery huddled throughout the town, and every time one of them got through to us on the radio we put our fire right where he wanted it, no questions asked. We knocked down bridges and sank boats. We leveled shops and bars along the river. We pulverized hotels and houses, floor by floor, street by street, block by block. I saw the map, I knew where the shells were going, but I didn't think of our targets as homes where exhausted and frightened people were praying for their lives. When you're afraid you will kill anything that might kill you. Now that the enemy had the town, the town was the enemy ...

For the next couple of days we plastered the town. Then the jets showed up. Their run into My Tho took them right over our compound, sometimes low enough that we could see the rivets on their skin. Such American machines, so boss-looking, so technical, so loud. *Phantoms.* When they slowed overhead to lock into formation the roar of their engines made speech impossible. Down here I was in a deranged and malignant land, but when I raised my eyes to those planes I could see home. They dove screaming on the town, then pulled out and banked around and did it again. Their bombs sent tremors pulsing up through our legs. When they used up all their bombs they flew off to get more. Flames gleamed on the underside of the pall of smoke that overhung My Tho, and the smell of putrefaction soured the breeze, and still we served the guns, dropping rings of ruination around every frightened man with a radio transmitter.

None of this gave me pause. Only when we finally took the town back, when the last sniper had been blasted off his rooftop, did I see what we had done, we and the VC together. The place was a wreck, still smoldering two weeks later, still reeking sweetly of corpses. The corpses were everywhere, lying in the streets, floating in the reservoir, buried and half buried in collapsed buildings, grinning, blackened, fat with gas, limbs missing or oddly bent, some headless, some burned almost to the bone, the smell so thick and foul we had to wear surgical masks scented with cologne, aftershave, deodorant, whatever we had, simply to move through town. Hundreds of corpses and the count kept rising. Gangs of diggers sifted through the rubble, looking for survivors. They found some, but mostly they found more corpses. These they rolled up in tatami mats and left by the roadside for pickup. One day I passed a line of them that went on for almost a block, all children, their bare feet protruding from the ends of the mats. My driver told me that we'd bombed a school building where they had been herded together to learn revolutionary history and songs.

I didn't believe it. It sounded like one of those stories that always make the rounds afterward. But it could have been true.

Now that the danger was past I could permit myself certain feelings about what we had done, but I knew even then that they would vanish at the next sign of danger. How about the VC? I used to wonder. Were they sorry? Did they love their perfect future so much that they could without shame feed children to it, children and families and towns – their own towns? They must have, because they kept doing it. And in the end they got their future. The more of their country they fed to it, the closer it came.

As a military project the Tet failed; as a lesson it succeeded. The VC came into My Tho and all the other towns knowing what would happen. They knew that once they were among the people we would abandon our pretence of distinguishing between them. We would kill them all to get at one. In this way they taught the people that we did not love them and would not protect them; that for all our talk of partnership and brotherhood we disliked and mistrusted them, and that we would kill every last one of them to save our own skins. To believe otherwise was self-deception. They taught that lesson to the people, and also to us. At least they taught it to me.

IN PHARAOH'S ARMY: MEMORIES OF A LOST WAR, 1994

VERA BRITTAIN

WHENEVER I THINK OF THE WEEKS that followed news of Roland's death, a series of pictures, disconnected but crystal clear, unroll themselves like a kaleidoscope through my mind.

A solitary cup of coffee stands before me on a hotel breakfast-table; I try to drink it, but fail ignominiously.

Outside, in front of the promenade, dismal grey waves tumble angrily over one another on the windy Brighton shore, and, like a slaughtered animal that still twists after life has been extinguished, I go on mechanically worrying because his channel-crossing must have been so rough.

In an omnibus, going to Keymer, I look fixedly at the sky; suddenly, the pale light of a watery sun streams out between the dark, swollen clouds, and I think for one crazy moment that I have seen the heavens opened …

At Keymer a fierce gale is blowing and I am out alone on the brown winter ploughlands, where I have been driven by a desperate desire to escape from the others. Shivering violently, and convinced that I am going to be sick, I take refuge behind a wet bank of grass from the icy sea-wind that rushes, screaming, across the sodden fields.

It is late afternoon; at the organ of the small village church, Edward is improvising a haunting memorial hymn for Roland, and the words: 'God walked in the garden in the cool of the evening,' flash irrelevantly into my mind.

I am back on night-duty at Camberwell after my leave; in the chapel, as the evening voluntary is played, I stare with swimming eyes at the lettered wall, and remember reading the words: 'I am the Resurrection and the Life,' at the early morning communion service before going to Brighton.

I am buying some small accessories for my uniform in a big Victoria Street store, when I stop, petrified, before a vase of the tall pink roses that Roland gave me on the way to *David Copperfield*; in the warm room their melting sweetness brings back the memory of that New Year's Eve, and suddenly, to the perturbation of the shop-assistants, I burst into uncontrollable tears, and find myself, helpless and humiliated, unable to stop crying in the tram all the way back to the hospital.

It is Sunday, and I am out for a solitary walk through the dreary streets of Camberwell before going to bed after the night's work. In front of me on the frozen pavement a long red worm wriggles slimily. I remember that, after our death, worms destroy this body

– however lovely, however beloved – and I run from the obscene thing in horror.

It is Wednesday, and I am walking up the Brixton Road on a mild, fresh morning of early spring. Half-unconsciously I am repeating a line from Rupert Brooke:

'*The deep night, and birds singing, and clouds flying ...* '

For a moment I have become conscious of the old joy in rainwashed skies and scuttling, fleecy clouds, when suddenly I remember – Roland is dead and I am not keeping faith with him; it is mean and cruel, even for a second, to feel glad to be alive.

TESTAMENT OF YOUTH, 1933

SALVADOR DALI

I WAS TWENTY-THREE, living at my parents' house in Figueras. I was inspired, working on a large cubist painting in my studio. I had lost the belt to my dressing gown, which kept hampering my movements. Reaching for the nearest thing to hand I picked up an electric cord lying on the floor and impatiently wound it round my waist. At the end of the cord, however, there was a small lamp. Not wanting to waste time by looking further, and as the lamp was not very heavy, I used it as a buckle to knot the ends of my improvised belt together.

I was deeply immersed again in my work when my sister came to announce that there were some important people in the living-room who wanted to meet me. At this time I had considerable notoriety in Catalonia, less because of my paintings than because of several cataclysms that I had unwittingly precipitated. I tore myself ill-humoredly from my work and went into the living-room. I was immediately aware of my parents' disapproving glance at my paint-spattered dressing gown, but no one yet noticed the lamp which dangled behind me, right against my buttocks. After a polite introduction I sat down, crushing the lamp against the chair and causing the bulb to burst like a bomb. An unpredictable, faithful and objective hazard seems to have systematically singled out my life to make what are normally uneventful incidents violent, phenomenal and memorable.

THE SECRET LIFE OF SALVADOR DALI, 1942

MUHAMMAD ALI

O F ALL THE POEMS I WROTE, all the words I spoke, all the slogans I shouted – 'I'm the greatest!' ... 'I'm the prettiest!' ... 'I can't be beat!' ... 'He must fall in five!' – of all the controversies that aroused people against me or for me, none would have the effect on my life or change the climate around me like the 'poem' I read on a TV hookup one warm February afternoon in Miami, 1966.

I was in training and looking forward to my third defense of the World Heavyweight Title. This time against six-foot-six Ernie 'The Octopus' Terrell, so named because he wrapped his long arms like tentacles around his opponents, smothering their blows and hugging them half to death.

I had come out into the front yard of the little gray cement cottage that my White Southern Christian Millionaire Sponsors had rented in my name in the black section of Miami. A TV reporter had been set up to ask my reaction to the fact that the Louisville Draft Board had just promoted me from 1-Y, deferred status, to 1-A, making me eligible for immediate induction into the US Army.

I gave it: 'I ain't got no quarrel with the Viet Cong.' Later, when they kept asking the same question, I rhymed it for them:

Keep asking me, no matter how long
On the war in Viet Nam, I sing this song
I ain't got no quarrel with the Viet Cong ...

I said more than that, of course, much more, and all evening, but those were the only words it seemed the world wanted to hear from me. They broke out in headlines across America and overseas – in London, Paris, Berlin, Zurich, Madrid, Hong Kong, Rome,

Amsterdam – and for years afterwards their echo would rumble in the air around me. In fact, the rumbling began even before I got to sleep that night.

After the reporters left I took a ride over to a Miami Beach steakhouse, and when I came back my brother was in the doorway. He was beckoning me in a way I understood to mean he wanted no reporters to follow.

'The phones won't stop,' he whispered as I brushed past him. 'They gone crazy.'

We had three phones and all three were ringing. I was reaching for the nearest one.

'Wait a minute.' He tried to restrain me. 'Let me answer. They all insane.'

But I was already hearing a hard, mean voice on the other end of the line: 'This you, Cassius?'

'No, sir,' I said, feeling he should at least acknowledge my name. 'This is Muhammad Ali.'

'Muhammad, Cassius – whatever you call yourself, I heard you on TV!' he shouted. 'You cowardly, turncoat black rat! If I had a bomb I would blow you to hell! I've got a message for you and your kind …' I hung up, since I had already gotten the message, and picked up the kitchen phone. A woman's voice was hysterical: 'Cassius Clay? Is that you? You better'n my son? You black bastard, you! I pray to God they draft you tomorrow. Draft you and shoot you on the spot! Listen to me …'

I let her go to pick up the phone in the bedroom. This time it was a voice I knew. A deputy sheriff named Murphy who had escorted me around Miami Beach many times. He had a soft drawl, like a fatherly bigot: 'Now, Cassius, you just done gone too far now. Somebody's telling you wrong. Them Jews and Dagos you got around you. Now, some of my boys want to come down and talk to you, for your own good.'

I hung up and took the phone handed to me by my sparring partner, Cody Jones. There was only heavy breathing. Then: 'You gonna die, nigger, before the night's out! You gonna die for that!' and more heavy breathing.

Those who had always wanted me to disappear from the scene reacted quickest. The first calls came mostly from the white side of

Miami. But as the news spread across the time zones, other voices were saying, 'That was mighty fine' ... 'I'm glad you said that' ... 'It's time someone spoke out.'

And in the days that followed, calls came in from Kansas City, Omaha, St Louis, Las Vegas, New York, Philadelphia. Housewives and professionals and plain everyday people – who I never heard from except when I pulverized somebody in the ring – thanked me for what I said. Students called from campuses, urging me to come and speak. It was a strange new feeling, and now, without planning or even wanting it, I was an important part of a movement I hardly knew existed.

For days I was talking to people from a whole new world. People who were not even interested in sports, especially prizefighting. One in particular I will never forget: a remarkable man, seventy years older than me but with a fresh outlook which seemed fairer than that of any white man I had ever met in America.

My brother Rahaman had handed me the phone, saying, 'Operator says a Mr Bertrand Russell is calling Mr Muhammad Ali.' I took it and heard the crisp accent of an Englishman: 'Is this Muhammad Ali?' When I said it was, he asked me if I had been quoted correctly.

I acknowledged that I had been, but wondered out loud, 'Why does everyone want to know what I think about Viet Nam? I'm no politician, no leader. I'm just an athlete.'

'Well,' he said, 'this is a war more barbaric than others, and because a mystique is built up around a champion fighter, I suppose the world has more than incidental curiosity about what the World Champion thinks. Usually he goes with the tide. You surprised them.'

I liked the sound of his voice, and told him I might be coming to England soon to fight the European champ, Henry Cooper, again.

'If I fight Cooper, who'd you bet on?'

He laughed. 'Henry's capable, you know, but I would pick you.'

I gave him back a stock answer I used on such occasions: 'You're not as dumb as you look.' And I invited him to ringside when I got to London.

He couldn't come to the fight, but for years we exchanged cards and notes. I had no idea who he was (the name Bertrand Russell had never come up in Central High in Louisville) until two years later when I was thumbing through a *World Book Encyclopaedia* in the *Muhammad Speaks* newspaper office in Chicago and saw his name and picture. He was described as one of the greatest mathematicians and philosophers of the twentieth century. That very minute I sat down and typed out a letter of apology for my offhand remark, 'You're not as dumb as you look,' and he wrote back that he had enjoyed the joke.

A short time after I fought Cooper, when I had another fight prospect in London, I made plans for Belinda and me to visit him, but I had to explain to him that the outcome of my fight against being drafted to Viet Nam might hold me up. The letter he wrote was sent to me in Houston:

> *I have read your letter with the greatest admiration and personal respect.*
>
> *In the coming months there is no doubt that the men who rule Washington will try to damage you in every way open to them, but I am sure you know that you spoke for your people and for the oppressed everywhere in the courageous defiance of American power. They will try to break you because you are a symbol of a force they are unable to destroy, namely, the aroused consciousness of a whole people determined no longer to be butchered and debased with fear and oppression. You have my wholehearted support. Call me when you come to England.*
>
> *Yours sincerely,*
> *Bertrand Russell*

By the time I got his letter I had been convicted and my passport lifted, just as his had been in World War I. Four years later, when my passport was returned, the friend I had made with my remark in my front yard had died. I thought of him whenever I visited England and for years I kept a picture of his warm face and wide eyes. 'Not as dumb as he looks.'

THE GREATEST: MY OWN STORY, 1975

NOEL COWARD

SUCCESS ALTERED THE FACE OF LONDON for me. Just for a little the atmosphere felt lighter. I'm not sure whether or not the people who passed me in the street appeared to be more smiling and gay than they had been hitherto, but I expect they did. I do know that very soon life began to feel overcrowded. Every minute of the day was occupied and I relaxed, rather indiscriminately, into a welter of publicity. No Press interviewer, photographer or gossip writer had to fight in order to see me, I was wide open to them all; smiling and burbling bright witticisms, giving my views on this and that, discussing such problems as whether or not the modern girl would make a good mother, or what would be my ideal in a wife, etc. My opinion was asked for, and given, on current books and plays. I made a few adequately witty jokes which were immediately misquoted or twisted round the wrong way, thereby denuding them of any humour they might originally have had. I was photographed in every conceivable position. Not only was *I* photographed, but my dressing-room was photographed, my car was photographed, my rooms in Ebury Street were photographed. It was only by an oversight, I am sure, that our lodgers escaped the camera.

I took to wearing coloured turtle-necked jerseys, actually more for comfort than for effect, and soon I was informed by my evening paper that I had started a fashion. I believe that to a certain extent this was really true; at any rate, during the ensuing months I noticed more and more of our seedier West End chorus boys parading about London in them.

I found people difficult to cope with in my new circumstances. Their attitude to me altered so swiftly and so completely. Naturally my intimates and the few friends I happened to know well remained the same, but ordinary acquaintances to whom I had nodded and spoken casually for years, gummed strong affection to me like fly-paper and assumed tacit proprietary rights. Apparently they had always known that I was clever, talented, brilliant and destined for great things. 'How does it feel,' they cried, 'to be a genius?' To reply to this sort of remark without either complacency or offensive modesty was impossible, and so I chose the latter as being the less troublesome course and wore a permanent blush of self-deprecation for quite a long while. I can indeed still call it into use if necessary. Sometimes I became so carried away by my performance that I alluded to my success as luck! This monumental insincerity was received with acclaim. People were actually willing and eager to believe that I could throw out of my mind all memories of heartbreaks, struggles, disillusionments, bitter disappointments, and work, and dismiss my hard-earned victory as luck. Just glorious chance. An encouraging pat on the back from kindly Fate. I can only imagine that this easy belief in a fundamental schism in my scale of values must have been a comfort to them, an implication that such a thing might happen to anybody.

The legend of my modesty grew and grew. I became extraordinarily unspoiled by my great success. As a matter of fact, I still am. I have frequently been known to help old friends in distress and, odd as it may seem, I have actually so far forgotten my glory as to give occasional jobs to first-rate actors whom I knew in my poorer days. Gestures such as these cause widespread astonishment. The general illusion that success automatically transforms ordinary human beings into monsters of egotism has, in my case, been shattered. I am neither conceited, overbearing, rude, nor insulting to waiters. People often refer to me as being 'simple' and 'surprisingly human'. All of which is superficially gratifying but, on closer analysis, quite idiotic. Conceit is more often than not an outward manifestation of an inward sense of inferiority. Stupid people are frequently conceited because they are subconsciously frightened of being found out; scared that some perceptive eye will pierce through their façade and discover the timid confusion behind it. As a general rule, the most uppish people I have met have been those who have never achieved anything whatsoever.

I am neither stupid nor scared, and my sense of my own importance to the world is relatively small. On the other hand, my sense of my own importance to myself is tremendous. I am all I have, to work with, to play with, to suffer and to enjoy. It is not the eyes of others that I am wary of, but my own. I do not intend to let myself down more than I can possibly help, and I find that the fewer illusions that I have about me or the world around me, the better company I am for myself.

Naturally in 1925 my reasoning on myself was not as clear as it is now, but the nucleus was fortunately there. I opened my arms a little too wide to everything that came, and enjoyed it. Later on, just a little while later, three years to be exact, circumstances showed me that my acceptance has been a thought too credulous. The 'darling' of the London Theatre received what can only be described as a sharp kick in the pants. And while my over-trusting behind was still smarting, I took the opportunity to do a little hard thinking.

Perhaps, after all, in the above paragraphs I have been a little stingy with my gratitude. I hereby render deep thanks to those booing hysterical galleryites and those exultant, unkind critics and journalists for doing me more constructive good than any of their cheers or praises have ever done.

PRESENT INDICATIVE, 1937

J.M. COETZEE

WHAT IS WRONG WITH HIM is that he is not prepared to fail. He wants an A or an alpha or one hundred per cent for his every attempt, and a big Excellent! in the margin. Ludicrous! Childish! He does not have to be told so: he can see it for himself. Nevertheless. Nevertheless he cannot do it. Not today. Perhaps tomorrow. Perhaps tomorrow he will be in the mood, have the courage.

If he were a warmer person he would no doubt find it all easier: life, love, poetry. But warmth is not in his nature. Poetry is not written out of warmth anyway. Rimbaud was not warm, Baudelaire was not warm. Hot, indeed, yes, when it was needed – hot in life, hot in love – but not warm. He too is capable of being hot, he has not ceased to believe that. But for the present, the present indefinite, he is cold: cold, frozen.

And what is the upshot of this lack of heat, this lack of heart? The upshot is that he is sitting alone on a Sunday afternoon in an upstairs room in a house in the depths of the Berkshire countryside, with crows cawing in the fields and a grey mist hanging overhead, playing chess with himself, growing old, waiting for evening to fall so that he can with a good conscience fry his sausages and bread for supper. At eighteen, he might have been a poet. Now he is not a poet, not a writer, not an artist. He is a computer programmer, a twenty-four-year-old computer programmer in a world in which there are no thirty-year-old computer programmers. At thirty one is too old to be a programmer: one turns oneself into something else – some kind of businessman – or one shoots oneself. It is only because he is young, because the neurons in his brain are still firing more or less infallibly, that he has a toehold in the British computer industry, in British society, in Britain itself.

YOUTH, 2002

PRIMO LEVI

I WAS CAPTURED BY THE FASCIST MILITIA on 13 December 1943. I was twenty-four, with little wisdom, no experience and a decided tendency – encouraged by the life of segregation forced on me for the previous four years by the racial laws – to live in an unrealistic world of my own, a world inhabited by civilized Cartesian phantoms, by sincere male and bloodless female friendships. I cultivated a moderate and abstract sense of rebellion.

It had been by no means easy to flee into the mountains and to help set up what, both in my opinion and in that of friends little more experienced than myself, should have become a partisan band affiliated with the Resistance movement *Justice and Liberty*. Contacts, arms, money and the experience needed to acquire them were all missing. We lacked capable men, and instead we were swamped by a deluge of outcasts, in good or bad faith, who came from the plain in search of a non-existent military or political organization, of arms, or merely of protection, a hiding place, a fire, a pair of shoes.

At that time I had not yet been taught the doctrine I was later to learn so hurriedly in the Lager: that man is bound to pursue his own ends by all possible means, while he who errs but once pays dearly. So that I can only consider the following sequence of events justified. Three Fascist Militia companies, which had set out in the night to surprise a much more powerful and dangerous band than ours, broke into our refuge one spectral snowy dawn and took me down to the valley as a suspect person.

During the interrogations that followed, I preferred to admit my status of 'Italian citizen of Jewish race'. I felt that otherwise I would be unable to justify my presence in places too secluded even for an evacuee; while I believed (wrongly as was subsequently seen) that the admission of my political activity would have meant torture and certain death. As a Jew, I was sent to Fossoli, near Modena, where a vast detention camp, originally meant for English and American prisoners-of-war, collected all the numerous categories of people not approved of by the new-born Fascist Republic.

At the moment of my arrival, that is, at the end of January 1944, there were about one hundred and fifty Italian Jews in the camp, but within a few weeks their number rose to over six hundred. For the most part they consisted of entire families captured by the Fascists or Nazis through their imprudence or following secret accusations. A few had given themselves up spontaneously, reduced to desperation by the vagabond life, or because they lacked the means to survive, or to avoid separation from a captured relation, or even – absurdly – 'to be in conformity with the law'. There were also about a hundred Jugoslavian military internees and a few other foreigners who were politically suspect.

The arrival of a squad of German SS men should have made even the optimists doubtful; but we still managed to interpret the novelty in various ways without drawing the most obvious conclusions. Thus, despite everything, the announcement of the deportation caught us all unawares.

On 20 February, the Germans had inspected the camp with care and had publicly and loudly upbraided the Italian commissar for the defective organization of the kitchen service and for the scarce amount of wood distribution for heating; they even said that an infirmary would soon be opened. But on the morning of the 21st we learned that on the following day the Jews would be leaving. All the Jews, without exception. Even the children, even the old, even the ill. Our destination? Nobody knew. We should be prepared for a fortnight of travel. For every person missing at the roll-call, ten would be shot.

Only a minority of ingenuous and deluded souls continued to hope; we others had often spoken with the Polish and Croat refugees and we knew what departure meant.

For people condemned to death, tradition prescribes an austere ceremony, calculated to emphasize that all passions and anger have died down, and that the act of justice represents only a sad duty towards society which moves even the executioner to pity for the victim. Thus the condemned man is shielded from all external cares, he is granted solitude and, should he want it, spiritual comfort; in short, care is taken that he should feel around him neither hatred nor arbitrariness, only necessity and justice, and by means of punishment, pardon.

But to us this was not granted, for we were many and time was short. And in any case, what had we to repent, for what crime did we need pardon? The Italian commissar accordingly decreed that all services should continue to function until the final notice: the kitchens remained open, the corvées for cleaning worked as usual, and even the teachers of the little school gave lessons until the evening, as on other days. But that evening the children were given no homework.

And night came, and it was such a night that one knew that human eyes would not witness it and survive. Everyone felt this: not one of the guards, neither Italian nor German, had the courage to see what men do when they know they have to die.

All took leave from life in the manner which most suited them. Some praying, some deliberately drunk, others lustfully intoxicated for the last time. But the mothers stayed up to prepare the food for the journey with tender care, and washed their children and packed the luggage; and at dawn the barbed wire was full of children's washing hung out in the wind to dry. Nor did they forget the diapers, the toys, the cushions and the hundred other small things which mothers remember and which children always need. Would you not do the same? If you and your child were going to be killed tomorrow, would you not give him to eat today?

In hut 6A old Gattegno lived with his wife and numerous children and grandchildren and his sons- and daughters-in-law. All the men were carpenters; they had come from Tripoli after many long journeys, and had always carried with them the tools of their trade, their kitchen utensils and their accordions and violins to play and dance to after the day's work. They were happy and pious folk. Their women were the first to silently and rapidly finish the preparations for the journey in order to have time for mourning. When all was ready, the food cooked, the bundles tied together, they unloosened their hair, took off their shoes, placed the Yahrzeit candles on the ground and lit them according to the customs of their fathers, and sat on the bare soil in a circle for the lamentations, praying and weeping all the night. We collected in a group in front of their door, and we experienced within ourselves a grief that was new for us, the ancient grief of the people that has no land, the grief without hope of the exodus which is renewed every century.

IF THIS IS A MAN / SURVIVAL IN AUSCHWITZ, 1947

FREDERICK DOUGLASS

I WAS BORN IN TUCKAHOE, near Hillsborough, and about twelve miles from Easton, in Talbot County, Maryland. I have no accurate knowledge of my age, never having seen any authentic record containing it. By far the larger part of the slaves know as little of their ages as horses know of theirs, and it is the wish of most masters within my knowledge to keep their slaves thus ignorant. I do not remember to have ever met a slave who could tell of his birthday. They seldom come nearer to it than planting-time, harvest-time, cherry-time, spring-time, or fall-time. A want of information concerning my own was a source of unhappiness to me even during childhood. The white children could tell their ages. I could not tell why I ought to be deprived of the same privilege. I was not allowed to make any inquiries of my master concerning it. He deemed all such inquiries on the part of a slave improper and impertinent, and evidence of a restless spirit. The nearest estimate I can give makes me now between twenty-seven and twenty-eight years of age. I come to this, from hearing my master say, some time during 1835, I was about seventeen years old.

NARRATIVE OF THE LIFE OF FREDERICK DOUGLASS, AN AMERICAN SLAVE, 1845

LADY DAIBU

I USED TO BE AMUSED by the various love affairs I saw around me or heard about, though I myself had no thought of following everybody else in such behavior. But among the many men who used to mingle with us at all times of the day and night, just like other ladies-in-waiting, there was one in particular who made approaches to me, though after seeing and hearing of other people's unhappy affairs I felt I ought not to let anything of that sort happen to me. Destiny, however, is not to be avoided, and in spite of my resolve, I also came to know love's miseries.

Once, while this affair was causing me a great deal of heartache, I was at my home, lost in thought and gazing westward into the distance. The light of the evening sun was fading on the treetops and this filled me with melancholy. Then the sky darkened and the fitful winter rain began to fall. As I looked out at this, I felt:

Caught in the last rays
Of the setting sun, the treetops
Darken in the chilling rain:
So too my heart is dimmed
And clouded over in its misery.

THE POETIC MEMOIRS OF LADY DAIBU, C.1174–C.1232

GIACOMO CASANOVA

I T WAS AT ONE HOUR AFTER SUNSET that I took up my position by the statue of the hero Colleoni. She had told me to go there at the second hour, but I wanted to have the gentle pleasure of waiting for her. The night was cold but magnificent, and without the slightest breeze in the air.

At two hours after sunset precisely, I saw a gondola with two oars pull up and a figure wearing a mask get out. After speaking to the oarsman in the prow, the figure made its way to the statue. Seeing a masked man, I am alarmed; I step out of his path and berate myself for not carrying my pistols. The mask walks around the statue and approaches me, holding out a hand peacefully, leaving me no room for doubt. I recognize my angel dressed as a man. She laughs at my surprise, rests her arm in mine, and without exchanging a word, we walk towards St Mark's Square; we cross it and go to the small house that could not have been more than a hundred paces from the Teatro San Moisè.

There everything is arranged as I had ordered. We climb the stairs and I quickly take off my mask, but MM takes pleasure in walking slowly around every nook of the delicious place that she was being welcomed into, enchanted too that I was contemplating her in profile, and often, facing her, the full grace of her person, and that I, who should be the lover to possess her, admired her in her finery. She was surprised at the marvel that made her see her form everywhere, and simultaneously, even though she stood still, from a hundred different points of view. Her multiple portraits offered up by the mirrors in the light of all the candles placed for this purpose, presented her with a new spectacle that made her fall in love with herself. Seated on a stool, I examined attentively all the elegance of her finery. A cloak of smooth velvet the colour of roses, trimmed with embroidered spangles of gold, a matching hand-embroidered waistcoat, richer than anything you have ever seen, breeches in black satin, lace-work in needlepoint, buckles studded with precious stones, an expensive solitaire on her little finger, and on her other hand a ring that displayed only a surface of white taffeta covered in a convex crystal. Her hooded cape of black blonde-lace was as beautiful as it could be in terms of its fineness and its design. She came and stood in front of me so that I could see her better. I look in her pockets and find there a snuffbox, a box for sweets, flask, wallet for toothpicks, lorgnette, and handkerchiefs that exuded a scent that filled the air. I study attentively the wealth and the work of her two watches and her beautiful pendant seals attached to delicate chains with little carats. I look in her side pockets and find two flintlock pistols of the finest English workmanship ...

'Wait here while I go and take my disguise off alone.'

A quarter of an hour later, she appeared before me, her hair done up as a man, with her beautiful locks unpowdered, whose long curls at the front come down to the bottom of her cheeks.

A black ribbon tied them at the back and a loose plait like a tail reached down to her legs ...

Overcome by so many charms, I felt that I might be ill. I threw myself on the sofa to support my head.

'I've lost all confidence,' I tell her, 'you will never be mine; even tonight some fatal setback will tear you from my desires; a miracle devised perhaps by your divine husband who has become jealous of this mortal. I feel crushed. In a quarter of an hour perhaps I will no longer exist.'

'Are you mad? I am yours here and now, if you so wish. Though I have been fasting, I do not need to dine. Let us go to bed.'

She was cold. We sat by the fire. She told me that she was not wearing a waistcoat. I unbuckled a heart of brilliants that held her frill closed and my hands sensed, before my eyes saw, that there was only her shirt between the air and the two sources of life enhancing her chest. I became ardent; she needed only to kiss me once to calm me and to say two words: 'After dinner.'

STORY OF MY LIFE, 1789–1792

JOHN LENNON

Wonsaponatime there was two Balloons called Jock and Yono. They were strictly in love-bound to happen in a million years. They were together man. Unfortunatimetable they both seemed to have previous experience – which kept calling them one way oranother (you know howitis). But they battled on against overwhelming oddities, includo some of there beast friends. Being in love they cloong even the more together man – but some of the poisonessmonster of outrated buslodedshithrowers did stick slightly and they occasionally had to resort to the drycleaners. Luckily this did not kill them and they weren't banned from the olympic games. They lived hopefully ever after, and who could blame them.

'TWO VIRGINS', 1986

P.J. KAVANAGH

I HAD TEN POUNDS A WEEK and Sally had four, a present from her mother who'd given her in trust the savings she'd made from her books. We found a flat, a dank one in Pimlico that smelled of hamsters, and fixed a date to be married. And then, as so often with Sally, the right things began to happen at the right time, like music. We'd neither asked for help nor expected any, but once we'd committed ourselves to a place and a date the help came. An aunt of Sally's who lived in the country decided to buy a house in London and rented it to us cheaply. We converted the top floor into a flat, rented that to a friend, and so we were married and lived rent free in a house of our own. What a joy that was! And marriage itself was like those dreams of flying; you believe so purely and completely that you can, suddenly there you are, circling round the room. It had seemed like a happy end, but it turned out to be only a beginning. I woke each morning to my great good luck, which was itself like a house, endlessly clear and bright, with rooms that continually opened out into larger, brighter ones, unsuspected with Sally singing softly in all of them; that astonishing, musical, heart-easing sound.

Our lives for the next year and a half were too simple to talk about. Sally did odd jobs to help bring in the money. A brief one was looking after some energetic children. That night we came back from some friends and I was unexpectedly and uncharacteristically sick. Sally felt fine but during the night she had a miscarriage. I took her to the hospital and she was very clouded. I paid her an unexpected visit before work, crept into the ward at seven in the morning. The others were asleep but she was awake, staring at the ceiling. She scarcely recognized me; within seconds she was telling me about the others in the ward, their names, their family histories; not observed, entirely entered into. After a while I realized that many were now awake, smiling on their pillows towards her, not greeting or speaking, just quietly smiling; it was a world she'd made in a couple of days, with her at the centre because of the sheer force of her participation in it. I went out into the courtyard and could have yelled for joy – whereas I suppose I should have been hurt, she'd hardly remembered to say goodbye – but everything I wasn't she so completely was: our one and one didn't make two but two thousand.

THE PERFECT STRANGER, 1966

J.R. ACKERLEY

A USEFUL VANTAGE POINT for observing my father and myself together is the Bois de Boulogne in the spring of 1923. My parents were in Paris with my sister, who was working as a mannequin for one of the fashion houses, and I joined them there, coming up from Ragusa, where I had been with a young artist friend. At this time I had a flat in St John's Wood.

I remember sitting with my father one afternoon in the Bois, watching the procession of people go by. If I had known and thought about him then as much as I have learnt and thought about him since his death, what an interesting conversation we might have had. For here was the city of his romantic youth … The place must have been full of memories for him, happy and sad, and if I could have that day again, I hope I should make better use of it. But although it was jolly sitting with him in the Bois, we had no interesting talk; instead we were watching a dog's large turd, just pointed out by him, which lay in the middle of the path in front of us. Which of the people passing along would be the first to tread on it? That was our curiosity, and thus, whether it was dogs' turds, or 'yarns', or other trivialities, did all our life together senselessly slip away.

MY FATHER AND MYSELF, 1968

JOHN RUSKIN

C ALAIS IS PROPERLY A FLEMISH, not French town (of course the present town is all, except belfry and church, built in the seventeenth century, no vestige remaining of Plantagenet Calais); it has no wooden houses, which mark the essential French civic style, but only brick or chalk ones, with, originally, most of them, good indented Flemish stone gables and tiled roofs. True French roofs are never tiled, but slated, and have no indented gables, but bold dormer windows rising over the front, never, in any pretty street groups of them, without very definite expression of pride. Poor little Calais had indeed nothing to be proud of, but it had a quaint look of contentment with itself on those easy terms; some dignity in its strong ramparts and drawbridge gates; and, better than dignity, real power and service in the half-mile of pier, reaching to the low-tide breakers across its field of sand.

Sunset, then, seen from the pier-head across those whispering fringes; belfry chime at evening and morning; and the new life of that year, 1846, was begun.

After our usual rest at Champagnole, we went on over the Cenis to Turin, Verona, and Venice; whereat I began showing my father all my new discoveries in architecture and painting. But there began now to assert itself a difference between us I had not calculated on. For the first time I verily perceived that my father was older than I, and not immediately nor easily to be put out of his way of thinking in anything. We had been entirely of one mind about the carved porches of Abbeville, and living pictures of Vandyck; but when my father now found himself required to admire also flat walls, striped like the striped calico of an American flag, and oval-eyed saints like the figures on a Chinese teacup, he grew restive. Farther, all the fine writing and polite *éclat* of [my book] *Modern Painters* had never reconciled him to my total resignation of the art of poetry; and beyond this, he entirely, and with acute sense of loss to himself, doubted and deplored my now constant habit of making little patches and scratches of the sections and fractions of things in a notebook which used to live in my waistcoat pocket, instead of the former Proutesque or Robertsian outline of grand buildings and sublime scenes. And I was the more viciously stubborn in taking my own way, just because everybody was with him in these opinions; and I was more and more persuaded every day, that everybody was always wrong.

Often in my other books – and now, once for all, and finally here – I have to pray my readers to note that this continually increasing arrogance was not founded on vanity in me, but on sorrow. There is a vast difference – there is all the difference – between the vanity of displaying one's own faculties, and the grief that other people do not use their own. Vanity would have led me to continue writing and drawing what everyone praised; and disciplining my own already practised hand into finer dexterities. But I had no thought but of learning more, and teaching what truth I knew – assuredly then, and ever since, for the student's sake, not my own fame's; however sensitive I may be to the fame, also, afterwards.

Meantime, my father and I did not get on well in Italy at all, and one of the worst, wasp-barbed, most tingling pangs of my memory is yet of a sunny afternoon at Pisa, when, just as we were driving past my pet La Spina chapel, my father, waking out of a reverie, asked me suddenly, 'John, what shall I give the coachman?' Whereupon I, instead of telling him what he asked me, as I ought to have done with much complacency at being referred to on the matter, took upon me with impatience to reprove, and lament over, my father's hardness of heart, in thinking at that moment of sublunary affairs. And the spectral Spina of the chapel has stayed in my own heart ever since.

Nor did things come right that year till we got to Chamouni, where, having seen enough by this time of the upper snow, I was content to enjoy my morning walks in the valley with Papa and Mamma; after which, I had more than enough to do among the lower rocks and woods till dinner time, and in watching phases of sunset afterwards from beneath the slopes of the Breven.

PRAETERITA: OUTLINES OF SCENES AND THOUGHTS PERHAPS WORTHY OF MEMORY IN MY PAST LIFE, 1885–1889

DAVE EGGERS

THE AUTHOR WOULD LIKE TO ACKNOWLEDGE that he does not look good in red. Or pink, or orange, or even yellow – he is not a spring. And until last year he thought Evelyn Waugh was a woman, and that George Eliot was a man. Further, the author, and those behind the making of this book, wish to acknowledge that yes, there are perhaps too many memoir-sorts of books being written at this juncture, and that such books, about real things and real people, as opposed to kind-of made up things and people, are inherently vile and corrupt and wrong and evil and bad, but would like to remind everyone that we could all do worse, as readers and as writers.

ANECDOTE: midway through the writing of this ... this ... *memoir*, an acquaintance of the author's accosted him at a Western-themed restaurant/bar, while the author was eating a hearty plate of ribs and potatoes served fried in the French style. The accoster sat down opposite, asking what was new, what was *up*, what was he working on, etc. The author said Oh, well, that he was kind of working on a book, kind of mumble mumble. Oh great, said the acquaintance, who was wearing a sport coat made from what seemed to be (but it might have been the light) purple velour. What kind of book? asked the acquaintance. (Let's call him, oh, 'Oswald'.) What's it about? asked Oswald. Well, uh, said the author, again with the silver tongue, it's kind of hard to explain, I guess it's kind of a memoir-y kind of thing – *Oh no!* said Oswald, interrupting him, loudly. (Oswald's hair, you might want to know, was feathered.) *Don't tell me you've fallen into that trap!* (It tumbled down his shoulders, Dungeons & Dragons-style.) *Memoir! C'mon, don't pull that old trick, man!* He went on like this for a while, using the colloquial language of the day, until, well, the author felt sort of bad. After all, maybe Oswald, with the purple velour and the brown corduroys, was right – maybe memoirs were *Bad*. Maybe writing about actual events, in the first person, if not from Ireland and before you turned seventy, was *Bad*. He had a point! Hoping to change the subject, the author asked Oswald, who shares a surname with the man who killed a president, what it was that *he* was working on. (Oswald was some sort of professional writer.) The author, of course, was both expecting and dreading that Oswald's project would be of grave importance and grand scope – a renunciation of Keynesian economics, a reworking of *Grendel* (this time from the point of view of nearby conifers), whatever. But do you know what he said, he of the feathered hair and purple velour? What he said was: a screenplay. He didn't italicize it then but we will here: *a screenplay*. What sort of screenplay? the author asked, having no overarching problem with screenplays, liking movies enormously and all, how they held a mirror to our violent society and all, but suddenly feeling slightly better all the same. The answer: a screenplay 'about William S. Burroughs, and the drug culture.' Well, suddenly the clouds broke, the sun shone, and once again, the author knew this: that even if the idea of relating a true story is a bad idea, and even if the idea of writing about deaths in the family and delusions as a result is unappealing to everyone but the author's high school classmates and a few creative writing students in New Mexico, there are still ideas that are *much, much worse*. Besides, if you are bothered by the idea of this being real, you are invited to do what the author should have done, and what authors and readers have been doing since the beginning of time: PRETEND IT'S FICTION.

A Heartbreaking Work of Staggering Genius: A Memoir Based on a True Story, 2000

BENJAMIN FRANKLIN

I HAD BEGUN IN 1733 TO STUDY LANGUAGES. I soon made myself so much a Master of the French as to be able to read the Books with Ease. I then undertook the Italian. An Acquaintance, who was also learning it, us'd often to tempt me to play Chess with him. Finding this took up too much of the Time I had to spare for Study, I at length refus'd to play any more, unless on this Condition, that the Victor in every Game should have a Right to impose a Task, either in Parts of the Grammar to be got by heart, or in Translation, &c., which Tasks the Vanquish'd was to perform upon Honour before our next Meeting. As we play'd pretty equally, we thus beat one another into that Language. I afterwards with a little Pains-taking, acquir'd as much of the Spanish as to read their books also. I have already mention'd that I had only one Year's Instruction in a Latin School, and that when very young, after which I neglected that Language entirely. But, when I had attained an Acquaintance with the French, Italian, and Spanish, I was surpriz'd to find, on looking over a Latin Testament, that I understood so much more of that Language than I had imagined;

which encouraged me to apply myself again to the Study of it, & I met with more Success, as those preceding Languages had greatly smooth'd my Way. From these Circumstances, I have thought, that there is some Inconsistency in our common Mode of Teaching Languages. We are told that it is proper to begin first with the Latin, and having acquir'd that it will be more easy to attain those modern Languages which are deriv'd from it; and yet we do not begin with the Greek, in order more easily to acquire the Latin. It is true, that if you can clamber & get to the top of a Stair-Case without using the Steps, you will more easily gain them in descending; but certainly, if you begin with the lowest you will with more Ease ascend to the Top. And I would therefore offer it to the Consideration of those who superintend the Educating of our Youth, whether, since many of those who begin with the Latin quit the same after spending some Years without having made any great Proficiency, and what they have learnt becomes almost useless, so that their time has been lost, it would not have been better to have begun them with the French, proceeding to the Italian, &c. for, tho' after spending the same time they should quit the Study of Languages & never arrive at the Latin, they would, however, have acquir'd another Tongue or two, that being in modern Use, might be serviceable to them in common Life.

THE AUTOBIOGRAPHY, 1788

CLAUDE MONET

THE PROGRESS I MADE WAS RAPID. Three years later I was showing at exhibitions. The two seascapes that I had sent off were given top billing and hung prominently. It was a great success. In 1866, there was the same unanimous praise for a large portrait that was displayed at Durand-Ruel for a long time, called *The Woman in Green*. The newspapers transported my name all the way back to Le Havre. My family finally gave me its respect. With the respect the allowance was reinstated. I bathed in opulence, provisionally at least, because we were to fall out again later on, and I threw myself recklessly into painting in the open air.

It was a dangerous novelty. No one had done anything like it up to that point, not even Manet who tried it only later, after me. His painting was still very classical then, and I always remember the scorn with which he spoke about my early works. It was in 1867: my style had taken shape, but it was nothing revolutionary, all things considered. I was far from having adopted the principle of dividing colours that turned so many people against me, but I was starting to try it out a little and I was playing with the effects of light and colour that clashed with received ideas. The selection committee, which had welcomed me so well at the beginning, turned on me, and I was ignominiously blackballed when I presented this new painting at the Salon.

Nonetheless, I found a way of exhibiting but elsewhere. Touched by my pleas, a dealer who had his shop on Rue Auber agreed to display a seascape that had been turned down by the *Palais de l'Industrie*. There was a general clamour of indignation. One evening, I stopped in the street in the middle of a crowd of onlookers, to hear what they were saying about me, when I saw Manet arrive with two or three of his friends. The group stopped, looked, and Manet, shrugging his shoulders, called out disdainfully: 'Can you see this young man who wants to paint in the open air? As if the old masters had never thought of it!'

Manet held an old grudge against me. At the Salon of 1866, the day of the opening, he had been met, from the beginning, with acclaim. 'Excellent, my dear, your painting!' And people had shaken his hand, said bravo, congratulations. Manet, as you can imagine, was exultant. Imagine his surprise when he noticed that the canvas they were congratulating him for was mine. It was *The Woman in Green*. And as bad luck would have it, as he tried to slip away, he stumbled on a group that included Bazille and myself. 'How are you?' said one of our friends. 'Ah! my dear fellow, it's disgusting, I am furious. They're complimenting me on a picture that isn't mine. One would think it's a hoax.'

When Astruc, the next day, informed him that he had voiced his displeasure in front of the artist who had done the painting and that he wanted to introduce him to me, Manet, with a sweep of his hand, refused. He harboured a grudge at the trick I had played on him, even though I hadn't realized I was doing so. For once, people had congratulated him on a masterstroke and this masterstroke belonged to someone else. What a bitter blow to someone as sharply sensitive as Manet.

It was only in 1869 that I saw him again and this time we became friends immediately. From the first meeting, he invited me to come and spend every evening with him at Café des Batignolles, where he and his friends met up to chat after leaving their studios. There I met Fantin-Latour and Cézanne, Degas, who came shortly after returning from Italy, the art critic Duranty, Émile Zola who was starting out in the literary world then, and several others. I myself brought along Sisley, Bazille and Renoir. There was nothing more interesting than these conversations, with their perpetual collision of opinions. We would spur each other on, we would push each other to explore new avenues of research; we made enthusiastic plans that would sustain us for weeks and weeks until we could definitively execute the idea. We would always leave feeling more engrossed, more determined, our thinking more defined and clear.

'AN INTERVIEW', 1900

NOEL COWARD

MY DETERMINATION THAT IN THIS NARRATIVE the reader shall take the rough with the smooth impels me to relate that, two days before rehearsals for the American production of *This Year of Grace* were due to begin, I was operated on for piles.

This meant postponing everything for two weeks, during which I lay, in bad pain and worse temper, in a nursing home.

The newspapers described the affair with light-hearted reticence as 'a minor operation', and I couldn't help reflecting that if that were a minor operation, I should have been far happier with a Caesarian.

The night before I was to go under the knife, having been respectfully shaved and offered some barley sugar, I was left dejectedly alone in a small bed in a minute white room. Realizing that after the anaesthetic I should probably have all, if not more, the sleep that I was usually accustomed to, I passed the long hours until dawn pleasantly enough by writing the second act of *Bitter Sweet*, and in the morning consciousness that I had accomplished a considerable job of work upheld me throughout the routine indignities that I had to endure.

The nursing home was conservative to a degree, and so nineteenth century in atmosphere that I fully expected the nurses to come in in crinolines.

There was one bathroom on the fourth floor which contained, in addition to the usual offices, a forbidding geyser. This snarled angrily at those patients who were strong enough to survive a long, frightening ascent in a lift which, I imagine, must assuredly have been the pride of the *Arts and Crafts Exhibition* at Earl's Court in 1842.

I had several visitors during my convalescence, all of whom were kind and sympathetic, and seldom referred, except obliquely, to the mortifying nature of my complaint.

Marie Tempest was the exception. She came a lot to see me, and we discussed every detail with enthusiasm, and I need hardly say that her visits were far and away the most welcome of all.

It was my first experience of nursing-home life, and once the acuter discomforts were over I settled down to enjoy it. There was, first and foremost, a pleasant sense of timelessness. The moment the early-morning washing and prinking were done with I could sink back in clean pyjamas on to a freshly made bed with the heavenly sensation that there was no hurry and no necessity to do anything whatever.

There came a beaten-up egg in milk at eleven, and possibly a visit from the surgeon at twelve; apart from these minor interruptions the hours stretched lazily ahead towards lunch, my afternoon snooze, one or two amiable visitors, an early supper and then the night.

The nights were the nicest of all. When the bed had been remade, the curtains drawn, the dark-green shade put over the light, and the night nurse had whisked out of the room, a different kind of peace descended. There was no obligation to sleep. I had rested a lot during the day and could rest more on the following day. A gentle dimness enveloped me, a detachment from affairs. The life outside seemed incredibly remote.

Occasionally a taxi drew up on the other side of the road. I could hear the screech of the tyres, the sound of the door opening and shutting, a murmur of voices, a sharp little ting as the driver reset the fare meter, then the grinding of gears and a diminishing hum until there was silence again. I pictured, without envy, those strangers letting themselves into their houses, switching on the lights in the dining-room and finding the usual decanter, siphon, glasses, and sandwiches curling slightly at the edges in spite of having been covered with a plate.

I imagined problems for them. Jealousy perhaps, suspicions of infidelity, a business crisis to be dealt with the next day, a brief to be prepared, or a political speech. Sleep was essential to them, they must get to bed and sleep because Time was whirling them along too fast. Not for them the luxury of lying still and making faces out of the shadows on the ceiling. Not for them the delight of a sudden cup of tea at three in the morning with a couple of Marie biscuits and one chocolate one. They had to be active and energetic and get things done, as I should have to in a week or so, but in the meantime I could relax, comfortably aware that I was not imprisoned by a long illness and that I should be up and about again before this delicious enforced rest had had time to become tedious.

PRESENT INDICATIVE, 1937

ISADORA DUNCAN

AFTER A SUCCESSFUL SEASON IN STOCKHOLM, we returned to Germany by water. On the boat I became quite ill, and I realized that it would be better for me to cease making any more tours for the time being. Anyway, I had a great longing to be alone, and to retire far from the gaze of human beings.

In the month of June, after a short visit to my School, I had an intense desire to be near the sea. I went first to The Hague, and from there to a little village called Nordwyck, on the shores of the North Sea. Here I rented a little white villa in the dunes, called Villa Maria.

I was so inexperienced as to think that having a baby was a perfectly natural process. I went to live in this villa, which was a hundred miles from any town, and I engaged a village doctor. In my ignorance I was quite content to have this village doctor who, I think, was only used to peasant women.

From Nordwyck to the nearest village, Kadwyck, was about three kilometres. Here I lived, all by myself. Each day I walked from Nordwyck to Kadwyck and back. Always I had this longing for the sea; to be alone in Nordwyck, in the little white villa, quite isolated among the sand dunes which stretched for miles on either side of the lovely country. I lived in the Villa Maria for June, July and August …

The child asserted itself now, more and more. It was strange to see my beautiful marble body softened and broken and stretched and deformed. It is an uncanny revenge of Nature, that the more refined the nerves, the more sensitive the brain, the more all this tends to suffering. Sleepless nights, painful hours. But joy too. Boundless, unlimited joy, when I strode every day over the sands between Nordwyck and Kadwyck, with the sea, the great waves, looming on one side, and the swelling dunes on the other, along the deserted beach. Almost always, on that coast, the wind blows, sometimes a gentle, billowing zephyr, sometimes a breeze so strong that I had to struggle against it. Occasionally the storms grew terrific, and the Villa Maria was rocked and buffeted all night like a ship at sea.

I grew to dread any society. People said such banalities. How little is appreciated the sanctity of the pregnant mother. I once saw a woman walking alone along the street, carrying a child within her. The passers-by did not regard her with reverence, but smiled at one another derisively, as though this woman, carrying the burden of coming life, was an excellent joke.

I closed my doors to every visitor except a good and faithful friend who came over from The Hague on his bicycle, bringing me books and magazines, and cheering me with his discourses on recent art, music and literature. At that time he was married to a great poetess of whom he spoke often with worshipful tenderness. He was a methodical man. He came on certain days, and even a big storm did not deter him from his schedule. Except for him, I was mostly alone with the sea and the dunes and the child, who seemed already to have a great, strong impatience to enter the world.

As I walked beside the sea, I sometimes felt an excess of strength and prowess, and I thought this creature would be mine, mine alone, but on other days, when the sky was grey and the cold North Sea waves were angry, I had sudden, sinking moods, when I felt myself some poor animal in a mighty trap, and I struggled with an overwhelming desire to escape, escape. Where? Perhaps even into the midst of the sullen waves. I struggled against such moods and bravely overcame them, not did I ever let anyone suspect what I felt, but nevertheless, such moods were waiting for me at odd hours, and were difficult to avoid …

From now on, I confess, I began to be assailed with all sorts of fears. In vain I told myself that every woman had children. My grandmother had eight. My mother had four. It was all in the course of life, etc. I was, nevertheless, conscious of fear. Of what? Certainly not of death, nor even of pain – some unknown fear, of what I did not know.

August waned. September came. My burden had become very heavy. Villa Maria was perched on the dunes. One mounted by a flight of almost one hundred steps. Often I thought of my dancing, and sometimes a fierce regret for my Art assailed me. But then I would feel three energetic kicks, and a form turning within me. I would smile and think, after all, what is Art but a faint mirror for the Joy and Miracle of Life?

MY LIFE, 1927

MARGARET OLIPHANT

WHEN I LOOK BACK ON MY LIFE, among the happy moments which I can recollect is one which is so curiously common and homely, with nothing in it, that it is strange even to record such a recollection, and yet it embodied more happiness to me than almost any real occasion as might be supposed for happiness. It was the moment after dinner when I used to run upstairs to see that all was well in the nursery, and then to turn into my room on my way down again to wash my hands, as I had a way of doing before I took up my evening work, which was generally needlework, something to make for the children. My bedroom had three windows in it, one looking out upon the gardens … the other two into the road. It was light enough with the lamplight outside for all I wanted. I can see it now, the glimmer of the outside lights, the room dark, the faint reflection in the glasses, and my heart full of joy and peace – for what? – for nothing – that there was no harm anywhere, the children well above stairs and their father below. I had few of the pleasures of society, no gaiety at all. I was eight-and-twenty, going downstairs as light as a feather, to the little frock I was making. My husband also gone back for an hour or two after dinner to his work, and well – and the bairns well. I can feel now the sensation of that sweet calm and ease and peace.

I have always said it is in these unconsidered moments that happiness is – not in things or events that may be supposed to cause it. How clear it is over these more than thirty years!

THE AUTOBIOGRAPHY OF MARGARET OLIPHANT, 1864–1894

AZAR NAFISI

O N JANUARY 26, 1984, my daughter Negar was born, and on September 15, 1985, my son Dara. I have to be precise in terms of the day, month and year of their births, details that twinkle and tease every time I think of their blessed births, and have no compunction in becoming sentimental over their coming into this world. This blessing, like other blessings, was mixed. For one thing, I became more anxious. Until then I had worried for the safety of my parents, husband, brother and friends, but my anxiety for my children overshadowed all. When my daughter was born I felt I was given a gift, a gift that in some mysterious way preserved my sanity. And so it was with the birth of my son. Yet it was a source of constant regret and sorrow to me that their childhood memories of home, unlike my own, were so tainted.

My daughter, Negar, blushes every time I tell her that her particular brand of obstinacy, her passionate defense of what she considers to be justice, comes from her mother's reading too many nineteenth-century novels when she was pregnant with her. Negar has a way of throwing her head to the right and back in one move and pursing her lips just a little in defiance of whatever authority she is protesting at the moment. I embarrass her, and she wants to know, Why do I say such impossible things? Well, don't they say that what a mother eats during her pregnancy, as well as her moods and emotions, all have an effect on the child. While I was pregnant with you, I read too much Jane Austen, too much of the Brontës, George Eliot and Henry James. Look at your two favorite novels of all time: *Pride and Prejudice* and *Wuthering Heights*. But *you*, I add with glee, *you* are pure Daisy Miller. I don't know who this Daisy or Maisie or whatever of yours is, she tells me, pursing her lips, and I won't like James, *I know*. Yet she *is* like Daisy: a mixture of vulnerability and courage that accounts for these gestures of defiance, her way of throwing her head back which I first noticed when she was barely four, in the waiting room of a dentist's office of all places.

And when Dara jokingly asks, What about me? What did you do when you were pregnant with me? I tell him, Just to defy me, you turned out to be all that I imagined you would not be. And the moment I say this, I begin to believe it. Even in the womb, he took upon himself the task of proving my nightmarish anxieties wrong. While I was pregnant with him, Tehran was the object of continual bombings and I had become hysterical. There were stories about how pregnant women gave birth to crippled children, how their mother's anxiety had affected the unborn fetus in irremediable ways, and I imagined mine to be infected with all those maladies – that is, if we were spared and lived to see the birth of this child. How could I know that instead of my protecting him, he was coming into the world to protect me?

READING LOLITA IN TEHRAN: A MEMOIR IN BOOKS, 2003

JEAN-JACQUES ROUSSEAU

AFTER TWO YEARS OF SILENCE and patience, despite my resolutions, I take up my pen again. Reader, suspend your judgment on the reasons that have forced me to do this. You may only judge them after having read what I have to say.

We have seen my peaceful youth pass by in a fairly steady, fairly sweet way, without major setbacks or major windfalls. This mediocrity was in large part due to my lively but feeble nature, which was less keen to venture than easy to discourage: rousing from its rest in fits and starts, but slumping back again by laziness and by inclination, and which, always returning me to the idle and tranquil life which I felt myself born to, far from the great virtues and even farther from the great vices, never allowed me to try anything significant, good or bad.

What a different picture I should soon paint! Fate, which for thirty years indulged my whims, stopped them in their tracks for the next thirty, and from this continual opposition between my situation and my inclinations, we will see the birth of enormous errors, incredible misfortunes, and all the virtues, except strength, that could honour adversity.

The first part of my book was wholly written from memory and I must have made many mistakes. Forced to write the second from memory also, I will probably make many more. The delicate memories of my beautiful years, spent with as much tranquillity as innocence, left me a thousand charming impressions that I love to recall endlessly. We will soon see how different are those of the rest of my life. To recall them is to renew the bitterness. Far from sharpening the bitterness of my situation by these sad journeys into the past, I push the memories aside as much as I can, and often I succeed to the point where I cannot recover them again when I need to. This facility for forgetting the bad things is a consolation that the heavens have devised for me; in among those that fate would one day pile upon me. My memory, which retraces solely pleasant objects, is the happy counterweight to my frightened imagination, which makes me foresee only cruel futures.

All the papers that I had gathered together to supplement my memory and guide me in this enterprise, passed into other hands and will no longer return to mine. I have only one faithful guide on whom I can count; it is the chain of feelings that has marked the succession of my being, and through those feelings, that of the events which have been their cause or effect. I easily forget my misfortunes; but I cannot forget my faults, and I am even less likely to forget my good intentions. Their memory is too dear to me ever to be erased from my heart. I can make omissions in the facts, transpositions, errors in dates; but I cannot be wrong about that which I felt, nor about that which my feelings made me do; and this is principally what it is about. The central object of my confessions is to make known exactly my innermost self in all the situations of my life. It is the history of my soul that I promised, and to write it faithfully I have no need for other memories; it is enough to return into myself as I have done to this point.

THE CONFESSIONS, 1782–1789

ROSAMOND LEHMANN

WHEN I CAME ROUND FROM THE ANAESTHETIC that late afternoon in January, 1934, there was no nurse or doctor in the room. She and I were alone. I heard her before I saw her. She was making strong, broken noises of protest, sorrow, from some unidentifiable region near my bed. 'Yes, yes. I know,' I said. 'Never mind. I know … ' Immediately she was silent, listening. In this soundless naught, recognition started to vibrate, like a fine filament, between us; quickened, tautened. I swung in living darkness, emptiness; in the beginning of the deepest listening of my life.

When, probably quite soon, Sister came in and said loudly: 'Here's your baby, dear – a lovely daughter – don't you want to see her?' I started to sob: I suppose for happiness. There were shadows over her birth time and the period before; and I had not been able to imagine a joyful conclusion to these unreal months. Particularly I had schooled myself not to expect a daughter, which was what I longed for.

THE SWAN IN THE EVENING: FRAGMENTS OF AN INNER LIFE, 1967

VLADIMIR NABAKOV

YOU KNOW, I STILL FEEL IN MY WRISTS certain echoes of the pram-pusher's knack, such as, for example, the glib downward pressure one applied to the handle in order to have the carriage tip up and climb the curb. First came an elaborate mouse-gray vehicle of Belgian make, with fat autoid tires and luxurious springs, so large that it could not enter our puny elevator. It rolled on sidewalks in slow stately mystery, with the trapped baby inside lying supine, well covered with down, silk and fur; only his eyes moved, warily, and sometimes they turned upward with one swift sweep of their showy lashes to follow the receding of branch-patterned blueness that flowed away from the edge of the half-cocked hood of the carriage, and presently he would dart a suspicious glance at my face to see if the teasing trees and sky did not belong, perhaps to the same order of things as did rattles and parental humor. There followed a lighter carriage, and in this, as he spun along, he would tend to rise, straining at his straps; clutching at the edges; standing there less like the groggy passenger of a pleasure boat than like an entranced scientist in a spaceship; surveying the speckled skeins of a live, warm world; eyeing with philosophic interest the pillow he had managed to throw overboard; falling out himself when a strap burst one day. Still later he rode in one of those small contraptions called strollers; from initial springy and secure heights the child came lower and lower, until, when he was about one and a half, he touched ground in front of the moving stroller by slipping forward out of his seat and beating the sidewalk with his heels in anticipation of being set loose in some public garden.

SPEAK, MEMORY: AN AUTOBIOGRAPHY REVISITED, 1966

ST AUGUSTINE

B UT WHEN A PROFOUND REFLECTION HAD, from the secret depths of my soul, drawn together and heaped up all my misery before the sight of my heart, there arose a mighty storm, accompanied by as mighty a shower of tears. Which, that I might pour forth fully, with its natural expressions, I stole away from [my friend] Alypius; for it suggested itself to me that solitude was fitter for the business of weeping. So I retired to such a distance that even his presence could not be oppressive to me. Thus was it with me at that time, and he perceived it; for something, I believe, I had spoken, wherein the sound of my voice appeared choked with weeping, and in that state had I risen up. He then remained where we had been sitting, most completely astonished. I flung myself down, how, I know not, under a certain fig-tree, giving free course to my tears, and the streams of mine eyes gushed out, an acceptable sacrifice unto Thee. And, not indeed in these words, yet to this effect, spake I much unto Thee – 'But Thou, O Lord, how long?' 'How long, Lord? Wilt Thou be angry for ever? Oh, remember not against us former iniquities'; for I felt that I was enthralled by them. I sent up these sorrowful cries – 'How long, how long? Tomorrow, and tomorrow? Why not now? Why is there not this hour an end to my uncleanness?'

I was saying these things and weeping in the most bitter contrition of my heart, when, lo, I heard the voice of a boy or a girl, I know not which, coming from a neighbouring house, chanting, and oft repeating, 'Take up and read; take up and read.' Immediately my countenance was changed, and I began most earnestly to consider whether it was usual for children in any kind of game to sing such words; nor could I remember ever to have heard the like. So, restraining the torrent of my tears, I rose up, interpreting it no other way than as a command to me from Heaven to open the book, and to read the first chapter I should light upon. For I had heard of Antony, that, accidentally coming in whilst the gospel was being read, he received the admonition as if what was read were addressed to him, 'Go and sell that thou hast, and give to the poor, and thou shalt have treasure in heaven; and come and follow me.' And by such oracle was he forthwith converted unto Thee. So quickly I returned to the place where Alypius was sitting; for there I had put down the volume of the apostles, when I rose thence. I grasped, opened, and in silence read that paragraph on which my eyes first fell – 'Not in rioting and drunkenness, not in chambering and wantonness, not in strife and envying; but put ye on the Lord Jesus Christ, and make not provision for the flesh, to fulfil the lusts thereof.' No further would I read, nor did I need; for instantly, as the sentence ended – by a light, as it were, of security into my heart – all the gloom of doubt vanished away.

Closing the book, then, and putting either my finger between, or some other mark, I now with a tranquil countenance made it known to Alypius. And he thus disclosed to me what was wrought in him, which I knew not. He asked to look at what I had read. I showed him; and he looked even further than I had read, and I knew not what followed. This it was, verily, 'Him that is weak in the faith, receive ye'; which he applied to himself, and discovered to me. By this admonition was he strengthened; and by a good resolution and purpose, very much in accord with his character (wherein, for the better, he was always far different from me), without any restless delay he joined me. Thence we go in to my mother. We make it known to her – she rejoiceth. We relate how it came to pass – she leapeth for joy, and triumpheth, and blesseth Thee, who art 'able to do exceedingly abundantly above all that we ask or think'; for she perceived Thee to have given her more for me than she used to ask by her pitiful and most doleful groanings. For Thou didst so convert me unto Thyself, that I sought neither a wife, nor any other of this world's hopes – standing in that rule of faith in which Thou, so many years before, had showed me unto her in a vision. And Thou didst turn her grief into a gladness, much more plentiful than she had desired, and much dearer and chaster than she used to crave, by having grandchildren of my body.

THE CONFESSIONS OF ST AUGUSTINE, 397–400

ST TERESA OF AVILA

A T THIS TIME I WAS GIVEN St Augustine's *Confessions,* seemingly by the ordainment of the Lord. I did not ask for it myself, nor had I ever seen it. I am most devoted to Saint Augustine, because the convent in which I lived before taking my vows was of his Order, and also because he had been a sinner. I derived great comfort from those saints who have sinned and yet whom the Lord has drawn to Himself. I thought that I could obtain help from them, and that as the Lord had pardoned them he might pardon me. But one thing that I have already mentioned disturbed me. The Lord had called them only once and they had not sinned again, but my relapses were so many that it distressed me. Yet when I remembered the love He bore me I took fresh courage, for I never doubted His mercy, though I very often doubted myself.

O my Lord, I am amazed that my soul was so stubborn when I received such help from You! It frightens me to think how little I could do by myself and of those attachments that hindered my resolution to give myself entirely to God. When I began to read the *Confessions* I seemed to see myself portrayed there, and I began to commend myself frequently to that glorious saint. When I came to the tale of his conversion, and read how he heard the voice in the garden, it seemed exactly as if the Lord had spoken to me. So I felt in my heart. For some time I was dissolved in tears, in great inward affliction and distress. How a soul suffers, O my Lord, by losing its liberty! Once it was mistress of itself, and now what torments it endures! I was amazed today that I was ever able to live under such torture. Praise be to God, who gave me life to escape from so absolute a death.

The Life of St Teresa of Avila by herself, 1562–1565

JONATHAN EDWARDS

ONCE, AS I RID OUT INTO THE WOODS for my health, Anno 1737, and having lit from my horse in a retired place, as my manner commonly has been, to walk for divine contemplation and prayer, I had a view, that for me was extraordinary, of the glory of the Son of God, as mediator between God and man, and His wonderful, great, full, pure and sweet grace and love, and meek and gentle condescension. This grace, that appeared to me so calm and sweet, appeared great above the heavens. The person of Christ appeared ineffably excellent, with an excellency great enough to swallow up all thought and conception, which continued, as near as I can judge, about an hour, which kept me, the bigger part of the time, in a flood of tears, and weeping aloud. I felt withal an ardency of soul to be, what I know not otherwise how to express, than to be emptied and annihilated; to lie in the dust, and to be full of Christ alone; to love Him with a holy and pure love; to trust in Him; to live upon Him; to serve and follow Him; and to be totally wrapt up in the fullness of Christ; and to be perfectly sanctified and made pure with a divine and heavenly purity. I have several other times had views very much of the same nature and that have had the same effects.

'PERSONAL NARRATIVE', 1765

P.T. BARNUM

WHILE IN EUROPE, I was constantly on the look-out for novelties. Not a fair was held, within a reasonable distance, that I did not visit, with a view to buy or hire such exhibitions as I thought would 'pay' in the United States.

I obtained verbally through a friend the refusal of the house in which Shakspeare [sic] was born, designing to remove it in sections to my Museum in New York; but the project leaked out, British pride was touched, and several English gentlemen interfered and purchased the premises for a Shakspearian Association. Had they slept a few days longer, I should have made a rare speculation, for I was subsequently assured that the British people, rather than suffer that house to be removed to America, would have bought me off with twenty thousand pounds …

Having heard, while in London in 1844, of a company of 'Campanalogians, or Lancashire Bell Ringers', performing in Ireland, I induced them to meet me in Liverpool, and there engaged them for an American tour. One of my stipulations was, that they should suffer their moustaches to grow, assume a picturesque dress, and be known as the 'Swiss Bell Ringers'. They at first objected, in the broad and almost unintelligible dialect of Lancashire, because, as they said, they spoke only the English language, and could not pass muster as Swiss people; but the objection was withdrawn when I assured them, that if they continued to speak in America as they had just spoken to me, they might safely claim to be Swiss, or any thing else, and no one would be any the wiser.

As in other cases, so in this, the deception as to birth-place was of small account, and did no injury. Those seven men were really admirable performers, and by means of their numerous bells, of various sizes, they produced the most delicious music. They attracted much attention in various parts of the United States, in Canada, and in Cuba.

As a compensation to England for the loss of the Bell Ringers, I dispatched an agent to America for a party of Indians, including squaws. He proceeded to Iowa, and returned to London with a company of sixteen.

THE LIFE OF P.T. BARNUM, WRITTEN BY HIMSELF, 1855

MICHAEL ONDAATJE

WHAT BEGAN IT ALL WAS the bright bone of a dream I could hardly hold onto. I was sleeping at a friend's house. I saw my father, chaotic, surrounded by dogs, and all of them were screaming and barking into the tropical landscape. The noises woke me. I sat up on the uncomfortable sofa and I was in a jungle, hot, sweating. Street lights bounced off the snow and into the room through the hanging vines and ferns at my friend's window. A fish tank glowed in the corner. I had been weeping and my shoulders and face were exhausted. I wound the quilt around myself, leaned back against the head of the sofa, and sat there for most of the night. Tense, not wanting to move as the heat gradually left me, as the sweat evaporated and I became conscious again of brittle air outside the windows searing and howling through the streets and over the frozen cars hunched like sheep all the way down towards Lake Ontario. It was a new winter and I was already dreaming of Asia.

Once a friend had told me that it was only when I was drunk that I seemed to know exactly what I wanted. And so, two months later, in the midst of the farewell party in my growing wildness – dancing, balancing a wine glass on my forehead and falling to the floor twisting round and getting up without letting the glass tip, a trick which seemed only possible when drunk and relaxed – I knew I was already running. Outside the continuing snow had made the streets narrow, almost impassable. Guests had arrived on foot, scarved, faces pink and frozen. They leaned against the fire-place and drank.

I had already planned the journey back. During quiet afternoons I spread maps onto the floor and searched out possible routes to Ceylon. But it was only in the midst of this party, among my closest friends, that I realized I would be travelling back to the family I had grown from – those relations from my parents' generation who stood in my memory like frozen opera. I wanted to touch them into words. A perverse and solitary desire. In Jane Austen's *Persuasion* I had come across the lines, 'she had been forced into prudence in her youth – she learned romance as she grew older – the natural sequence of an unnatural beginning'. In my mid-thirties I realized I had slipped past a childhood I had ignored and not understood.

Asia. The name was a gasp from a dying mouth. An ancient word that had to be whispered, would never be used as a battle cry. The word sprawled. It had none of the clipped sound of Europe, America, Canada. The vowels took over, slept on the map with the S. I was running to Asia and everything would change. It began with that moment when I was dancing and laughing wildly within the comfort and order of my life. Beside the fridge I tried to communicate some of the fragments I knew about my father, my grandmother. 'So how *did* your grandmother die?' 'Natural causes.' 'What?' 'Floods.' And then another wave of the party swirled me away.

RUNNING IN THE FAMILY, 1982

WALT WHITMAN

IN 1848, '49, I WAS OCCUPIED AS EDITOR of the 'daily Eagle' newspaper, in Brooklyn. The latter year went off on a leisurely journey and working expedition (my brother Jeff with me) through all the middle States, and down the Ohio and Mississippi rivers. Lived awhile in New Orleans, and work'd there on the editorial staff of 'daily Crescent' newspaper. After a time plodded back northward, up the Mississippi, and around to, and by way of the great lakes, Michigan, Huron, and Erie, to Niagra Falls and lower Canada, finally returning through central New York and down the Hudson; traveling altogether probably 8000 miles this trip, to and fro. '51, '53 occupied in house-building in Brooklyn. (For a little of the first part of that time in printing a daily and weekly paper, 'the Freeman'.) '55, lost my dear father this year by death. Commenced putting *Leaves of Grass* to press for good, at the job printing office of my friends, the brothers Rome, in Brooklyn, after many MS [manuscript] doings and undoings. (I had great trouble in leaving out the stock 'poetical' touches, but succeeded at last.) I am now (1856–7) passing through my 37th year.

'SPECIMEN DAYS', 1882

BRIAN KEENAN

I HAD, OF COURSE, LIKE ALL OF US, seen prison cells. We have all seen films about prisoners, or read books about prison life. Some of the great stories of escape and imprisonment are part of our history. It seems much of our culture is laden with these stories. But when I think back to that cell, I know that nothing that I had seen before could compare with that most dismal of places. I will describe it briefly to you, that you may see it for yourself.

It was built very shoddily of rough-cut concrete blocks haphazardly put together and joined by crude slapdash cement-work. Inside, and only on the inside, the walls were plastered over with that same dull grey cement. There was no paint. There was no colour, just the constant monotony of rough grey concrete. The cell was six feet long and four feet wide. I could stand up and touch those walls with my outstretched hands and walk those six feet in no more than four paces. On the floor was a foam mattress. With the mattress laid out I had a pacing stage of little more than a foot's width.

In one corner there was a bottle of water which I replenished daily when I went to the toilet, and in another corner was a bottle for urine, which I took with me to empty. There was also a plastic cup in which I kept a much abused and broken toothbrush. On the mattress was an old, ragged, filthy cover. It had originally been a curtain. There was one blanket which I never used, due to the heat, the filth and the heavy smell, stale and almost putrid, of the last person who had slept here. The cell had no windows. A sheet steel door was padlocked every day, sounding like a thump on the head to remind me where I was. At the head of the mattress I kept my briefcase with my school text books. Behind the briefcase I hid my shoes. I was forever afraid that I would lose those shoes. If I did, I felt it would be a sure sign that I would never leave that cell. I was insistent that they should not have them. They had taken everything else by now, but the shoes I guarded with jealous and vicious determination. The foolish things one clings to. A pair of cheap shoes off a street trader's stall! Since the day they had given me *Time* and *Newsweek* I also treasured these magazines. Initially to read, reread and look at the pictures and read again. But later they served a more needy purpose.

Come now into the cell with me and stay here and feel if you can and if you will that time, whatever time it was, for however long, for time means nothing in this cell. Come, come in.

I am back from my daily ablutions. I hear the padlock slam behind me and I lift the towel which has draped my head from my face. I look at the food on the floor. The round of Arab bread, a boiled egg, the jam I will not eat, the slice or two of processed cheese and perhaps some humus. Every day I look to see if it will change, if there will be some new morsel of food that will make this day different from all the other days, but there is no change. This day is the same as all the days in the past and as all the days to come. It will always be the same food sitting on the floor in the same place.

I set down my plastic bottle of drinking water and the other empty bottle. From bottle to bottle, through me, this fluid will daily run. I set the urine bottle at the far corner away from the food. This I put in a plastic bag to keep it fresh. In this heat the bread rapidly turns stale and hard. It is like eating cardboard. I pace my four paces backwards and forwards, slowly feeling my mind empty, wondering where it will go today. Will I go with it or will I try to hold it back, like a father and an unruly child? There is a greasy patch on the wall where I lay my head. Like a dog I sniff it.

I begin as I have always begun these days to think of something, anything upon which I can concentrate. Something I can think about and so try to push away the crushing emptiness of this tiny, tiny cell and the day's long silence. I try with desperation to recall the dream of the night before or perhaps to push away the horror of it. The nights are filled with dreaming. The cinema of the mind, the reels flashing and flashing by and suddenly stopping at some point when with strange contortions it throws up some absurd drama that I cannot understand. I try to block it out. Strange how in the daytime the dreams that we do not wish to remember come flickering back into the conscious mind. Those dreams that we desperately want to have with us in the daylight will not come to us but have gone and cannot be enticed back. It is as if we are running down a long empty tunnel looking for something that we left behind but cannot see in the blackness.

The guards are gone. I have not heard a noise for several hours now. It must be time to eat. I tear off a quarter of the unleavened bread and begin to peel the shell from the egg. The word 'albumen' intrigues me for a while and I wonder where the name came from. How someone decided once to call that part of the egg 'albumen'. The shape of an egg has lost its fascination for me. I have exhausted thinking about the form of an egg. A boiled egg with dry bread is doubly tasteless. I make this meaningless remark to myself every day and don't know why.

I must ration my drinking water for I am always fearful that I might finish it and then wake in the middle of the night with a raging thirst that I cannot satiate. I think of rabies and the raging thirst of mad dogs and I know how easy it would be to go mad from thirst. Now I know the full meaning of the expression so frequently used in our daily lives: 'He was mad with thirst.' If I were to knock over this water-bottle there would be nothing I could do because there is no one here. Until tomorrow there will be silence in this tomb of a place so far down under the ground.

Then it begins, I feel it coming from out of nowhere. I recognize it now, and I shrink into the corner to await its pleasure. What will it be today? That slow down-dragging slide and pull into hopeless depression and weariness. The waters of the sea of despair are heavy and thick and I think I cannot swim through them. But today is a day of euphoria. A day in which I will not walk my four paces but in which I will glide, my feet hardly touching the ground. Up snakes and down ladders my mind is maniacally playing games with me and I cannot escape. Today it is teasing me, threatening me, so far without the full blast of its fury. I squat and rock backwards and forwards reciting a half-remembered nursery rhyme like a religious mantra. I am determined I will make myself more mad than my mind.

Blackness, the light has gone. There will be none for ten hours. They have given me candles. Small, stubby candles. I will not light them. I fear the dark so I save the candles. It's stupid, it's ridiculous. There are a dozen or so hidden under my bed. I will not light them, yet I hate the dark and cannot abide its thick palpable blackness. I can feel it against my skin.

I am going crazier by the day. In the thick sticky darkness I lie naked on the mattress. The blanket reeks, full of filth. It is pointless to try to shield myself from the mosquitoes drooling and humming, their constant buzz, buzz, buzz everywhere, as if it is inside my ears and inside my head. In the thick black invisibility it is foolishness to hope to kill what you cannot see but only feel when it is too late, upon your flesh.

Always in the morning I see the marks of the night's battle. Red lumps like chicken pox, all raging to be itched and scratched. I sit trying to prevent myself from scratching. The more I try to resist, the more difficult it becomes and the more demanding is my body for the exquisite pain of my nails tearing my own flesh. For some reason I do not understand, the feet and the backs of my fingers suffer the most from these insistent fleas. The pain of the bites on these tender areas can be excruciating. At times I exchange one pain for another. Deciding feverishly to tear and scratch the skin from my feet, and with it the pain of the bite, knowing that in the morning my feet will be a bloody mess and I will be unable to walk on this filthy floor. It's all so purposeless. I am naked in the dark and I try to wipe the perspiration from my skin. The night noise of these insects is insidious. I cannot bear much more. I thrust my body back upon the mattress and pull the filthy curtain over it to keep these things from feeding on my flesh. I cannot bear the heat and smell of this rag over my body like a shroud. I must content myself, let the mosquitoes feed and hope that having had a fill of me they will leave me alone to find some sleep.

AN EVIL CRADLING, 1992

SALVADOR DALI

I AM THIRTY-SEVEN YEARS OLD. It is July 30th, 1941, the day I promised my publisher I would finish this manuscript.

I am completely naked and alone in my room at Hampton Manor. I approach the wardrobe mirror and look at myself: my hair is still black as ebony, my feet have not yet known the degrading stigma of a single corn; my body exactly resembles that of my adolescence, except for my stomach which has grown bigger. I am not on the eve of a voyage to China, nor am I about to get a divorce; neither am I thinking of committing suicide, nor of jumping over a cliff clutching the warm placenta of a silk parachute to attempt to be reborn; I have no desire to fight a duel with anyone or with anything; I want only two things: first, to love Gala, my wife; and second, that other inescapable thing, so difficult and so little desired – to grow old.

THE SECRET LIFE OF SALVADOR DALI, 1942

ABRAHAM COWLEY

WITH THESE AFFECTIONS OF MIND, and my heart wholly set upon letters, I went to the university; but was soon torn from thence by that violent public storm which would suffer nothing to stand where it did, but rooted up every plant, even from the princely cedars to me, the hyssop. Yet I had as good fortune as could have befallen me in such a tempest; for I was cast by it into the family of one of the best persons, and into the court of one of the best princesses of the world. Now though I was here engaged in ways most contrary to the original design of my life, that is, into much company, and no small business, and into a daily sight of greatness, both militant and triumphant (for that was the state then of the English and French Courts) yet all this was so far from altering my opinion, that it only added the confirmation of reason to that which was before but natural inclination. I saw plainly all the paint of that kind of life, the nearer I came to it; and that beauty which I did not fall in love with, when, for aught I knew, it was real, was not like to bewitch or entice me when I saw that it was adulterate. I met with several great persons, whom I liked very well, but could not perceive that any part of their greatness was to be liked or desired, no more than I would be glad or content to be in a storm, though I saw many ships which rid safely and bravely in it. A storm would not agree with my stomach, if it did with my courage. Though, I was in a crowd of as good company as could be found anywhere, though I was in business of great and honourable trust, though I ate at the best table, and enjoyed the best conveniences for present subsistence that ought to be desired by a man of my condition in banishment and public distresses; yet I could not abstain from renewing my old schoolboy's wish in a copy of verses to the same effect.

> Well then; I now do plainly see,
> This busy world and I shall ne'er agree, etc.

And I never then proposed to myself any other advantage from His Majesty's happy restoration, but the getting into some moderately convenient retreat in the country, which I thought in that case I might easily have compassed, as well as some others, with no greater probabilities or pretences have arrived to extraordinary fortunes. But I had before written a shrewd prophesy against myself, and I think Apollo inspired me in the truth, though not in the elegance of it.

> Thou, neither great at court nor in the war,
> Nor at th' Exchange shalt be, nor at the wrangling Bar;
> Content thyself with the small barren praise
> Which neglected Verse does raise, etc.

However, by the failing of the forces which I had expected, I did not quit the design which I had resolved on; I cast myself into it *A Corps Perdu*, without making capitulations or taking counsel of fortune. But God laughs at a man who says to his soul, 'Take thy ease': I met presently not only with many little encumbrances and impediments, but with so much sickness (a new misfortune to me) as would have spoiled the happiness of an emperor as well as mine. Yet I do neither repent nor alter my course.

'OF MYSELF', 1668

MALCOLM X

ANYTHING I DO TODAY, I regard as urgent. No man is given but so much time to accomplish whatever is his life's work. My life in particular never has stayed fixed in on one position for very long. You have seen how throughout my life, I have often known unexpected drastic changes.

I am only facing the facts when I know that any moment of any day, or any night, could bring me death. This is particularly true since that last trip that I made abroad. I have seen the nature of things that are happening, and I have heard things from sources which are reliable.

To speculate about dying doesn't disturb me as it might some people. I have never felt that I would live to become an old man. Even before I was a Muslim – when I was a hustler in the ghetto jungle, and then a criminal in prison, it always stayed on my mind that I would die a violent death. In fact, it runs in my family. My father and most of his brothers died by violence – my father because of what he believed in. To come right down to it, if I take the kind of things in which I believe, then add to that the kind of temperament I have, plus the one hundred percent dedication I have to whatever I believe in – these are ingredients which make it just about impossible for me to die of old age.

THE AUTOBIOGRAPHY OF MALCOLM X, 1964

HENRY DAVID THOREAU

MEANWHILE MY BEANS, the length of whose rows, added together, was seven miles already planted, were impatient to be hoed, for the earliest had grown considerably before the latest were in the ground; indeed they were not easily to be put off. What was the meaning of this so steady and self-respecting, this small Herculean labor, I knew not. I came to love my rows, my beans, though so many more than I wanted. They attached me to the earth, and so I got strength like Antaeus. By why should I raise them? Only Heaven knows. This was my curious labor all summer – to make this portion of the earth's surface, which had yielded only cinquefoil, blackberries, johnswort, and the like, before, sweet wild fruits and pleasant flowers, produce instead this pulse. What shall I learn of beans or beans of me? I cherish them, I hoe them, early and late I have an eye to them; and this is my day's work. It is a fine broad leaf to look on. My auxiliaries are the dews and rains which water this dry soil, and what fertility is in the soil itself, which for the most part is lean and effete. My enemies are worms, cool days, and most of all woodchucks. The last have nibbled for me a quarter of an acre clean. But what right had I to oust johnswort and the rest, and break up their ancient herb garden? Soon, however, the remaining beans will be too tough for them, and go forward to meet new foes.

When I was four years old, as I well remember, I was brought from Boston to this my native town, through these very woods and this field, to the pond. It is one of the oldest scenes stamped on my memory. And now tonight my flute has waked the echoes over that very water. The pines still stand here older than I; or, if some have fallen, I have cooked my supper with their stumps, and a new growth is rising all around, preparing another aspect for new infant eyes. Almost the same johnswort springs from the same perennial root in this pasture, and even I have at length helped to clothe that fabulous landscape of my infant dreams, and one of the results of my presence and influence is seen in these bean leaves, corn blades, and potato vines.

I planted about two acres and a half of upland; and it was only about fifteen years since the land was cleared, and I myself had got out two or three cords of stumps; I did not give it any manure; but in the course of the summer it appeared by the arrow-heads which I turned up in hoeing, that an extinct nation had anciently dwelt here and planted corn and beans ere white men came to clear the land, and so, to some extent, had exhausted the soil for this very crop.

Before yet any woodchuck or squirrel had run across the road, or the sun had got above the shrub-oaks, while all the dew was on, though the farmers warned me against it – I would advise you to do your work if possible while the dew is on – I began to level the ranks of haughty weeds in my bean-field and throw dust upon their heads. Early in the morning I worked barefooted, dabbling like a plastic artist in the dewy and crumbling sand, but later in the day the sun blistered my feet. There the sun lighted me to hoe beans, pacing slowly backward and forward over that yellow gravelly upland, between the long green rows, fifteen rods, the one end terminating in a shrub-oak copse where I could rest in the shade, the other in a blackberry field where the green berries deepened their tints by the time I had made another bout. Removing the weeds, putting fresh soil about the bean stems, and encouraging this weed which I had sown, making the yellow soil express its summer thought in bean leaves and blossoms rather than in wormwood and piper and millet grass, making the earth say beans instead of grass – this was my daily work.

WALDEN, OR LIFE IN THE WOODS, 1854

BILLIE HOLIDAY

I 'VE BEEN TOLD THAT NOBODY SINGS the word 'hunger' like I do. Or the word 'love'.

Maybe I remember what those words are all about. Maybe I'm proud enough to *want* to remember Baltimore and Welfare Island, the Catholic institution and the Jefferson Market Court, the sheriff in front of our place in Harlem and the towns from coast to coast where I got my lumps and scars, Philly and Alderson, Hollywood and San Francisco – every damn bit of it.

All the Cadillacs and minks in the world – and I've had a few – can't make it up or make me forget it. All I've learned in all those places from all those people is wrapped up in those two words. You've got to have something to eat and a little love in your life before you can hold still for any damn body's sermon on how to behave.

Everything I am and everything I want out of life goes smack back to that.

Look at my big dream! It's always been to have a big place of my own out in the country someplace where I could take care of stray dogs and orphan kids, kids that didn't ask to be born; kids that didn't ask to be black, blue, or green or something in between.

I'd only want to be sure of one thing – that nobody in the world wanted these kids. Then I would take them. They'd have to be illegit, no mama, no papa.

I'd have room for twenty-five or thirty, with three or four big buxom loving women just like my mom to take care of them, feed them, see to it the little bastards go to school; knock them in the head when they're wrong, but love them whether they're good or bad.

We'd have a crazy big kitchen with a chartreuse stove and a refrigerator to match, and I'd supervise the cooking and baking. We might have a doctor and a nurse and a couple of tutors. But I'd always be around to teach them my kind of teaching – not the kind that tells them how to spell Mississippi, but how to be glad to be who you are and what you are.

When they grow up enough to go out and do babysitting and take little jobs or start on their own, away they'd go. And then there would always be more.

Grown-ups can make it some kind of way. They might have a little more or a little less to eat than the next guy – a little more or a little less love, and it isn't fatal.

But kids? Take me, I didn't ask Clarence Holiday and Sadie Fagan to get together in that Baltimore hallway and have me and then have to leave me to get pushed around and hassle with life on my own. Sure, my old lady took care of me the best she could and she was the greatest. But she was only a kid herself. Her hassle was worse than mine. She was just a young kid trying to raise a young kid.

Anyway, that's my dream and there is another dream too.

All my life I've wanted my own club. A small place where I can walk in, have my own piano, drums, and a swinging guitar. I'd want it to be crowded if there were one hundred and twenty-five people there – that's how intimate I want it.

I've fought all my life to be able to sing what I wanted the way I wanted to sing it. Before I die I want a place of my own where nobody can tell me *when* to go on. I might go on at nine, or four in the morning; I might sing forty-nine songs or one song. I might even get up and stop the band in the middle of a number and sing something I felt like singing.

But it would be a place where my friends could come and really relax and enjoy themselves – sleep if they wanted to sleep, and eat if they wanted to eat.

And I'd run that kitchen myself. I might not actually cook everything, but I'd oversee it and taste it and see that it's my kind of cooking and that it's straight. I used to laugh when Mom talked about having her own place, but look at me now.

I could have had a dozen clubs in my time, but I'd always have been fronting for something else. Even today there are promoters willing to get behind a club of mine. But I wouldn't take somebody else's money even if they were fool enough to give it to me. I'd always be scared someone would come in and plant some stuff in my place, have me raided and busted.

Besides, it would have to be proven to me that it was mine, all mine, before the law would let me sing in it. And I would have to know it was mine before I could sing in it anyway.

Although people sometimes act like they think so, a singer is not like a saxophone. If you don't sound right, you can't go out and get some new reeds, split them just right. A singer is only a voice, and a voice is completely dependent on the body God gave you. When you walk out there and open your mouth, you never know what's going to happen.

I'm not supposed to get a toothache, I'm not supposed to get nervous; I can't throw up or get sick to my stomach; I'm not supposed to get the 'flu or have a sore throat. I'm supposed to go out there and look pretty and sing good and smile and I'd just better.

Why? Because I'm Billie Holiday and I've been in trouble.

LADY SINGS THE BLUES, 1956

BLAKE MORRISON

HE ISN'T DRINKING, ISN'T EATING. He wears his trousers open at the waist, held up not by a belt but by pain and swelling. He looks like death, but he is not dead, and won't be for another four weeks. He has driven down from Yorkshire to London. He has made it against the odds. He is still my father. He is still here.

'I've brought some plants for you.'

'Come and sit down first, Dad, you've been driving for hours.'

'No, best get them unloaded.'

It's like Birnam Wood coming to Dunsinane, black plastic bags and wooden boxes blooming in the back seat, the rear window, the boot: herbs, hypericum, escallonia, cotoneaster, ivies, potentillas. He directs me where to leave the different plants – which will need shade, which sun, which shelter. Like all my father's presents, they come with a pay-off – he will not leave until he has seen every one of them planted: 'I know you. And I don't want them drying up.'

We walk round the house, the expanse of rooms, so different from the old flat. 'It's wonderful to see you settled at last,' he says, and I resist telling him that I'm not settled, have never felt less settled in my life. I see his eyes taking in the little things to be done, the leaky taps, the cracked paint, the rotting window-frames.

'You'll need a new switch unit for the mirror light – the contact has gone, see.'

'Yes.'

'And a couple of two-inch Phillips screws will solve this.'

'I've got some. Let's have a drink now, eh.'

'What's the schedule for tomorrow?' he asks, as always, and I'm irritated, as always, at his need to parcel out the weekend into a series of tasks, as if without a plan of action it wouldn't be worth his coming, not even to see his son or grandchildren. 'I don't think I'll be much help to you,' he says, 'but I'll try.' By nine-thirty he is in bed and asleep.

I wake him next day at nine, unthinkably late, with a pint-mug of tea, unthinkably refused. After his breakfast of strawberry Complan he comes round the house with me, stooped and crouching over his swollen stomach. For once it's me who is going to have to do the hammering and screwing. We go down to the hardware shop in Greenwich, where he charms the socks off the black assistant, who gives me a shrug and a pat at the end, as if to say, 'Where d'you get a dad like this from?' Back home again, he decides that the job for him is to get the curtains moving freely on their rails. 'You know the best thing for it?' he says. 'Furniture polish. Get me a can of it and I'll sort it for you.' He teeters on a wooden kitchen stool at each of the windows in the house, his trousers gaping open, and sprays polish on the rail, and wipes it over with a dirty rag. His balance looks precarious. I try to talk him down, but he is stubborn.

'No, it needs doing. And every time you pull the curtains from now on, you can think of me.'

I ask him about the operation: is he apprehensive?

'No point in being. They have to have a look. I expect it's an infarct, and they'll be able to cure that, but if not … well, I've had a good life and I've left everything in order for you.'

'I'd rather you than order.'

'Too true.'

I make sure there are only two light but time-consuming jobs for us. The first is to fix a curtain pole across the garden end of the kitchen, over the glazed door, and we spend the best part of two hours bickering about the best way to do this: there's a problem on the left-hand side because the kitchen cupboards finish close to the end wall, six inches or so, and you can't get an electric drill in easily to make the holes for the fixing bracket. The drill keeps sheering off, partly because I'm unnerved by him below, drawing something on the back of an envelope. I get down and he shows me his plan: a specially mounted shelf in the side wall to support the pole rather than a fixing bracket for it on the end. Sighing and cursing, I climb back up and follow his instructions in every detail – not just the size of screws and Rawlplugs needed, but how to clasp the hammer.

'Hold it at the end, you daft sod, not up near the top.'

'Christ, Dad, I'm forty-one years old.'

'And you still don't know how to hold a hammer properly – or a screwdriver.'

Infuriatingly, his plan works – the shelf mounting, the pole, the curtain, all fine. I try not to give him the satisfaction of admitting it.

We bicker our way into the next room and the other job: to hang the chandelier inherited from Uncle Bert. At some point in the move, many of the glass pieces have become separated, and now, in the dim November light behind the tall sash-window, we spend the afternoon working out where they belong, re-attaching them to the wire that joins them, and then strengthening the candelabra from which they dangle. 'This really needs soldering,' he says, meaning that he will find an alternative to soldering them, since to solder would mean going out and spending money on a soldering iron when he has a perfectly good one at home. I watch him bowed over the glass diamonds, with pliers and fractured screw-threads and nuts and bits of wire – the improviser, the amateur inventor – and I think of all the jobs he's done for me down the years, and how sooner or later I'll have to learn to do them for myself. The metal clasps joining glass ball to glass ball are like the clasps on his King Edward cigar boxes, and the clasps on his student skeleton, Janet.

'I think that's it,' he says, attaching a last bauble. 'Three pieces missing, but no one will notice.' He stands at the foot of the stepladder holding the heavy chandelier while I connect the two electrical wires to the ceiling rose, tighten the rose-cover and slip the ring-attachment over the dangling hook. He lets go tentatively – 'Gently does it' – unable to believe, since he has not done the fixing himself, that the chandelier will hold. It holds. We turn the light on, and the six candle-bulbs shimmer through the cage of glass, the prison of prisms. 'Let there be light,' my father says, the only time I can ever remember him quoting anything, though I can recall some joke he used to tell, about failed footlights at Turf Moor, a visiting Chinese football team, and the punch-line 'Many hands make light work'. We stand there gawping upwards for a moment, as if we had witnessed a miracle, or as if this were a grand ballroom, not a suburban dining-room, and the next dance, if we had the courage to take part in it, might be the beginning of a new life. Then he turns the switch off and it's dark again and he says, 'Excellent. What's the next job, then?'

AND WHEN DID YOU LAST SEE YOUR FATHER? 1993

OSCAR WILDE

WHEN FIRST I WAS PUT INTO PRISON some people advised me to try and forget who I was. It was ruinous advice. It is only by realizing what I am that I have found comfort of any kind. Now I am advised by others to try on my release to forget that I have ever been in a prison at all. I know that would be equally fatal. It would mean that I would always be haunted by an intolerable sense of disgrace, and that those things that are meant for me as much as for anybody else – the beauty of the sun and moon, the pageant of the seasons, the music of daybreak and the silence of great nights, the rain falling through the leaves, or the dew creeping over the grass and making it silver – would all be tainted for me, and lose their healing power and their power of communicating joy. To regret one's own experiences is to arrest one's own development. To deny one's own experiences is to put a lie into the lips of one's own life. It is no less than a denial of the soul.

For just as the body absorbs things of all kinds, things common and unclean no less than those that the priest or a vision has cleansed, and converts them into swiftness or strength, into the play of beautiful muscles and the moulding of fair flesh, into the curves and colours of the hair, the lips, the eye; so the soul in its turn has its nutritive functions also, and can transform into noble moods of thought and passions of high import what in itself is base, cruel and degrading; nay, more, may find in these its most august modes of assertion, and can often reveal itself most perfectly through what was intended to desecrate or destroy.

The fact of my having been the common prisoner of a common gaol I must frankly accept, and, curious as it may seem, one of the things I shall have to teach myself is not to be ashamed of it. I must accept it as a punishment, and if one is ashamed of having been punished, one might just as well never have been punished at all. Of course there are many things of which I was convicted that I had not done, but then there are many things of which I was convicted that I had done, and a still greater number of things in my life for which I was never indicted at all. And as the gods are strange, and punish us for what is good and humane in us as much as for what is evil and perverse, I must accept the fact that one is punished for the good as well as for the evil that one does. I have no doubt that it is quite right one should be. It helps one, or should help one, to realize both, and not to be too conceited about either. And if I then am not ashamed of my punishment, as I hope not to be, I shall be able to think, and walk, and live with freedom.

Many men on their release carry their prison about with them into the air, and hide it as a secret disgrace in their hearts, and at length, like poor poisoned things, creep into some hole and die. It is wretched that they should have to do so, and it is wrong, terribly wrong, of society that it should force them to do so. Society takes upon itself the right to inflict appalling punishment on the individual, but it also has the supreme vice of shallowness, and fails to realize what it has done. When the man's punishment is over, it leaves him to himself; that is to say, it abandons him at the very moment when its highest duty towards him begins. It is really ashamed of its own actions, and shuns those whom it has punished, as people shun a creditor whose debt they cannot pay, or one on whom they have inflicted an irreparable, an irredeemable wrong. I can claim on my side that if I realize what I have suffered, society should realize what it has inflicted on me; and that there should be no bitterness or hate on either side.

Of course I know that from one point of view things will be made different for me than for others; must indeed, by the very nature of the case, be made so. The poor thieves and outcasts who are imprisoned here with me are in many respects more fortunate than I am. The little way in grey city or green field that saw their sin is small; to find those who know nothing of what they have done they need go no further than a bird might fly between the twilight at dawn and the dawn itself: but for me the world is shrivelled to a hand's breadth, and everywhere I turn my name is written on the rocks in lead. For I have come, not from obscurity into the momentary notoriety of crime, but from a sort of eternity of fame to a sort of eternity of infamy, and sometimes seem to myself to have shown, if indeed it required showing, that between the famous and the infamous there is but one step, if as much as one.

Still, in the very fact that people will recognize me wherever I go, and know all about my life, as far as its follies go, I can discern something good for me. It will force on me the necessity of again asserting myself as an artist, and as soon as I possibly can. If I can produce only one beautiful work of art I shall be able to rob malice of its venom, and cowardice of its sneer, and to pluck out the tongue of scorn by the roots.

And if life be, as it surely is, a problem to me, I am no less a problem to life. People must adopt some attitude towards me, and so pass judgment both on themselves and me. I need not say I am not talking of particular individuals. The only people I would care to be with now are artists and people who have suffered: those who know what beauty is, and those who know what sorrow is: nobody else interests me. Nor am I making any demands on life. In all that I have said I am simply concerned with my own mental attitude towards life as a whole; and I feel that not to be ashamed of having been punished is one of the first points I must attain to, for the sake of my own perfection, and because I am so imperfect.

Then I must learn how to be happy.

DE PROFUNDIS, 1905

JOHN MORTIMER

THE CRACKS SPREAD ACROSS THE CEILING in our North London house like ever-widening rivers on a map, and the plaster powdered the stair-carpets. Step-daughters, who had been lurking with lovers in the shadowy upper stories, left home. In spite of the simplicities of the law I used to practise, there is no one cause you can write on the death certificate of a marriage; the patient is at the mercy of a multiplicity of sicknesses, and when two writers in one house are involved resistance may be seriously weakened. I knew how my clients felt at the end of a long and familiar life and their fear at the prospect of unaccustomed freedom. For a long time every effort is made to keep the true facts from the family. Meanwhile there is a constant and increasingly hopeless search for a cure.

At one period of history we might have put our affairs in the hands of priests or vicars. Nowadays the dissolution of marriage seems to be attended by grave and sympathetic chartered accountants. The affluent sixties brought, I'm sure, a great increase in the number of psychoanalysts. Such doctors, a red-faced Scot with a breezy commonsense manner, or a pale and uncommunicative Central European who sat by the gas fire in the house he never left, while his family listened uneasily to the opening of the front door and the tentative footstep on the stair, become the third parties in our lives. They were the rivals, granted the long private hours of self-examination, whose enigmatic advice could be repeated and, perhaps, improved upon. Bred to a scepticism which found the Book of Genesis, the Oedipus Complex and the Collective Unconscious merely myths of varying usefulness, I found my visits to these doctors puzzling. The breezy Scotsman, for instance, suggested that the situation might improve were I to take up golf. It seemed, at a time of advancing despair, an extreme but probably fruitless remedy.

I had, I suppose, reached that moment when well-settled people set out for a second visit to their youth. Mine was a place I had never seen before, having been too involved with children, 'undefendeds', overdrafts and getting on in the law. Gauguin gave up his bourgeois life and set sail for Tahiti. Many men, I imagine, travel the same route, and if their South Sea island is only the adolescence they never enjoyed, it is subject to the same disadvantages, heat, disease, disillusion, loneliness and the slow disintegration of life in the tropics. I suppose it's possible that Gauguin might have painted his pictures of the South Seas while still living with his Danish wife and during his spare time from the bank. Such considerations never dissuade anyone from attempting the journey, however much they may regret arriving at their destination.

These thoughts, confused and hardly understood, were half exhilarating and half paralysing to the will. It became an enormous effort to open letters, still more to do an 'undefended', and much time seemed to be spent in watching the cracks trace their slow way across the ceiling. Some sort of new start was clearly necessary, but I had no idea where to begin.

CLINGING TO THE WRECKAGE: A PART OF LIFE, 1982

MARCUS AURELIUS ANTONINUS

WILT THOU, THEN, MY SOUL, never be good and simple and one and naked, more manifest than the body which surrounds thee? Wilt thou never enjoy an affectionate and contented disposition? Wilt thou never be full and without a want of any kind, longing for nothing more, nor desiring anything, either animate or inanimate, for the enjoyment of pleasures? nor yet desiring time wherein thou shalt have longer enjoyment, or place, or pleasant climate, or society of men with whom thou mayest live in harmony? but wilt thou be satisfied with thy present condition, and pleased with all that is about thee, and wilt thou convince thyself that thou hast everything and that it comes from the gods, that everything is well for thee, and will be well whatever shall please them, and whatever they shall give for the conservation of the perfect living being, the good and just and beautiful, which generates and holds together all things, and contains and embraces all things which are dissolved for the production of other like things? Wilt thou never be such that thou shalt so dwell in community with gods and men as neither to find fault with them at all, nor to be condemned by them?

THE MEDITATIONS, 167

ANNIE BESANT

L OOKING BACK TODAY OVER MY LIFE, I see that its keynote – through all the blunders, and the blind mistakes, and clumsy follies – has been this longing for sacrifice to something felt as greater than the self. It has been so strong and so persistent that I recognize it now as a tendency brought over from a previous life and dominating the present one; and this is shown by the fact that to follow it is not the act of a deliberate and conscious will, forcing self into submission and giving up with pain something the heart desires, but the following it is a joyous springing forward along the easiest path, the 'sacrifice' being the supremely attractive thing, not to make which would be to deny the deepest longings of the soul, and to feel oneself polluted and dishonoured. And it is here that the misjudgment comes in of many generous hearts who have spoken sometimes lately so strongly in my praise. For the efforts to serve have not been painful acts of self-denial, but the yielding to an overmastering desire. We do not praise the mother who, impelled by her protecting love, feeds her crying infant and stills its wailings at her breast; rather should we blame her if she turned aside from its weeping to play with some toy. And so with all those whose ears are opened to the wailings of the great orphan

Humanity; they are less to be praised for helping than they would be to be blamed if they stood aside. I now know that it is those wailings that have stirred my heart through life, and that I brought with me the ears open to hear them from previous lives of service paid to men. It was those lives that drew for the child the alluring pictures of martyrdom, breathed into the girl the passion of devotion, sent the woman out to face scoff and odium, and drove her finally into the Theosophy that rationalizes sacrifice, while opening up possibilities of service beside which all other hopes grow pale.

ANNIE BESANT: AN AUTOBIOGRAPHY, 1893

EDWARD W. SAID

DURING THE LAST FEW MONTHS of my mother's life, she would tell me plaintively and frequently about the misery of trying to fall asleep. She was in Washington, I in New York; we would speak constantly, see each other about once a month. Her cancer was spreading, I knew. She refused to have chemotherapy: '*Ma biddee at adthab*,' she would say, 'I don't want the torture of it.' Years later I was to have four wasting years of it with no success, but she never buckled, never gave in even to her doctor's importunings, never had chemotherapy. But she could not sleep at night. Sedatives, sleeping pills, soothing drinks, the counsel of friends and relatives, reading, praying: none, she said, did any good. 'Help me to sleep, Edward,' she once said to me with a piteous trembling in her voice that I can still hear as I write. But then the disease spread into her brain, and for the last six weeks she slept all the time. Waiting by her bed for her to awaken, with my sister Grace, was for me the most anguished and paradoxical of my experiences with her.

Now I have divined that my own inability to sleep may be her last legacy to me, a counter to her struggle *for* sleep. For me sleep is something to be gotten over as quickly as possible. I can only go to bed very late, but I am up literally at dawn. Like her I don't possess the secret of long sleep, though unlike her I have reached the point where I do not want it. For me, sleep is death, as is any diminishment in awareness. During my last treatment – a twelve-week ordeal –

I was most upset by the drugs I was given to ward off fever and shaking chills, and manifestly upset by the induced somnolence, the sense of being infantilized, the helplessness that many years ago I had conceded as that of a child to my mother and, differently, to my father. I fought the medical soporifics bitterly, as if my identity depended on that resistance even to my doctor's advice.

Sleeplessness for me is a cherished state to be desired at almost any cost; there is nothing for me as invigorating as immediately shedding the shadowy half-consciousness of a night's loss, than the early morning, re-acquainting myself with or resuming what I might have lost completely a few hours earlier. I occasionally experience myself as a cluster of flowing currents. I prefer this to the idea of a solid self, the identity to which so many attach so much significance. These currents, like the themes of one's life, flow along during the waking hours, and at their best, they require no reconciling, no harmonizing. They are 'off' and may be out of place, but at least they are always in motion, in time, in place, in the form of all kinds of strange combinations moving about, not necessarily forward, sometimes against each other, contrapuntally yet without one central theme. A form of freedom, I'd like to think, even if I am far from being totally convinced that it is. That skepticism too is one of the themes I particularly want to hold on to. With so many dissonances in my life I have learned actually to prefer being not quite right and out of place.

OUT OF PLACE: A MEMOIR, 1999

MICHEL DE MONTAIGNE

I HAVE, AS TO THE REST, a strong and thickset body; a face, not fat, but full; a temperament between jovial and melancholy, moderately sanguine and hot,

> *Whence 'tis my thighs so rough and bristled are,*
> *And that my breast is so thick set with hair; [Martial]*

vigorous and lively health, rarely troubled by ailments until well on in years. Such I was, for I am not considering myself at this moment

when I am moving along the avenues of old age, having long since
passed forty:

> By small degrees old age breaks down their strength
> And their full vigor, and dissolves into decay. [Lucretius]

What I shall be from this time forward will be but a half being, it will
no longer be myself. I escape and steal away from myself every day,

> The parting years steal all things from us one by one. [Horace]

Dexterity and agility I have never had, and yet I am the son of a very
nimble father whose sprightliness lasted until his extreme old age. He
found hardly a man of his condition who was equal in bodily
exercises; just as I have found hardly any who have not excelled me,
except in running, at which I was fair. In music, either vocal, for which
my voice is very unfit, or instrumental, they could never teach me
anything. In dancing, tennis, or wrestling I have been able to acquire
only very slight and ordinary ability; in swimming, fencing, vaulting,
and jumping, none at all. My hands are so clumsy that I cannot even
write legibly enough for myself; so that I had rather do over what I
have scribbled than give myself the trouble to untangle it. And I do
not read much better. I feel that I weigh on my listeners. Otherwise, a
good scholar. I cannot properly fold up a letter, nor could I ever cut a
pen, nor carve at table worth a hang, nor saddle a horse, nor carry a
bird correctly and let it fly, nor talk to dogs, birds, or horses.

In fine, my bodily qualities agree very closely with those of my
soul. There is no sprightliness; there is only a full and firm vigor. I
hold out well under hard work, but it is only if I go voluntarily to it,
and as much as my desire guides me to it,

> Excitement gently lightening the irksome toil. [Horace]

Otherwise, if I am not allured with some pleasure, and I have a
different guide than my own pure free will, I am good for nothing.
For I have reached the point where, except for health and life, there
is nothing for which I would bite my nails and that I would purchase
at the price of torment of mind and constraint,

May all the sands of shady Tagus and the gold
It rolls into the sea be not that dear to me: [Juvenal]

extremely idle, extremely independent, both by nature and by art. I would as willingly lend a man my blood as my pains.

I have a soul all its own, accustomed to guide itself in its own fashion. Having hitherto never had either master or governor imposed upon me, I have gone as far as I pleased and at my own pace. This has made me soft and useless for the service of others and no use to anyone but myself. And for my sake there was no need of forcing this heavy, lazy, and do-nothing disposition. For having enjoyed from birth such a degree of fortune that I had reason to be contented with it, and as much sense as I felt I had occasion for, I have sought nothing, and I have also acquired nothing:

I am not wafted by the swelling gales
Of winds propitious, with expanded sails,
Nor do I guide my life 'mid adverse gales;
In strength, wit, beauty, virtue, place, and wealth,
I'm last among the first, and first among the last. [Horace]

I have had need only of sufficiency to content myself, which, nevertheless, is a well-ordered state of mind, to take it right, equally difficult in every sort of human lot, and that we see by experience even more easily found in want than in abundance; perhaps because, as with our other passions, the hunger for riches is sharpened more by their use than by the lack of them, and because the virtue of moderation is more rare than that of patience. And I have never had need of anything but pleasantly to enjoy the good things that God in His bounty had put into my hands. I have never tasted of any kind of tedious work. I have had hardly anything to handle except my own affairs; or, if I have, it has been on condition of handling them at my own times and in my own way, committed to my trust by people who trusted me, who knew me, and who did not press me. For experts get some service out of even a restive and broken-winded horse.

Even my childhood was guided in a free and gentle manner and exempt from any rigorous subjection. All this has shaped in me a delicate disposition, incapable of enduring cares; to such a degree that I like to have my losses and the disorders that concern me concealed from me. I put down to the account of my expenses what it costs me to nourish and maintain my nonchalance,

> *Those things of course, superfluous, which pass*
> *The master unperceived and profit thieves. [Horace]*

I prefer not to know the count of what I have in order to feel my loss less exactly. I entreat those who live with me, when they lack affection for me and honest dealing, to deceive me and pay me with decent appearances. For want of firmness enough to support the annoyance of the adverse accidents to which we are subject, and from being unable to keep up the strain of regulating and managing my affairs, I foster all I can in myself this idea, while abandoning myself to fortune, of expecting the worst in all things and resolving to bear that worst mildly and patiently. It is for that alone that I labor, and it is the goal to which I direct all my meditation.

In a danger I do not so much consider how I shall escape it as of how little importance it is whether I escape it. Even if I should be left on the spot, what would it matter? Not being able to govern events, I govern myself, and I adapt myself to them if they do not adapt themselves to me. I have hardly enough skill to be able to evade Fortune and to escape from her or to force her, and by prudence to direct and conduct things to my own purpose. I have still less patience to stand the harsh and painful care that it requires. And the most painful situation for me is to be in suspense about urgent matters and to be agitated between hope and fear. Deliberation, even in things of lightest moment, is very troublesome to me; and I find my mind more put to it to stand the varied agitation and shocks of doubt and deliberation than to settle down and acquiesce to any course whatever after the die is thrown. Few passions have troubled my sleep, but as for deliberations, the slightest one troubles it. Just as in roads I preferably avoid the sloping and slippery sides and take to the beaten track, however muddy and boggy, where I can fall no lower, and there seek my safety; so do I like pure misfortunes which do not torment and harass me any more, after the uncertainty about setting them right has passed, and which at the first leap plunge me directly into suffering:

Uncertain ills torment us most. [Seneca]

When actions are taking place, I carry myself like a man; in their conduct, like a child. The fear of the fall gives me a greater fever than the fall. The game is not worth the candle. The covetous man suffers more from his passion than the poor man, and the jealous man [more] than the cuckold. And often there is less harm in losing your vineyard than in going to law about it. The lowest step is the firmest. It is the seat of constancy. There you have need only of yourself. It is there founded and leans wholly upon itself.

'OF PRESUMPTION', 1580

INGMAR BERGMAN

DURING THE 1960s, Charlie Chaplin was on a visit to Stockholm to publicize his recent autobiography. Lasse Bergström, his publisher, asked me if I would like to meet the great man at the Grand Hotel, and indeed I would. One morning at ten o'clock, we knocked on the door, and it was immediately opened by Chaplin himself, impeccably dressed in a dark well-tailored suit, the Legion of Honour's little button in his lapel. That hoarse multi-toned voice politely welcomed us, and his wife, Oona, and two young daughters, as lovely as gazelles, came out of an inner room.

We at once started talking about his book. I asked him when he had found out for the first time that he caused laughter, that people laughed at him in particular. He nodded eagerly and willingly told me.

He had been employed by Keystone in a group of artists who went under the name of the Keystone Kops. They did hazardous numbers before a static camera, like a variety show on a stage. One day they were told to chase a huge bearded villain who was made-up white. It was, you might say, a routine assignment.

After a great deal of running and falling about, by the afternoon they had managed to catch the villain and he was seated on the ground surrounded by policemen hitting him on the head with their truncheons. Chaplin had the idea of not banging repeatedly with his truncheon as he had been told. Instead he made sure he was in a visible place in the circle. There he spent a long time carefully aiming his truncheon. He started on the penultimate blow several times, but always stopped at the last moment. When, gradually and after careful preparation, he let the blow fall, he missed and fell over. The film was shown at a Nickelodeon. He went to see the result.

The movie audience, seeing the blow miss its target, laughed for the first time at Charlie Chaplin.

THE MAGIC LANTERN, 1987

TRUMAN CAPOTE

Q: SUPPOSE YOU WERE DROWNING. What images, in the classic tradition, do you envision rolling across you mind?

A: A hot Alabama day in, oh, 1932, so I must be eight, and I am in a vegetable garden humming with bees and heat waves, and I am picking and putting into a basket turnips and slushy scarlet tomatoes. Then I am running through pine and honeysuckle woods toward a deep cool creek, where I bathe and wash the turnips, the tomatoes. Birds, bird-music, leaf-light, the stringent taste of raw turnip on my tongue: pleasures everlasting, hallelujah. Not far away a snake, a cotton-mouth moccasin, writhes, ripples across the water; I'm not afraid of it.

Ten years later. New York. A wartime jazz joint on West 52nd Street. The Famous Door. Featuring my most beloved American singer – then, now, forever: Miss Billie Holiday. *Lady Day*. Billie, an orchid in her hair, her drug-dimmed eyes shifting in the cheap lavender light, her mouth twisting out the words: 'Good mornin', Heartache – you're here again to stay –'

June, 1947. Paris. Having a *fine l'eau* at a sidewalk café with Albert Camus, who tells me I must learn to be less sensitive to criticism. (Ah!

If he could have lived to see me now.)

Standing at the window of a *pension* on a Mediterranean island watching the afternoon passenger boat arrive from the mainland. Suddenly, there on the wharf carrying a suitcase is someone I know. Very well. Someone who had said goodbye to me, in what I took to be final tones, not many days prior. Someone who had apparently had a change of mind. So: is it the real turtle soup? – or only the mock? Or is it at long last love? (It was.)

A young man with black cowlicked hair. He is wearing a leather harness that keeps his arms strapped to his sides. He is trembling; but he is speaking to me, smiling. All I can hear is the roar of blood in my ears. Twenty minutes later he is dead, hanging from the end of a rope.

Two years later. Driving down from the April snows of the Alps into the valleys of an Italian spring.

Visiting, at Père Lachaise in Paris, the grave of Oscar Wilde – overshadowed by Epstein's rather awkward rendition of an angel; I don't think Oscar would have cared for it much.

Paris, January, 1966. The Ritz. An unusual friend comes to call, bringing as gifts masses of white lilac and a baby owl in a cage. The owl, it seems, must be fed live mice. A waiter at the Ritz very kindly sent it to live with his farm-family in Provence.

Oh, but now the mental slides are moving very fast. The waves are closing over. Picking apples on an autumn afternoon. Nursing to life a bulldog puppy ill-to-death with distemper. And she lives. A garden in the California desert. The surf-sound of wind in the palm trees. A face, close by. Is it the Taj Mahal I see? Or merely Asbury Park? Or is it at long last love? (It wasn't – God no, was it ever not.)

Suddenly, everything is again spinning backward; my friend Miss Faulk is making a scrap-quilt, the design is of roses and grapes, and now she is drawing the quilt up to my chin. There is a kerosene lamp by the bed; she wishes me happy birthday, and blows out the light.

And at midnight when the church-bell chimes I'm eight.

Once more, the creek. The taste of raw turnip on my tongue, the flow of summer water embracing my nakedness. And there, *just* there, swiveling, tangoing on the sun-dappled surface, the exquisitely limber and lethal cotton-mouth moccasin. But I'm not afraid; am I?

'SELF-PORTRAIT', 1972

LEO TOLSTOY

M Y LIFE HAD COME TO A SUDDEN STOP. I was able to breathe, to eat, to drink, to sleep. I could not, indeed, help doing so; but there was no real life in me. I had not a single wish to strive for the fulfilment of what I could feel to be reasonable. If I wished for anything, I knew beforehand that, were I to satisfy the wish, nothing would come of it; I should still be dissatisfied. Had a fairy appeared and offered me all I desired, I should not have known what to say. If I seemed to have, at a given moment of excitement, not a wish, but a mood resulting from the tendencies of former wishes, at a calmer moment I knew that it was a delusion, that I really wished for nothing. I could not even wish to know the truth, because I guessed what the truth was.

The truth lay in this – that life had no meaning for me. Every day of life, every step in it, brought me nearer the edge of a precipice, whence I saw clearly the final ruin before me. To stop, to go back, were alike impossible; nor could I shut my eyes so as not to see the suffering that alone awaited me, the death of all in me, even to annihilation. Thus I, a healthy and happy man, was brought to feel that I could live no longer, that an irresistible force was dragging me down into the grave. I do not mean that I had an intention of committing suicide. The force that drew me away from life was stronger, fuller, and concerned with far wider consequences than any mere wish; it was a force like that of my previous attachment to life, only in a contrary direction. The idea of suicide came as naturally to me as formerly that of bettering my life. It had so much attraction for me that I was compelled to practise a species of self-deception, in order to avoid carrying it out too hastily. I was unwilling to act hastily, only because I had determined first to clear away the confusion of my thoughts, and, that once done, I could always kill myself. I was happy, yet I hid away a cord, to avoid being tempted to hang myself by it to one of the pegs between the cupboards of my study, where I undressed alone every evening, and ceased carrying a gun because it offered me too easy a way of getting rid of life. I knew not what I wanted; I was afraid of life; I shrank from it, and yet there *was* something I hoped far from it.

Such was the condition I had come to, at a time when all the circumstances of my life were pre-eminently happy ones, and when I had not reached my fiftieth year. I had a good, a loving, and a well-beloved wife, good children, a fine estate, which, without much trouble on my part, continually increased in my income; I was more than ever respected by my friends and aquaintances; I was praised by strangers, and could lay claim to having made my name famous without much self-deception. Moreover, my mind was neither deranged nor weakened; on the contrary, I enjoyed a mental and physical strength which I have seldom found in men of my class and pursuits; I could keep up with a peasant in mowing, and could continue mental labour for ten hours at a stretch, without any evil consequences.

The mental state in which I then was seemed to me summed up in the following: my life was a foolish and wicked joke played upon me by I knew not whom.

'MY CONFESSION', 1884

STENDHAL

WHAT KIND OF MAN AM I? Do I have good sense? Do I have good sense with great depth?

Do I have remarkable wit? In truth, I have absolutely no idea. With everything that happens to me from day to day, I rarely think about these fundamental questions, and so my judgments change like my mood. My judgments are only throwaway remarks.

Let us see if – in conducting my examination of my conscience, my pen in my hand – I will arrive at something *positive* that holds *true for a long time* for me. What will I think about what I decide to write when I re-read it in 1835, if I live? Will it be the same as with my published works? I have a deep sense of sadness when, for want of another book, I re-read them.

For the month that I have been thinking about it, I feel a real repugnance towards writing only on the subject of myself – the number of my shirts, the buffeting of my self-esteem. What's more, I am a long way from France; I have read every book that has reached this country [Italy]. The whole inclination of my heart was to write a fictional book about a love affair which took place in Dresden in August 1813, in a house next door to mine, but the minor duties of my job interrupt me fairly often, or, more accurately, I can never be certain, when taking up pen and paper, of spending an hour without being interrupted. This little inconvenience completely dampens my imagination. When I pick up my fiction, I am disgusted by what I was thinking. To which a wise man will reply that one has to overcome one's self. I will reply: it is too late, I am forty something years old; after so many adventures it is time to dream of rounding off my life, as best I can.

My principal objection to doing this was not the vanity that there is writing about one's life. A book on such a subject is like any other; you forget it quickly, if it is boring. I was concerned about deflowering those happy moments I have encountered, by describing them, by anatomizing them. This is what I will not do; I will pass over the happy times.

The poetic genius is dead, but the genius of suspicion has arrived in the world. I am profoundly convinced that the only antidote that will allow the reader to forget the author's eternal *I*'s, is a perfect sincerity.

Will I have the courage to relate humiliating aspects without endlessly excusing them in prefaces? I hope so.

MEMOIRS OF AN EGOTIST, 1892

DIRK BOGARDE

AND THEN, QUITE SUDDENLY, as happens in this oddest of climates, it was spring. Almost overnight the whole area was clothed in tender green and starred about with a million wild anemones: hazed here and there with long drifts of grape hyacinths and violets, and a willow which I had planted by the pond hung golden in the still air; broom and bramble were in bud, and I bought a small plastic bag of goldfish from the local Monoprix and set them free to swim among my Salvator Rosa rocks, and awoke one brilliant morning to find that I had reached my half-century.

I was fifty.

I was not particularly surprised by this event: after all I had been expecting it for a number of years. Now that the moment had arrived it didn't seem to me that any fearful metamorphosis had taken place overnight. My hair had not instantly gone white: I was still able to hold my razor unassisted, the lines and bags scattered about my face had been with me for some time now, and were familiar: and even though the face which peered back at me from the steam-misted mirror was, without any doubt, that of a middle-aged man, the innermost heart, I knew, was still unnervingly that of a mildly retarded sixteen-year-old.

So much for being fifty.

Forwood called up from the terrace. 'Marie says it's mince, sprouts and mashed for lunch. Or would you rather go out somewhere? You won't be fifty again.'

So to the Colombe d'Or, lunch in the sun under the budding fig tree with Vivienne and Paddy Glenavy (Patrick Campbell), the former a very old friend from the early Ealing Studios days and now happily re-discovered as a close neighbour, Simone Signoret and Yves Montand and, later, James Baldwin, who very sensibly suggested champagne for such a rare occasion.

A perfectly balanced table, a perfectly pleasant way of easing into one's second half. No standards had been lowered.

An Orderly Man, 1983

QUENTIN CRISP

I AM NOT A DROP-OUT; I was never in.

I have not spent my life hacking my way through the constraints of a bourgeois existence. I was always free – appallingly free.

For my first fifty years I was like someone standing alone in a landscape which led to infinite possibilities in all directions but in which there was an arena surrounded by an insurmountable wall. Over this floated shouts and cheers provoked by an Olympiad from which I keenly felt my exclusion both as spectator and player. In England this perpetual tournament has no name; Americans call it 'the big time'.

These games are incapable of sharper definition than this because their rules are rearranged by each person who goes on to the field and the rewards of victory are not entirely measurable – not wholly of this world.

If you beat your head against this high wall or, indeed, against any wall, after a while it will crumble but such a course of action requires at least a positive temperament. This, if I ever had it, I lost in childhood. At a time when my two brothers aspired to be splendid icons of manliness such as firemen or ships' captains, all I wanted was to be a chronic invalid. For this vocation I had a certain flair. Unfortunately my parents decided that, as a career, it would prove too expensive. Now I could obtain a grant but then I was forced to strike out of my heart all hope of becoming a kinky Mrs Browning. Even so, nothing that has happened to me since that unhappy time has been the result of healthy, vigorous action on my part. I have always proceeded cautiously. However, even if you only lean limply against a wall and you happen to live a very long time, gradually it will begin to give way.

HOW TO BECOME A VIRGIN, 1981

GEORGE SAND

IT IS QUITE NATURAL THAT, having lived for half a century, a person should see herself deprived of a number of those she has held close to her heart; but we are living through an age in which violent, moral shocks have jolted us all and left every family in mourning. For the past few years in particular, revolutions, which spark dreadful days of civil war, which weaken vested interests and rouse passions, which seem fatally to call down great epidemics after the crises of anger and suffering, after the proscriptions of some, the tears or terror of others, revolutions which bring forth great wars, and which, as they follow one another, destroy the souls of some and harvest the lives of others, have driven one half of France into mourning for the other.

For my part, it is no longer by the dozens but by the hundreds that I count the bitter losses I have experienced these past years. My heart is a cemetery, and if I do not feel myself dragged into the tomb that has engulfed half my life, in a sort of contagious vertigo, it is because the other life is peopled for me with so many loved ones that it is confused at times with my present life, to the point where it becomes an illusion. This illusion is not without a certain austere charm, and my thoughts now converse as often with the dead as with the living.

STORY OF MY LIFE, 1854–1855

ANDREW CARNEGIE

THE YEAR 1886 ENDED IN DEEP GLOOM for me. My life as a happy careless young man, with every want looked after, was over. I was left alone in the world. My mother and brother passed away in November, within a few days of each other, while I lay in bed under a severe attack of typhoid fever, unable to move and, perhaps fortunately, unable to feel the full weight of the catastrophe, being myself face to face with death.

I was the first stricken, upon returning from a visit in the East to our cottage at Cresson Springs on top of the Alleghanies where my mother and I spent our happy summers. I had been quite unwell for a day or two before leaving New York. A physician being summoned, my trouble was pronounced typhoid fever. Professor Dennis was called from New York and he corroborated the diagnosis. An attendant physician and trained nurse were provided at once. Soon after my mother broke down and my brother in Pittsburgh also was reported ill.

I was despaired of, I was so low, and then my whole nature seemed to change. I became reconciled, indulged in pleasing meditations, was without the slightest pain. My mother's and brother's serious condition had not been revealed to me, and when I was informed that both had left me forever it seemed only natural that I should follow them. We had never been separated; why should we be now? But it was decreed otherwise.

I recovered slowly and the future began to occupy my thoughts. There was only one ray of hope and comfort in it. Toward that my thoughts always turned. For several years I had known Miss Louise Whitfield. Her mother permitted her to ride with me in the Central

Park. We were both very fond of riding. Other young ladies were on my list. I had fine horses and often rode in the park and around New York with one or the other of the circle. In the end the others all faded into ordinary beings. Miss Whitfield remained alone as the perfect one beyond any I had met. Finally I began to find and admit to myself that she stood the supreme test I had applied to several fair ones in my time. She alone did so of all I had ever known ...

My advances met with indifferent success. She was not without other and younger admirers. My wealth and future plans were against me. I was rich and had everything and she felt she could be of little use or benefit to me. Her ideal was to be the real helpmeet of a young, struggling man to whom she could and would be indispensable, as her mother had been to her father. The care of her own family had largely fallen upon her after her father's death when she was twenty-one. She was now twenty-eight; her views of life were formed. At times she seemed more favorable and we corresponded. Once, however, she returned my letters saying she felt she must put aside all thought of accepting me.

Professor and Mrs Dennis took me from Cresson to their own home in New York, as soon as I could be removed, and I lay there some time under the former's personal supervision. Miss Whitfield called to see me, for I had written her the first words from Cresson I was able to write. She saw now that I needed her. I was left alone in the world. Now she could be in every sense the 'helpmeet'. Both her heart and head were now willing and the day was fixed. We were married in New York, April 22,1887, and sailed for our honeymoon which was passed on the Isle of Wight.

THE AUTOBIOGRAPHY OF ANDREW CARNEGIE, 1920

EDWARD GIBBON

WHEN I CONTEMPLATE the common lot of mortality, I must acknowledge that I have drawn a high prize in the lottery of life. The far greater part of the globe is overspread with barbarism or slavery: in the civilized world, the most numerous class is condemned to ignorance and poverty; and the double fortune of my birth in a free and enlightened country, in an honourable and wealthy family, is the lucky chance of an unit against millions. The general probability is about three to one, that a new-born infant will not live to complete his fiftieth year. I have now passed that age, and may fairly estimate the present value of my existence in the three-fold division of mind, body and estate.

1. The first and indispensable requisite of happiness is a clear conscience, unsullied by the reproach or remembrance of an unworthy action ... I am endowed with a cheerful temper, a moderate sensibility, and a natural disposition to repose rather than to activity: some mischievous appetites and habits have perhaps been corrected by philosophy or time. The love of study, a passion which derives fresh vigour from enjoyment, supplies each day, each hour, with a perpetual source of independent and rational pleasure; and I am not sensible of any decay of the mental faculties. The original soil has been highly improved by cultivation; but it may be questioned, whether some flowers of fancy, some grateful errors, have not been eradicated with the weeds of prejudice. 2. Since I have escaped from the long perils of my childhood, the serious advice of a physician has seldom been requisite. 'The madness of superfluous health' I have never known, but my tender constitution has been fortified by time, and the inestimable gift of the sound and peaceful slumbers of infancy may be imputed both to the mind and body. 3. I have already described the merits of my society and situation; but these enjoyments would be tasteless or bitter if their possession was not assured by an annual and adequate supply. According to the scale of Switzerland, I am a rich man; and I am indeed rich, since my income is superior to my expense, and my expense is equal to my wishes.

MEMOIRS OF MY LIFE AND WRITINGS, 1796

SPALDING GRAY

WHAT WOULD AN AVERAGE DAY be like back then? Oh, I'd wake up, usually after seven hours' sleep, 7:30, 8:00. Then I take my morning pee, and as I am peeing, I hear that little old voice in my head, every morning, say, 'Remember, you are going to die.'

Imagine, I forgot that for seven hours. This usually causes an erection and I have very anxious sex with Ramona to try work off the anxiety of death, and then after lying there in a stupefied heap of *petite morte*, I talk about my dreams, or maybe get out the *Mayo Clinic Family Health Book* to see if I have any symptoms of disease. I mean, there are 2,740 diseases in that book, how could I not have one? Then I do my yoga stretches, have some breakfast, some coffee, write in my journal. But what would I write? Maybe something like I'm telling you now. Then I'd go to my little bookshelf and take out a book for morning reading, maybe *Becker's The Denial of Death*, underlined profusely in red, and read:

> *The irony of man's condition is that the deepest need is to be free of the anxiety of death and annihilation – but it is life itself that awakens this anxiety, and so we shrink from being fully alive.*

Closing the book, I go out for a walk in New York City to try to be fully alive. I'm not interested in buying anything anymore, I don't look in shop windows, I'm tired of the architecture, I'm searching for a park. I don't want to go up to Central Park because I don't want to ride on the subway, I want to walk to a park. So I walk to Washington Square Park. Basically a dysfunctional fountain with broken benches around it. And I walk around that fountain, obsessing on what I could do to feel more fully alive. Well, okay, so I'm obsessing on where I could go to turn right on skis, thinking about Kathie, a woman I had met on the road who had moved to New York and had sent me her phone number. Should I call her, should I 'touch base' with her? Drop in for some tea? And I'm dwelling on the fact that I'm going to turn fifty-two years old, and I'm thinking about Mom, and how she committed suicide at fifty-two, and did that mean I was gonna do it, too?

Around that dysfunctional fountain I go, peeling the onion of my mind, running into the same Jamaican drug dealers each time around, trying to sell me the same drugs each time, not recognizing I'm the same person. Saying, 'Hey, man, what's happening?'

'Hey, good question, what *is* happening?' I reply.

IT'S A SLIPPERY SLOPE, 1997

SIMONE DE BEAUVOIR

O LD AGE. From a distance you take it to be an institution; but they are all young, these people who suddenly find that they are old. One day I said to myself: 'I'm forty!' By the time I recovered from the shock of that discovery I had reached fifty. The stupor that seized me then has not left me yet.

I can't get around to believing it. When I read in print Simone de Beauvoir, it is a young woman they are telling me about, and who happens to be me. Often in my sleep I dream that in a dream I'm fifty-four, I wake and find I'm only thirty. 'What a terrible nightmare I had!' says the young woman who thinks she's awake. Sometimes, too, just before I come back to reality, a giant beast settles on my breast: 'It's true! It's my nightmare of being more than fifty that's come true!' How is it that time, which has no form or substance, can crush me with so huge a weight that I can no longer breathe? How can something that doesn't exist, the future, so implacably calculate its course? My seventy-second birthday is now as close as the Liberation Day that happened yesterday.

FORCE OF CIRCUMSTANCE, 1963

MICHEL DE MONTAIGNE

G OD IS MERCIFUL TO THOSE WHOSE LIFE he withdraws bit by bit; that is the only benefit of old age. The last death will be so much the less complete and painful; by then it will kill only a half or quarter of a man. Here is a tooth that has just fallen out, without pain, without effort; that was the natural term of its duration. Both that part of my being and several others are already dead, others half dead, even among the most active, which held the highest rank in the prime of my life. Thus do I melt and steal away from myself. What folly it would be on the part of my understanding to feel the last plunge of this fall, already so far advanced, just as if it were the whole way! I hope I shall not.

In truth, I gain one principal consolation in meditating on my death, that it will be normal and natural, and that henceforth I cannot in this matter seek or hope for any but illegitimate favor from destiny. Men delude themselves into believing that in former times their lives, like their stature, had a bigger span. But Solon, who belongs to those old times, nevertheless limits the extreme duration of life to threescore and ten years. Shall I, who in every way have worshipped so much that *golden mean* of ancient times and have taken the moderate measure for the most perfect, aspire to an immoderate and prodigious old age? Whatever happens contrary to the course of Nature may be troublesome, but what happens according to her should always be pleasant.

All things that happen according to nature should be accounted good. [Cicero]

Thus, says Plato, the death which is occasioned by wounds or maladies may be called violent, but that which takes us by surprise while old age is leading us to it is the easiest of all and in a way delightful.

Young men have their lives taken away by violence, old men by ripeness. [Cicero]

Death mingles and blends with our life throughout. Decline anticipates death's hour and makes its way even into the course of our growth. I have portraits of myself at twenty-five and thirty-five years of age; I compare them with one of the present: how many times over it is no longer myself. How much more remote is my present picture from those than from that of my death! It is too much of an abuse of Nature to fret her so far that she is constrained to leave us and abandon our guidance – our eyes, our teeth, our legs, and the rest – to the mercy of foreign assistance begged by us, and to resign us to the hands of art, weary of following us.

I am not excessively fond of either salads or fruits, except melons. My father hated all sorts of sauces; I love them all. Eating

too much troubles me, but I have as yet no really certain
knowledge that any kind of food disagrees with me because of its
nature; even as I do not distinguish a full or waning moon, or
spring from autumn. There are changes going on in us, irregular
and unknown. For radishes, for example, I first found agreed
with me, then later disagreed, now they agree again. In several
things I feel my stomach and appetite keep on varying that way:
I have changed back from white wine to claret, and then from
claret to white. I am a great lover of fish, and the lean days
become my fat days, and the fast days my feasts. I believe what
some people say, that it is easier to digest than meat. As it is
contrary to my conscience to eat meat on fish days, so it is
contrary to my taste to mix fish and meat; the difference between
them seems to me too great.

Ever since my youth I have at times omitted a meal, either to
sharpen my appetite for the next day, for, as Epicurus used to fast
and to make lean meals in order to accustom his appetite to do
without abundance, I do it, on the contrary, to train my appetite
to take better advantage and make more cheerful use of
abundance; or I fasted to conserve my vigor for the benefit of
some action of body or mind; for both of these become cruelly
sluggish in me through repletion, and I hate above all things the
stupid coupling of so healthy and sprightly a goddess with that
little, unruly, belching god, all bloated with the fumes of his
liquor; or to cure my sick stomach; or for want of fit company, for
I say, like that same Epicurus, that we should not so much
consider what we eat as with whom we eat, and I commend Chilo
because he would not promise to be at Periander's feast till he
was informed who were the other guests. There is no preparation
so sweet to me, nor sauce so appetizing as that which is derived
from society.

I think it healthier to eat more leisurely and less, and to eat
oftener. But I want to make the most of appetite and hunger. I
should take no pleasure in dragging out three or four wretched
meals a day, restricted in the manner of a doctor's regimen. Who
would assure me that I would find again at supper the gaping
appetite that I had in the morning? Let us take – especially the old
men – let us take the first opportune time that comes our way. Let

us leave daily schedules to almanac-makers and doctors.

The greatest benefit that I get from good health is sensual pleasure; let us take hold of the first that is present and known.

'*Of Experience*', 1588

HARRIET MARTINEAU

I AM, IN TRUTH, VERY THANKFUL for not having married at all. I have never since been tempted, nor have suffered any thing at all in relation to that matter which is held to be all-important to woman – love and marriage. Nothing, I mean, beyond occasional annoyance, presently disposed of. Every literary woman, no doubt, has plenty of importunity of that sort to deal with; but freedom of mind and coolness of manner dispose of it very easily: and since the time I have been speaking of, my mind has been wholly free from all idea of love affairs. My subsequent literary life in London was clear from all difficulty and embarrassment – no doubt because I was evidently too busy, and too full of interests of other kinds to feel any awkwardness ... I can easily conceive how I might have been tempted – how some deep springs in my nature might have been touched, then as earlier; but, as a matter of fact, they never were; and I consider the immunity a great blessing, under the liabilities of a moral condition such as mine was in the olden time. If I had had a husband dependent on me for his happiness, the responsibility would have made me wretched. I had not faith enough in myself to endure avoidable responsibility. If my husband had *not* depended on me for his happiness, I should have been jealous. So also with children. The care would have so overpowered the joy – the love would have so exceeded the ordinary chances of life – the fear on my part would have so impaired the freedom on theirs, that I rejoice not to have been involved in a relation for which I was, or believed myself, unfit. The veneration in which I hold domestic life has always shown me that that life was not for those whose self-respect had been early broken down, or had never grown. Happily, the majority are free from this disability. Those who suffer under it had better be as I – as my observation of married, as well as single life assures me. When I see what conjugal love is, in the extremely rare cases in which it is seen in its perfection, I feel that there is a power of attachment in me that has never been touched. When I am among little children, it frightens me to think what my idolatry of my own children would have been. But, through it all, I have ever been thankful to be alone. My strong will, combined with anxiety of conscience, makes me fit only to live alone; and my taste and liking are for living alone. The older I have grown, the more serious and irremediable have seemed to me the evils and disadvantages of married life, as it exists among us at this time: and I am provided with what it is the bane of single life in ordinary cases to want – substantial, laborious and serious occupation. My business in life has been to think and learn, and to speak out with absolute freedom what I have thought and learned. The freedom is itself a positive and never-failing enjoyment to me, after the bondage of my early life. My work and I have been fitted to each other, as is proved by the success of my work and my own happiness in it. The simplicity and independence of this vocation first suited my infirm and ill-developed nature, and then sufficed for my needs, together with family ties and domestic duties, such as I have been blessed with, and as every woman's heart requires. Thus, I am not only entirely satisfied with my lot, but think it the very best for me – under my constitution and circumstances: and I long ago came to the conclusion that, without meddling with the case of the wives and mothers, I am probably the happiest single woman in England.

HARRIET MARTINEAU'S AUTOBIOGRAPHY, 1877

BENVENUTO CELLINI

ALL MEN OF EVERY SORT, who have done something that is virtuous, or something so truly that it could have been done by the Virtues themselves, should, if they are truthful and good, describe their own life in their own hand; however, they should not begin such a fine undertaking before they have passed the age of forty. Now that I journey on past my fifty-eighth year, such a thing has happened to me, and being in my native Florence, I remember the many adversities that have happened to me, as happen to anyone who lives; but being freer from adversities than I have ever been up to this point, it seems to me that I am happier in spirit and healthier in body than I ever was before; and recalling the few pleasant good things and the inestimable bad things, which, looking back at them, shock me completely that I have reached this age of fifty-eight years old, and, through the grace of God, so happily journey on through life.

MY LIFE, 1558–1562

VLADIMIR NABOKOV

I WAS GROSSLY LATE for my last public lecture at Cornell: it had been difficult to park the car because of the interest in a controversial novel; my wife and I had been cruising around and around in the hope that somebody would leave, until we realized that all available space near the lecture-hall would remain occupied until the performance, my performance, was over. Finally we had to seek out a rather remote spot, and started at a brisk walk, almost a run, for the lighted building.

People were waiting there – everyone had come, except a last runner; for on the way we were suddenly overtaken by a lone Japanese who sprinted past us at a pace far surpassing anything we could attain. There was something uncanny about his solitary velocity and streamlined shape as he made for the porch and dashed up the steps and plunged into a crowded place which existed for him at the moment only insofar as it included the lecturer. But the lecturer was still outside, almost paralysed by the weird feeling that a ghost must feel when debarred from the events of his relivable past.

FROM THE NOTES FOR A SECOND VOLUME OF SPEAK, MEMORY: SPEAK ON, MEMORY, 1968–1971

~TOWARDS THE END ~

AGES 60–100

'An autobiography is an obituary
in serial form with the last
instalment missing.'

QUENTIN CRISP,
THE NAKED CIVIL SERVANT, 1968

KAMO NO CHŌMEI

NOW THAT I HAVE REACHED THE AGE of sixty, and my life seems about to evaporate like the dew, I have fashioned a lodging for the last leaves of my years. It is a hut where, perhaps, a traveler might spend a single night; it is like the cocoon spun by an aged silkworm. This hut is not even a hundredth the size of the cottage where I spent my middle years.

Before I was aware, I had become heavy with years, and with each remove my dwelling grew smaller. The present hut is of no ordinary appearance. It is a bare ten feet square and less than seven feet high. I did not choose this particular spot rather than another ... I laid a foundation and roughly thatched a roof. I fastened hinges to the joints of the beams, the easier to move elsewhere should anything displease me. What difficulty would there be in changing my dwelling? A bare two carts would suffice to carry off the whole house, and except for the carter's fee there would be no expenses at all.

Since first I hid my traces here in the heart of Mount Hino, I have added a lean-to on the south and a porch of bamboo ... Above the sliding door that faces north I have built a little shelf on which I keep three or four black leather baskets that contain books of poetry and music and extracts from the sacred writings ...

Along the east wall I have spread long fern fronds and mats of straw which serve as my bed for the night. I have cut open a window in the eastern wall, and beneath it have made a desk. Near my pillow is a square brazier in which I burn brushwood. To the north of the hut I have staked out a small plot of land which I have enclosed with a rough fence and made into a garden. I grow many species of herbs there.

This is what my temporary hut is like. I shall now attempt to describe its surroundings. To the south there is a bamboo pipe which empties water into the rock pool I have laid. The woods come close to my house, and it is thus a simple matter for me to gather brushwood. The mountain is named Toyama. Creeping vines block the trails and the valleys are overgrown, but to the west is a clearing, and my surroundings thus do not leave me without spiritual comfort. In the spring I see waves of wisteria like purple clouds, bright in the west. In the summer I hear the cuckoo call, promising to guide me on the road of death. In the autumn the voice of the evening insects fills my ears with a sound of lamentation for this cracked husk of a world. In winter I look with deep emotion on the snow, piling up and melting away like sins and hindrances to salvation ...

At the foot of this mountain is a rough-hewn cottage where the guardian of the mountain lives. He has a son who sometimes comes to visit me. When I am bored with whatever I am doing, I often go for a walk with him as my companion. He is sixteen and I sixty: though our ages greatly differ we take pleasure in each other's company.

Sometimes I pick flowering reeds or the wild pear, or fill my basket with berries and cress. Sometimes I go to the rice fields at the foot of the mountain and weave wreaths of the fallen ears. Or, when the weather is fine, I climb the peak and look out toward Kyoto, my old home, far, far away. The view has no owner and nothing can interfere with my enjoyment ...

If the evening is still, in the moonlight that fills the window I long for old friends or wet my sleeve with tears at the cries of the monkeys. Fireflies in the grass thickets might be mistaken for fishing-lights off the island of Maki; the dawn rains sound like autumn storms blowing through the leaves. And when I hear the pheasants' cries, I wonder if they call their father or their mother; when the wild deer of the mountain approach me unafraid, I realize how far I am from the world. And when sometimes, as is the wont of old age, I waken in the middle of the night, I stir up the buried embers and make them companions in solitude.

'AN ACCOUNT OF MY HUT', 1212

GERTRUDE STEIN

BEFORE ONE IS SUCCESSFUL that is before any one is ready to pay money for anything you do then you are certain that every word you have written is an important word to have written and that any word you have written is as important as any other word and you keep everything you have written with great care. And then it happens sometimes sooner and sometimes later that it has a money value I had mine very much later and it is upsetting because when nothing had any commercial value everything was important and when something began having a commercial value it was upsetting, I imagine this is true of any one.

Before anything you write had commercial value you could not change anything that you had written but once it had commercial value well then changing or not changing was not so important. All this is true and now I will tell how it all happened to me as it did.

I was getting older when I wrote *The Autobiography* [of Alice B. Toklas], not that it makes much difference how old you are because the only thing that is any different is the historical fact that you are older or younger. One thing is certain the only thing that makes you younger or older is that nothing can happen that is different from what you expected and when that happens and it mostly does happen everything is different from what you expected then there is no difference between being younger or older. Just the other day they thought well anyway America thought that there was going to be war again in Europe and they called me up on the telephone to ask me what I thought about it. I said I do not believe that there is going to be another European war just now but as I am most generally always wrong perhaps there is. When I was very small we always used to say let us toss up a coin to decide and then as it came down we always said and now let's do the other way. That is a natural way and if you are that way then anything is a surprise and if anything is a surprise then there is not much difference between older or younger because the only thing that does make anybody older is that they cannot be surprised. I suppose there are some people who get so that they cannot be surprised so that things happen as they think they will happen. It always has been a game with me to think if something is going to happen just all the possible ways a thing is going to happen and then when it does happen it always does happen in a way I had never thought of. That is why I like detective stories, I never know ever how they are going to happen and anybody ought to yes I realize that anybody really ought to.

Well anyway it was a beautiful autumn in Bilignin and in six weeks I wrote *The Autobiography of Alice B. Toklas* and it was published and it became a best seller and first it was printed in the *Atlantic Monthly* and there is a nice story about that but first I bought myself a new eight-cylinder Ford car and the most expensive coat made to order by Hermes and fitted by the man who makes horse covers for race horses for Basket the white poodle and two collars studded for Basket. I had never made any money before in my life and I was most excited.

EVERYBODY'S AUTOBIOGRAPHY, 1937

WILLIAM STYRON

A PHENOMENON THAT A NUMBER OF PEOPLE have noted while in deep depression is the sense of being accompanied by a second self – a wraithlike observer who, not sharing the dementia of his double, is able to watch with dispassionate curiosity as his companion struggles against the oncoming disaster, or decides to embrace it. There is a theatrical quality about all this, and during the next several days, as I went about stolidly preparing for extinction, I couldn't shake off a sense of melodrama – a melodrama in which I, the victim-to-be of self-murder, was both the solitary actor and lone member of the audience. I had not as yet chosen the mode of my departure, but I knew that step would come next, and soon, as inescapable as nightfall.

I watched myself in mingled terror and fascination as I began to make the necessary preparation: going to see my lawyer in the nearby town – there rewriting my will – and spending part of a couple of afternoons in a muddled attempt to bestow upon posterity a letter of farewell. It turned out that putting together a suicide note, which I felt obsessed with a necessity to compose, was the most difficult task of writing that I had ever tackled. There were too many people to acknowledge, to thank, to bequeath final bouquets. And finally I couldn't manage the sheer dirge-like solemnity of it; there was something I found almost comically offensive in the pomposity of such a comment as 'For some time now I have sensed in my work a growing psychosis that is doubtless a reflection of the psychotic strain tainting my life' (this is one of the few lines I recall verbatim), as well as something degrading in the prospect of a testament, which I wished to infuse with at least some dignity and eloquence, reduced to an exhausted stutter of inadequate apologies and self-serving explanations. I should have used as an example the mordant statement of the Italian writer Cesare Pavese, who in parting wrote simply: *No more words. An act. I'll never write again.*

But even a few words came to seem to me too long-winded, and I tore up all my efforts, resolving to go out in silence. Late one bitterly cold night, when I knew that I could not possibly get myself through the following day, I sat in the living room of the house bundled up against the chill; something had happened to the furnace. My wife had gone to bed, and I had forced myself to watch the tape of a movie in which a young actress, who had been in a play of mine, was cast in a small part. At one point in the film, which was set in late nineteenth-century Boston, the characters moved down the hallway of a music conservatory, beyond the walls of which, from unseen musicians, came a contralto voice, a sudden soaring passage from the Brahms *Alto Rhapsody.*

This sound, which like all music – indeed, like all pleasure – I had been numbly unresponsive to for months, pierced my heart like a dagger, and in a flood of swift recollection I thought of all the joys the house had known: the children who had rushed through its rooms, the festivals, the love and work, the honestly earned slumber, the voices and the nimble commotion, the perennial tribe of cats and dogs and birds 'laughter and ability and Sighing, / And Frocks and Curls'. All this I realized was more than I could ever abandon, even as what I had set out so deliberately to do was more than I could inflict on those memories, and upon those, so close to me, with whom the memories were bound. And just as powerfully I realized I could not commit this desecration on myself. I drew upon some last gleam of sanity to perceive the terrifying dimensions of the mortal predicament I had fallen into. I woke up my wife and soon telephone calls were made. The next day I was admitted to the hospital.

DARKNESS VISIBLE: A MEMOIR OF MADNESS, 1990

ANTHONY TROLLOPE

IT WILL NOT, I TRUST, BE SUPPOSED by any reader that I have intended in this so-called autobiography to give a record of my inner life. No man ever did so truly – and no man ever will. Rousseau probably attempted it, but who doubts but that Rousseau has confessed in much the thoughts and convictions rather than the facts of his life? If the rustle of a woman's petticoat has ever stirred my blood, if a cup of wine has been a joy to me, if I have thought tobacco at midnight in pleasant company to be one of the elements of an earthly paradise, if now and again I have somewhat recklessly fluttered a £5 note over a card table, of what matter is that to any reader? I have betrayed no woman. Wine has brought me to no sorrow. It has been the companionship of smoking that I have loved rather than the habit. I have never desired to win money and I have lost none. To enjoy the excitement of pleasure, but to be free from its vices and ill effects; to have the sweet and to leave the bitter untasted – that has been my study. The preachers tell us that this is impossible. It seems to be that hitherto I have succeeded fairly well. I will not say that I have never scorched a finger, but I carry no ugly wounds.

For what remains to me of my life I trust for my happiness still chiefly to my work – hoping that when the power for work be over with me God may be pleased to take me from a world in which according to my view there can be no joy; secondly, to the love of those who love me; and then to my books. That I can read and be happy when I am reading is a great blessing. Could I have remembered, as some men do, what I read I should have been able to call myself an educated man. But that power I have never possessed. Something is always left – something dim and inaccurate – but still something sufficient to preserve the taste for more. I am inclined to think it is so with most readers.

AN AUTOBIOGRAPHY, 1883

WIFI is changing at WPL.
Please ask staff for
information and
new log-in details.

User name: BALACHANDAR, VIDYA

Title: The Middle East & South Asia
Author: Russell, Malcolm B.
Item ID: T1536001383565
Date due: 11/20/2015,23:59

Title: Woman's day (New York, N.Y.)
Item ID: M1536000135314
Date due: 11/6/2015,23:59

Title: Queen Elizabeth the Queen Mother
Item ID: T1536001378995
Date due: 11/20/2015,23:59

Title: The Queen : 50 years-- a celebrati
n
Author: Allison, Ronald.
Item ID: T1536001323078
Date due: 11/20/2015,23:59

Title: The book of life : a compendium o
the best autob
Item ID: T1536001532371
Date due: 11/20/2015,23:59

Visit Us Online 24/7
www.windsorpubliclibrary.com
or Call us at 519-255-6770

MARK TWAIN

M Y PARENTS REMOVED TO MISSOURI in the early 'thirties; I do not remember just when, for I was not born then and cared nothing for such things. It was a long journey in those days, and must have been a rough and tiresome one. The home was made in the wee village of Florida, in Monroe County, and I was born there in 1835. The village contained a hundred people and I increased the population by one per cent. It is more than many of the best men in history could have done for a town. It may not be modest in me to refer to this, but it is true. There is no record of a person doing as much – not even Shakespeare. But I did it for Florida, and it shows that I could have done it for any place – even London, I suppose.

Recently some one in Missouri has sent me a picture of the house I was born in. Heretofore I have always stated that it was a palace, but I shall be more guarded now.

I used to remember my brother Henry walking into a fire outdoors when he was a week old. It was remarkable in me to remember a thing like that, and it was still more remarkable that I should cling to the delusion, for thirty years, that I *did* remember it – for of course it never happened; he would not have been able to walk at that age. If I had stopped to reflect, I should not have burdened my memory with that impossible rubbish so long. It is believed by many people that an impression deposited in a child's memory within the first two years of its life cannot remain there five years, but that is an error. The incident of Benvenuto Cellini and the salamander must be accepted as authentic and trustworthy; and then that remarkable and indisputable instance in the experience of Helen Keller – however, I will speak of that at another time. For many years I believed that I remembered helping my grandfather to drink his whisky toddy when I was six weeks old, but I do not tell about that any more, now; I am grown old and my memory is not as active as it used to be. When I was younger I could remember anything, whether it had happened or not; but my faculties are decaying now, and soon I shall be so I cannot remember any but the things that never happened. It is sad to go to pieces like this, but we all have to do it.

MARK TWAIN'S AUTOBIOGRAPHY, 1924

NUALA O'FAOLAIN

M Y HANDS IN FRONT OF ME on the keyboard are veined and freckled. I am aware of my physical being all the more intensely because all I do is write. There's the complex feel of my body – the curve of my belly against my thighs, my bare feet on the wood of the floor, the slight ache in my buttocks from long hours sitting on this wooden chair, the tension in my right hand from holding it, hollowed, over the laptop's mouse. There's the hot, still air on my skin. All summer there were the noises of children running and laughing between bikes and swings out there, and when the last of their calls died away, after nightfall, there was sometimes in the silence the approaching whisper of a heavy shower of rain. It is raining now. That means that in the morning when the dog and I go down the grassy slope to the lake, my canvas shoes will squelch with wet even before I get wet myself. I think I will remember forever the feel of the wooden dock here – how it tilts slightly forward as I walk out along it, how the cold water slides across the warm planks. I slip in, trying not to disturb the sheen of the water. The ducks paddle calmly past my nose. The dog is crouched above the bushes on the shore, fascinated by the traffic of bees. I go back up to the apartment and shower, and walk between one small room and another, putting on a kettle for tea, looking around for a comb, hitting a key on the laptop to light the screen so as to frown over the last few sentences I've written, matching them against their ideal shape in my head. There's one CD I play a lot, of cello and piano sonatas by Beethoven. Sometimes I'm the cello and sometimes the piano. The big refrigerator whines. You can open its door for a moment to get a waft of cool.

Oh, let me have a long time yet in this beautiful world and let him stay by me and not get tired of my difficulties! I rang up the Central Statistics Office in Dublin. Yes, statistically, an Irishwoman who is my age now will live to seventy-eight and three quarters. That gives me sixteen and a half years. By then maybe I'll be willing to die. It depends, I suppose, on who has gone before. A child does leave a playground, however reluctantly, when all the friends he's been playing with have gone home.

ALMOST THERE: THE ONWARD JOURNEY OF A DUBLIN WOMAN,
2003

GWEN RAVERAT

W HEN I LOOK BACK ON THOSE YEARS when I was neither fish nor flesh, between the ages of sixteen and twenty-two, I remember them as an uncomfortable time, and sometimes a very unhappy one. Now that I have attained the status of Good Red Herring, I may at last be allowed to say: Oh dear, Oh dear, how horrid it was being young, and how nice it is being old and not having to mind what people think.

PERIOD PIECE: A CAMBRIDGE CHILDHOOD, 1952

JEAN-JACQUES ROUSSEAU

'I BECOME OLD, AS I CONTINUE TO LEARN.' Solon often repeated this line in his old age. In a sense I could say it in mine too; it is a sorry body of knowledge that the experience of the last twenty years has given me: ignorance would even be preferable. Perhaps adversity is a great teacher, but he charges a high price for his lessons, and often the profit we take from them is not worth the price they have cost us. Moreover, before we have acquired all this knowledge from such belated lessons, their relevance to us passes. Youth is the time to study wisdom; old age is the time to practise it. Experience always instructs us, I confess; but she profits only in respect to the time we have left ahead of us. Is this the time, when we are on the verge of dying, to learn how we should have lived?

Ah, what is the use of shining lights so late and so painfully acquired on my destiny and on the passions of others who have made it what it is! I have learned to understand men better only to feel better the misery into which they have plunged me, and even though this knowledge uncovered all their traps it did not help me avoid any of them. Why did I not always remain in that state of imbecilic but gentle confidence that made me for so many years the prey and the plaything of my noisy friends, without ever having the slightest suspicion of all the plots they were weaving around me. I was their dupe and their victim, it is true, but I believed myself loved by them, and my heart rejoiced in the friendship they inspired in me, all the while attributing the same feelings to them. These gentle illusions have been destroyed. The sad truth that time and reason have revealed to me in making me experience my misfortune, has made me see that there is no remedy and that the only thing to do is to resign myself. Thus, all the experiences of my old age are in my present state useless to me, and without benefit in the future.

We enter the race at birth, we leave it at death. What use is it to learn how to drive your chariot better when you are at the end of your career? The only thing left to do is to wonder how you will make your exit. If there is anything left for an old man to study, it is solely to learn how to die, and it is precisely this that we do least at my age; you think of anything besides that. All old men hold onto life more dearly than children and leave it with worse grace than young people. It is because all their work has been for this same life, and they see at its end that it has all been in vain. They leave everything when they depart, all their cares, all their goods, all the fruits of their laborious endeavours. They have not dreamed of acquiring anything during their lives that they can take with them at death …

But patience, gentleness, resignation, integrity, and impartial justice are goods we can take with us, and with which we can enrich ourselves endlessly, without fear that death itself will make us lose their value. It is to this unique and useful study that I devote the rest of my old age. I will be happy if, through my self-improvement, I learn to leave life, not better, for that is impossible, but more virtuous than I entered it.

THE REVERIES OF A SOLITARY WALKER, 1782

MALCOLM COWLEY

I REMEMBER A MORNING MANY YEARS AGO when I was backing out of the parking lot near the railroad station in Brewster, New York. There was a near collision. The driver of the other car jumped out and started to abuse me; he had his fists ready. Then he looked hard at me and said, 'Why, you're an old man.' He got back into his car, slammed the door, and drove away, while I stood there fuming.

'I'm only 65,' I thought. 'He wasn't driving carefully. I can still take care of myself in a car, or in a fight, for that matter.'

My hair was whiter – it may have been in 1974 – when a young woman rose and offered me her seat in a Madison Avenue bus. That message was kind and also devastating. 'Can't I even stand up?' I thought as I thanked her and declined the seat. But the same thing happened twice the following year, and the second time I gratefully accepted the offer, though with a sense of having diminished myself. 'People are right about me,' I thought while wondering why all those kind gestures were made by women. Do men now regard themselves as the weaker sex, not called upon to show consideration? All the same, it was a relief to sit down and relax.

THE VIEW FROM EIGHTY, 1980

MARLON BRANDO

I SUPPOSE THE FIRST MEMORY I have was when I was too young to remember how young I was. I opened my eyes, looked around in the mouse-colored light and realized that Ermi was still asleep, so I dressed myself as best I could and went down the stairs, left foot first on each step. I had to scuff my way to the porch because I couldn't buckle my sandals. I sat on the one step in the sun at the dead end of Thirty-second Street and waited. It must have been spring because the big tree in front of the house was shedding pods with two wings like a dragonfly. On days when there wasn't any wind, they would spin around in the air as they drifted softly to the ground.

I watched them float all the way down, sitting with my neck craned back until my mouth opened and holding out my hand just in case, but they never landed on it. When one hit the ground I'd look up again, my eyes darting, waiting for the next magical event, the sun warming the yellow hairs on my head.

Waiting like that for the next magic was as good a moment as any other that I can remember in the last sixty-five years.

BRANDO: SONGS MY MOTHER TAUGHT ME, 1994

MARGARET THATCHER

O N 28 NOVEMBER 1990, as I left 10 Downing Street for the last time eleven years, six months and twenty-four days after I first set foot there as Prime Minister, I was tormented by a whirl of conflicting and confused thoughts and emotions. I had passed from the well-lit world of public life where I had lived so long into ... what? Yet, though I may have leapt – or been pushed – into the dark, I was not in free fall. I had my family and my health. I also found that there was an abundance of friends to give me moral and practical help.

Alistair McAlpine lent me his house in Great College Street, close to the Palace of Westminster, to serve as a temporary office. When Denis, Mark and I arrived there, I found a little sitting room for me to work in. John Whittingdale, who had been my Political Secretary as Prime Minister, and several other old and new faces were waiting to greet me. As for our own house, which Denis and I had bought in Dulwich partly as an investment and partly to provide for emergencies (although we had hardly foreseen this one), neither of us really wanted to keep it. It was too far from Westminster and somehow in spite of all that had happened we both assumed that whatever else I was to do, 'retirement' was not an option. I wanted and probably needed to earn a living. In any case, I would have gone mad without work.

It took some time before we found somewhere suitable to live; to begin with we were lent a lovely flat in Eaton Square by Mrs Henry Ford. But finding work to do was certainly no problem. There were countless letters to write in answer to messages of commiseration, which had deeply moved me. Some of my correspondents were in despair. I, myself, was merely depressed.

THE PATH TO POWER, 1995

HAROLD BRODKEY

O CTOBER 25, 1995: it is my birthday. And for the first time in my adult life, it matters to me that the age I have reached is a specific number. I am sixty-five years old, but it is not so much that

I am sixty-five as the idea of birth and near old age and now death. I do not know at what rate of speed I am moving toward my death. The doctors cannot tell me – the only hard medical fact with AIDS is death. The hard social fact is the suffering. One approaches the end of consciousness – or the end of consciousness approaches one – and strange alterations of the self occur: a hope of cure, a half-belief in treatments that could extend life. (By a year, by two years? Three years is so vast a time, one thinks of life as being extended indefinitely if one can hope to live three more years.)

The less luck one has, the stronger is one's new conviction in one's luck. This while the doctors back away. They have nothing more to offer. They conserve their energies and the hospital's medical resources, but what it feels like is being locked out of the house when I was six years old. The experience is closer to the early, angrier descriptions of AIDS than I had expected it would be for me or others after all these years.

I am sleeping without a detritus of dreams or symbols now, without images, not lions or tigers, not flowers or light, not Jesus or Moses – but a few memories, chiefly of childhood, perhaps because of the night sweats, which I have all day long sometimes. I am rolling down the grassy hill behind the house in Alton. It is twilight. Dark shapes flit in the air – bats, I say now, like a schoolchild answering a question in class. And the birdsong! The pre-DDT birdsong: I had no idea I missed it so harshly. Sing! Chitter! A train travels on the tracks below the cliff, below the limestone bluff. Chug-a-chug, chuff-chuff. The grown-ups sit in those heavy wooden lawn chairs of the 1930s: so still, so handsome. And I, a pudgy child who will not use words yet, this soon after his mother's death, in high-sided shoes and white socks, I am shouting, yelling, in my own sort of birdsong, yelling and grumbling as I roll; stones and pebbles bite into my ribs. I am magnifying my size with the sound I make. Faster and faster I go, then either my father stops me or I curl up against a tree trunk, I'm not sure which.

The change in momentum changed everything, how the light darkened and had a name, like dusk; how the trees and faces emerged and could be named. I remember feeling large from the adventure but small as well, factually small. And because I was in my own mind no one thing, large or small or boy or son of this household, I remember the dreamlikeness of being no one, of being lifted and of being of no important weight. The smells, the grass, my father's shirt – they were more important than I was. I was no one and nothing, about to be devoured by sleep.

THIS WILD DARKNESS: THE STORY OF MY DEATH, 1996

DAVID HUME

IN SPRING, 1775, I WAS STRUCK WITH A DISORDER in my bowels, which at first gave me no alarm, but has since, as I apprehend it, become mortal and incurable. I now reckon upon a speedy dissolution. I have suffered very little pain from my disorder; and, what is more strange, have, notwithstanding the great decline of my person, never suffered a moment's abatement of my spirits; insomuch that were I to name a period of my life which I should most choose to pass over again, I might be tempted to point to this later period. I possess the same ardour as ever in study, and the same gaiety in company. I consider, besides, that a man at sixty-five, by dying, cuts off only a few years of infirmities; and though I see many symptoms of my literary reputation's breaking out at last with additional lustre, I know that I could have but very few years to enjoy it. It is difficult to be more detached from life than I am at present.

To conclude historically with my own character. I am, or rather was (for that is the style I must now use in speaking of myself, which emboldens me the more to speak my sentiments) I was, I say, a man of mild disposition, of command of temper, of an open, social, and cheerful humour, capable of attachment, but little susceptible of enmity, and of great moderation in all my passions. Even my love of literary fame, my ruling passion, never soured my temper, notwithstanding my frequent disappointments. My company was not acceptable to the young and careless, as well as to the studious and literary; and as I took a particular pleasure in the company of modest women, I had not reason to be displeased with the reception I met with from them. In a word, though most men, anywise eminent, have found reason to complain of calumny, I never was touched, or even attacked, by her baleful tooth; and though I wantonly exposed myself to the rage of both civil and religious factions, they seemed to be disarmed in my behalf of their wonted fury. My friends never had occasion to vindicate any one circumstance of my character and conduct: not but that the zealots, we may well suppose, would have been glad to invent and propagate any story to my disadvantage, but they could never find any which they thought would wear the face of probability. I cannot say there is no vanity in making this funeral oration of myself; but I hope it is not a misplaced one; and this is a matter of fact which is easily cleared and ascertained.

THE LIFE OF DAVID HUME, ESQ. WRITTEN BY HIMSELF, 1776

T. H. HUXLEY

THE LAST THING THAT IT WOULD BE proper for me to do would be to speak of the work of my life, or to say, at the end of the day, whether I think I have earned my wages or not. Men are said to be partial judges of themselves – young men may be, I doubt if old men are. Life seems terribly foreshortened as they look back; and the mountain they set themselves to climb in youth turns out to be a mere spur of immeasurably higher ranges, when, with failing breath, they reach the top. But if I may speak of the objects I have had more or less definitely in view since I began the ascent of my hillock, they are briefly these: to promote the increase of natural knowledge and to forward the application of scientific methods of investigation to all the problems of life to the best of my ability, in the conviction – which has grown with my growth and strengthened with my strength – that there is no alleviation for the sufferings of mankind except veracity of thought and action, and the resolute facing of the world as it is, when the garment of make-believe, by which pious hands have hidden its uglier features, is stripped off.

It is with this intent that I have subordinated any reasonable or unreasonable ambition for scientific fame, which I may have permitted myself to entertain, to other ends; to the popularization of science; to the development and organization of scientific education; to the endless series of battles and skirmishes over evolution; and to untiring opposition to that ecclesiastical spirit, that clericalism, which in England, as everywhere else, and to whatever denomination it may belong, is the deadly enemy of science.

In striving for the attainment of these objects, I have been but one among many, and I shall be well content to be remembered, or even not remembered, as such.

AUTOBIOGRAPHY, 1889

ELIE WIESEL

'MEMOIRS?' PEOPLE ASK. 'WHAT'S THE HURRY? Why don't you wait awhile?' It puzzles me. Wait for what? And for how long? I fail to see what age has to do with memory. I am sixty-six years old, and I belong to a generation obsessed by a thirst to retain and transmit everything. For no other has the commandment *Zachor* – Remember! – had such meaning.

You have plenty of time, people tell me. Time for what – to let oblivion wipe out the victims' final traces? To explore the planet, witnessing its degradation?

To write your memoirs is to draw up a balance sheet of your life so far. Am I ready for a final reckoning? Memory, after all, may well prove voracious and intrusive. Remembering means to shine a merciless light on faces and events, to say 'No' to the sands that bury words and to forgetfulness and death. Is that not too ambitious?

It's been years since I was young. But I would love to rediscover, to recapture, if not the anguish and exaltation that I once felt, then at least the road leading to them.

ALL RIVERS RUN TO THE SEA: MEMOIRS, 1994

MARY AUGUSTA WARD

DO WE ALL BECOME GARRULOUS and confidential as we approach the gates of old age? Is it that we instinctively feel, and cannot help asserting, our one advantage over the younger generation, which has so many over us? – the one advantage of *time*!

After all, it is not disputable that we have lived longer than they. When they talk of past poets, or politicians, or novelists, whom the young still deign to remember, of whom for once their estimate agrees with ours, we can sometimes put in a quiet, 'I saw him' – or, 'I talked with him' – which for the moment wins the conversational race. And as we elders fall back before the brilliance and glitter of the New Age, advancing 'like an army with banners', this mere prerogative of years becomes in itself a precious possession. After all, we cannot divest ourselves of it, if we would. It is better to make friends with it – to turn it into a kind of *panache* – to wear it with an air, since wear it we must.

So as the years draw on toward the Biblical limit, the inclination to look back, and to tell some sort of story of what one has seen, grows upon most of us. I cannot hope that what I have to say will be very interesting to many. A life spent largely among books, and in the exercise of a literary profession, has very obvious drawbacks, as a subject-matter, when one comes to write about it. I can only attempt it with any success, if my readers will allow me a large psychological element. The thoughts and opinions of one human being, if they are sincere, must always have an interest for some other human beings. The world is there to think about; and if we have lived, or are living, with any sort of energy, we *must* have thought about it, and about ourselves in relation to it – thought 'furiously' often. And it is out of the many 'thinkings' of many folk, strong or weak, dull or far-ranging, that thought itself grows. For progress surely, whether in men or nations, means only a richer knowledge; the more impressions, therefore, on the human intelligence that we can seize and record, the most sensitive becomes that intelligence itself.

But of course the difficulty lies in the seizing and recording – in the choice, that is, of what to say, and how to say it. In this choice, as I look back over more than half a century, I can only follow – and trust – the same sort of instinct that one follows in the art of fiction. I shall be telling what is primarily true, or as true as I can make it, as distinguished from what is primarily imagination, built on truth. But the truth one uses in fiction must be interesting! Milton expresses that in the words 'sensuous' and 'passionate' which he applies to poetry in the *Areopagitica*. And the same thing applies to autobiography, where selection is even more necessary than in fiction. Nothing ought to be told, I think, that does not interest or kindle one's own mind in looking back; it is the only condition on which one can hope to interest or kindle other minds. And this means that one ought to handle things broadly, taking only the salient points in the landscape of the past, and of course with as much detachment as possible. Though probably in the end one will have to admit – egotists that we all are! – that not much detachment *is* possible.

A WRITER'S RECOLLECTIONS, 1918

CHARLES DARWIN

AFTER SEVERAL FRUITLESS SEARCHES in Surrey and elsewhere, we found this house and purchased it. I was pleased with the diversified appearance of the vegetation proper to a chalk district, and so unlike what I had been accustomed to in the Midland counties; and still more pleased with the extreme quietness and rusticity of the place. It is not, however, quite so retired a place as a writer in a German periodical makes it, who says that my house can be approached only by mule-track! Our fixing ourselves here has answered admirably in one way which we did not anticipate, namely, by being very convenient for frequent visits from our children, who never miss an opportunity of doing so when they can.

Few persons can have lived a more retired life than we have done. Besides short visits to the houses of relations, and occasionally to the seaside and elsewhere, we have gone nowhere. During the first part of our residence we went a little into society, and received a few friends here; but my health almost always suffered from the excitement, violent shivering and vomiting attacks being thus brought on. I have therefore been compelled for many years to give up all dinner-parties; and this has been something of a deprivation to me, as such parties always put me into high spirits. From the same cause I have been able to invite here very few scientific acquaintances. Whilst I was young and strong I was capable of very warm attachments, but of late years, though I still have very friendly feelings towards many persons, I have lost the power of becoming deeply attached to anyone, not even so deeply to my good and dear friends Hooker and Huxley, as I should formerly have been. As far as I can judge this grievous loss of feeling has gradually crept over me, from the expectation of much distress afterwards from exhaustion having become firmly associated in my mind with seeing and talking with anyone for an hour, except my wife and children.

My chief enjoyment and sole employment throughout life has been scientific work; and the excitement from such work makes me for the time forget, or drives quite away, my daily discomfort.

'RECOLLECTIONS OF THE DEVELOPMENT OF MY MIND AND CHARACTER', 1876

ALBERT EINSTEIN

HERE I SIT IN ORDER TO WRITE, at the age of sixty-seven, something like my own obituary. I am doing this not merely because Dr Schilpp has persuaded me to do it, but because I do, in fact, believe that it is a good thing to show those who are striving alongside of us how our own striving and searching appears in retrospect. After some reflection, I felt how imperfect any such attempt is bound to be. For, however brief and limited one's working life may be, and however predominant may be the way of error, the exposition of that which is worthy of communication does nonetheless not come easy – today's person of sixty-seven is by no means the same as was the one of fifty, of thirty, or of twenty. Every reminiscence is colored by one's present state, hence by a deceptive point of view. This consideration could easily deter one. Nevertheless much can be gathered out of one's own experience that is not open to another consciousness.

AUTOBIOGRAPHICAL NOTES, 1949

MARGARET MEAD

As THE YEARS WENT BY, I had carefully not let myself hope that I would have grandchildren, as I knew before [my daughter] Catherine had children I would be old enough to be a great-grandmother. Great-grandmotherhood is something we do not think of as a likely possibility of the human condition, even now when it is becoming more common.

But I did think how delightful it would be, if it happened, to see my daughter with a child. And I wondered what kind of child Catherine and Barkev Kassarjian would have – she with her long ancestry from the British Isles and he with his long Armenian heritage in the Middle East, she with her English fairness and he with his dark eyes and black hair. Thinking back to my grandmother and my mother and the kind of mother I had tried to be and remembering all the different kinds of mothering people who had cared for my daughter in her childhood – her English nanny, her lovely young aunt Mary, and her devoted godmother, Aunt Marie, who brought in the generation of my grandmother's day when people respected heirlooms and passed their dolls on from generation to generation – I wondered what kind of child my daughter would have and what kind of mother she would be.

Rather carefully I also did not think too much about the kind of father my son-in-law would be, just as, earlier, I had not permitted myself to daydream about a son-in-law. When Biddy Barlow asked me, just before Catherine was married, 'Whose side are you going to take?' I realized with a jolt that such a contingency had not occurred to me. So carefully had I restricted my day-dreaming to what Barkev meant to Catherine that I had left myself out. It was an added delight, then, to discover that I enjoyed him very much. I appreciated and took great pleasure in his analytical mind, his keen enjoyment of all the concrete details of life, his sensitive regard for persons and lively respect for the nature of things.

When Catherine and Barkev lost their first baby in the Philippines – Martin, who was born too soon and lived only long enough to be christened and registered as a citizen – I knew that they both wanted a child very much. I knew also that bereavement had catapulted Catherine into the same position in which I had been placed by a long series of disappointed hopes; just as I had been, she was potentially an overprotective mother. And as I had done, she would have to school herself to give her child the freedom to take risks. I could feel again the terrible tingle in the calves of my legs that I had felt when Cathy became an intrepid climber of tall pine trees …

The baby was due in September. Like so many other people in the United States, Catherine and Barkev planned to move just before the baby was born, and so added to other complications all the confusion of making a new home.

When they moved in, the newly remodeled house – in which there was a small apartment for a baby-sitting young professional couple – was not finished. Teaching began, and the baby was not yet born. In the end, in spite of careful planning, something went wrong with the telephone connection to Barkev, a few blocks away, and Catherine was taken to the hospital in the fire chief's car summoned from the concerned fire department across the street. It was a modern version of having the baby born while the mother is out fishing in a canoe, far from the village and the waiting midwife.

When the news came that Sevanne Margaret was born, I suddenly realized that through no act of my own I had become biologically related to a new human being. This was one thing that had never come up in discussions of grandparenthood and had never before occurred to me. In many primitive societies grandparents and grandchildren are aligned together. A child who has to treat his father with extreme respect may joke with his grandfather and playfully call his grandmother 'wife'. The tag that grandparents and grandchildren get along so well because they have a common enemy is explicitly faced in many societies. In our own society the point most often made is that grandparents can enjoy their grandchildren because they have no responsibility for them, they do not have to discipline them and they lack the guilt and anxiety of parenthood. All these things were familiar. But I had never thought how strange it was to be involved at a distance in the birth of a biological descendant …

In the presence of grandparent and grandchild, past and future merge in the present. Looking at a loved child, one cannot say, 'We must sacrifice this generation for the next. Many must die now so that later others may live.' This is the argument that generations of old men, cut off from children, have used in sending young men out to die in war. Nor can one say, 'I want this child to live well no matter how we despoil the earth for later generations.' For seeing a child as one's grandchild, one can visualize that same child as a grandparent, and with the eyes of another generation one can see other children, just as light-footed and vivid, as eager to learn and know and embrace the world, who must be taken into account – now. My friend Ralph Blum has defined the human unit of time as the space between a grandfather's memory of his own childhood and a grandson's knowledge of those memories as he heard about them. We speak a great deal about a human scale; we need also a human unit in which to think about time.

BLACKBERRY WINTER: MY EARLIER YEARS, 1972

KURT VONNEGUT

I DON'T CARE IF I AM REMEMBERED OR NOT when I am dead. (A scientist I knew at General Electric, who was married to a woman named Josephine, said to me, 'Why should I buy life insurance? If I die, I won't care what's happening to Jo. I won't care about anything. I'll be dead.')

I am a child of a Great Depression (just like my grandchildren). In a Great Depression any job is a miracle. Back in the 1930s, if somebody got a job there was a big celebration. Around about midnight somebody would finally inquire as to the nature of the job. A job was a job. To me writing books or whatever is just another job. When my cash cows the slick magazines were put out of business by TV, I wrote industrial advertising and then sold cars instead, and invented a new board game, and taught in a private school for fucked-up rich kids, and so on. I didn't think I owed it to the world or to myself or to anything to get back to writing, if I could. Writing was just a job I'd lost. When a child of a Great Depression loses a job, it is sort of like losing a billfold or a key to the front door. You go get another one.

(One jocular Great Depression answer to the question about what kind of job you got was, 'Cleaning birdshit out of cuckoo clocks.' Another one was, 'It's in a bloomer factory. I'll be pulling down five thousand a year.')

Most people my age and of my social class, no matter what job they held, are retired now. So it seems redundant (even silly) for critics to say, as so many do, that I am not the promising writer I used to be. If they think I am a disappointment, they should see what the passage of time has done to Mozart, Shakespeare, and Hemingway.

The older my father was (and he died at seventy-two), the more absent-minded he became. People forgave him for that, and I think people should forgive me, too. (I never meant anybody any harm, and neither did he.) Toward the end, Father actually called me Bozo several times. Bozo was a wire-haired fox terrier we had when I was a little boy. (Bozo wasn't even my dog. Bozo belonged to my big brother Bernard.) Father apologized for calling me Bozo. Ten minutes later he called me Bozo again.

During the last three days of his life (which I did not see) he would look through drawers and in cupboards for some sort of document. It was obviously important to him, but it was also a secret. He wouldn't tell anybody what it was. He never found it, and neither did we, so we will never know what it was.

(I can never forget the dying words of the actor John Barrymore, according to Gene Fowler in his *Good Night, Sweet Prince*: 'I am the illegitimate son of Buffalo Bill.')

FATES WORSE THAN DEATH: AN AUTOBIOGRAPHICAL COLLAGE OF THE 1980S, 1991

LADY DAIBU

THOUGH LIFE HAS BROUGHT ME NOTHING but painful recollections one after another, the years have piled upon me, and in the course of this vain existence I have written down little by little those things that have chanced to come to mind. Once in a while people would ask me whether I had any such writings, but what I had written was so much my own personal thoughts that I felt embarrassed, and would copy out just a little to show to them. I wrote these things, intending that my eyes alone should look on them; and now, as I gaze at them years later, I feel:

Grief enough
To break one's heart!
Yet as I gather up my thoughts
To write them down.
I feel the pain anew

THE POETIC MEMOIRS OF LADY DAIBU, C.1174–C.1232

COLLEY CIBBER

A MAN WHO HAS PASS'D above Forty Years of his Life upon a Theatre, where he has never appear'd to be Himself, may have naturally excited the Curiosity of his Spectators to know what he really was when in no body's Shape but his own; and whether he, who by his Profession had so long been ridiculing his Benefactors, might not, when the Coat of his Profession was off, deserve to be laugh'd at himself; or from his being often seen in the most flagrant and immoral Characters, whether he might not see as great a Rogue when he look'd into the glass Himself as when he held it to others.

It was doubtless from a Supposition that this sort of Curiosity would compensate their Labours that so many hasty Writers have been encourag'd to publish the lives of the late Mrs Oldfield, Mr Wilks, and Mr Booth, in less time after their Deaths than one could suppose it cost to transcribe them.

Now, Sir, when my Time comes, less they shou'd think it worth while to handle my Memory with the same Freedom, I am willing to prevent its being so oddly besmear'd (or at best but flatly white-wash'd) by taking upon me to give the Publick This, as true a Picture of myself as natural Vanity will permit me to draw: For to promise you that I shall never be vain, were a Promise that, like a Looking-glass too large, might break itself in the making: Nor am I sure I ought wholly to avoid that Imputation, because if Vanity be one of my natural Features, the Portrait wou'd not be like me without it. In a Word, I may palliate and soften as much as I please; but upon an honest Examination of my Heart, I am afraid the same Vanity which makes even homely People employ Painters to preserve a flattering Record of their Persons, has seduced me to print off this *Chiaro Oscuro* of my Mind.

And when I have done it, you may reasonably ask me of what Importance can the History of my private Life be to the Publick? To this, indeed, I can only make you a ludicrous Answer, which is, that the Publick very well knows my Life has not been a private one; that I have been employ'd in their Service ever since many of their Grandfathers were young Men; And tho' I have voluntarily laid down my Post, they have a sort of Right to enquire into my Conduct (for which they have so well paid me) and to call for the Account of it during my Share of Administration in the State of the Theatre. This Work, therefore, which I hope they will not expect a Man of hasty Head shou'd confine to any regular Method: (For I shall make no scruple of leaving my History when I think a Digression may make it lighter for my Reader's Digestion.) This Work, I say, shall not only contain the various Impressions of my Mind, (as in Louis the Fourteenth his Cabinet you have seen the growing Medals of his Person from Infancy to Old Age), but shall likewise include with them the *Theatrical History of My Own Time*, from my first Appearance on the Stage to my last *Exit*.

If then what I shall advance on that Head may any ways contribute to the Prosperity or Improvement of the Stage in Being, the Publick must of consequence have a Share in its Utility.

This, Sir, is the best Apology I can make for being my own Biographer.

AN APOLOGY FOR THE LIFE OF MR COLLEY CIBBER, WRITTEN BY HIMSELF, 1740

ALEC GUINNESS

WHETHER IT WAS THE INTENSELY BRIGHT moonlight that woke me in the early hours of the morning or a desperate attempt to escape from a nightmare I cannot tell. Merula [my wife] and I were staying in a charming small hotel in Connemara, on a long arm of the sea which reached in from the Atlantic a mile to the west. We had a ground-floor semi-suite which faced a vivid green lawn surrounded by bushes of battered October roses, yet the wind only seemed to reach the top of the trees that enclosed us. The moonlight so disturbed me that, reluctant to shut the curtains, I put on a dressing-gown to sit by the window, and for an hour contemplated the shadows on the now milky-blue grass, the fading globes of pale hydrangeas, and a few leggy, pastel-coloured geraniums. The fir trees had become silent and only the tall eucalyptus behind them swayed furiously. Sitting here at a round table I comforted myself with the beauty of the night and tried to shake off my foolish dream.

In my dream I was eighty years old; ten years older than I am at the time of writing. I was in Hollywood to play a very small part, for which I was being paid handsomely, in a movie directed by David Lean. If I was eighty he must have been getting on for eighty-seven, but he was as lithe and handsome as ever. He appeared to be riding on some giant camera which resembled a combine-harvester. On this strange apparatus were various seats, canvas chairs, slings and steel bars on which were perched a dozen assistant directors I have known in the past, together with camera crews, continuity girls, producers and press representatives. I was heavily made up, with a very black beard, curly black wig, and dressed as some sort of tramp. My part consisted of a few lines, mostly gibberish, and required me to be killed in a train crash. The huge camera was facing a railway truck tilted on its side, about fifteen feet up in the air, and David, wearing his smart blue collarless jacket, had his eye glued to a lens. 'When he arrives,' he said, 'put him in the truck but don't let it fall until we do a take.' 'I suppose we are properly insured,' said a producer I didn't recognize, 'should anything happen.' 'For God's sake,' piped up someone else, 'he's eighty, so what's it matter?' Maggie Unsworth, a delightful continuity girl who always smoothed over awkward situations with great tact, whispered to David, 'Alec is here.' David unfocussed his eye from the lens and re-focussed on me. 'Where have you been?' he asked irritably. 'Crossing the Atlantic and the United States. I got in two hours ago. As you see, I am made up. But I don't appear to have a dressing-room. I changed in a passage.' All the assistant directors jumped off the camera. 'No dressing-room?' they chorused. 'The last time I was at MGM

Studios,' I said over-modestly, 'I was given Spencer Tracy's room. Of course I wouldn't expect anything like that now: that was forty years ago and I was starring with Grace Kelly.' 'Oh, we know, we know!' David said. It struck me that no one else knew: the press representatives were feeling for their notebooks. 'Well, climb in the truck,' David said, 'and we'll have a go. When you've said your speech – blah, blah, blah – the camera eases in and the truck falls over. End of you.' 'How do I get in?' I asked. The assistants ran in circles, David thumped his head with his fists and everyone left the set to have coffee. 'I think I'll go home now,' I said to no one in particular. At that moment the truck fell over, doing a lot of damage. Looking at the wreckage I realized that had I been in the truck I would have been crushed to death. 'What a fucking way to die!' I said. Then I saw my *doppelgänger*, spread-eagled on the railway-line, its head separated from its body. 'Is the make-up okay?' the head asked. 'The beard is too black,' I replied to the head. I turned to look for David, to ask his opinion, but by now they were all making another film, in a different location, and were no longer concerned with me. I woke, shielding my eyes from the arc-lamp of the moon.

BLESSINGS IN DISGUISE, 1985

NELSON MANDELA

I AWOKE ON THE DAY OF MY RELEASE after only a few hours' sleep at 4:30 AM. February 11 was a cloudless, end-of-summer Cape Town day. I did a shortened version of my usual exercise regimen, washed, and ate breakfast. I then telephoned a number of people from the ANC and the UDF in Cape Town to come to the cottage to prepare for my release and work on my speech. The prison doctor came by to give me a brief checkup. I did not dwell on the prospect of my release, but on all the many things I had to do before then. As so often happens in life, the momentousness of an occasion is lost in the welter of a thousand details.

There were numerous matters that had to be discussed and resolved with very little time to do so. A number of comrades from the reception committee, including Cyril Ramaphosa and Trevor

Manuel, were at the house bright and early. I wanted initially to address the people of Paarl, who had been very kind to me during my incarceration, but the reception committee was adamant that that would not be a good idea: it would look curious if I gave my first speech to the prosperous white burghers of Paarl. Instead, as planned, I would speak first to the people of Cape Town at the Grand Parade in Cape Town.

One of the first questions to be resolved was where I would spend my first night of freedom. My inclination was to spend the night in the Cape Flats, the bustling black and Coloured townships of Cape Town, in order to show my solidarity with the people. But my colleagues and, later, my wife argued that for security reasons I should stay with Archbishop Desmond Tutu in Bishop's Court, a plush residence in a white suburb. It was not an area where I would have been permitted to live before I went to prison, and I thought it would send the wrong signal to spend my first night of freedom in a posh white area. But the members of the committee explained that Bishop's Court had become multiracial under Tutu's tenure, and symbolized an open, generous nonracialism.

The prison service supplied me with boxes and crates for packing. During my first twenty or so years in prison, I accumulated very few possessions, but in the last few years I had amassed enough property – mainly books and paper – to make up for previous decades. I filled over a dozen crates and boxes.

My actual release time was set for 3 PM, but Winnie and Walter and the other passengers on the chartered flight from Johannesburg did not arrive till after two. There were already dozens of people at the house, and the entire scene took on the aspect of a celebration. Warrant Officer Swart prepared a final meal for all of us, and I thanked him not only for the food he had provided for the last two years but the companionship. Warrant Officer James Gregory was also there at the house, and I embraced him warmly. In the years that he had looked after me from Pollsmoor through Victor Verster, we had never discussed politics, but our bond was an unspoken one and I would miss his soothing presence. Men like Swart, Gregory, and Warrant Officer Brand reinforced my belief in the essential humanity even of those who had kept me behind bars for the previous twenty-seven and a half years.

There was little time for lengthy farewells. The plan was that Winnie and I would be driven in a car to the front gate of the prison. I had told the authorities that I wanted to be able to say goodbye to the guards and warders who had looked after me and I asked that they and their families wait for me at the front gate, where I would be able to thank them individually.

At a few minutes after three, I was telephoned by a well-known SABC presenter who requested that I get out of the car a few hundred feet before the gate so they could film me walking toward freedom. This seemed reasonable, and I agreed to do it. This was my first inkling that things might not go as calmly as I had imagined.

By 3:30, I began to get restless, as we were already behind schedule. I told the members of the reception committee that my people had been waiting for me for twenty-seven years and I did not want to keep them waiting any longer. Shortly before four, we left in a small motorcade from the cottage. About a quarter of a mile in front of the gate, the car slowed to a stop and Winnie and I got out and began to walk toward the prison gate.

At first, I could not really make out what was going on in front of us, but when I was within one hundred fifty feet or so, I saw a tremendous commotion and a great crowd of people: hundreds of photographers and television cameras and newspeople as well as several thousand well-wishers. I was astounded and a little bit alarmed. I had truly not expected such a scene; at most, I had imagined there would be several dozen people, mainly the warders and their families. But this proved to be only the beginning; I realized we had not thoroughly prepared for all that was about to happen.

Within twenty feet or so of the gate, the cameras started clicking, a noise that sounded like some great herd of metallic beasts. Reporters started shouting questions; television crews began crowding in; ANC supporters were yelling and cheering. It was a happy, if slightly disorienting chaos. When a television crew thrust a long, dark, furry object at me, I recoiled slightly, wondering if it were some newfangled weapon developed while I was in prison. Winnie informed me that it was a microphone.

When I was among the crowd I raised my right fist and there was a roar. I had not been able to do that for twenty-seven years and it gave me a surge of strength and joy. We stayed among the crowd for only a few minutes before jumping back into the car for the drive to Cape Town. Although I was pleased to have such a reception, I was greatly vexed by the fact that I did not have a chance to say goodbye to the prison staff. As I finally walked through those gates to enter a car on the other side, I felt – even at the age of seventy-one – that my life was beginning anew. My ten thousand days of imprisonment were over.

LONG WALK TO FREEDOM, 1994

ARTHUR MILLER

'I STILL FEEL – KIND OF TEMPORARY ABOUT MYSELF,' Willy Loman says to his brother Ben. I smiled as I wrote the line in the spring of 1948, when it had not yet occurred to me that it summed up my own condition then and throughout my life. The here and now was always melting before the head of a dream coming toward me or its tail going away. I would be twenty before I learned how to be fifteen, thirty before I knew what it meant to be twenty, and now at seventy-two I have to stop myself from thinking like a man of fifty who has plenty of time ahead.

TIMEBENDS: A LIFE, 1987

AKIRA KUROSAWA

I AM SHORT-TEMPERED AND OBSTINATE. These defects are still pronounced, and when I was an assistant director they gave rise to some very serious problems. I recall one occasion when we were particularly pressed for time on the shooting of a film. For more than a week we had not had a full half-hour for lunch, and what made it worse was that we had to make do with the box lunches the company provided. These box lunches consisted of riceballs and giant radish pickles.

More than a week of riceballs and radish pickles is unbearable. The crew began to complain, so I went to the company administrative offices and requested a little consideration. 'At least wrap the riceballs in dried seaweed,' I begged. The production office agreed to my request, so I returned to the set and announced to the crew that the next day the box lunches would contain something different. The grumbling ceased.

However, the box lunches the next day consisted of riceballs and radish pickles. One of the enraged crew picked up his lunch and threw it at me. I very nearly flew into a rage myself at that, but I controlled myself, picked up the lunch I had been hit with and set out for the production office. We were shooting on an open set a good ten-minute walk from the studio buildings. As I walked, I kept saying to myself, 'Don't fly off the handle, you mustn't fly off the handle ...' But the longer I walked, the shorter my fuse got, and by the time I reached the door of the production office I was just a few seconds from exploding. When I stood before the chief of the production office, it happened. In a flash the production chief got the box lunch right in the face and was covered with sticky grains of rice.

There was another incident when I was assistant director for Fushimizu Shū, who had been an assistant director for Yama-san before me. We had to shoot a starry night scene, and I had clambered up to the top of the set to string together the spangles representing the stars. But the threads kept getting tangled and twisted, and finally my patience was at an end. Fushimizu himself, watching from below in his position next to the camera, was also getting irritated. 'Can't you hurry it up a little?' he shouted.

That was it. As if I wasn't annoyed enough already! I grabbed a silver-colored glass ball that was in the box of spangles and threw it at Fushimizu. 'OK, here's a *shooting* star for you!' I yelled. Later he said to me, 'You're still a child. Just a short-tempered child.'

Fushimizu may have been right. Even though I have passed the age of seventy, I haven't been able to cure my quick temper. Now I sometimes put on a fireworks display, but that's all it is. I'm like a space satellite that flies around but doesn't leave behind any radioactivity, so I consider that my short temper is of a rather good quality.

Another time we had to record the sound of someone being hit in the head. We tried socking all kinds of things, but the mixer didn't find anything that was suitable. Finally I exploded and hit the microphone with my fist. The blue light signaling 'OK' flashed on.

I have a distaste for argumentation, and I can't stand people who spout all kinds of strung-together logic. One argumentative screenwriter used some syllogistic reasoning to prove to me that his script was right. I became annoyed and countered that, no matter how logically he defended it, what was dull was still dull, so forget it. We fought.

Once when I was in charge of the second-unit shooting we were terribly pressured. We had finished a particular take and I was dead on my feet, so I sat down to rest. The cameraman came to ask me where to set up for the next shot, and I pointed to a spot near where I was sitting. The cameraman, an argumentative fellow, demanded an explanation of the theoretical basis for my decision to select that spot. I became annoyed (this seems to happen a lot, and it always gets me in trouble) and told him the theoretical basis for my selection of that particular camera position was that I was exhausted and didn't want to move. This cameraman loved to fight, so imagine my surprise when he had no reply to this reasoning.

Anyway, I used to get annoyed very easily. According to my assistant directors, when I get angry my face turns red, but the end of my nose is drained of pigmentation – an anger that would lend itself well to color film, they say. Since I have never got angry in front of a mirror, I don't know if what they say is true or not. But for my assistants this is a danger signal, so it's not likely their observations would be wrong.

SOMETHING LIKE AN AUTOBIOGRAPHY, 1982

HARPO MARX

I'VE PLAYED PIANO IN A WHOREHOUSE. I've smuggled secret papers out of Russia. I've spent an evening on the divan with Peggy Hopkins Joyce. I've taught a gangster mob how to play Pinchie Winchie. I've played croquet with Herbert Bayard Swope while he kept Governor Al Smith waiting on the phone. I've gambled with Nick the Greek, sat on the floor with Greta Garbo, sparred with

Benny Leonard, horsed around with the Prince of Wales, played ping-pong with George Gershwin. George Bernard Shaw has asked me for advice. Oscar Levant has played private concerts for me at a buck a throw. I have golfed with Ben Hogan and Sam Snead. I've basked on the Rivera with Somerset Maugham and Elsa Maxwell. I've been thrown out of the casino at Monte Carlo.

Flush with triumph at the poker table, I've challenged Alexander Woollcott to anagrams and Alice Duer Miller to a spelling match. I've given lessons to some of the world's greatest musicians. I've been a member of the two most famous Round Tables since the days of King Arthur – sitting with the finest creative minds of the 1920s at the Algonquin in New York, and with Hollywood's sharpest professional wits at the Hillcrest ...

The truth is, I had no business doing any of these things. I couldn't read a note of music. I never finished the second grade. But I was having too much fun to recognize myself as an ignorant upstart.

HARPO SPEAKS, 1961

WALT WHITMAN

A BOUT MYSELF AT PRESENT. I will soon enter upon my 73rd year, if I live – have pass'd an active life, as country schoolteacher, gardener, printer, carpenter, author and journalist, domicil'd in nearly all the United States and principal cities, North and South – went to the front (moving about and occupied as army nurse and missionary) during the Secession War, 1861 to '65, and in the Virginia hospitals and after the battles of that time, tending the Northern and Southern wounded alike – work'd down South and in Washington city arduously three years – contracted the paralysis which I have suffer'd ever since – and now live in a little cottage of my own, near the Delaware in New Jersey. My chief book, unrhym'd and unmetrical (it has taken thirty years, peace and war, 'a borning') has its aim as once said, 'to utter the same old human *critter* – but now in Democratic American modern and scientific conditions.' Then I have publish'd two prose works *Specimen Days*, and a late one *November Boughs*. (A little volume *Goodbye My Fancy* is soon to be out, wh' will finish the matter.) I do not propose here to enter the much-fought field of the literary criticism of any of those works.

But for a few portraiture or descriptive bits. Today in the upper of a little wooden house of two stories near the Delaware River, east shore, sixty miles up from the sea, is a rather large 20-by-20 low ceiling'd room something like a big old ship's cabin. The floor, three-quarters of it with an ingrain carpet, is half cover'd by a deep litter of books, papers, magazines, thrown-down letters and circulars, rejected manuscripts, memoranda, bits of light or strong twine, a bundle to be 'express'd', and two or three venerable scrapbooks. In the room stand two large tables (one of ancient St Domingo mahogany with immense leaves) cover'd by a jumble of more papers, a varied and copious array of writing materials, several glass and china vessels or jars, some with cologne-water, others with real honey, granulated sugar, a large bunch of beautiful fresh yellow chrysanthemums, some letters and envelopt papers ready for the post office, many photographs, and a hundred indescribable things besides. There are all around many books, some quite handsome editions, some half cover'd by dust, some within reach, evidently used, (good-sized print, no type less than long primer,) some maps, the Bible (the strong cheap edition of the English crown,) Homer, Shakspare [sic], Walter Scott, Emerson, Ticknor's *Spanish Literature*, John Carlyle's *Dante*, Felton's *Greece*, George Sand's *Consuelo*, a very choice little Epictetus, some novels, the latest foreign and American monthlies, quarterlies, and so on. There being quite a strew of printers' proofs and slips, and the daily papers, the place with its quaint old fashion'd calmness has also a smack of something alert and of current work. There are several trunks and depositories back'd up at the walls; (one well-bound and big box came by express lately from Washington city, after storage there for nearly twenty years.) Indeed the whole room is a sort of result and storage collection of my own past life. I have here various editions of my own writings, and sell them upon request; one is a big volume of complete poems and prose, 1000 pages, autograph, essays, speeches, portraits from life, &c. Another is a little *Leaves of Grass*, latest date, six portraits, morocco bound, in pocket-book form.

Fortunately the apartment is quite roomy. There are three windows in front. At one side is the stove, with a cheerful fire of oak wood, nearby a good supply of fresh sticks, whose faint aroma is plain. On another side is the bed with white coverlid and woollen blankets. Toward the windows is a huge armchair (a Christmas present from Thomas Donaldson's young daughter and son, Philadelphia), timber'd as by some stout ship's spars, yellow polish'd, ample, with rattan-woven seat and back, and over the latter a great wide wolf-skin of hairy black and silver, spread to guard against cold and draught. A time-worn look and scent of old oak attach both to the chair and the person occupying it.

'MEMORANDA', 1891

GIROLAMO CARDANO

I AM A MAN OF MEDIUM HEIGHT; my feet are short, wide near the toes, and rather too high at the heels, so that I can scarcely find well-fitting shoes; it is usually necessary to have them made to order. My chest is somewhat narrow and my arms slender. The thickly fashioned right hand has dangling fingers, so that chiromantists have declared me a rustic; it embarrasses them to know the truth. The line of life upon my palm is short, while the line called Saturn's is extended and deep. My left hand, on the contrary, is truly beautiful with long, tapering, well-formed fingers and shining nails.

A neck a little long and inclined to be thin, cleft chin, full pendulous lower lip, and eyes that are very small and apparently half closed; unless I am gazing at something ... such are my features. Over the eyebrow of my left eye is a blotch or wart, like a small lentil, which can scarcely be noticed. The wide forehead is bald at the sides where it joins the temples. My hair and beard were blond; I am wont to go rather closely clipped. The beard, like my chin, is divided, and the part of it beneath my chin always was thick and long, seeming to have a more abundant growth thereunder. Old age has wrought changes in this beard of mine, but not much in my hair.

A rather too shrill voice draws upon me the censure of those who pretend to be my friends, for my tone is harsh and high; yet when I am lecturing it cannot be heard at any distance. I am not inclined to speak in the least suavely, and I speak too often.

I have a fixed gaze as if in meditation. My complexion varies, turning from white to red. An oval face, not too well filled out, the head shaped off narrowly behind and delicately rounded, complete a picture so truly commonplace that several painters who have come from afar to make my portrait have found no feature by which they could so characterize me, that I might be distinguished. Upon the lower part of my throat is a swelling like a hard ball, not at all conspicuous, and coming to me as an inheritance from my mother.

THE BOOK OF MY LIFE, 1576

CHARLES CHAPLIN

I REALIZE THAT TIME AND CIRCUMSTANCES have favored me. I have been cosseted in the world's affections, loved and hated. Yes, the world has given me its best and a little of its worst. Whatever were my ill vicissitudes, I believe that fortune and ill fortune drift upon one haphazardly as clouds. Knowing this, I am never too shocked at the bad things that happen and am agreeably surprised at the good. I have no design for living, no philosophy – whether sage or fool, we must all struggle with life. I vacillate with inconsistencies; at times small things will annoy me and catastrophes will leave me indifferent.

Nevertheless, my life is more thrilling today than it ever was. I am in good health and still creative and have plans to produce more pictures – perhaps not with myself, but to write and direct them for members of my family – some of whom have quite an aptitude for the theater. I am still very ambitious; I could never retire. There are many things I want to do; besides having a few unfinished cinema scripts, I should like to write a play and an opera – if time will allow.

Schopenhauer said happiness is a negative state – but I disagree. For the last twenty years I have known what happiness means. I have the good fortune to be married to a wonderful wife. I wish I could write more about this, but it involves love, and perfect love is the most beautiful of all frustrations because it is more than one can express. As I live with Oona, the depth and beauty of her character are a continual revelation to me. Even as she walks ahead of me along the narrow sidewalks of Vevey with simple dignity, her neat little figure straight, her dark hair smoothed back showing a few silver threads, a sudden wave of love and admiration comes over me for all that she is – and a lump comes into my throat.

With such happiness, I sometimes sit out on our terrace at sunset and look over a vast green lawn to the lake in the distance, and beyond the lake to the reassuring mountains, and in this mood think of nothing and enjoy their magnificent serenity.

MY AUTOBIOGRAPHY, 1964

P.G. WODEHOUSE

IN ADDITION TO WATCHING HIS DIET the septuagenarian must, of course, have exercise, and there I am fortunately situated. In Remsenburg we enjoy a number of amenities such as fresh air, fresh eggs and an attractive waterfront on the Great South Bay, but we have not progressed on the path of civilization so far as to have postmen. I walk two miles to the post office every day to get the afternoon mail, accompanied by Poona the cat and Bill the foxhound, who generally packs up after the first furlong or so. (Someone tells me that this is always the way with foxhounds. They have to do so much bustling about in their younger days that when of riper years their inclination is to say 'Ah the hell with it' and just lie around in the sun. But Poona and I are made of sterner stuff, and we trudge the two miles there and two miles back singing a gipsy song. This keeps me in rare fettle.)

Also I still do my getting-up exercises before breakfast, as I have done since 1919 without missing a day, though it is an open secret that I now find a difficulty in touching my toes, and I catch – or try to catch – Poona the cat each night. We let her out at about 10 pm for a breath of air, and once out she hears the call of the old wild life and decides to make a night of it. This means that, unless caught and returned to store, she will hit the high spots till five in the morning, when she will come and mew at my bedroom window, murdering sleep as effectively as ever Macbeth did. And I have the job of catching her.

When you are in your middle seventies you have passed your

peak as a cat-catcher. There was a time – say between 1904 and 1910 – when it would have been child's play for me to outstrip the fleetest cat, but now the joints have stiffened a trifle and I am less quick off the mark. The spirit is willing but the flesh doesn't seem to move as it did. The thing usually ends in a bitter 'All right, be a cad and *stay out!*' from me and a quiet smile from Poona. And then the reproachful mew outside my window as the clocks are striking five. And if I leave the fly-screen open so that she can come in through the window, she jumps on my bed and bites my toes. There seems no way of beating the game.

Still, things have brightened a good deal lately owing to Poona having been bitten in the foot by another cat – no doubt in some night-club brawl – and being able to operate only on three legs. One more such episode, and the thing, as I see it, will be in the bag. I may not be the sprinter I once was, but I feel confident of being able to overtake a cat walking on two hind legs.

Meanwhile, the exercise is doing me a world of good, for apart from the running there is the falling. Owing to the activities of hurricane Carol many of the trees on the estate are shored up with wire ropes, and any Harley Street physician will tell you there is nothing better for the liver than to trip over a wire rope when going all out after a receding cat and come down like a sack of coals. It amuses the cat too.

OVER SEVENTY: AN AUTOBIOGRAPHY WITH DIGRESSIONS, 1957

M.F.K. FISHER

I T USED TO BE CALLED AGING, or the Aging Process if one was more discreet in speech and wording. It meant *getting old*, or *growing older*.

What it amounts to, in my mind at least and about midway in my seventy-seventh year (I was born July 3, 1908, and this is January 23, 1984, for computer's sake), is that I seem almost unconsciously, or perhaps only will-nilly, to be winding down. It is like being a wound clock: I have the original mechanism, but the ticking is slower, and some of the intricate tiny artful gears have worn down with long usage, so that now and then the ticking may falter. (This is known in some circles as *attrition*.)

I notice, and have done for some time, a slowing and faultier rhythm in my walk, my speech now and then, and lately my daily routine. For instance, today I meant to have the bimonthly laundry ready. I got up early, stripped the bed and pillows, brought fresh linen, got out the old laundry in its basket and added to it from bathroom and kitchen. I put the lapboard with its usual folded paper on top of the used linens, and got a pin out so that I could attach it as usual to the bag. I planned to do this at noon after my typist left – which she did at precisely 11:55.

It was then that the bookkeeper called: she would be here at 1:00 instead of 4:00, because her new baby was awake then.

So, at 3:44 PM the laundry man has come, leaving his bundle of clean linens but taking none away, so that I'll have to try to reach his outlet office about the next pickup. My bookkeeper has come and gone. I have not yet eaten the salad I meant to eat before she came. (It smells good.) I have fed Charlie, and am ready to eat, but the telephone has rung often and I have made two appointments for next month, and the fire is not yet laid and I have not given an extra-food watering to the plants on the two balconies and inside, as I meant to do yesterday. I have not located a check for $1,000 that I must send my agent, to whom it should have been sent in the first place. I have not written to dear neglected generous friends. I must send off some checks and cash others, and perhaps thank my stars that I can pay the bills. I must rest a little, this late afternoon, after some wilted lunch.

But I know that this compulsive attempt to stay upright, as Rudyard Kipling might have put it, is futile. I am winding down. I don't protest the process, because it is inevitable. I regret it because I wish I had more time to observe its progress and perhaps comment on it. That is plainly not meant to be.

So I'll eat some tired salad and take a little nap, and wind down some more. Perhaps the laundry man will call, to remind me of the neglected rendezvous with dirty linens—

But how long can this last?

'WINDING DOWN', 1984

BERTRAND RUSSELL

THREE PASSIONS, simple but overwhelmingly strong, have governed my life: the longing for love, the search for knowledge, and unbearable pity for the suffering of mankind. These passions, like great winds, have blown me hither and thither, in a wayward course, over a deep ocean of anguish, reaching to the very verge of despair.

I have sought love, first, because it brings ecstasy – ecstasy so great that I would often have sacrificed all the rest of life for a few hours of this joy. I have sought it, next, because it relieves loneliness – that terrible loneliness in which one shivering consciousness looks over the rim of the world into the cold unfathomable lifeless abyss. I have sought it, finally, because in the union of love I have seen, in a mystic miniature, the prefiguring vision of the heaven that saints and poets have imagined. This is what I sought, and though it might seem too good for human life, this is what – at last – I have found.

With equal passion I have sought knowledge. I have wished to understand the hearts of men. I have wished to know why the stars shine. And I have tried to apprehend the Pythagorean power by which number holds sway above the flux. A little of this, but not much, I have achieved.

Love and knowledge, so far as they were possible, led upward toward the heavens. But always pity brought me back to earth. Echoes of cries of pain reverberate in my heart. Children in famine, victims tortured by their oppressors, helpless old people a hated burden to their sons, and the whole world of loneliness, poverty, and pain make a mockery of what human life should be. I long to alleviate the evil, but I cannot, and I too suffer.

This has been my life. I have found it worth living, and would gladly live it again if the chance were offered to me.

THE AUTOBIOGRAPHY OF BERTRAND RUSSELL, 1967–1969

C.G. JUNG

MY LIFE IS A STORY of the self-realization of the unconscious. Everything in the unconscious seeks outward manifestation, and the personality too desires to evolve out of its unconscious conditions and to experience itself as a whole. I cannot employ the language of science to trace this process of growth in myself, for I cannot experience myself as a scientific problem.

What we are to our inward vision, and what man appears to be *sub specie aeternitatis*, can only be expressed by way of myth. Myth is more individual and expresses life more precisely than does science. Science works with concepts of averages which are far too general to do justice to the subjective variety of an individual life.

Thus it is that I have now undertaken, in my eighty-third year, to tell my personal myth. I can only make direct statements, only 'tell stories'. Whether or not the stories are 'true' is not the problem. The only question is whether what I tell is *my* fable, *my* truth.

An autobiography is so difficult to write because we possess no standards, no objective foundation, from which to judge ourselves. There are really no proper bases for comparison. I know that in many things I am not like others, but I do not know what I really am like. Man cannot compare himself with any other creature; he is not a monkey, not a cow, not a tree. I am a man. But what is it to be that? Like every other being, I am a splinter of the infinite deity, but I cannot contrast myself with any animal, any plant or any stone. Only a mythical being has a range greater than man's. How then can a man form definite opinions about himself?

We are a psychic process which we do not control, or only partly direct. Consequently, we cannot have any final judgment – about ourselves or our lives. If we had, we would know everything – but at most that is only a pretense. At bottom we never know how it has come about. The story of a life begins somewhere, at some particular point we happen to remember; and even then it was already highly complex. We do not know how life is going to turn out. Therefore the story has no beginning, and the end can only be vaguely hinted at.

The life of man is a dubious experiment. It is a tremendous phenomenon only in numerical terms. Individually, it is so fleeting, so insufficient, that it is literally a miracle that anything can exist and develop at all. I was impressed by that fact long ago, as a young medical student, and it seemed to me miraculous that I should not have been prematurely annihilated.

Life has always seemed to me like a plant that lives on its rhizome.

Its true life is invisible, hidden in the rhizome. The part that appears above ground lasts only a single summer. Then it withers away – an ephemeral apparition. When we think of the unending growth and decay of life and civilizations, we cannot escape the impression of absolute nullity. Yet I have never lost a sense of something that lives and endures underneath the eternal flux. What we see is the blossom, which passes. The rhizome remains.

In the end the only events in my life worth telling are those when the imperishable world irrupted into this transitory one. That is why I speak chiefly of inner experiences, amongst which I include my dreams and visions. These form the *prima materia* of my scientific work. They were the fiery magma out of which the stone that had to be worked was crystallized.

All other memories of travel, people and my surroundings have paled beside these interior happenings. Many people have participated in the story of our times and written about it; if the reader wants an account of that, let him turn to them or get somebody to tell it to him. Recollection of the outward events of my life has largely faded or disappeared. But my encounters with the 'other' reality, my bouts with the unconscious, are indelibly engraved upon my memory. In that realm there has always been wealth in abundance, and everything else has lost importance by comparison.

Similarly, other people are established inalienably in my memories only if their names were entered in the scrolls of my destiny from the beginning, so that encountering them was at the same time a kind of recollection.

Inner experiences also set their seal on the outward events that came my way and assumed importance for me in youth or later on. I early arrived at the insight that when no answer comes from within to the problems and complexities of life, they ultimately mean very little. Outward circumstances are no substitute for inner experience. Therefore my life has been singularly poor in outward happenings. I cannot tell much about them, for it would strike me as hollow and insubstantial. I can understand myself only in the light of inner happenings. It is these that make up the singularity of my life, and with these my autobiography deals.

MEMORIES, DREAMS, REFLECTIONS, 1961

FLORIDA SCOTT-MAXWELL

ANOTHER DAY TO BE FILLED, to be lived silently, watching the sky and the lights on the wall. No one will come probably. I have no duties except to myself. That is not true. I have a duty to all who care for me – not to be a problem, not to be a burden. I must carry my age lightly for all our sakes, and thank God I still can. Oh that I may to the end. Each day then, must be filled with my first duty, I must be 'all right'. But is this assurance not the gift we all give to each other, daily, hourly?

I wonder if we need be quite so dutiful. With one friend of my own age we cheerfully exchange the worst symptoms, and our black dreads as well. We frequently talk of death, for we are very alert to the experience of the unknown that may be so near and it is only to those of one's own age that one can speak frankly. Talking of one's health, which one wants to do, is generally full of risks. Ill health is unpleasant to most healthy people as it makes them feel helpless, threatened, and it can feel like an unjustified demand for sympathy. Few believe in the pains of another, and if the person in pain has nothing to show, can forget the pain when interested, then where is the reality of it? In one's self, where it ought to be kept I suppose. Disabilities crowd in on the old; real pain is there, and if we have to be falsely cheerful, it is part of our isolation.

Another secret we carry is that though drab outside – wreckage to the eye, mirrors a mortification – inside we flame with a wild life that is almost incommunicable. In silent, hot rebellion we cry silently – 'I have lived my life haven't I? What more is expected of me?' Have we got to pretend out of *noblesse oblige* that age is nothing, in order to encourage the others? This we do with a certain haughtiness, realizing now that we have reached the place beyond resignation, a place I had no idea existed until I had arrived here.

It is a place of fierce energy. Perhaps passion would be a better word than energy, for the sad fact is this vivid life cannot be used. If I try to transpose it into action I am soon spent. It has to be accepted as passionate life, perhaps the life I never lived, never guessed I had it in me to live. It feels other and more than that. It feels like the far side of precept and aim. It is just life, the natural intensity of life, and when old we can have it for our reward and undoing. It can – at moments – feel as though we had it for our glory. Some of it must go beyond good and bad, for at times – though this comes rarely, unexpectedly – it is a swelling clarity as though all was resolved. It has no content, it seems to expand us, it does not derive from the body, and then it is gone. It may be a degree of consciousness which lies outside activity, and which when young we are too busy to experience.

I wonder if living alone makes one more alive. No precious energy goes in disagreement or compromise. No need to augment others, there is just yourself, just truth – a morsel – and you. You went through those long years when it was pain to be alone, now you have come out on the good side of that severe discipline. Alone you have your own way all day long, and you become very natural. Perhaps this naturalness extends into heights and depths, going further than we know; as we cannot voice it we must just treasure it as the life that enriches our days.

THE MEASURE OF MY DAYS, 1968

PABLO CASALS

ON MY LAST BIRTHDAY I was ninety-three years old. That is not young, of course. In fact, it is older than ninety. But age is a relative matter. If you continue to work and to absorb the beauty in the world about you, you find that age does not necessarily mean getting old. At least, not in the ordinary sense. I feel many things more intensely than ever before, and for me life grows more fascinating.

Not long ago my friend Sasha Schneider brought me a letter addressed to me by a group of musicians in the Caucasus Mountains in the Soviet Union. This was the text of the letter:

DEAR HONORABLE MAESTRO
I have the pleasure on behalf of the Georgian Caucasian Orchestra to invite you to conduct one of our concerts. You will be the first musician of your age who receives the distinction of conducting our orchestra.

Never in the history of our orchestra have we permitted a man under one hundred years to conduct. All of the members of our orchestra are over one hundred years old. But we have heard of your talents as a conductor, and we feel that, despite your youthfulness, an exception should be made in your case.

We expect a favorable response as soon as possible.

We pay travel expenses and of course shall provide living accommodations during your stay with us.

Respectfully,

ASTAN SHLARBA

President, 123 years old

Sasha is a man with a sense of humor; he likes to play a joke. That letter was one of his jokes; he had written it himself. I must admit I took it seriously at first. And why? Because it did not seem implausible that there should be an orchestra composed of musicians older than a hundred. And, indeed, I was right! That portion of the letter was not a joke. There is such an orchestra in the Caucasus. Sasha had read about it in the London *Sunday Times*. He showed me the article, with photographs of the orchestra. All of its members were more than a hundred years old. There were about thirty of them – they rehearse regularly and give periodic concerts. Most of them are farmers who continue to work in the fields. The oldest of the group, Astan Shlarba, is a tobacco grower who also trains horses. They are splendid-looking men, obviously full of vitality. I should like to hear them play sometime – and, in fact, to conduct them, if the opportunity arose. Of course I am not sure they would permit this, in view of my inadequate age.

There is often something to be learned from jokes, and it was so in this case. In spite of their age, those musicians have not lost their zest for life. How does one explain this? I do not think the answer lies simply in their physical constitutions or in something unique about the climate in which they live. It has to do with their attitude toward life; and I believe that their ability to work is due in no small measure to the fact they *do* work. Work helps prevent one from getting old. I, for one, cannot dream of retiring. Not now or ever. Retire? The word is alien and the idea inconceivable to me. I don't believe in retirement for anyone in my type of work, not while the spirit remains. My work is my life. I cannot think of one without the other. To 'retire' means to me to begin to die. The man who works and is never bored is never old. Work and interest in worthwhile things are the best remedy for age. Each day I am reborn. Each day I must begin again.

For the past eighty years I have started each day in the same manner. It is not a mechanical routine but something essential to my daily life. I go to the piano, and I play two preludes and fugues of Bach. I cannot think of doing otherwise. It is a sort of benediction on the house. But that is not its only meaning for me. It is a rediscovery of the world of which I have the joy of being a part. It fills me with awareness of the wonder of life, with a feeling of the incredible marvel of being a human being. The music is never the same for me, never. Each day it is something new, fantastic and unbelievable. That is Bach, like nature, a miracle!

I do not think a day passes in my life in which I fail to look with fresh amazement at the miracle of nature. It is there on every side. It can be simply a shadow on a mountainside, or a spider's web gleaming with dew, or sunlight on the leaves of a tree. I have always especially loved the sea. Whenever possible, I have lived by the sea, as for these past twelve years here in Puerto Rico. It has long been a custom of mine to walk along the beach each morning before I start to work. True, my walks are shorter than they used to be, but that does not lessen the wonder of the sea. How mysterious and beautiful is the sea! how infinitely variable! It is never the same, never, not for one moment to the next, always in the process of change, always becoming something different and new.

JOYS AND SORROWS: REFLECTIONS, 1970

MANNY SHINWELL

WE LIVE IN A WORLD OF CONSTANT CHANGE. I express curiosity about the future, that is understandable. I have always wished to see what was on the other side of the hill. On those issues of theological concern, where for centuries controversy, violence, even persecution have harassed mankind, my tongue remains silent.

In periods of meditation I have wondered about one's purpose in life. I read, I listen, engage in conversation, respect the sincerely held beliefs of others: nevertheless, I confess failure in reaching a conclusion. In this vast illimitable universe, so incomprehensible, all one can claim with limited mental apparatus is to reflect on the mystery of it all. To quote on those lines of the poet Keats:

> – *then on the shore*
> *Of the wide world I stand alone, and think*
> *Till love and fame to nothingness do sink.*

To have survived the vicissitudes and strifes of a long life, frustrations, moments of desperation, even tragedy in the departure of loved ones, and even though in later periods of life one is accompanied by ailments, solitude and other penalties, one must be grateful. A long life has enabled one to widen experience, gain knowledge, the preface to understanding. That it is accompanied by periods of trauma when memory overcomes reason, I admit. So how do I live now, when in my ninety-sixth year? Until a few months ago I alternated between my typewriter and my kitchen. Now, apart from attendance at the House of Lords, a few functions – less now than ever – I am engaged in the dictation of a book, a task I was reluctant to undertake, and have only done so under pressure; more of a challenge than an adventure.

When the House of Lords terminates its proceedings some time in the evening, but not too late, I repair to my flat and, depending on the mood, devote myself as much to the kitchen as to the typewriter. Indeed, I confess that I often meet with disaster with both. Domestic help is minimal. I do not mind being alone and enjoy meditation about world problems; the past and people I have admired and loved, and gratitude for the services of experts in the medical profession; and when faced by periods of melancholy aware that one is better off than most; sometimes off-colour, but try hard to shake it off. If, when not in good form, I have to make a speech or ask a question in the Lords I feel much better. It is stimulating, even if one's speech is unacceptable or even ignored.

LEAD WITH THE LEFT: MY FIRST NINETY-SIX YEARS, 1981

MARGARET MURRAY

I N ALL COUNTRIES AND IN ALL PERIODS old age has been credited with wisdom born of experience, and it has always been acknowledged that to women have been given certain gifts which are denied to men. Therefore on account of both sex and age I claim that my opinions may be worth consideration. I claim that I have no more than that gift which is so identified with women that it is known as 'a woman's intuition', but at the age of one hundred my consecutive memory goes back farther than the memory of all but a very few.

My own personal recollections take me back to the Franco-German war of 1870–71, with the downfall of France and the triumph of Germany. This is a period which has now gone into the mists of historical research and rouses as little interest as the Battle of Crecy. But as an archaeologist my range of vision is not limited to my personal knowledge but extends even beyond that of the historian into that far period when man began his first struggle upwards. And my special line of research has always been in religion, in that groping towards something higher and better than the human being. The material evidence which remains is now all that we have to show the mental and spiritual rise of the human race. The material objects show that advance in material comfort, and if rightly judged can show also that imponderable, intangible element, the spiritual advance which, more than any other element, has differentiated man from the animals.

I am often asked, 'Do you see much change in the world of the present day and the world as you knew it when you were young?' 'Do you think things are better or worse than they were?'

To the first question I should answer, 'Yes!' And I should go so far as to quote the line from that well-known hymn, 'Change and decay in all around I see,' for the two things must go together. In this world there is nothing permanent, therefore certain customs and beliefs must decay and fall out of use. But they are usually replaced by something higher and better, and the loss of them indicates an advance. Decay is the natural process by which what is useless and worn out is so quietly removed that its loss is hardly noticed. 'Change and decay in all around I see.' Yes, and I am glad to see it.

In answer to the second question, I am definitely of opinion that there is no comparison, the change for the better is so great. At my age I stand, as it were, on a high peak alone. I have no contemporaries with whom I can exchange memories or views. But that very isolation gives me a less biased view of that vast panorama of human life which is spread before the eyes of a centenarian, still more when those eyes are the eyes of an archaeologist. It is true that much of the far distance is shrouded in cloud and mist, but every here and there the fog thins a little and one can see clearly the advance of mankind.

MY FIRST HUNDRED YEARS, 1963

~ BIOGRAPHIES ~

J.R. ACKERLEY (1896–1967) English editor and writer. *My Father and Myself* (1968)

Joseph Randolph Ackerley published a novel, a play, a travel book and poems, and served for many years as the editor of *The Listener* magazine where he nurtured the writings of E.M. Forster, Virginia Woolf, W.H. Auden, Christopher Isherwood and Stephen Spender, amongst others. But it is for his memoir, *My Father and Myself*, that he is lastingly remembered. Ackerley's coming-of-age story – and depiction of his relationship with his distant and often disdainful father – describes the homosexual longings of his schooldays, his experiences during the First World War, the beginnings of his writing career and his agonizing search for love. It is also Ackerley's attempt to come to terms with his father, who, on his death in 1929, left Ackerley a letter revealing that he had a long-time French mistress and second family in France. Ackerley also finds evidence that leads him to believe that his father had homosexual lovers in his youth. Ackerley died at the age of 71 in 1967, and left instructions for the manuscript of *My Father and Myself* to be published after his death. He was also the author of a memoir of his dog, *My Dog Tulip*, 1968, to whom *My Father and Myself* is dedicated.

HENRY ADAMS (1838–1918) American historian and writer. *The Education of Henry Adams* (1907)

Henry Adams came from a long line of eminent Americans, including two presidents: John Adams and John Quincy Adams. His father, Charles Adams, was a Congressman and then US ambassador to England during the American Civil War. But Henry, who was born in Boston in 1838, was determined not to go into the family business.

After graduating from Harvard, Adams went to England with his father as his personal secretary, but began writing articles, returning to America to take up the position of professor of history at Harvard and to edit the *North American Review*. He went on to publish histories, biographies, essays and two novels. Then, in 1907, at the age of 69, he privately printed his memoirs, *The Education of Henry Adams*, which he circulated amongst friends and family. In this classic work of American autobiography, Adams describes the development of his sensibility, from his schooldays through Harvard and beyond, as he attempts to establish a philosophy of history for the times. The book is told in the third person, which serves to distance Adams from his narrative, but also brilliantly anticipates the ironic and embittered tones of American modernism. The memoir was properly published after Adams' death in 1918, to acclaim, and a posthumous Pulitzer Prize.

MUHAMMAD ALI (1942–) American boxer and humanitarian.
The Greatest: My Own Story (1975)

Muhammad Ali's 1975 autobiography – co-written with the journalist Richard Durham and published at the peak of Ali's boxing career – was the result of six years' collaboration between the writer and subject. The book begins with Ali's 1973 return to his hometown of Louisville, Kentucky, just after his humiliating loss to Ken Norton. In numerous flashbacks, Ali then recounts the most important events of his life – his discovery of boxing at the age of 12, his gold medal at the 1960 Olympics, his conversion to Islam leading to his name change from Cassius Clay, his 1967 refusal to be drafted into the army, at which point he was taken to court and stripped of his heavyweight title. The book culminates with Ali's dramatic defeats of George Foreman, in Zaire, in 1974 and of Joe Frazier, in Manila, in 1975. Ali kept boxing until 1981. Three years after announcing his retirement, he was diagnosed with Parkinson's disease. He remains active in advocating for children and war victims, and in promoting humanitarian causes. In 2004 he published a new memoir, co-written with one of his nine children and called *The Soul of the Butterfly: Reflections on Life's Journey*.

REINALDO ARENAS (1943–1990) Cuban writer. *Before Night Falls: A Memoir* (1992)

Reinaldo Arenas dictated his memoir into a tape-machine, too weak to physically write as he was terminally ill with AIDS. He completed the work just months before his suicide in 1990, at the age of 47. The memoir begins with Arenas' impoverished childhood in rural Cuba where he was born in 1943. Abandoned by his father, the family was often too poor to eat, but the freedom Arenas was afforded as a child set a precedent for the rest of his life. As a teenager Arenas fought in the Cuban Revolution for Castro, and in 1961 moved to Havana where he studied and began to write. Arenas was outspoken in his political beliefs and his homosexuality, and before long, his writings were systematically censored and suppressed. In 1973, he was sent to prison for 'ideological deviation'; later he was tortured and forced to renounce his work. In 1980, Arenas exiled himself to New York City where he was later diagnosed with AIDS. Despite Castro's best efforts, Arenas produced ten novels, five novellas, many short stories, essays, theatre pieces and poems, in addition to *Before Night Falls*. His memoir remains a vivid testament of the writer's struggle to remain free – artistically, sexually and politically.

ELIZABETH ASHBRIDGE (1713–1755) American preacher. *Some Account of the Fore-part of the Life of Elizabeth Ashbridge* (1774)

Although Elizabeth Ashbridge began to write the *Account* of her life in 1746, it wouldn't appear in print until nearly 20 years after her death in 1755. It was preserved by her husband, Aaron Ashbridge, who published it under the above title in 1774. As Ashbridge describes in her Account she was born Elizabeth Sampson in Cheshire, England, in 1713, and brought up by her mother while her father was away at sea. When she was 14, Elizabeth eloped, marrying a man who died a few months later. Her father, still furious with his daughter for running away, refused to take her back and she left England to stay with her mother's relatives in Ireland. She found herself in a Quaker household, which did not suit Ashbridge's 'wild and airy' temperament – she loved to dance, which was forbidden – so she left to live in the west of Ireland, where she met a woman who was emigrating to America. Ashbridge sailed with her, not realizing that she was being sold as an indentured servant. She arrived in New York in 1782 at the age of 19, but after three years of service, she managed to buy her freedom. At 22, she remarried to a man who – as the author tells us – fell in love with her for her dancing. It was an unhappy union; he was drunken and violent, and the couple fell out over Ashbridge's new-found devotion to Quakerism, a religion she finally embraced. In 1740, her husband left to serve as a soldier in Cuba, where he died. Ashbridge's *Account* ends at this point, so we do not hear about the last part of her life, her happy marriage to Aaron Ashbridge in 1746, and her career as a successful Quaker preacher. She died in 1755, in Ireland, where she had returned to preach.

ANDREA ASHWORTH (1969–) English academic and writer. *Once in a House on Fire* (1998)

Andrea Ashworth was born in Manchester in 1969 and published her memoir, *Once in a House on Fire*, at the age of 28. The book begins with the death of the author's father, by drowning, when she is five. After this, her mother remarries twice, and two physically abusive stepfathers cast dark shadows over the family. Their mother, although loving, is ineffectual, and so it is left to Ashworth to try to protect herself and her sisters. An intelligent and resilient child, Ashworth discovers she can retreat into the world of books and at 18 escapes to Oxford, where her memoir ends. *Once In a House on Fire* is narrated in the voice first of a child and then of a young woman who has managed to prevail. After Oxford, Ashworth won a scholarship to Yale University, where she wrote her memoir, returning to become a research fellow at Jesus College, Oxford.

ST AUGUSTINE (354–430) Roman bishop. *The Confessions of St Augustine* (397–400).

The Confessions of St Augustine, the first ever full-length autobiography, remains one of the most impassioned works of self-examination in the canon. Augustine was born Aurelius Augustinus in 354, in the Roman outpost of Thagaste (Souk Ahras in modern-day Algeria). He began work on his *Confessions* in 397, while serving as the bishop of Hippo (Annaba in modern-day Algeria). Augustine's *Confessions* were written in Latin and take the form of an extended prayer to God for grace and forgiveness. The first ten books cover Augustine's childhood, his education, youth and early manhood in Carthage, Rome and Milan. Initially, the young Augustine ignores the efforts of his Christian mother to save him from sinfulness, but finally she succeeds and he converts to Christianity at the age of 32. At this point, he gives up teaching and begins a life of religious contemplation. Here, the autobiographical narrative ends – the last three chapters of *The Confessions* are concerned solely with the author's religious beliefs. Augustine died in 430 while Hippo was under siege to the Vandals, and although the city burned to the ground, Augustine's library, containing his many manuscripts, was miraculously saved. Augustine's theories of sin and grace became a cornerstone of the Roman Catholic Church, but his influence on subsequent autobiographers is perhaps just as profound. The narrative rhythm of *The Confessions*, which follows Augustine's progress from sinfulness to conversion to spiritual enlightenment, establishes a pattern that generations of autobiographers will either react against or echo.

JAMES BALDWIN (1924–1987) African-American writer and civil rights activist. *'The Devil Finds Work'* (1976)

James Arthur Baldwin was born in Harlem, New York, in 1924. 'The story of my childhood is the usual bleak fantasy,' he wrote in his 'Autobiographical Notes', included with his essays, *Notes of a Native Son* (1955), 'and we can dismiss it with the restrained observation that I certainly would not consider living it again.' In fact, Baldwin did not dismiss his childhood entirely from his writings – descriptions from his youth find their way into his great essays, which are invariably personal in tone. The excerpt included in this anthology is the title essay from *The Devil Finds Work*, Baldwin's 1976 collection of investigations into racism in American movies, in which the writer deals with films as diverse as *Lawrence of Arabia* and *The Exorcist*. Baldwin produced six novels and three plays, as well as essays, poems and short stories in his lifetime. As a result of his participation in the Civil Rights struggles of the 60s, Baldwin came under surveillance by the FBI, and so it is perhaps not surprising that he chose to spend so many years in France, a place he first visited in 1948. He died in St Paul-de-Vence, at the age of 63.

P.T. BARNUM (1810–1891) American entrepreneur and showman. *The Life of P.T. Barnum, written by himself* (1855)

Phineas Taylor Barnum was born in Bethel, Connecticut in 1810. At the age of 15, his father died, leaving the family bankrupt. Barnum began his career as a teenager, first working as a lottery agent, then as a newspaper editor and shop owner. In 1835, however, he heard about a woman claiming to be the former nurse of George Washington, and decided to pay for exclusive rights to 'exhibit' the woman, calculating she would have to be 161 years old for the claim to be true. His career as America's 'Prince of Humbugs' had commenced. In 1841, Barnum acquired the American Museum in Manhattan and proceeded to transform it into the most successful venture of its kind in America, exhibiting, amongst other delights, a real-life mermaid from Fiji. The excerpts from his autobiography included in this book are from the original 1855 version of *The Life of P.T. Barnum* – its author rewrote his life story numerous times, and it sometimes appears under the name *Struggles and Triumphs*. Later in life, Barnum helped create the three-ring Barnum and Bailey circus, 'the greatest show on earth'. He died in Bridgeport, Connecticut, in 1891, where he had built a large estate from the profits of his labours.

SIMONE DE BEAUVOIR (1908–1986) French intellectual and feminist. *The Prime of Life* (1960) and *Force of Circumstance* (1963)

Simone de Beauvoir's four-volume autobiographical project began in 1958 with the publication of her *Memoirs of a Dutiful Daughter*. The book deals with the first 20 years of de Beauvoir's life: her upbringing in a bourgeois Parisian family and the development of her mind, as well as her early meetings as a student with Jean-Paul Sartre, the man who remained her lover and companion for the next 50 years. *The Prime of Life* covers de Beauvoir's time after her graduation and leading up to the Second World War, as she began work on her early novels and essays. *Force of Circumstance* (1963) starts with the liberation of Paris in 1945, and describes the period during which de Beauvoir wrote her famous history of the oppression of women, *The Second Sex* (1949); it finishes with the author's musings on her distaste for growing old (she was 54 when the book was completed). The last in the sequence – *All Said and Done* (1972) – covers the decade from 1962 to 1972, a period when she became increasingly involved with social reform and the women's liberation movement she had helped to inspire. Taken as a whole, the sequence is a remarkable account of a woman who, despite the strictures of her times, was determined to be a writer, an intellectual and to remain free (although Sartre proposed, he was refused, and de Beauvoir never married). Towards the end of her life, de Beauvoir wrote two autobiographical accounts: *A Very Easy Death* (1964) on her mother's dying, and *Adieux: A Farewell to Sartre* (1981), an account of the last ten years of their relationship. She died in Paris in 1986.

ALAN BENNETT (1934–) English playwright, actor, director. *'The Treachery of Books'* (1994)

Alan Bennett was born in Yorkshire, England, in 1934, the son of a butcher. He gained a degree in history from Oxford University; around the same time he met Peter Cook, Dudley Moore and Jonathan Miller, with whom he began to write and perform the sketches included in *Beyond the Fringe*, the revolutionary comedy revue that stormed the stages of London and New York in the early 60s. His first stage play, *Forty Years On*, was performed in 1968 and was followed by 19 plays for television, three films, as well as numerous stage works and short stories, many of them deriving inspiration from the Northern working-class world of his youth. *Writing Home*, a collection of Bennett's journalism, lectures, diaries and essays, was published in 1994 by way of a memoir – and a sequel, *Untold Stories*, appeared in 2005. *Writing Home* commences with the autobiographical essay 'The Treachery of Books', about his Leeds childhood and how books influenced (and often misled) him as a boy, an excerpt from which is included in this compendium.

INGMAR BERGMAN (1918–) Swedish film and theatre director. *The Magic Lantern* (1987)

In his autobiography, *The Magic Lantern*, Ingmar Bergman cuts back and forth in time, as if perhaps envisioning a storyboard for the film of his life. Bergman was born in Uppsala, Sweden, in 1918, the son of a Lutheran minister. He experienced particularly intense relations with both his parents – in the memoir he mines the kinds of complicated familial dramas he so often explored in his films (while managing to remain tellingly silent on the subject of his five marriages). After graduating from the University of Stockholm, Bergman began to work in the theatre and in opera, writing his first screenplay in 1944 and going on to make 50 films, including such classics of European cinema as *The Seventh Seal* (1957) and *Fanny and Alexander* (1982). The great director has produced a further autobiographical work, *Images: My Life in Film* (1993).

ANNIE BESANT (1847–1933) Social campaigner and theosophist. *Annie Besant: An Autobiography* (1893)

Annie Besant's autobiography tells the story of a woman who had already repeatedly reinvented herself by the time she wrote her life story at the age of 46. She was born Annie Wood in London in 1847. At the age of 19 she married the Reverend Frank Besant, but the new Mrs Besant found her husband's religious dogmatism stifling, and when she refused to take communion, he ordered her to leave the household. She fled back to London. She was 23. Soon afterwards, Annie Besant had rejected religion entirely, joining the National Secular Society and beginning to write articles on secularism and women's rights. After narrowly escaping a prison sentence for promoting birth control, Besant published the pioneering *Laws of Population*, in which she continued to argue the case for family planning. Next Besant turned her attentions to workers' rights, campaigning on behalf of women factory workers and the trade union movement. She was elected to the London School Board in 1889, initiating sweeping reforms of the educational system. Then, in 1887, Besant met Madame Blavatsky – a Russian émigré and founder of the Theosophical Society – a meeting that caused her to abandon her atheism for a system of religious belief based on ancient Indian spirituality. When Blavatsky died in 1891, the school of theosophy split into two branches and Besant became president of one of them. It was at this point she began work on her memoir. Later, Besant moved to India, and became involved in the campaign for Indian home rule. She died in Madras, in 1933, at the age of 86, convinced she would be quickly reincarnated.

AMBROSE BIERCE (1842–C.1914) American writer. *'What I Saw of Shiloh'* (1881)

Ambrose Gwinnett Bierce was born in Ohio in 1842. At the age of 19, he enlisted with the Union army, fighting in some of the bloodiest battles of the Civil War. After the war, Bierce briefly worked for the government, before moving to San Francisco, and beginning to write. He became a successful newspaper editor and satirist, and was nicknamed 'Bitter Bierce' for his biting wit. Bierce's extraordinary depiction of the 1862 Battle of Shiloh, 'What I Saw of Shiloh', was first published as an article in 1881, and the author's surreal treatment of the brutality of war set a new precedent for writings on the subject. He is perhaps most famous for his brilliantly satirical definitions of common words in *The Devil's Dictionary*. The book was first published in 1906 as *The Cynic's Word Book*, in which he defined 'cynic' as 'A blackguard whose faulty vision sees things as they are, not as they ought to be.' The circumstances of Bierce's later years are unknown. In 1913, he disappeared in Mexico, where, legend has it, he died in the Mexican Revolution.

DIRK BOGARDE (1921–1999) English actor and writer. *An Orderly Man* (1983)

In later life, the actor Dirk Bogarde began to write, producing no less than seven volumes of autobiography, *A Postilion Struck by Lightning* (1977), *Snakes and Ladders* (1978), *An Orderly Man* (1983), *Back Cloth* (1986), *Great Meadow* (1992), *A Short Walk from Harrods* (1993), and *Cleared for Take-off* (1995). He also wrote six novels and published collections of his journalism and letters. Born Derek Van den Bogaerde in London in 1921, the son of a newspaper editor and an actress, Bogarde served in the Second World War, before beginning his acting career on the London stage. His breakthrough in films came in 1950, playing a murderer in *The Blue Lamp*, and he went on to appear in over 60 features during his lifetime. The excerpt from his autobiographies included in this compendium is from the third volume, *An Orderly Man*, which takes up where the second, *Snakes and Ladders* left off, at the conclusion of the filming of Luchino Visconti's *Death in Venice* (1971). It is 1970, and Bogarde has decided to retreat from the acting world after three decades of almost continual work. On the verge of turning 50, the author has bought a dilapidated farmhouse in the South of France, and *An Orderly Man* follows his progress as he struggles to rescue the house and land from years of neglect. Bogarde continued to act and write into his 70s. He died in London in 1999.

GERTRUDE SIMMONS BONNIN (1876–1938) Native American writer and campaigner. *Impressions of an Indian Childhood* (1900)

Gertrude Simmons was born on a Sioux reservation, in South Dakota. At the age of eight, against her mother's wishes, she agreed to leave the reservation to study at a Quaker school in Indiana, learning English and becoming largely assimilated. A talented violinist, she attended the Boston Conservatory to study music. After she graduated, she gave herself the Native American name, Zitkala-Sa, meaning 'red bird', and began to publish her autobiographical sketches. From 1900 to 1902 she wrote her memoirs, articles and versions of Sioux legends, becoming one of the first Native American women to write about her background without an ethnographer. There is no doubt that Bonnin saw herself as preserving the ways of her people, dangerously dispossessed and shrinking in numbers, even though she had long since left the reservation of her childhood behind. In 1902 she married Raymond Bonnin, who worked for the Bureau of Indian Affairs, and her writing career came to an abrupt halt. Although she produced no other major literary works after her marriage, she spent her life working for Native American rights. She remains the only Native American to have written an opera (*Sun Dance*, 1913).

PAUL BOWLES (1910–1999) American composer and writer. *Without Stopping* (1972)

The title of Paul Bowles' autobiography, *Without Stopping*, gives the reader some idea of the pace of the story to follow. Bowles' tale begins with his four-year-old epiphany that he was an individual and continues at an unrelenting clip till we join him in his adopted home of Tangiers, Morocco. Bowles was born in New York in 1910. He began writing poetry at an early age and published his first poem at 17. Two years later, while studying at the University of Virginia, he decided to run away to Europe, returning to America briefly before setting out again on travels, which would continue for most of his adult life. During the late 30s and 40s, Bowles' career as a composer flourished and he became a prominent music critic. He first visited Morocco in 1931 on the suggestion of Gertrude Stein, and made his home in Tangiers from 1947 onwards. Then, in 1949, at the age of 39, he published his first and most famous novel, *The Sheltering Sky*. He began work on his autobiography in 1970, considering it a necessary chore. Although *Without Stopping* is rich in anecdote, exotic locales and famous names (Bowles can name-drop most of the important artists of his era, it seems), those looking for personal revelations about the artist's life should purchase a biography. Bowles' friend and fellow writer William Burroughs joked that the autobiography should have been called 'Without Telling'.

MARLON BRANDO (1924–2004) American film actor.
Brando: Songs My Mother Taught Me (1994)

According to Robert Lindsey, the co-author of *Brando: Songs My Mother Taught Me*, Marlon Brando had said that he wanted nothing left out of his autobiography, with the exception of his three marriages and nine children. It's true that much is left out of *Brando* – at the time of starting work on the book, Brando's son was in prison for manslaughter and his daughter would soon commit suicide – but nonetheless the passages on the actor's childhood are especially revealing. Brando endured a difficult start in life, growing up with drunken and abusive parents in California, Illinois and Omaha, Nebraska, where he was born in 1924. Acting provided a means of escape, and when he arrived in New York at the age of 19, he immediately enrolled in classes with the method-acting coach, Stella Adler. His first and only stage appearance was in Tennessee Williams' *A Streetcar Named Desire*, on Broadway in 1947, in the role that launched his career. Brando appeared in scores of films, including triumphs such as *The Godfather* (1972) and disasters like *Mutiny on The Bounty* (1962). In his autobiography he is consistently offhand about his achievements – of his famous role in *On the Waterfront* (1954), he says it was 'actor-proof'. His passion is reserved for his activism – including for the civil rights movement and Native American causes – and his pets, devoting an entire chapter to them. Brando died in 2004, at the age of 80.

VERA BRITTAIN (1893–1970) English writer. *Testament of Youth* (1933)

Testament of Youth is Vera Brittain's famous account of her early years and time as a nurse during the First World War. It was written with the intention of illuminating, not just Brittain's own story, but that of an entire generation – young men and women whose lives were devastated and, in many cases, ended by the war. She was born in Newcastle-under-Lyme in 1893, and grew up in a middle-class English family who initially refused to let her attend university. When war broke out, Brittain was at Oxford, and she immediately volunteered to serve as a nurse, first in Malta and then France before returning to London. Her fiancé, Roland Leighton, and her brother, Edward Brittain, were both killed at the Front, as well as several close friends – the excerpt included in this compendium describes her grief following Leighton's death. After the end of the war, she returned to Oxford, where she met the writer Winifred Holtby, the subject of a second memoir, *Testament of Friendship* (1940). Holtby and Brittain moved to London where they began to write, Brittain producing novels and journalism. She was briefly married to an American, George Catlin, but returned to live with Holtby again until the writer's untimely death in 1935. Brittain produced a further work of autobiography, *Testament of Experience* (1957), which takes up her story from 1925 to 1950 and recounts her involvement in the British peace movement. She was a confirmed pacifist who opposed the Second World War and who helped to found the Campaign for Nuclear Disarmament in 1957. She continued to work for peace until her death in London in 1970.

HAROLD BRODKEY (1930–1996) American writer. *This Wild Darkness: The Story of My Death* (1996)

Harold Brodkey was diagnosed with AIDS in the spring of 1993, and announced his diagnosis in *The New Yorker* soon afterwards. His reports and diary entries from his deathbed were published in the magazine over the next three years and then gathered into a book, *This Wild Darkness: The Story of My Death*. In his final work, Brodkey looks back at his life, his mother's death when he was still a baby, his childhood in St Louis, and the abuse he suffered at the hands of his adoptive father. He also reflects on his homosexual affairs, the last of which he believes infected him, even though it occurred 20 years previously. *This Wild Darkness* forms a chronicle of the disease, its physical effects and the politics surrounding it, and the approach of death itself. Brodkey, who was born Aaron Weintraub in 1930, published his first collection of short stories in 1954, then spent 30 years writing his first novel, *The Runaway Soul* (1991). He published a second, final novel, *Profane Friendship* in 1994. *This Wild Darkness* was published in 1996, the year of his death, and dedicated to his wife, the novelist Ellen Schwamm.

CHRISTY BROWN (1932–1981) Irish writer and painter. *My Left Foot* (1954)

Christy Brown's autobiography begins in Dublin, Ireland, in 1932, with the author's birth. One of 13 children of a devoted mother and a bricklayer father, Brown was born with cerebral palsy and grew up with severe physical limitations – as a child he could only move his left foot. Nonetheless, his mother was convinced that it was only his body that was afflicted and not his mind, and thanks to her perseverance, Brown managed to learn to read, write and paint. At the age of 18, Brown started rehabilitation classes where he was taught to speak and type with his hands – but during this period, he was forbidden to use his left foot. In the excerpt included in this book, Brown is learning to live without using his foot, and so he begins writing his autobiography by dictating it to his brother. *My Left Foot* was published four years later. Brown also published novels and collections of poetry. In later years he lived in County Kerry, Ireland, and Somerset, England, with his wife, Mary Karr, until his death in 1981.

TRUMAN CAPOTE (1924–1984) American writer. *'Self-Portrait'* (1972)

In his 'Self-Portrait', Truman Capote interviews a major American literary celebrity – namely, himself. The interview, included in a collection of Capote's incidental pieces entitled *The Dogs Bark: Public People & Private Places* (1973), is an amusing back and forth between author and author. To his first question: 'If you had to live in just one place – without ever leaving – where would it be?' this distinctly Southern writer replies: 'New York.' Truman Strekfus Persons was born in New Orleans, Louisiana, in 1924, and was brought up in Alabama by his aunts and cousins, until, in his mid-teens, he was sent to live in New York with his mother and stepfather (at this point, he took his stepfather's name). At the age of 17, Capote found work as an office boy at *The New Yorker* magazine, and began to write professionally soon afterwards. His first novel, *Other Voices, Other Rooms*, was published in 1948, and he would later capture the life of his favourite city in the novella, *Breakfast At Tiffany's* (1958). Towards the end of 'Self-Portrait', Capote vividly imagines himself drowning, his life flashing before him. One of the images that emerges is of a 'young man with black cow-licked hair' – this is Perry Smith, the real-life murderer featured in Capote's *In Cold Blood* (1966), which told the story of the 1959 killings of a Kansas family. It was a book that spawned a new genre, the non-fiction novel. Capote died in 1984 at the age of 59, in Los Angeles, California.

GIROLAMO CARDANO (1501–1576) Italian astronomer, doctor, philosopher and mathematician. *The Book of My Life* (1576)

Born in Pavia, Italy, in 1501, Girolamo Cardano wrote his account of his life on the verge of his death at the age of 74. Considered one of the greatest physicians of his day, Cardano produced his first writings on mathematics in 1539, the beginning of a prolific output that included best-selling books on medicine, natural philosophy, theology, astronomy and morals, as well as one of the earliest investigations into theories of probability. His *Book of My Life* is a masterwork of Renaissance autobiography – based on Cardano's horoscope, it describes the author's life aspect by aspect. The result is a highly idiosyncratic collection of Cardano's musings on such diverse subjects as his dreams and appetites, his physiognomy and sexual impotence, the execution of his son for murder in 1560 and his own imprisonment for heresy in 1570. After Cardano was released, he was forbidden to publish, and it was at this point that he began work on his autobiography. Although completed before his death in 1576, *The Book of My Life* didn't appear in print until 1643, when a French scholar discovered the manuscript.

THOMAS CARLYLE (1795–1881) Scottish historian and biographer. *Reminiscences* (1881)

Thomas Carlyle was born in Dumfriesshire, Scotland, in 1795. After attending the University of Edinburgh, he trained as a minister, but abandoned the vocation to devote himself to teaching, studying and writing. Carlyle became one of the most significant voices of the Victorian era – his voluminous output beginning with *Sartor Resartus* (1833), a fictional work in the form of an autobiography. This was followed by, amongst other works, his mammoth history of *The French Revolution* (1837) and 21 volumes of *Friedrich II of Prussia: Called Fredrick the Great* (1858–1865). Carlyle's memoirs – known as *Reminiscences* – existed as separate essays written privately over a period of years, and were prompted by the death of his father, James Carlyle in 1832, and the death of his wife, Jane Welsh Carlyle in 1866. Then, when Carlyle was on his deathbed, his friend and biographer, J.A. Froude helped prepare to put them into print. They include essays on his father, his wife, and others including the poet William Wordsworth. *Reminiscences* was published in the month of Carlyle's death, February 1881. The book caused much consternation when it first appeared – commentators were taken aback by its author's lack of discretion in describing those he had known.

ANDREW CARNEGIE (1835–1919) Scottish-American industrialist and philanthropist. *Autobiography of Andrew Carnegie* (1920)

Andrew Carnegie began work on his autobiography after his retirement, and gave up writing it at the onset of the First World War. With a good degree of exuberance Carnegie tells his rags to riches story, beginning with his birth, in Dunfermline, Scotland, in 1835. Carnegie's father was a skilled weaver but was unable to find work, prompting the family's move to America in 1848. Here the young Carnegie began working in a textile mill and telegraph office, before getting a job on the railroads. He rose through the ranks until, at the age of 30, he left his position to found his own company, becoming the first American industrialist to realize the potential of steel. An emotional low-point arrived in 1886, when both his mother and brother died while Carnegie was sick with typhoid. He married the following year, at the age of 51. The Carnegie holdings continued to grow until, in 1901 when he sold Carnegie Steel, he had become the richest man in the world – Carnegie was in an elite group of industrialists who helped make America an economic superpower. As his subsequent biographers have pointed out, his *Autobiography* is a sugar-coated version of Carnegie's story – although he portrays himself as a friend of the working man, in fact his steelworkers were treated dismally. Nonetheless, it remains one of the more enjoyable and colourful memoirs to be written by a businessman, especially in his descriptions of how he began to give his money away – 'the man who dies rich, dies disgraced,' he famously stated. Carnegie's millions went to fund education, pension plans for teachers, the cause of world peace, and thousands of libraries around the world. When he died in 1919, in Lenox, Massachusetts, he had already successfully dispensed with 90 per cent of his fortune. His autobiography was published posthumously in 1920.

PABLO CASALS (1876–1973) Spanish cellist, conductor and composer. *Joys and Sorrows: Reflections* (1970)

Pablo Casals said he would never write an autobiography, claiming that his life wasn't worthy of self-scrutiny. However, in his 94th year he relented, agreeing to reflect on his long life in conversation with the writer Albert E. Khan. *Joys and Sorrows* covers Casals' lifetime in music, a career spanning the best part of a century – as a young man he played for Queen Victoria, towards the end of his life for President Kennedy. Casals was born in Catalonia, Spain, in 1876 and performed on the violin in public for the first time at the age of eight. Soon afterwards, he switched to the cello and began 'a long and cherished companionship', making his debut as a soloist at age 14. At the outset of the Spanish Civil War in 1936, Casals exiled himself to France. When Francisco Franco came to power, the cellist refused to play in any country where the regime was officially recognized – throughout his life, Casals continued to promote the causes of peace and democracy. He was also a prominent composer and conductor – one of his final public appearances was at the United Nations, conducting his composition *Hymn of the United Nations*, just before his 95th birthday. Casals died in 1973 in his adopted home of Puerto Rico. After the death of Franco in 1979, his remains were finally laid to rest in Catalonia.

GIACOMO CASANOVA (1725–1798) Italian writer and adventurer. *Story of My Life* (1789–1792)

Giacomo Casanova began work on *Story of My Life* in 1789. 'I am writing my life to laugh at myself,' he wrote in a letter dated 1791, 'and I am succeeding.' Casanova's gloriously eventful memoirs, unfinished at the time of his death, comprise 12 volumes and describe 122 sexual conquests. They also provide as evocative a guide as is available to the world of 18th-century Europe. Casanova was born in Venice in 1725 – his parents were actors who wanted their son to become a priest, but Casanova was a hedonist of the highest order, addicted to the pleasures of drink, gambling and beautiful women, and he was soon expelled from the seminary. After training to become a lawyer and serving in the Venetian army, Casanova worked as a violinist, but throughout his life he resisted limiting himself to one occupation. He wrote poetry, fiction and history; he worked as a secretary, a translator, a spy, a diplomat and an entrepreneur. He was a nomad by inclination, exiling himself from Italy after he escaped from a Venetian prison in 1755. Then, nearing 60 and after years of wandering, he accepted the post of librarian at the castle of a Bohemian count. Here he began to write about his life in his adopted language of French and on his death in 1798, he had already produced 3,600 pages. The original manuscript was sold to a German publisher and appeared in censored form in German in 1822. A largely inaccurate French edition was published in 1838. The complete French text finally appeared in print in 1960.

BENVENUTO CELLINI (1500–1571) Italian goldsmith and sculptor. *My Life* (1558–1562)

For Benvenuto Cellini, the necessary seclusion to write his autobiography arrived in 1558, while he was under house arrest on charges of sodomy. It was also a time when the master goldsmith was keen to promote his own legend, having been omitted from Giorgio Vasari's biographical *Lives of the Artists* (1550). But although *My Life* was written to secure his place in art history, Cellini's rambunctious storytelling reveals the author to be much more in fact a man of impetuosity, complexity, rebelliousness and frequent violence (he commits murder twice in the course of the narrative). Cellini was born in Florence in 1500 and apprenticed to a Florentine goldsmith at the age of 15. His work was frequently interrupted by his frequent arrests, duels and tempestuous disputes, most of which, but not all, are described in his autobiography. The book is divided into two parts – his life before his religious conversion in 1539 while imprisoned in Rome, and his life afterwards, when he began work on his famous statue of Perseus holding the head of Medusa. This was completed in 1554 and is one of the triumphs of Renaissance art. Although *My Life* was finished in 1562, it wasn't published in the sculptor's lifetime. After his death in Florence in 1571, it languished until it was rediscovered and put into print in 1728.

PATRICK CHAMOISEAU (1953–) French-Caribbean writer. *School Days* (1994)

Patrick Chamoiseau was born on the French-Caribbean island of Martinique in 1953. He is the author of novels and essays, and has also produced two works of autobiography, *School Days* (1994) and *Childhood* (1996). Both books are written in the third person with Chamoiseau referring to himself as 'the boy'. In *School Days*, 'the boy' receives a classic French primary school education, despite the fact that he lives in the tropics and speaks Creole. Inside the schoolroom, the children learn about Napoleon and Cinderella, out in the playground, they retell Creole stories of zombies, sprites and sorceresses. In the excerpt included in this compendium, the children's teacher is trying to cure them of their Creole. Chamoiseau followed *School Days* with *Childhood*, a memoir of his earliest years before his teacher's attempt to make him unlearn his native tongue and traditions. Although both the books are written in French, they consciously evoke the rhythms and vocabulary of Creole and dramatize the child's need to retain his native identity while adopting the French language as a means of adaptation.

JUNG CHANG (1952–) Chinese writer and academic. *Wild Swans: Three Daughters of China* (1991)

Jung Chang's *Wild Swans* tells the story not only of Chang herself, but also of her grandmother and mother. Written in English, and in the first person throughout, Chang takes her readers on a journey that begins in 1909 with the birth of her grandmother, and spans almost 70 years of Chinese history. The experiences of the three women are dramatically different, and yet each woman lived during a period of enormous upheaval. Chang's grandmother was a concubine to a warlord; her mother became an important Communist official, and was later denounced, along with Chang's father, during the Cultural Revolution. Chang herself, born in 1952, served in Chairman Mao's Red Guard, before becoming a peasant doctor, then a steelworker and electrician. The author went on to study English at Sichuan University – the excerpt included in this compendium describes her hunger for forbidden Western texts while a student. In 1978, Chang left China to study in England, where she became the first person from the People's Republic of China to receive a British PhD, and where she has lived ever since.

CHARLES CHAPLIN (1889–1977) English film actor and director. *My Autobiography* (1964)

My Autobiography begins in 1889, in Victorian London, with the birth of Charles Spencer Chaplin. Although the first few years of Chaplin's life were spent in relative comfort, at the age of seven, Charlie, his brother Sidney and their mother were forced into the workhouse. For a time, the Chaplin sons went to live with their violent and drunken father. Then, when Charles was 12, his father died and his mother was admitted to an asylum, leaving the Chaplin sons to fend for themselves. Both boys found work in various vaudeville productions until, in 1912, on a tour of the United States and Canada with a variety act called the Karno Troupe, Charlie decided to stay in America. He signed a contract with Keystone Films Studio – and so started his career in the movies. Soon afterwards, Chaplin developed the character of the little tramp, and began to star in and direct his own films. My Autobiography traces the course of Chaplin's childhood, his career on stage and screen, and his eventual exile from America in 1953 during the Communist witch-hunts. The narrative ends in the early 1960s, at which time Chaplin was living happily with his wife Oona and their eight young children in the village of Corsair, Switzerland. He continued to make films into his 70s, published another volume of autobiography, My Life in Pictures (1974), and died in Switzerland in 1977. He was 88.

CHARLOTTE CHARKE (1713–1760) English actress and businesswoman. *A Narrative of the Life of Mrs Charlotte Charke* (1755)

The daughter of the actor and theatre manager Colley Cibber, Charlotte Charke was born in London in 1713. Following her father's example, she went onto the stage, making her debut at the age of 17. After her father published his autobiography in 1740, Charke decided to write her own memoir. She had risen to fame playing 'breeches parts', or roles for men. But after becoming estranged from her father, and finding it difficult to get acting work, Charke embarked on a new life as a businesswoman – her ventures included founding a puppet theatre in London's Haymarket. Disowned by her father, and with her businesses failing, Charke began to wear men's clothing off-stage. Dressed as a man, she courted an heiress in order to cheat her out of money; became a waiter at a pub, a valet for a lord, and worked as a travelling player. Charke hoped her startling memoir would make her fortune, but she sold the copyright for pennies and died in poverty five years after its publication, at the age of 47.

KAMO NO CHŌMEI (C.1155–1216) Japanese poet and monk. *'An Account of My Hut'* (1212)

Born in Kyoto, Japan, around 1155, Kamo No Chōmei came from a family of Shinto priests. He began his career as a poet at the

Imperial court, later renouncing court life to become a Buddhist monk. His autobiographical essay, 'An Account of My Hut', written after he had left Kyoto to live as a hermit, begins with a chronicle of the author's times. Chōmei describes the four natural disasters of his lifetime – the great fire of Kyoto in 1177, the tornado that further devastated the city in 1180, the subsequent famine that lasted for the next two years, as well as a terrible earthquake in 1185. He also describes how, in 1205, at the age of 50, he decided to live in seclusion, and how, at the age of 60, he built a simple ten-foot-square hut in the mountains where he awaited the end of his life. In the light of the devastation Chōmei had witnessed, his withdrawal from the world is poignant – in solitude, and without attachments, he hopes to no longer experience grief. He died in 1216 at the age of 61.

WINSTON CHURCHILL (1874–1965) English statesman and writer. *My Early Life / A Roving Commission* (1930)

Winston Churchill was 55 years old and yet to become Prime Minister when he began to write his autobiography. Working from articles previously published in magazines, he produced an account of his first 30 years in a matter of months. His English publisher called the book *My Early Life* and his American publisher, *A Roving Commission* – both were published in 1930. In the autobiography Churchill describes his aristocratic childhood and his school years at Harrow – he was a far from exceptional student and it took him three tries before he was accepted into Sandhurst Military Academy. In *My Early Life* Churchill charts his early military career and his time as a correspondent during the Boer War. On his return to Britain, he was elected to parliament at the age of 26, beginning a career in politics that would last for the next 62 years. In 1940, ten years after the publication of *My Early Life* and with Britain at war, Churchill became Prime Minister. A prolific writer of histories and biographies, he won the Nobel Prize for Literature in 1953. He retired from the Commons in 1964 and died the following year at the age of 90.

COLLEY CIBBER (1671–1757) English actor-manager, playwright and Poet Laureate. *An Apology for the Life of Mr Colley Cibber, written by himself* (1740)

Colley Cibber's autobiography was written on his retirement, after nearly 30 years at the helm of the Drury Lane Theatre, London. Cibber's chatty and meandering memoir started a vogue for gossipy, actor autobiographies that continues to this day. Written to inflate his reputation, the *Apology* is nonetheless a very vivid depiction of the world of theatrical London after the Restoration. Cibber, who was born in London in 1671, began his stage career at the age of 19. Although he was not initially successful, he later became famous for playing fops after starring in his own play, *Love's Last Shift or Virtue Rewarded* (1696), for which he wrote himself a large part. He was a controversial figure, not always well beloved – he was the model for the head Dunce in Alexander Pope's *Dunciad* (1728) – but nonetheless was appointed Poet Laureate in 1730. Cibber made his final appearance, playing King John, at the age of 74. He was the father of the actress Charlotte Charke, whose memoir writings are also included in this compendium.

J.M. COETZEE (1940–) South African writer. *Youth* (2002)

John Maxwell Coetzee was born in Cape Town, South Africa, to German-Afrikaans but English-speaking parents. His experiences growing up during apartheid are described in his first autobiographical work, *Boyhood: Scenes from Provincial Life* (1997). Coetzee's sequel, *Youth*, takes up the story in 1959 when the 19-year-old Coetzee began making plans to leave his family and the divided community of Cape Town behind him. He moved to London where he worked for a time as a computer programmer. In the excerpt included in this compendium, Coetzee is 24 and about to leave England to take up graduate work in America, at which point the book ends. Both *Boyhood* and *Youth* are written in the third person, with Coetzee making clear to the reader that when reconstructing himself from fragments of the past, he is creating a character in much the same way as he would a fictional one. In addition to the two memoirs, Coetzee is the author of eight novels as well as works of criticism and translation. He won the Nobel Prize for Literature in 2003.

SARA COLERIDGE (1802–1852) English writer. *'Memoir'* (1873)

Sara Coleridge was the only daughter of the poet Samuel Taylor Coleridge. Towards the end of her life, and very ill, Sara recounted her memories of childhood to her daughter, Edith Coleridge, in a letter. Eight months later, in 1852, Sara died before she could finish her recollections, and her daughter published the letter posthumously under the title *Memoir and Letters of Sara Coleridge* (1873). Sara was born in 1802 and grew up in the Lake District, close to the home of William Wordsworth. The brief 'Memoir' gives a marvellous child's eye view of the major Romantic poets – including Sara's uncle, Robert Southey. We see them not as men of history, but rather as fathers and friends. Sara married her cousin Henry Coleridge in 1829. Her own poems and a fairy tale written for her children were published and became popular during her lifetime. She also produced a number of works in translation. When Henry died in 1843, it fell to Sara to edit and look after her father's work.

CO-OPERATIVE WORKING WOMEN: MRS SCOTT JP, MRS F.H. SMITH, MRS WRIGLEY (DATES UNKNOWN). *Life As We Have Known It*, by Co-operative Working Women and edited by Margaret Llewelyn Davies (1931)

Life As We Have Known It was first published by Leonard and Virginia Woolf's Hogarth Press in 1931. The book is made up of memoirs written by members of the Women's Co-operative Guild, an organization founded in 1883 to educate and empower working women. At the time the book was published, the guild had 67,000 members and 1400 branches. In six essays and extracts from their letters, the women write movingly about their memories of impoverished childhoods, the harshness of working life, the sacrifices of their marriages and many children, as well as the liberating impact of their involvement with the guild. These rare examples of female working-class testimonials are particularly vivid for having been written by the women themselves, rather than recorded by an intermediary. The book's editor was the guild's long-serving general secretary, Margaret Llewelyn Davies, who persuaded her friend and guild supporter Virginia Woolf to provide an introduction to the book.

NOEL COWARD (1899–1973) English playwright, songwriter and actor. *Present Indicative* (1937)

Noel Coward wrote three volumes of autobiography: *Present Indicative* (1937), *Future Indefinite* (1954) and *Past Conditional* (incomplete at the time of his death in 1973). He was born Noel Pierce Coward in 1899, in Middlesex, England, just before Christmas (hence his name). At the age of 12 he got his first acting job and his first play was produced when its author was just 18. In 1924, Coward's *Vortex*, a play about sex and drug-use amongst the upper classes, was staged to considerable acclaim. By 25, he was famous. Over a period of five decades, Coward wrote and appeared in scores of plays, musicals and films, his wit and urbanity as much his trademarks as the silk dressing gown and cigarette he was usually photographed posing with. Although his autobiographies mention his male friends, he never publicly discussed his homosexuality. When pressed to come out, he replied: 'There are still a few old ladies in Worthing who don't know.' He died at his home in Port Maria, Jamaica, at the age of 74.

ABRAHAM COWLEY (1618–1667) English poet and essayist. *'Of Myself'* (1668)

Abraham Cowley was born in London, in 1618, the son of a merchant. As he describes in his autobiographical essay 'Of Myself', he was a solitary child who fell in love with literature at an early age. By 12 he had read the whole of Edmund Spenser's *The Faerie Queen* (1590) and at 15 published his first volume of poems. Cowley went up to Cambridge in 1637, but 'was soon torn from thence by that violent storm which would suffer nothing to stand where it did'. This was the English Civil War. As a Royalist, Cowley was unable to take up his fellowship in Cambridge, so he settled for a while at Oxford. In 1646 he left England to join the court of Queen Henrietta Maria in France, returning to England in 1654, where he was arrested a year later as a Royalist agent. He remained on bail until 1660, the year of the Restoration, but in the meantime, Cowley ceased his resistance to the Roundheads. When Charles II took the throne, the new king refused to reward the poet, and merely forgave him his lapse in loyalty. Eventually, Cowley obtained a small grant and withdrew to the countryside. His essays were all written in this period of seclusion, when he had become almost completely overlooked as a poet. 'Of Myself' was published the year after his death and is one of the earliest personal essays in English.

MALCOLM COWLEY (1898–1989) American writer, poet, editor and critic. *The View from Eighty* (1980)

In 1978, Malcolm Cowley wrote an article called 'The View from Eighty' on the subject of turning 80 for *Life* magazine. Then, after a deluge of enthusiastic letters from fellow octogenarians, he expanded the piece to create a short book on the subject of aging, also called *The View from Eighty*. Cowley was born in 1898 and served in the First World War as a young man. When Cowley returned to America from the Front in 1918, he graduated from Harvard and began to write poetry and book reviews. In 1921 he returned to France, where he met such writers as Ernest Hemingway, Ezra Pound and Gertrude Stein, whose dilemmas and disillusion he would describe in *Exile's Return* (1934), his famous memoir of the 'lost generation'. In 1923 Cowley settled in America, becoming the literary editor of the *New Republic* and, later, literary advisor to Viking Press. He continued to write literary history, criticism and poems for the rest of his life.

WILLIAM COWPER (1731–1800) English poet and hymnist. *Memoir of the Early Life of William Cowper Esq, written by himself* (1767)

William Cowper was born in Hertfordshire, England, in 1731. As he describes in his *Memoir* – written around 1767 but published posthumously in 1816 – his mother died when he was only six and he was sent away to school where he was severely bullied. After completing his studies, he trained as a barrister and at the age of 21 was admitted to London's Inner Temple. But in 1763 he suffered a terrible breakdown, and after failing to commit suicide he was placed in a private asylum. It was here that Cowper experienced his religious conversion, ascribing his miraculous recovery to the grace of God. The volume ends with Cowper redeemed and his suffering behind him. However, in 1773 the poet broke down again, suffering from crippling bouts of depression for the rest of his life, convinced he was being refused God's grace. He died of 'a worn-out constitution' in 1800 at the age of 69, leaving behind him a large body of poems, as well as the famous 'Olney' hymn cycle, written with the Anglican evangelical preacher John Newton.

QUENTIN CRISP (1908–1999) English writer. *The Naked Civil Servant* (1968) and *How to Become A Virgin* (1981)

Quentin Crisp was born Denis Charles Pratt in Surrey, England, in 1908. As he writes in *The Naked Civil Servant*: 'From the dawn of my history I was so disfigured by the characteristics of a certain kind of homosexual that, when I grew up, I realised that I could not ignore my predicament.' As a young man, Crisp fled the suburbs for London, where he studied journalism and art and discovered the gay coffee-houses of 1920s Soho. After leaving college, he lived in virtual obscurity and frequent penury – working as a tap dance teacher, a freelance designer, and, most famously, an art school model – until his autobiography was published when he was 60. The book, with its acerbic and unapologetic portrayal of a gay, effeminate man, appearing only a year after homosexuality was partially decriminalized in England, was later turned into a television drama series. Its author became a celebrity. Thirteen years later, Crisp published a second volume of autobiography, *How to Become A Virgin*, about the chain of circumstances that led him to write his memoirs and his subsequent fame – enabling his move in 1981 to New York, the city he adopted and adored. He lived in Manhattan, writing and performing until his death in 1999 at the age of 90, while on tour in England with his one-man show, *An Evening With Quentin Crisp*.

ROALD DAHL (1916–1990) Welsh-born writer. *Boy: Tales of Childhood* (1984)

Boy: Tales of Childhood was written in the latter years of Roald Dahl's life. Aimed at a young audience, the author recalls his childhood adventures, including his plot to murder the nasty old lady who owned the local sweet shop – just the kind of macabre tale that one might expect to find in his fiction. Born in Llandaff, Wales, to Norwegian immigrant parents, Dahl was sent to Llandaff Cathedral School at seven, and two years later, to boarding school in England, where he encountered the seemingly commonplace brutalities of an English public school in the 1920s. *Boy* ends in 1937, after the author had finished his education and was setting sail for East Africa, where he worked for the Shell company. *Going Solo* (1986), a sequel to *Boy*, describes Dahl's time in Africa and with the Royal Air Force during the Second World War – at which time he also began to write about his experiences. After the war he wrote a first novel. But it was only after his marriage in 1953 and when he had a family that he started to concentrate on writing for children in earnest, beginning with *James and the Giant Peach* in 1961. He continued to produce classic works of children's literature throughout the 60s, 70s and 80s. Dahl died in Oxford, England, in 1990.

LADY DAIBU (c.1157–c.1232) Japanese poet and courtier. *The Poetic Memoirs of Lady Daibu* (c.1174–c.1232)

The earliest sections of *The Poetic Memoirs of Lady Daibu* were begun in 1174, while Kenreimon-in Ukyo no Daibu was serving as a lady-in-waiting to the Empress Tokuku, in Kyoto, Japan. A combination of prose and poetry – with elements of the diary and memoir forms – it provides an emotional account of Daibu's inner life over a period of nearly 60 years, during one of the most turbulent times in Japanese history. Although Daibu had many love affairs, central to the memoirs is a single difficult relationship with an unnamed lover that lasted for many years and ended when he died in the civil war which broke out in 1180. Interestingly, Daibu makes only passing reference to the conflict – as a female courtier, she had no language for describing either politics or violence, but her intense suffering after her lover dies is testament enough to the cost of the conflict. The war marked the end of 300 years of the Heian period, and when Daibu returned to court around 1191, a new family dominated. Little is known of Daibu's life after this, except that in 1232, some time before her death, she assembled her poems and writings so they would tell the story of a lifetime of love and loss.

HIS HOLINESS THE DALAI LAMA OF TIBET (1935–)
spiritual and political leader of the Tibetan people. *My Land and My People* (1962)

The 14th Dalai Lama of Tibet completed his autobiography when he was just 27 years old and living in exile in India. *My Land and My People* tells the remarkable story of his beginnings – he was born in 1935, in the small village of Taktser in north-eastern Tibet, the son of a farmer. At the age of two, he was identified as the reincarnation of the 13th Dalai Lama, an incarnation of the Buddha of Compassion. At the age of five, he was enthroned in the Tibetan capital of Lhasa and began his education. As he describes in his autobiography, it was a happy childhood that ended abruptly when, at 16, he was called upon to lead his country after China invaded Tibet. Although the Dalai Lama attempted to bring about a peaceful resolution with the Chinese, and although the Tibetan people rose up in resistance, he was forced to flee along with thousands of refugees in 1959. Since 1960 the Dalai Lama has lived in Dharamsala, the seat of the Tibetan government in exile, where he continues to work to preserve Tibetan ways of life and for the non-violent liberation of Tibet. He won the Nobel Peace Prize in 1989.

SALVADOR DALI (1904–1989) Spanish painter. *The Secret Life of Salvador Dali* (1942)

Salvador Dali was born in Figueras, Spain, in 1904, and began to paint at an early age. As a young student in Madrid he saw works by the new French Surrealists and travelled to Paris to join their ranks – at which time he met his future wife and muse, Gala Eluard. After the onset of the Second World War, Dali and Gala escaped to New York. The couple quickly captured the imagination of the American public, in large part due to Dali's exotic eccentricities, but also thanks to Gala's natural aptitude for publicizing her husband's talents. In 1941 Dali had his first major retrospective, at the Museum of Modern Art in New York, and his legend was further enhanced by the publication of his autobiography the following year. In the richly inventive and frequently bizarre *Secret Life*, Dali remembers, amongst many other incidents, the time he spent in his mother's womb. The artist lived another 47 years after the publication of his life story, during which time he rejected Surrealism and embraced Catholicism, creating paintings of religious and hallucinatory content. In the 1960s, Parkinson's disease began to hamper Dali's ability to paint, and after Gala's death in 1982, he retreated completely. He died in 1989 at the castle he had built in his Spanish birthplace.

JEAN DANIEL (1920–) French intellectual and journalist. *'Dwelling on Images'* (1997)

Jean Daniel was born in Blida, Algeria, and is of Sephardic origin. After graduating from the Sorbonne in Paris, he began his career in journalism, founding the *Caliban* review in 1947 and becoming editor-in-chief of the French newspaper *L'Express* from 1954 to 1964, during which time he covered the war in Algeria and travelled extensively in Cuba. He went on to become the Paris correspondent of the American magazine *New Republic* and a contributor to the French newspaper *Le Monde*. In 1964, he founded the French news magazine *Le Nouvel Observateur*. In a long and distinguished career he has covered the end of colonization in Africa, amongst many other subjects. He is also the author of novels, short stories and essays. The excerpt included in this book is from the autobiographical essay 'Dwelling on Images' contributed to *An Algerian Childhood: A Collection of Autobiographical Narratives*, edited by Leila Sebbar and first published in 1997.

CHARLES DARWIN (1809–1882) English naturalist. *'An Autobiographical Fragment'* (1838) and *'Recollections of the Development Of My Mind and Character'* (1876)

In 1876, at the age of 67, Charles Darwin decided to set down a record of his life for his children and grandchildren under the title 'Recollections of the Development Of My Mind and Character'. His intention was that the writings would remain private, but after his death, his family published them in a highly edited version. In 1958 Darwin's granddaughter republished them in complete form. Also included in this compendium is an excerpt from an autobiographical fragment Darwin wrote when he was 28 – again, for personal use. The fragment was later found and first published in an edition of his letters in 1903. Together, these autobiographical works tell the story of a remarkable life. After a childhood spent in Shropshire, Darwin briefly studied medicine at Edinburgh, but left due to lack of interest. Next he attended Cambridge University, where his father hoped he would prepare for a vocation in the clergy. Instead, most of Darwin's time as a student was spent hunting, playing cards and beetle-collecting. In 1831, at the age of 22, Darwin set sail aboard the HMS *Beagle* as a naturalist, bound for South America. For the next 40 years, he devoted himself to the study of species, developing his landmark theories of natural and sexual selection. *The Origin of Species* appeared in 1859 and *The Descent of Man* in 1871, for ever altering the way we understand the world. Darwin continued to write and study until his death at his home in Downe, Kent, in 1882.

CHARLES DICKENS (1812–1870) English novelist.
'Autobiographical Fragment' (1847)

In 1847, Charles Dickens started to write an autobiography at the suggestion of his friend and future biographer, John Forster. Soon afterwards he abandoned the project, telling Forster he found it too painful to write about his childhood. His early boyhood had been happy enough, but then, at the age of nine, Dickens' father lost his job and moved the family to London, where the boy was forced to leave school and take a job at a shoe-polish factory to help support the family. In 1824, his parents were sent to debtors' prison and Charles became the family's sole source of income. Although he later returned to school, going on to have a successful career as a journalist and then novelist, it was this former, traumatic period of his life that Dickens wrote about and showed to Forster. While Dickens did not continue with the autobiography, immediately afterwards he began work on his most personal novel, *David Copperfield* (1849), in which the shoe-polish factory reappears as Murdstone & Grinby's warehouse and his parents are transformed into Mr and Mrs Micawber. During his lifetime Dickens never revealed the details of his childhood experiences to his readers, and so it was only in 1872, after his death, when Forster published the 'Autobiographical Fragment' in *The Life of Charles Dickens*, that readers learned that the author had not only written about childhood privations, he had lived them too.

ARIEL DORFMAN (1942–) Chilean-American writer. *Heading South, Looking North: A Bilingual Journey* (1998)

In *Heading South, Looking North*, Ariel Dorfman charts his family's many exiles and his own gradual acceptance of himself as a writer in two languages. He was born Vladimiro Ariel Dorfman, in Buenos Aires in 1942 – his parents were Eastern European Jews who had fled from Tsarist pogroms when they were children. Dorfman's father was a Marxist, and after the Juan Peron-led coup in Argentina, the family left for New York where Dorfman grew up speaking English. Then in 1953, during the Communist witch-hunts, his father, who worked for the United Nations, was dispatched to Santiago, Chile, where Dorfman had to learn Spanish. After he graduated from the University of Santiago, Dorfman became a Chilean citizen and married a Chilean woman. During Salvador Allende's brief period in power, he was cultural advisor to the new Socialist government. Then in 1973, came General Augusto Pinochet's coup in which Allende died and from which Dorfman barely escaped with his life. First Dorfman settled in Paris, then Amsterdam, before moving back to America, where he achieved international fame as a writer of poetry, essays, fiction and plays. He is currently professor of literature and Latin American studies at Duke University, North Carolina. *Heading South, Looking North* was written in both English and Spanish.

FREDERICK DOUGLASS (c.1818–1895) American writer and abolitionist. *Narrative of the Life of Frederick Douglass, An American Slave* (1845)

This is generally considered the finest of the hundreds of slave narratives that were published in America and Europe during the 19th century. Douglass was born Frederick Augustus Washington Bailey, in Maryland, around 1818. His mother was a slave whose white owner may have been Douglass's father. As a boy, Douglass experienced the manifold degradations of slave life – he was brutally beaten and frequently starved. As soon as he was old enough, Douglass resolved to escape, and in 1838, while working at a shipyard, he fled to New York, posing as a sailor and changing his name to protect his identity. He settled in Massachusetts where he became involved in the abolitionist movement. When the *Narrative* appeared, Douglass was still a fugitive, and he risked re-enslavement by publishing. After its publication, Douglass left for a lecture tour of Britain where he managed to raise the funds to pay for his legal emancipation. The author devoted the rest of his life to publishing and public life. He owned and edited a number of newspapers; during the Civil War he advised Abraham Lincoln and recruited Northern blacks for the Union army; after the war he continued to fight for the civil rights of African-Americans and held various government appointments, including the consul general of Haiti. He died at his home in Washington DC in 1895.

ISADORA DUNCAN (1878–1927) American dancer and choreographer. *My Life* (1927)

Isadora Duncan finished her autobiography shortly before her tragic, early death in a car accident in Nice in 1927. She was born Angela Duncan, in San Francisco, in 1878. Her parents divorced when she was a baby and her father was largely absent. As a child Duncan taught dance classes to help support the family and she began to perform professionally in her teens. In 1899, at the age of 21, she moved with her mother and siblings to London and then to Paris, where her evolving philosophy of dance – fluid, instinctual, and inspired by the images she had seen on Greek vases in the British Museum – found a more sympathetic audience. By 1904, Duncan was so successful that she established her first dance school in Germany, where children from poor families could come to be educated. She had two children, a daughter with the painter Gordon Craig and a son with the millionaire Paris Singer. Tragically, in 1913, both children died in a drowning accident. Duncan stopped dancing for a time and concentrated on her schools, adopting six of her young students. She was briefly married to the Russian poet Sergei Yesenin in 1922, only agreeing to marry him so she could bring him to the USA, where she was booed from the stage for her Communist sympathies. She left America and settled in Nice, where she died at age 49. Her autobiography, considered shocking on its publication for Duncan's sexual revelations, remains fascinating for the author's sheer self-confidence in her own opinions and artistry.

GERALD DURRELL (1925–1995) English conservationist, zoologist and writer. *My Family and Other Animals* (1956)

Gerald Durrell was born in Jamshedpur, India, in 1925. When he was three years old, his father died and his mother decided to move her four children back to England. It is here that Durrell's classic memoir starts on a rainy day in Bournemouth in 1935, with eldest brother Larry suggesting that the family relocate to the sunnier climes of Corfu. The Durrells uproot to Greece, taking the family dog with them, and ten-year-old Gerald is allowed to freely roam the island, discovering its inhabitants, both animal and human. It was the beginning of a vocation. In 1945, inspired by his love of the natural world, Durrell joined the staff of England's Whipsnade Park as a zoo keeper. A year later he led his first animal-collecting expedition to the Cameroons, the first of many travels throughout Africa and Latin America to find and conserve rare species. Durrell went on to found the Jersey Zoological Park and the Jersey Wildlife Preservation Trust. He was first encouraged to write about his life by his brother, the novelist Lawrence Durrell, and in 1953 he published *The Overloaded Ark*, which dealt with his time collecting animals for zoos. He went on to write 37 best-selling books about his life and work.

JONATHAN EDWARDS (1703–1758) American Puritan pastor and writer. *'Personal Narrative'* (1765)

Jonathan Edwards was born in the then colony of Connecticut in 1703, his father a reverend, his mother the daughter of a reverend. Edwards was deeply studious and religious throughout his youth, and at the age of 26, he took over his grandfather's parish of Northampton, Massachusetts. An orthodox Calvinist, Edwards served as the pastor of Northampton for the next 25 years, starting a religious revival that spread throughout the state, and producing a body of religious works that remains amongst the most influential in the American canon. His autobiographical account was written some time after 1739, but never published in his lifetime. Edwards' motives for writing his narrative are unknown, although it was very common for American revivalists to recount testimonials of religious experiences at their meetings. In the 'Personal Narrative', Edwards describes the kind of deeply felt belief he encouraged in his parishioners – he wanted them to fully immerse themselves in their faith and to be utterly transformed by it. But Edwards' religious passion proved to be his downfall. In 1750, he criticized some of the most important families in

Northampton as being insufficiently devoted, and he was dismissed from his church. In 1758, soon after taking the position of president at the College of New Jersey (later Princeton University), he took an inoculation for smallpox and died from the disease. His life story was first published in 1765 in a book entitled *The Life and Character of the late Rev. Mr Jonathan Edwards.*

DAVE EGGERS (1970–) American writer and publisher. *A Heartbreaking Work of Staggering Genius: A Memoir based on a True Story* (2000)

This memoir begins with the illness and death of Dave Eggers' mother from cancer, just months after his father's death from the same disease. Eggers was 22 at the time, and consequently becomes unofficial guardian of his eight-year-old brother, Toph. *A Heartbreaking Work* shows Eggers as he leaves his hometown to move to San Francisco. Here the author develops an unconventional parenting style, helps to found a magazine called *Might*, fails to win a place on MTV's *Real World* and eventually returns to his home where he rapidly unravels. The excerpt included in this compendium is from the author's expertly self-conscious acknowledgements, which form a 34-page-long disclaimer at the start of the book: 'This is a work of fiction,' Eggers writes of his memoir, 'only in that many cases, the author could not remember the exact words said by certain people, and exact descriptions of certain things, so had to fill in gaps as best he could. Otherwise, all characters and incidents and dialogue are real, are not products of the author's imagination …' Eggers is the founder and editor of *McSweeney's*, the literary quarterly, and McSweeney's Books. He lives in San Francisco, California.

ALBERT EINSTEIN (1879–1955) German Swiss physicist. *Autobiographical Notes* (1949)

At the age of 67, during a period of illness in which he thought he would die, Albert Einstein sat down to write what he described as 'something like my own obituary'. Einstein's personal notes were written at the request of Dr Paul Arthur Schilpp, the editor of the *Library of Living Philosophers*, for inclusion in the volume devoted to Einstein that appeared in 1949. In the *Notes*, Einstein reveals the development of his mind, how his encounters with science influenced him and, consequently, how he began to make his own considerable mark on science. Einstein was born to Jewish parents in Ulm, Germany, and educated in both Germany and Switzerland. In 1905, in a doctorate paper, Einstein proposed his Theory of Relativity, in which he unified Newtonian mechanics with electrodynamics. He was soon recognized for his work and in 1921 was awarded the Nobel Prize for Physics. In 1932, a month before Hitler came to power, Einstein arrived in America, where he was made professor of theoretical physics at Princeton. Einstein worked devotedly for the cause of peace and was instrumental in founding the Hebrew University in Jerusalem. He died in Princeton in 1955.

OLAUDAH EQUIANO (1745–1797) African-English abolitionist and writer. *The Interesting Narrative of the Life of Olaudah Equiano, or Gustavus Vassa, the African, written by himself* (1789)

Olaudah Equiano's autobiography is one of the earliest examples of the slave narrative, a genre that was sparked by the 18th-century abolitionist movement and which would remain immensely popular into the 19th century in both America and Europe. First published in 1789, the *Narrative* starts in what is now Nigeria, Africa, where Equiano was born in 1745. Equiano was captured at the age of 11 and enslaved in Africa and the West Indies before being sent to Virginia, where he became the personal slave of a British navy captain. In 1763, he was bought by a Quaker merchant and was permitted to earn money for himself working as a clerk and captain's assistant on board slave ships. After purchasing his freedom at the age of 21, he landed in England, where he trained to be a barber and a musician. He soon found work as a seaman again, participating in an exploration of the Arctic. Equiano also became involved in the British abolitionist movement, but he was later fired from his job as steward on a ship taking freed slaves from London to Sierra Leone, for mistreatment of the men on board. To a large degree, the *Narrative* was written to clear his name. The book went into nine printings in the author's lifetime, and due to its success Equiano lectured across Britain. He died a wealthy man in London, in 1797.

M.F.K. FISHER (1908–1992) American food writer. *'Winding Down'* (1984)

Mary Frances Kennedy was born in 1908 in Michigan and grew up in northern California. A writer since childhood, she would later describe her early years in her 1970 memoir, *Among Friends*. Mary Frances met her future husband Alfred Fisher while they were both students at the University of California. They spent the first few years of their marriage in France, where she learned about the French food and wines that would later inform her writings. On their return to California, Fisher began to publish essays on food and cooking, and with her first book, *Serve It Forth* (1937), she achieved something as delectable as her subject matter – the elevation of food writing into a fine art. She divorced Alfred Fisher in 1938 and married the painter Dillwyn Parrish, who became seriously ill shortly afterwards and committed suicide in 1941. After her husband's death, Fisher worked as a screenwriter in Hollywood, before giving birth to a daughter in 1943. Later, she again married briefly and had another daughter, bringing up her two children alone in California and France, and continuing to write and publish. In the last years of her life she settled in northern California, where she died in 1992. In 'Winding Down' from *Last House: Reflections, Dreams, and Observations 1943–1991*, published posthumously in 1995, an elderly Fisher writes about aging.

JANET FRAME (1924–2004) New Zealand writer. *To the Is-land* (1982)

Janet Paterson Frame was born in Dunedin, on the South Island of New Zealand. The first volume in her trilogy of autobiographies,

To the Is-land, tells the story of Frame's childhood, schooldays and adolescence, growing up in an extended family. It was during this period that her two sisters died in separate drowning accidents, events which deeply affected Frame. The next volume, *An Angel at My Table* (1984), begins with her time at teacher training college, before a suicide attempt left her diagnosed with schizophrenia and in psychiatric hospitals for the best part of the following decade. In 1951, while still in an institution, Frame published her first book, a collection of short stories – thereby saving herself from brutal brain surgery, after a hospital worker read that she had won a literary prize and cancelled the operation. The final volume, *The Envoy From Mirror City* (1985), takes up Frame's story on her departure for Europe in 1956 – by this time, she was a successful novelist with a literary grant to fund her travels. It was in London that she learned she had been misdiagnosed with schizophrenia. Throughout these three volumes, the reader witnesses a writer discovering and reconstructing her fractured identity through the writing of autobiography. Frame returned to New Zealand in 1964 and was based there for the rest of her life. She died in 2004, at the age of 79.

BENJAMIN FRANKLIN (1706–1790) American statesman, publisher, inventor and writer. *The Autobiography* (1771–1778)

Benjamin Franklin's 'memoirs' as he described them (he never used the word autobiography) were written over a period of 17 years. The first part of the manuscript was completed in 1771, in England, where Franklin had been posted as an envoy to the colonies. The next section was written in France in 1784, during which time Franklin was serving as minister for the recently founded United States. The last two parts were written in Franklin's final years, before his death in 1790. The sections were later collected together and given the title, *The Autobiography*, which was first published in complete form in 1868. Together they form a fascinating if incomplete picture of an extraordinary life. Franklin was born in Boston in 1706, the tenth son of a candle- and soap-maker father. Although his first ambition was to run away to sea, Franklin was apprenticed to his brother, a printer. At the age of 17, Franklin left home for Philadelphia to make his way in the world, and by 22 he was the owner of a printing office. Before his retirement from business 20 years later, Franklin's achievements included publishing his own newspaper, creating a best-selling almanac, opening the first public library in Philadelphia, founding the city's Union Fire Company, being appointed postmaster of Philadelphia, helping to found the University of Philadelphia, inventing a stove, and publishing his findings on electricity. It is at this point that *The Autobiography* ends. What followed was Franklin's long and distinguished career in public life, as a diplomat in England and France, and as a founding father of America, a signer of both the Declaration of Independence and the Constitution.

SIGMUND FREUD (1856–1939) Austrian founder of psychoanalysis. *An Autobiographical Study* (1925)

In Sigmund Freud's *The Interpretation of Dreams* (1900) the father of psychoanalysis argued that our conscious thoughts and actions are provoked by unconscious desires. This kind of reading of motive, interestingly, is almost impossible in Freud's only wholly autobiographical work, with its conspicuous avoidance of personal revelation, conscious or otherwise. Ferociously private, Freud destroyed his personal papers at intervals during his life and resisted the advances of biographers. The *Autobiographical Study* – originally written for inclusion in a series of short memoirs by medical professionals and called *Contemporary Medicine in Self-Portrayals* – was designed to tell the story of the development of psychoanalysis, and Freud presents himself as the devoted scientist. 'No personal experiences of mine are of any interest in comparison to my relations with that science,' he writes. He was born in Moravia (now part of the Czech Republic) in 1856 to a Jewish family who later moved to Vienna. He studied medicine at the University of Vienna before establishing his private practice in 1886, the year of his marriage. He founded the International Psychoanalytical Society with C.G. Jung, and others, in 1908 in order to consolidate and popularize psychoanatlytical theories, although Freud and Jung went their separate ways in 1913, over their disagreement on the causes of neurosis. After Germany annexed Austria in 1938 Freud emigrated to London, where he died the following year.

STEPHEN FRY (1957–) English writer, comedian, actor and director. *Moab is My Washpot: An Autobiography* (1997)

Stephen Fry was born in 1957 and grew up in Norfolk. His autobiography was written when he was turning 40 and its title is a direct quotation from the curious lines in Psalm 60: 'Moab is my washpot; over Edom will I cast out my shoe.' The book begins with Fry's boyhood days and describes the pubescent torments of his boarding school, Uppingham, where he fell in love for the first time, with one of his schoolmates. While still at school Fry ran off with a stolen credit card, was caught and spent three months in prison. After his release, he managed to secure a place at Cambridge, at which point his autobiography ends. At Cambridge, Fry met his comedy partner Hugh Laurie and the two began to write and perform comedy revues, which lead to a hugely successful television, film and radio career. He is the author of novels, articles and histories, and has appeared as an actor in productions on both screen and stage. He made his debut as a film director and screenwriter with *Bright Young Things* (2003).

SHEN FU (1763–POST 1809) Chinese civil servant, painter and writer. *Six Records of a Floating Life* (1809)

Shen Fu was born in Shoochow, China, in 1763. His autobiography, *Six Records of a Floating Life*, was written around 1809, and discovered and published after his death. Only four of the 'six records' have survived, and it is possible Fu never finished his story. The first, called 'The Joys of the Wedding Chamber', deals with Fu's relationship with his wife, Yun, whom he married at the age of 13. The couple were well matched and their love for one another transcends the difficulties of their marriage. Fu trained as a scholar but found it hard to earn a living, and his portrayal of the tensions and delights of domestic life is remarkably realistic. In 'Pleasures of Leisure', Fu writes about his favourite pasttimes, which include working in his garden and discussing poetry and painting with friends. In 'The Sorrows of Misfortune', Yun becomes ill, and during a series of family conflicts and financial problems, her health worsens. Yun died in 1803 and Fu's father and son died soon afterwards. 'The Delights of Roaming Afar' describes Fu's travels after his wife's death, working as a government clerk. Nothing is known of Fu's life after 1809, but his *Six Records* form a lasting testament to his love for Yun.

MAHATMA GANDHI (1869–1948) Indian leader. *An Autobiography: The Story of My Experiments with Truth* (1927–1929)

When Mohandâs Karamchand Gandhi began work on his autobiography, he was 56 years old and had recently finished serving three years in prison for his opposition to British rule in India. Gandhi was born in 1869 to a Hindu family, in Gujarat, India. He was married at the young age of 13, studied law in London and returned to India in 1891 to practise. In 1893, he accepted a job in Natal, South Africa, where he became involved in the campaign for the rights of South African Indians. It was here that Gandhi developed his theories of non-violence, civil disobedience, domestic simplicity, vegetarianism and celibacy. Gandhi returned to India in 1914, taking up the cause of the Indian Nationalist Movement in 1919. The struggle for independence was still in progress at the time of writing his autobiography, so it was important that Gandhi set down the story of his life without succumbing to a very Western and individualistic form. Although lacking a full recounting of his activities to that point (1927), the book contains fascinating insights into the moral and spiritual integrity informing Gandhi's every action, whether public or private. Twenty years after the autobiography was published, in 1947 India secured its independence. Gandhi – or Mahatma, meaning 'great soul', a name that had been given him by the Indian people and that he never personally adopted – was assassinated a year later by a Hindu radical.

EDWARD GIBBON (1737–1794) English historian. *Memoirs of My Life and Writings* (1796)

The historian Edward Gibbon began writing his memoirs shortly after completing his life's work, *The Decline and Fall of the Roman Empire* (1776–88). He rewrote the memoirs six times, leaving the last draft unfinished at the time of his death in 1794. Gibbon's friend, Lord Sheffield, later edited the manuscripts and published them in *The Miscellaneous Works of Edward Gibbon* in 1796. It wasn't until almost a century later that the six original drafts appeared under the title *The Autobiographies* (1876). Although much bowdlerized, the Sheffield version is the most readable, and an excerpt from the end of this version is included in this compendium. Gibbon was born in London in into an eminent family who had fallen on hard times. In his memoirs he recounts his early love of reading and study, despite frequent illnesses that meant he went to school only intermittently. He was 14 when he went up to Oxford, but before graduating he was forced to leave after converting to Roman Catholicism – Catholics were still barred from the university. His father sent him off to Lausanne, Switzerland, where he reconverted to Protestantism. 'From my childhood, I had been fond of religious disputation,' he wrote, and his natural scepticism later scandalized his readers when he criticized Christianity in *Decline and Fall*. Gibbon's great work, the opus that defined his life, was conceived in Rome in 1764, at the age of 27, while he sat 'musing amidst the ruins of the Capitol, while the barefooted friars were singing Vespers in the temple of Jupiter ...' Twelve years later, the first volume of Gibbon's history was published; and five further volumes followed, covering a period of 13 centuries. From 1774 to 1783, while still at work on *Decline and Fall*, Gibbon served as a Member of Parliament. The last three volumes were published in 1788. In his memoirs, as in his life, Gibbon's *Decline and Fall* is the defining element, yet he also gives credit to the age in which he was born as allowing him the opportunity and prosperity necessary for a happy existence.

MAXIM GORKY (1868–1936) Russian writer. *My Childhood* (1913–1914), and *My Apprenticeship* (1916)

Maxim Gorky was born Aleksei Maksimovich Peshkov in Nizhny Novgorod in 1868 and is the most widely known and prolific of Russian autobiographers. His famous trilogy covers the first 20 years of his life, to the point when he began his career as a writer. The first volume, *My Childhood*, ends with the 11-year-old boy orphaned and venturing out into the world alone, after the death of his mother from tuberculosis (his father died of cholera when Gorky was four). The next volume, *My Apprenticeship*, sees him scraping a living by working odd jobs, on the river boats of the Volga, in a bakery, becoming an architect's apprentice, and often starving. The final volume, *My Universities* (1923), deals with his failure to get into Kazan University, and his self-education thereafter. It also describes Gorky's attempted suicide at the age of 19 – he shot himself in the chest, but missed his heart. As a young man Gorky wrote for newspapers and edited a literary journal, and helped to found a secret printing press. At odds with the Tsarist regime, he was exiled to central Russia in 1902, and after meeting Lenin, he travelled to America to raise funds for the Bolshevik cause. He returned in 1913, but was already disillusioned with Lenin, and after the Russian Revolution and subsequent civil war, he went into voluntary exile. On the invitation of Joseph Stalin, he returned to Russia in 1931 and became head of the Writers' Union. Gorky's 'socialist realism' – rough and naturalistic yet highly didactic became the presiding doctrine of Soviet literature. In 1936 Gorky died suddenly at the age of 68, possibly killed on Stalin's orders.

EDMUND GOSSE (1849–1928) English critic and poet. *Father and Son* (1907)

Edmund Gosse was born in London in 1849, the only child of the Victorian zoologist Philip Henry Gosse, a Christian fundamentalist, who publicly disputed the evolutionary theories of Charles Darwin (amongst others). In his classic memoir, Edmund describes his upbringing, the strict and stifling piety of his parents and his mother's death from cancer when he was eight. Even so, from a young age Gosse sensed he was different and when he went away to boarding school his world started to open up, causing a rift between father and son. Eventually, the Gosse men parted ways altogether, the son embracing the advances and possibilities of the future, the father hanging behind in the past. Gosse went on to serve on the library staff of the British Museum, was a translator for the Board of Trade for 30 years, and became librarian to the House of Lords. He was also the author of many volumes of literary history, poetry and biography, including a life of his father, *The Naturalist of the Sea-shore*, in 1890. When *Father and Son* was first published Philip Gosse had been dead for 20 years, and yet his son still felt it necessary to publish anonymously, concealing the identities of those described. He revealed he was the book's author in its fourth edition.

ROBERT GRAVES (1895–1985) English writer. *Good-bye to All That* (1929)

Robert Graves' autobiography was prompted by dramatic events. In April 1929, the American poet Laura Riding tried to kill herself by throwing herself out of a building – she was in love with a man who was in love with Graves' wife and who had rejected her. Graves, who was himself in love with Riding, also jumped from the same building, but was uninjured. At this point, Graves needed money to flee England with Riding, who he feared would be arrested for attempted suicide, so he decided to write his memoirs. The book was finished in two months and caused a scandal on its publication that same year, selling 20,000 copies in a week. *Good-bye to All That* contains Graves' scornful description of his stodgy upper middle-class childhood in London, where he was born in 1895. His schooldays at Charterhouse were miserable, and when the First World War broke out, Graves, who was 19, enlisted immediately. He began to write poetry about the war, and his autobiography also contains some of the most vivid depictions of trench life ever written. The excerpts included in this compendium are from the original 1929 edition of Graves' book – the author revised it considerably in 1957, removing all references to Riding, from whom he had since become estranged, and generally dulling the effect of one of the most acidic autobiographies ever written. Graves died in Majorca in 1985, at the age of 90.

SPALDING GRAY (1941–2004) American writer and actor. *It's A Slippery Slope* (1997)

Spalding Gray wrote over a dozen autobiographical monologues, a genre that he made his own, and all of them painfully introspective but mordantly comic. He started in 1979 with the subject of his childhood: *Sex and Death to the Age 14*. Gray was born in 1941 on Rhode Island. In 1967, when he was 25, his mother committed suicide, an event that haunted his life and work. After attending Emerson College in Boston, Gray became active in the downtown New York theatre world, co-founding the Wooster Group in 1979. He became well known in 1987 after his monologue, *Swimming to Cambodia* – about appearing as an actor in *The Killing Fields* (1984) – was made into a film. *It's A Slippery Slope* was his last monologue, dealing with his marriage to and rapid divorce from his long time girlfriend and his unexpected fathering of a child with another woman. The monologue is Gray's attempt to get a handle on his life, and on the process of aging – which he likens to hurtling down a ski slope (a new-found passion of his). In 2001, Gray sustained head injuries in a car accident in Ireland that exacerbated his depression. He went missing in January of 2004, and his body was recovered from the East River of New York in March that year, a presumed suicide. Gray once said that he hoped his epitaph would read: 'An American Original: Troubled, Inner Directed and Cannot Type'.

GRAHAM GREENE (1904–1991) English writer. *A Sort of Life* (1971)

'An autobiography is only "a sort of life",' wrote a 66-year-old Graham Greene in the preface to his memoirs. 'It may contain less errors of fact than a biography, but it is of necessity even more selective; it begins later and it ends prematurely.' Greene's *A Sort of*

Life begins with his memories of childhood, growing up in Hertfordshire, where he was born Henry Graham Greene. He describes the horrors of his schooldays – attending a school where his father was headmaster – and his adolescence, at which time he attempted suicide, went into psychoanalysis and experimented with Russian roulette. At Oxford he began to write, publishing poems and articles. It was here he met his wife and converted to Catholicism, one of the great turning-points in his life. On graduation he moved to London to work as a sub-editor at *The Times*, a job he left after his first novel was published. *A Sort of Life* ends with the 27-year-old Greene trying to complete his second novel (and having a miserable time of it) and about to join the staff at *The Spectator* magazine. During the Second World War, Green worked for the Foreign Office in intelligence and was posted to Africa. The circumstances that surrounded the creation of his major novels are described in a subsequent work of autobiography, *Ways of Escape* (1980). Greene died in Vevey, Switzerland, in 1991.

ALEC GUINNESS (1914–2000) English actor. *Blessings in Disguise* (1985)

A gifted writer as well as actor, Alec Guinness published two volumes of diaries, *My Name Escapes Me* (1996) and *A Positively Final Appearance* (1996), in addition to his autobiography. He was born in London in 1914. His absent father's name was left blank on his birth certificate, an unsolved mystery that troubled Guinness for the rest of his life. He made his stage debut in 1936 and married fellow actor Merula Salaman in 1938. During World War II he served in the Royal Navy, beginning his screen career upon returning home, with two films directed by David Lean – *Great Expectations* (1946) and *Oliver Twist* (1948) – the start of a long collaboration with that director. In *Blessings in Disguise*, Guinness writes just some of his reminiscences from his first 70 years. As he explains in his preface, the book is 'not so much a patchwork quilt of memoirs as a cat's cradle of reminiscences all tangled round myself'. To the disappointment of *Star Wars* fans, Guinness makes only passing mention of his appearance as Obi-Wan Kenobi. He died in 2000 at the age of 86.

ROY HATTERSLEY (1932–) English politician, journalist and writer. *A Yorkshire Boyhood* (1983)

The former deputy leader of the British Labour Party, Roy Hattersley served as a Member of Parliament for 33 years before becoming a Labour peer. He has written novels, biographies, histories, essays and two volumes of memoirs while also maintaining a career as a prolific columnist. The first of his memoirs, *A Yorkshire Boyhood*, takes place in Sheffield, where he was born in 1932 and grew up. An only child, Hattersley's three lifelong passions were established when he was a boy – football, cricket and politics. His father took him regularly to see Sheffield Wednesday football team, and his mother, who later became a Labour councillor and Lord Mayor of Sheffield, introduced him to electioneering. A second volume of memoirs, *Who Goes Home?: Scenes from a Political Life* (1995), is an account of his lifetime in the Labour Party. In 2001, however, Hattersley brought out a new edition of *A Yorkshire Boyhood*, and in his introduction he revealed a recent discovery – that his parents, Enid and Frederick, were unmarried when he was born, that Frederick was a Catholic priest when he met Enid, who was married to someone else at the time. Hattersley's parents were legally married in 1956, and ten years later their son was legitimized. The revelation did nothing to diminish Hattersley's fondness for his parents, nor his perception that his was a happy childhood, and so he decided to leave his memoir unchanged in its new edition.

KATHARINE HEPBURN (1907–2003) American film actress. *Me: Stories of My Life* (1991)

Katharine Hepburn's autobiography is written in unmistakably clipped Hepburnian tones – a voice once described by Tallulah Bankhead as sounding like 'nickels dropping in a slot machine'. She was born Katharine Houghton Hepburn to upper middle-class New England parents, and in her memoirs she describes her childhood with a great deal of tenderness. Evidently, her liberal parents and their milieu helped define her spirited persona both on screen and off. Hepburn began acting immediately after graduating from Bryn

Mawr college, and in the same year of 1928 she married a Philadelphia stockbroker, Ludlow Ogden Smith. Her first film, *A Bill Of Divorcement*, appeared in 1932 and she went on to make a further 42 screen appearances (although in *Me* she mentions only a handful of them). In 1942, while appearing in *Woman of the Year*, Hepburn met Spencer Tracy. The two became partners both in real life and in numerous films, and the autobiography includes Hepburn's moving last letter to Tracy before his death in 1967. The feisty actress continued to work into her 80s, publishing her memoirs at the age of 84. She died at her family home in Connecticut in 2003, at 96.

EVA HOFFMAN (1945–) Polish-American writer. *Lost in Translation: A Life in a New Language* (1989)

Eva Hoffman's *Lost in Translation* is the story of her personal experience as a Polish immigrant girl in Canada, and then as a young woman in the United States. Hoffman describes the trauma of displacement and the difficulties, and eventual rewards, of acquiring English as her second language. She was born Ewa Wydra, in Cracow, in 1945. Her parents, although Jewish, had survived the Second World War, which they spent in hiding in the Ukraine. In 1959 the family left for Vancouver, and their daughter began to experience the world in two languages, a slow process of accommodation and loss that Hoffman describes in eloquent detail in her memoir. Although a gifted pianist, she chose to study literature and become a writer, a decision that eventually helped to reconcile her with her new language. Hoffman worked as a journalist for *The New York Times* throughout the 1980s and moved to London in 1993. She is the author of histories, memoir essays and a novel. *Lost in Translation*, written in English, was published when Hoffman was 43.

JAMES HOGG (1770–1835) Scottish poet. '*Memoir of the Author's Life*' (1832)

Altrive Tales (1832) begins: 'I like to write about myself: in fact, there are few things which I like better; it is so delightful to call up old reminiscences.' Hogg's memoir, included in his book of prose writings *Altrive Tales* (1832), begins with his birth in 1772 in Ettrick, Scotland (in fact, according to the parish register, he was born in 1770, but Hogg's account is so exuberant, it seems unfair to pick holes). He lived on his father's farm until, when the boy was six, the family went bankrupt and young Hogg was forced to leave school and start work as a shepherd. At 15 he began to teach himself to read and write, and he was soon composing poetry. In 1807 his first collection appeared, around the same time as Hogg's treatise on sheep diseases. Although his writings were popular successes, as he points out in his memoir, when he did make money, he squandered it. He did, however, learn to capitalize on his humble beginnings, appearing in London wearing his shepherd's tartan and – although he had long since given up herding – continuing to refer to himself as 'the Ettrick Shepherd'. Hogg's delightful narrative also describes his first meeting with William Wordsworth whom he confuses for a Scottish horse-dealer of the same name. His second work of memoirs *Familiar Anecdotes of Sir Walter Scott* (1834), comprise his recollections of his friend and fellow Scotsman, and was written just weeks after Scott's death in 1832. Hogg died three years later at his farm in Altrive.

BILLIE HOLIDAY (1915–1959) American jazz vocalist. *Lady Sings the Blues* (1956)

Billie Holiday claimed she had never read her autobiography. The book was co-written with her friend William Dufty – and biographers continue to dispute its veracity. For her part, Holiday had hoped the book would be called 'Bitter Crop' (a phrase from the song 'Strange Fruit' which she had made famous) but her publishers preferred Lady Sings the Blues. Holiday was, of course, not a blues singer, but the definitive jazz vocalist of her times. Born Eleanora Fagan, in Baltimore, to teenage parents, she was marked from an early age by violence, poverty and abuse. She began her career in the nightclubs of New York and her autobiography recounts the racism and sexism she suffered as a young woman singer. But *Lady Sings the Blues* is also a remarkable and candid account of drug addiction and

Holiday's persecution by the authorities as a result. In 1946, Holiday made her first attempt to give up heroin, but in 1947 she was arrested for narcotics' possession and sentenced to a year in prison, where she went into withdrawal. Two years later – as she she writes in the autobiography – she was set up by police on a phoney drug charge and arrested again. This time she was acquitted. *Lady Sings the Blues* ends with Holiday released on bail, reflecting on her life, hopeful that she might kick her habit, and that she might be given the time and consideration to do so. Three years after the book was published, she was rushed to hospital with liver and heart problems. Heroin was allegedly found in her room and she was arrested in the hospital, with guards stationed by her bed so that she couldn't escape. She died the same year (1959) at the age of 44, with only a few hundred dollars to her name.

DAVID HUME (1711–1776) Scottish philosopher, economist and historian. *The Life of David Hume, Esq. written by himself* (1776)

David Hume's brief account of his life was written on his deathbed, his intention being to provide a useful preface to subsequent editions of his work. It is less than 3000 words in length. When it was published in a separate pamphlet the following year, critics were quick to point out what they felt was missing from his account – despite Hume's proximity to death, his final statement did not include any repudiation of his lifelong atheism. In his writings Hume explored the subjects of philosophy, history, politics and economics without recourse to religious thought, and he remained a sceptic to the last. He was born in Edinburgh in 1711, and studied at Edinburgh University before considering a career in law. After some years of private study, most of them spent in France, his first philosophical work, *A Treatise of Human Nature*, was published in 1739. *The Treatise* established a philosophical system based on the study of human nature, incorporating principles that fundamentally influenced the development of modern Western philosophy. Despite failing to secure chairs at the major Scottish universities – most likely because of his atheism – Hume continued to publish, including six volumes of his *History of England*. From 1763 Hume served as personal secretary to the British ambassador in Paris, where he met the major French Enlightenment figures. He died from an internal disorder in Edinburgh, in 1776.

T.H. HUXLEY (1825–1895) English scientist. *Autobiography* (1889)

Thomas Henry Huxley wrote his memoir under a degree of duress – at the request of an editor who wanted to write a biography, he penned a brief sketch of himself to prevent any unreliable account being written. Only 4000 words in length, the *Autobiography* is for the most part a list of the key events in his professional career and, as a result, omits many of the more intriguing aspects of his story. For example, Huxley fails to mention that his conversion to agnosticism – a term he in fact coined – came about while grieving for the death of his young son. Huxley was born in London in 1825 and studied medicine at the University of London. In 1846, he left England to serve as a surgeon on HMS *Rattlesnake*, bound for Australia. The research into marine life that he conducted while on this trip established him as a scientist. He was a man who believed that scientific thinking was the supreme means of understanding and improving the world; and he spent the rest of his life promoting science, its teaching in schools and universities, and to protecting the scientific advances of himself and his peers, particularly Charles Darwin, whose *Origin of Species* (1859) he staunchly defended, earning himself the title 'Darwin's bulldog'. He died in 1895, six years after writing his account of his life.

HENRY JAMES (1843–1916) American-English novelist. *A Small Boy and Others* (1913) and *The Middle Years* (1916)

In 1912, at the age of 69, Henry James began work on a memoir of his late elder brother, the philosopher William James, who had died two years previously. In the process of writing, however, James developed his original idea, and the result, *A Small Boy and Others*, is as much an extended musing on memory, childhood and the author as it is a description of William. As if to make up for this earlier digression, James published *Notes of a Son and Brother* in 1914, which did include portraits of both William and their father, the theologian Henry James Senior. A third instalment, *The Middle Years*, is an account of James' European tour begun in 1869 at the age of 26, and his first as an adult. All three volumes were written in the writer's distinctive late style, characterized by lengthy sentences, piling clause upon clause and deferring verbs before the reward of a full stop. In all three works, James is concerned not only with reproducing his memories, but also of conveying the act of recalling and recording memories, an extraordinary development in the history of memoir writing. James was born in New York in 1843. He studied law at Harvard, but left after a year to write. During the course of his life, James spent as much time in Europe as America, and in 1876 he settled in England. His great early novels were written in Europe, including *Daisy Miller* (1879) and *Portrait of a Lady* (1881); and his last complete novel, *The Golden Bowl*, was published in 1904. In 1915, James became a British citizen in protest against America's refusal to enter the First World War. He died in 1916 before *The Middle Years* was finished. It was puiblished posthumously in 1917.

C.G. JUNG (1875–1961) Swiss psychiatrist. *Memories, Dreams, Reflections* (1961)

Carl Gustav Jung's autobiographical work was published, at his request, after his death in 1961. Written in collaboration with his assistant Aniela Jaffe, the book was subsequently edited by Jaffe, Jung's family and its publisher, so there has since been some dispute as to how much of the work was actually approved by the author. Nonetheless, this remains one of Jung's most widely read books, a kind of primer on his life's work. It begins in childhood – he was born in Kesswil, Switzerland, in 1875 – and follows Jung to university in Basel, where he studied medicine and then psychiatry. In 1907 Jung met Sigmund Freud in Vienna, and the two men began to collaborate. Together, they founded the International Psychoanalytical Association, before dramatically parting ways soon afterwards – Jung disagreed with Freud's insistence that neurosis was caused by psychosexual problems. After the split from Freud, Jung suffered a breakdown, but used his own illness as case study. He went on to develop his theories of the collective unconscious, of mythic archetypes, and to establish his own school of psychology. As he describes in his prologue, his own story is nothing less than 'the story of the self-realization of the subconscious'; and, as such, *Memories, Dreams, Reflections* is concerned as much with Jung's dream life as any outward events. He died in 1961 at the age of 85.

MARY KARR (1965–) American writer. *The Liars' Club* (1995)

Mary Karr's best-selling book *The Liars' Club* is often credited with sparking a resurgence of the memoir form in America. The book takes the reader inside the mind of Karr's cantankerous seven- and eight-year-old self, growing up in a small Texas oil town in the 1960s. We are thrown into the heart of her family – Karr's feisty, sarcastic elder sister Leica, her artistic but hard-drinking mother, and her equally hard-drinking, oil worker father. It is Karr's father who is a member of a 'liars' club', a group of drinking buddies who sit round telling tall tales. Karr followed *The Liars' Club* with *Cherry* (2000), a memoir of her adolescence and the circumstances leading up to the day she says goodbye to her hometown, at the age of 17, bound for California. Karr eventually arrived at Goddard College in Vermont, where she studied under the great American memoirists Tobias Wolff and Frank Conroy. She has published three books of poetry as well as essays and criticism. Karr currently lives in upstate New York, where she is a professor at Syracuse University.

P.J. KAVANAGH (1931–) English poet, journalist and actor. *The Perfect Stranger* (1966)

P.J. Kavanagh was the author of one collection of poetry when he published his memoir, *The Perfect Stranger*, at the age of 35. He was born into an Irish family living in England, and *The Perfect Stranger* begins here, with his childhood before, during and after the Second World War. He also goes on to describe his national service, his term as a soldier in Korea and his return to England, at which time he went up to Oxford University. He met his future wife Sally Phillips after first hearing her footsteps on the stairs of his digs – she is the perfect stranger of the title, the woman he falls in love with and whose love transforms him. After they married, the couple settled briefly in London before leaving for Jakarta where Kavanagh took a position with the British Council, and where one summer's day in 1958 Sally suddenly dies. The circumstances of her death from polio are recounted in the book's final chapter, forcing the reader to accept that the preceding narrative has been an elegy. Kavanagh went on to publish another nine collections of poetry, four novels, two children's books and a travel book. He was a columnist for *The Spectator* magazine and the *Times Literary Supplement* for many years, and has appeared intermittently as a television actor. 'Not so much an autobiography as the story of a rescue,' Kavanagh wrote of *The Perfect Stranger*; it remains one of the most beguiling descriptions of happiness in love ever written.

BRIAN KEENAN (1950–) Irish academic and writer. *An Evil Cradling* (1992)

Brian Keenan was born in Belfast and studied at the University of Ulster. In 1985, he moved to Lebanon to take up a position in the English department of the American University of Beirut. Soon after his arrival he was kidnapped by Islamic militants and taken to a secret underground prison, where he was held in isolation, darkness and squalor for months. After this time, he was moved into a cell with John McCarthy, the British journalist who had been captured a week before him. In his memoir of his almost five years in captivity, Keenan describes the torture of his confinement, his frequent beatings and a rape. He writes of his relationship with his fellow captives, and also with his captors – young men who can be both unaccountably kind and horrendously brutal. Keenan was finally released in 1990. He began work on his memoir soon afterwards. Since that time he has published a novel, an account of his travels in Alaska, and a book about his journey through South America that he took with McCarthy.

HELEN KELLER (1880–1968) American writer. *The Story of My Life* (1903)

Helen Adams Keller was born in Alabama in 1880, the daughter of a prominent newspaper publisher. When she was a year and a half, due to an illness she lost her hearing, vision and ability to speak. Her life changed dramatically again in 1887 when she was taught how to speak through touch. Later, Keller was sent to study speech at a school for the deaf in Boston, learned Braille and went on to Radcliffe College, Cambridge, from which she graduated in 1904. While she was still at university, Keller wrote and published her autobiography and the book quickly became a best-seller. Keller published four subsequent works of memoir: *The World I Live In* (1908), about the ways in which she understood the physical and audible world; *My Religion* (1927), about her conversion to the spiritual ideas of Emanuel Swedenborg; *Midstream: My Later Life* (1929), in which she writes about her years after graduation; and *Teacher: Anne Sullivan Macy* (1955), about the woman who taught her to read, write and communicate. Keller was an active campaigner for social justice throughout her adult life, not just for the blind, but also for the equal rights of women and in the cause of pacifism. She died in Connecticut, in 1968.

MARGERY KEMPE (c.1373–c.1439) English mystic. *The Book of Margery Kempe* (1436–1438)

Margery Kempe's account of her life is one of the earliest surviving autobiographies in the English language. Parts of the medieval 'boke' were published in pamphlet form around 1501, but the full manuscript was presumed missing until 1934, when it was rediscovered and brought to light by scholars at the Victoria & Albert Museum in London. Since then, it has been established that Kempe was born Margery Brunham in King's Lynn, Norfolk, around 1373, the daughter of a prosperous middle-class family. She was married to John Kempe around 1394 and endured ill health and 14 pregnancies in the course of the next 20 years. After her first experience of childbirth, Kempe began to have powerful visions.

When she was 40, she decided to devote herself to a celibate, spiritual life and for the next five years she made pilgrimages, travelling to Jerusalem, to Spain, Italy, and around England. In the early 1430s, she began to dictate her book, perhaps to one of her sons. After the death of her husband, when she was around 60 years old, Kempe travelled by boat to Germany, returning by land. Once back in England, she became determined to have her book rewritten, taking a copy of the work to a priest, who produced a legible version and added a further section to encompass her latest travels. Kempe's story is particularly rivetting for its rich domestic narrative – she is a wife who squabbles with her husband, leaves him to become a pilgrim, and returns to nurse him and grumble about having to change his underwear. She died some time after she was admitted into a King's Lynn guild in 1439, the last record of her existence.

AKIRA KUROSAWA (1910–1998) Japanese film director. *Something Like An Autobiography* (1982)

Akira Kurosawa was born in Tokyo into a family that was descended from samurai. As a young man Kurosawa had aspirations to become a painter, but in his mid-20s, he began to work as an assistant director in the Japanese film industry, before starting to make his own films in 1943. In his autobiography he writes of the forces and experiences that shaped his films, from his earliest memories of childhood, through to the Second World War and the American occupation of Japan, leading up to the Venice Film Festival where his *Rashomon* (1950) earned the Grand Prix. Throughout his career Kurosawa wrote, directed and edited his work, making both historical and contemporary films that reflected on issues specific to Japan and of universal appeal. Famously single-minded, he was known to have total authority on the film set – earning him the nickname of 'Emperor'. Kurosawa continued to direct and write screenplays into his 80s. He died, aged 88, in 1998.

LAURIE LEE (1914–1997) English writer. *As I Walked Out One Midsummer Morning* (1969)

Laurie Lee's autobiographical trilogy begins with *Cider With Rosie* (1959), a book about his boyhood growing up in the village of Slad, in Gloucestershire, a place where rural ways of life had remained virtually unchanged for centuries up to the point of Lee's birth, but were rapidly vanishing as he began to write. Lee began writing poems as a teenager, but left school at 15 and worked as a builder's labourer for a time. *As I Walked Out One Midsummer Morning* is Lee's story of leaving his childhood home and walking to London at the age of 19, as well as his subsequent travels on foot through Spain. *A Moment of War* (1991) deals with his experiences in Spain during the civil war. His first collection of poetry, *The Sun My Monument*, was published in 1944, during a period when he was employed working for the BBC and the General Post Office Film Unit. Lee was also the author of travel books, essays, a radio play and short stories. He died in 1997.

ROSAMOND LEHMANN (1901–1990) English writer. *The Swan in the Evening: Fragments of an Inner Life* (1967)

Rosamond Nina Lehmann was born in Buckinghamshire in 1901, the daughter of a German-Jewish father and an American mother. After attending Cambridge University, she published her first novel, an autobiographical coming-of-age story, *Dusty Answer*, in 1928. The novel was considered scandalous for its depiction of the heroine's sexual adventures, including a liaison with another woman. That same year Lehmann split with her first husband to marry the artist Wogan Philipps, with whom she had two children, Hugh and Sally. Lehmann continued to produce novels, establishing herself as a pre-eminent modern writer. In later life, Lehmann wrote *The Swan in the Evening*, a book she subsequently described as '... my last testament. What else is left that I might say?' The memoir opens with flashes of childhood memory, before touching on the beginnings of her career as a writer, but the main body of the work is, in fact, a latter-day spiritual autobiography. In the ensuing chapters, Lehmann writes of the birth, and sudden death in 1958 of her daughter Sally, at the age of 24. After this traumatic event, Lehmann began to visit spiritualists and became increasingly convinced that communication was possible between this world and the afterlife. Lehmann joined the College of Psychic Studies, an organisation she became vice-president of in 1971. (Sally is also memorialised by her husband, P.J. Kavanagh, in his memoir, *The Perfect Stranger*.)

JOHN LENNON (1940–1980) English songwriter, musician, singer, writer. *'Two Virgins'* (1986)

John Winston Lennon was born in Liverpool in 1940. He started a band called The Quarrymen in 1955 and began writing his own *Daily Howl*, a mock newspaper of jokes and cartoons. When Lennon was 17 he met Paul McCartney and a songwriting dream team was born. After a stint playing the clubs of Hamburg with their new band, they returned to Liverpool and Lennon started writing a column called 'Beatcomber' for the *Mersey Beat* newspaper. His first book appeared in the wake of The Beatles' massive success: *In His Own Write* (1964) comprised his drawings and comical nonsense writings that owe a debt to Edward Lear, James Joyce and Lewis Carroll. *A Spaniard in the Works*, Lennon's next book in the same vein, appeared in 1965. Towards the end of The Beatles' era, Lennon became involved with Yoko Ono and the two married in 1969. The writings included in *Skywriting By Word of Mouth* (1986) were produced in the period after he met Ono, and include his story of their love affair, 'Two Virgins'. After Lennon was murdered in 1980, the manuscript was stolen and thought lost, but the papers were recovered and published in 1986. They constitute Lennon's most autobiographical work, telling the story of The Beatles' break-up, his drug dependence, his persecution by the Nixon administration due to his political activities, and his relationship with Ono.

PRIMO LEVI (1919–1987) Italian writer and chemist. *If This Is A Man / Survival in Auschwitz* (1947)

Primo Levi's extraordinary Holocaust testimonial, *If This Is A Man*, was first published in Italian in 1947. Levi finished the manuscript just two years after his liberation from the Nazi death camp, but had difficulties finding a publisher. In 1958, a longer version was produced and it was in this form that *If This Is A Man* or *Survival in Auschwitz* (its American title) became an international best-seller. Levi's depiction of his capture, deportation and enslavement by the Nazis, and his eventual liberation, is written with a sustained precision – unspeakable experiences described by a writer of pre-eminent skill. Levi was born in Turin in 1919. He studied chemistry at the University of Turin and began work for a pharmaceutical factory upon graduating. After the collapse of Mussolini's regime, Levi joined the Italian Resistance, but was captured in the mountains in the winter of 1943. Two months later, he was sent to Auschwitz. In *The Truce* (1963), Levi describes his long journey home from Auschwitz to Italy, where finally he was reunited with his family. After the war he resumed work as a chemist, while writing in his spare time. In 1961 Levi became the general manager of a factory producing paints. He retired in 1977 to become a full-time writer. His last work of autobiography, *The Drowned and the Saved*, was published in 1986. In it, Levi returned to the subject matter of his first book, fearful that the Holocaust was already being forgotten. The following year, at the age of 67, Primo Levi died from a fatal fall presumed to be a suicide.

HANNAH LYNCH (1862–1904) Irish writer. *Autobiography of A Child* (1899)

Hannah Lynch was born in Dublin in 1862. As a young woman, she was a prominent member of the Ladies' Land League, the organization founded in 1880 by Anna and Fanny Parnell, sisters of the Irish nationalist leader Charles Parnell. With Parnell imprisoned by the British, his sisters and others, including Lynch, continued to agitate for Irish Home Rule. When the British government banned the nationalist publication *United Ireland* in 1881, Lynch was charged with taking the journal to Paris, where she published and distributed it. She subsequently settled in Paris, spending long periods in France, Spain and Greece, working as a magazine and newspaper correspondent, publishing novels as well as books and articles on France and Spain. Her *Autobiography of A Child*, written when she was 37, is an early example of a memoir of unhappy childhood. Lynch tells the story of a girl who is treated cruelly by her mother and sister, and is sent to convent school where she continues to be abused. The book was first serialized in *Blackwood's Edinburgh Magazine* in 1899, and was published anonymously. It is not clear whether *Autobiography of A Child* is Lynch's story, or if an anonymous woman dictated it to her. She died in Paris, in 1904.

NAGUIB MAHFOUZ (1911–) Egyptian writer. *Echoes of an Autobiography* (1994)

The Nobel prize-winning writer Naguib Mahfouz was born in Cairo, Egypt, in 1911. From 1934 to 1971, he worked as a high-ranking civil servant for the Egyptian government, while beginning to publish his novels and stories – including his masterful *Cairo Trilogy* (1956–1957). The books in the trilogy, set on the streets of the city where he spent his formative years, are remarkable for their breadth and realism. His later work, however, has become increasingly experimental in form. *Echoes of an Autobiography* comprises a succession of personal memories and fantasies that flicker back and forth in time, and across a range of subjects: the fruits of a lifetime's experience. The story printed in this compendium is typical of the book's brevity, intensity and humour – the revolution Mahfouz describes is the 1919 uprising against the British. In 1994, the year of the book's publication, Mahfouz was stabbed in the neck by Egyptian Islamic militants but survived. Unable to write for several years, nonagenarian Mahfouz recently published stories based on the dreams from the period of his recuperation. He continues to live in Cairo.

NELSON MANDELA (1918–) South African statesman. *Long Walk to Freedom* (1994)

Nelson Mandela began work on his autobiography in 1964, the year he was first imprisoned by the South African apartheid government on Robben Island. The writing was done in secret, and when Mandela's manuscript was discovered, the prison authorities confiscated it, and it would have been lost if a copy had not been smuggled out of the prison by two of Mandela's fellow inmates. When Mandela was released 26 years later, at the age of 71, he resumed work on his memoir. Finally, in 1994, the year Mandela was elected President of South Africa, *Long Walk to Freedom* was published. Mandela tells the story of a man who sensed his calling from an early age, and the book is a recounting not only of a political awakening, but also of the emergence of a new South Africa. He was born Nelson Rolihlahla Mandela in the Eastern Cape of South Africa in 1918 and, despite the restrictions of apartheid, managed to attend university. His studies were halted when he was expelled for starting a student strike in 1940. He moved to Johannesburg where he worked as a policeman and studied first for his BA and then for the bar. In 1944 he joined the African National Congress, the organization whose youth league he helped to found, and he became its president in 1950. Throughout the 50s and early 60s he was repeatedly arrested, but managed to elude captivity. Then, in 1964, he was convicted and sentenced to life imprisonment. *Long Walk to Freedom* ends in 1990 when Mandela's release was sanctioned by President De Klerk, with whom he later shared the Nobel Peace Prize in 1993. He retired from the presidency in 1999 and withdrew from public life in 2004.

MARCUS AURELIUS ANTONINUS (121–180) Roman emperor. *The Meditations* (167)

Born Marcus Annius Catilius Severus in Rome in 121, this future emperor was the grandson of a Roman consul. Marcus's father died in his youth, and he was educated at the expense of his grandfather.

By the time he was 12, he had decided to devote himself to the study of rhetoric and philosophy, and at the age of 25 he discovered the writings of the Stoics, which were to exert an enormous influence on his life and thought. His mother's cousin, Emperor Antoninus Pius, adopted Marcus in 138 and Marcus succeeded him in 161. When he became emperor he was given the name Marcus Aurelius Antoninus – 'Aurelius' meaning 'golden'. For the most part, he was an exemplary ruler who encouraged the arts and social reform, even though he persecuted Christians, whom he feared were undermining traditional Roman beliefs. His *Meditations*, written in Greek and begun in 167, are primarily philosophical works, composed in aphoristic form and comprising 12 volumes. Although these were private, devotional notes and never meant for publication, the famous opening of Marcus's *Meditations*, included in this compendium, has been imitated by autobiographers as diverse as Robert Graves and Marlon Brando. He remained emperor until his death in 180.

HARRIET MARTINEAU (1802–1876) English writer. *Harriet Martineau's Autobiography* (1877)

Although Harriet Martineau suffered from three distinct disadvantages by Victorian standards – she was deaf, a woman and remained a spinster all her life – she was a prolific and successful author, publishing close to 40 books and pamphlets as well as thousands of columns and articles during her lifetime. Martineau tried to make a start on her autobiography twice, once in 1831, at the age of nearly 30, and again about ten years later, when she had been told she was dying of heart disease. Finally, at the age of 74 and in failing health, she felt she could not die in peace until the work was finished. Martineau was born in Norwich, England, in 1802, the daughter of a textile manufacturer. She began to lose her hearing at the age of 12 but obtained a decent education. However, when the Martineau brothers went off to university, Harriet and her sisters were not allowed to follow. In 1826 her father died, and the man to whom Harriet was engaged had a mental collapse and also died. The Martineau women were left almost destitute, and Harriet took it upon herself to earn the family living. She moved to London, where she began to write books intended to help explain religion, politics and economics to the common reader. They were extremely successful, giving Martineau complete financial independence. She went on to produce travel books, fiction, histories and a children's book. In 1845 Martineau moved to Ambleside in the Lake District, where she lived until her death in 1876. Her autobiography was published the following year.

HARPO MARX (1888–1964) Comedian and musician. *Harpo Speaks* (1961)

Born Adolph Arthur Marx in New York in 1888, the second eldest Marx Brother earned his nickname during a card game, when the dealer called him 'Harpo' because he played the harp. He was bullied at school and left at the age of eight to make his way on the streets of New York. The family was poor but ambitious, with the brothers following in the footsteps of their uncle, the comedian Al Shean, and taking to the vaudeville stage. Harpo was inspired to stop speaking after reading a review of one of his theatre performances: 'Adolph Marx performed beautiful pantomime which was ruined whenever he spoke.' After appearing on Broadway, Harpo met the theatre critic Alexander Woollcott through whom he became a member of the Algonquin Round Table, along with Dorothy Parker. In 1929 the Marx Brothers made their first film *The Cocoanuts*, a success that was followed by many others. The title of Harpo's 1961 autobiography written with Roland Barber is a reply to people who assumed the comedian really was mute. In it, he not only relates the story of the Marx brothers, their upbringing in New York, and their career on stage and on screen, but he also speaks of his life outside the troupe, his happy marriage to the actress Susan Fleming and their four adopted children. Harpo died shortly after *Harpo Speaks* was published, in 1964.

JOYCE MAYNARD (1953–) American writer. *Looking Back: A Chronicle of Growing Up Old in the Sixties* (1973)

When Joyce Marnard was 18 and in her first year at Yale University, she was asked to write a cover story for *The New York Times* magazine about life for a young person growing up in the 60s. 'An Eighteen-Year-Old Looks Back on Life' made such an impact that Maynard was asked to turn it into a book. She left Yale to do so and the result was *Looking Back: A Chronicle of Growing Up Old in the Sixties*. She was born in New Hampshire in 1953, a 'baby boomer' who became a kind of unofficial spokesperson for that generation. Maynard went on to write for newspapers and magazines, and to author novels. Then, in 1998, she published *At Home in the World*, a book that revealed the circumstances surrounding *Looking Back*'s composition. After Maynard's essay appeared in the *Times*, one of the hundreds of letters she received was from the reclusive author J.D. Salinger. The two began a correspondence that culminated in Maynard leaving Yale and going to live with Salinger, a man 35 years her senior. But just before *Looking Back* was published, after helping her to prepare the manuscript, Salinger abruptly terminated the relationship. *At Home in the World* follows Maynard's heartbreak after the end of the affair, her subsequent marriage, career and motherhood. The author currently lives in North California where she writes and teaches.

MARY MCCARTHY (1912–1989) American writer. *How I Grew* (1987)

In 1957 Mary McCarthy published her first book of memoirs – *Memories of a Catholic Girlhood* – a vivid reconstruction of the years before and after the deaths of her parents in the influenza epidemic of 1918. She was born Mary Therese McCarthy, in 1912. After her parents' deaths she was fostered, along with her siblings, by her aunt and uncle – a far from happy arrangement. She graduated from Vassar in 1933 and married, while beginning to work as a critic and editor. In 1938 she married again, this time to her fellow critic Edmund Wilson, the second of her four husbands. McCarthy's first of 16 novels appeared in 1942. Thirty years after writing *Memories of a Catholic Girlhood*, at the suggestion of her publisher, McCarthy wrote the story of her intellectual development, *How I Grew*. This second volume of memoirs traces McCarthy's teenage years at a Seattle high school until her graduation from Vassar at 21. She describes the first time she has sex, the first time she falls in love, her first attempts at writing, her first job, and her growing involvement in the world of books and ideas. McCarthy's memoirs are characterized by the author's questioning of the veracity of her memories – truth and authenticity are particularly important to this orphan, who felt she had lost primary access to her past when she lost her parents. McCarthy died in New York two years after the publication of *How I Grew*.

MARGARET MEAD (1901–1978) American anthropologist. *Blackberry Winter: My Earlier Years* (1972)

Margaret Mead was born in Philadelphia in 1901 and studied at Barnard College and Columbia University. In 1928 she published her ground-breaking work of anthropology, *Coming of Age in Samoa*, the result of her PhD fieldwork in Polynesia. The book, which became a best-seller, explained how prevailing culture shapes the development of adolescent women, and the extent to which sexual and gender-specific behaviour is learned not innate. Mead is one of a handful of anthropologists credited with popularizing their subject through books that were accessible to general readers. She encouraged people to bring her findings to bear on modern life, and her work on matriarchal societies became an inspiration to the feminist movement. Issues of child rearing, child development, gender and adolescence evidently fascinated Mead, and when she came to write her autobiography, *Blackberry Winter: My Earlier Years*, when she was in her early 70s, her preoccupations were not dissimilar. She writes at length about her own childhood and teenage years, the cultural forces that shaped her personality, and her experiences of being a mother to her daughter Catherine and grandmother to her granddaughter Sevanne. Mead died in New York in 1978, aged 76.

JOHN STUART MILL (1806–1873) English philosopher and political economist. *Autobiography* (1873)

John Stuart Mill was born in London in 1806 and his *Autobiography* was published in the year of his death. In fact, the book had been years in the writing, beginning three decades earlier when the author was ill and assumed he was going to die. He resumed work on it in 1758 after the death of his wife, the writer and social campaigner Harriet Taylor. The resulting *Autobiography* is an extended exploration of his intellectual and moral development. Under the tutelage of his ambitious father, Mill was reading Greek at age three and by the age of eight he had absorbed a large proportion of the classics and English history. His father, James Mill was a devotee of the political thinker Jeremy Bentham, and was brought up to continue the work of Bentham's staunch utilitarianism. After finishing his education, Mill edited Bentham's *Rationale of Judicial Evidence* (1827). But when he was 20, he entered a period of prolonged dissatisfaction, with both himself and his mentors. He had begun to immerse himself in the Romantic poets and writers, and together with his natural inclination for enquiry, this led Mill to what he describes in his *Autobiography* as his 'mental crisis', a period that lasted from 1826 to 1827. The latter part of the *Autobiography* deals with his relationship with Taylor, whom he married in 1851, after the death of her first husband and more than 20 years of friendship.

ARTHUR MILLER (1915–2005) American playwright. *Timebends: A Life* (1987)

Born Arthur Asher Miller in Brooklyn, New York, Miller was the son of Polish-Jewish immigrants who lost their money during the Great Depression. After he left school Miller worked at an auto-parts warehouse, eventually saving enough to study English and drama at the University of Michigan, where he wrote his earliest plays. Miller was 29 when his sixth play, *Death of a Salesman* – about Willy Loman and his sons – was first produced. It went on to win the Pulitzer Prize and become a modern classic. His next creation, *The Crucible*, first staged in 1953, was written in response to the Communist witch-hunts. Miller himself became a target, appearing before the House of Un-American Activities Committee in 1956. His autobiography, *Timebends: A Life*, published when he was 72, is a thoughtful depiction of his life in its many stages. He writes at length about his early days, the process of creating his major plays, his short-lived marriage to Marilyn Monroe, and his work for PEN, the international writers' advocacy organization, amongst other subjects. Miller's last and 26th play, *Finishing The Picture*, was produced in 2004. He died at his home in Roxbury, Connecticut, in 2005.

CZESLAW MILOSZ (1911–2004) Polish poet. *Native Realm: A Search for Self-Definition* (1958)

Czeslaw Milosz wrote his autobiography in the middle of his life, while exiled in Paris. It describes the poet's origins and ancestors in Eastern Europe and the many political upheavals of his lifetime, beginning with the German military advance into the then Russian province of Lithuania in 1914. Born to a Polish-speaking family in Lithuania, Milosz grew up in the capital Vilnius, where he studied law and literature at the university. He began to write poetry as a young man and published his first collection of poems in 1933. In 1935 he moved to Warsaw, where he was involved in the underground resistance during World War II. He served as a diplomat for the People's Republic of Poland, but when he fell from favour with the government he was forced to defect, settling in Paris. *Native Realm* uses Milosz's personal experiences of migration to tell a universal story of human displacement. In 1960 he moved to the United States, where he became a professor of Slavic at the University of California, Berkeley. He won the Nobel Prize for Literature in 1980. After the end of the cold war, he returned to Poland. He continued to publish until his death, at his home in Cracow, in 2004.

CLAUDE MONET (1840–1926) French painter. *'An Interview'* (1900)

In 1900, during the opening of one of his Parisian exhibitions, Claude Monet spoke at length to the journalist François Thiébault-Sisson and the interview was printed as a form of autobiography in the French newspaper *Le Temps* soon afterwards. In it, Monet describes his life to that point. He was born Oscar-Claude Monet in Paris in 1840 and when he was five, moved with his family to Le Havre in Normandy, where, contrary to his family's wishes, he began to paint and draw. It was in Normandy that he met Eugène Boudin who became his mentor and encouraged him to paint *'en plein air'*, as opposed to in a studio. After two years in the French army, Monet went to study art, joining the Parisian studio of the Swiss painter Charles Gleyre and the circle of Pierre-Auguste Renoir, Frederic Bazille and Alfred Sisley. Although the word Impressionism would not be used to describe the group's work until 1874, these men had begun to develop a style that would revolutionize modern painting. Monet counted amongst his acquaintances many of the great painters of the day, including Edouard Manet, whom he first encountered in 1863. During the early part of their careers, the two men were often muddled because of the similarity of their names, and in his 'Interview' Monet speaks of a mutual rivalry. After a period in England during the Franco-Prussian War, Monet moved in 1890 to a house in Giverny, where he planted a garden, painting there for the next 40 years. He died at Giverny in 1926.

MICHEL DE MONTAIGNE (1533–1592) French essayist and philosopher. *'Of the Education of Children'* (1580), *'Of Presumption'* (1580), *'Of Experience'* (1588)

The Renaissance philosopher Michel de Montaigne is generally credited with the invention of the personal essay, although the form had its precedents in the didactic works of antiquity, as Montaigne's frequent reference to classical authors makes clear. In placing himself as the central object of his investigations, however,

Montaigne was the first to probe so deeply or to reveal so much. Whether writing about his dietary habits or matters of moral virtue, Montaigne revels in his subjectivity, allowing his essays to echo the quirky rhythms of thought itself, often at the expense of the efficacy of his arguments. He was born Michel Eyquem de Montaigne in Périgord, France, at the family chateau in 1533. He studied philosophy at university and served in the courts of Bordeaux until he inherited the family estate on the death of his father in 1568. At this point, Montaigne retired to the chateau, beginning to write his essays in 1572. Shortly after the publication of his first book, in 1580, Montaigne was elected Mayor of Bordeaux, as was his father before him. Throughout this period, he continued work on the essays, revising them and perfecting them for publication. Montaigne died at his chateau in 1592, at the age of 59.

BLAKE MORRISON (1950–) English writer, poet and editor. *And When Did You Last See Your Father?* (1993)

Blake Morrison was born in Yorkshire in 1950 and attended the University of Nottingham and University College in London. He began his career as an editor at *The Times Literary Supplement*, going on to become the literary editor of *The Observer* and the *Independent on Sunday*. His first poetry collection, *Dark Glasses*, appeared in 1984. Morrison is also the author of a novel, a book about the James Bulger case, a children's book, a play, dramatic adaptations and numerous critical works. Morrison's first memoir *And When Did You Last See Your Father?* tells the story of the last few weeks of his father's life, before his sudden death from cancer. In it Morrison expertly invokes his father's past and his own complicated connection with him. Central to the book is an enquiry into the veracity of any depiction of his father, or whether a parent will always be viewed through the distorting lens of filial relationship. In the final chapter, included in this compendium, he recalls the last time he saw his father. A second volume of memoirs, *Things My Mother Never Told Me*, was published in 2002. Blake Morrison lives in London.

JOHN MORTIMER (1923–) English writer. *Clinging to the Wreckage: A Part of Life* (1982)

Besides his work as a playwright, screenwriter, journalist, novelist, barrister – and creator of Rumpole of the Bailey – John Mortimer is also an autobiographer. *Clinging to the Wreckage* describes his childhood and early adulthood. The beginnings of Mortimer's career as a divorce lawyer are described, as well as his first marriage and the time leading up to his own divorce and his switch to criminal law. *Clinging to the Wreckage* was followed by *Murderers and Other Friends: Another Part of Life* (1994), about his time as a QC defending everyone from the murderers of the title to the punk band, The Sex Pistols, as well as his second, happy marriage and the progress of his literary career. Mortimer's third work of memoir, *The Summer of a Dormouse: Another Part of Life* (2000) is a book about its author's 78th year, and the challenges and pleasures of old age. John Mortimer was born in Oxfordshire where he lives to this day.

JOHN MUIR (1838–1914) Scottish-American environmentalist. *The Story of My Boyhood and Youth* (1913)

Published in 1913 when its author was 75, *The Story of My Boyhood and Youth* is John Muir's re-creation of his childhood in Dunbar, Scotland, where he was born in 1838. It was here that Muir first attended school and fell in love with the natural world. When he was 11, his family emigrated to Wisconsin, USA, where Muir and his brothers helped their father to carve out a farm from the wilderness. Throughout his boyhood and youth, Muir was fascinated by nature – in his memoir he writes about learning to swim by watching frogs. As a young man, Muir attended the University of Wisconsin, but interrupted his studies to join the 'university of the wildness', walking the thousand miles from Indiana to Florida. He settled in California, where he worked as a sheep-herder, amongst other jobs, in the foothills of the Sierra Nevada. Muir went on to play a vital role in the movement to create America's national parks. His many writings on the American West are a lasting testament to the power and magnificence of that landscape. He died in 1914 soon after the publication of his memoir.

MARGARET MURRAY (1863–1963) English archaeologist, Egyptologist and folklorist. *My First Hundred Years* (1963)

In the introduction to her autobiography, Margaret Murray writes that she is about to set forth the details of a life 'without a single adventure'. In fact, it was a remarkably eventful 100 years. Born in Calcutta, India, to a British colonial family, Murray decided at the age of 20 that she would like to pursue a career. She trained as a nurse, and after her family returned to England in 1887, on the suggestion of her sister, she began to study at University College, London, at a time when it was extremely rare for women to have academic lives. After graduating she joined the faculty at University College, began to publish and met her mentor Sir William Finders Petrie. In 1902 she travelled to Egypt with him to work on her first dig, and by 1905 had published the first of many volumes on Egyptology. In 1921 she produced the first of her works on witchcraft and although these have long since been exposed as academically specious, Murray's descriptions of pre-Christian cults were so vivid that they are credited with providing the inspiration for the modern day neo-pagan and Wicca movements. Murray retired from academic life in 1935, but continued her excavation work in the Middle East. At the age of 90 she was made president of the Folklore Society, in recognition for her contributions to the study of the subject. The excerpt included in this compendium is from the last chapter of her autobiography, written when she was 100, and called 'Still Looking Forward'. She died very soon after its completion.

VLADIMIR NABOKOV (1899–1977) Russian-American writer. *Speak, Memory: An Autobiography Revisited* (1966), and from the notes for a second volume of *Speak, Memory: Speak On, Memory* (1968–1971)

Vladimir Nabokov initially published his series of autobiographical sketches in *The New Yorker* and other American magazines from 1948 to 1951. These were later collected into the volume *Conclusive Evidence: A Memoir* (1951) and then revised in the subsequent *Speak,*

Memory: An Autobiography Revisited. In *Speak, Memory* Nabokov meditates on memory, transcendence and imagination. The very act of remembering through writing allows the author to return to the place of his aristocratic Russian childhood – St Petersburg, where he was born in 1899 and a city that he would never return to in actuality. In 1919 the family had fled Russia in the aftermath of the Bolshevik Revolution. Nabokov then won a scholarship to Cambridge University and after graduating, went to live in Berlin, where he came to prominence with his writings in Russian. In 1924 he married and in 1934 his only child, Dmitri, was born. After Hitler's rise to power, the family moved to Paris. When the Nazis invaded France, the Nabokovs emigrated to New York, where he began to write in English. He taught at American universities until the publication of his controversial novel *Lolita* (1955), the book that transformed him into an international celebrity and allowed him to retire from academia and devote himself to writing. In 1960 he moved to Montreux, Switzerland, and, in the last decade of his life, began to work on a further volume of autobiography about his time in America. Nabokov never proceeded further than the notes stage, fearing that the more recent past would fall into a mere sequential recounting, rather than the lyrical unfolding of *Speak, Memory*. A finely wrought paragraph from the notes is included in this compendium. The author died in Switzerland in 1977.

AZAR NAFISI (1955–) Iranian academic and writer. *Reading Lolita in Tehran: A Memoir in Books* (2003)

Azar Nafisi was born in Tehran, Iran, in 1955. When she was 13 years old, her parents sent her to England to finish her studies. The Shah had imprisoned her father, once the Mayor of Tehran, and so when the 1979 Iranian Revolution took place, Nafisi returned with hope to her homeland. She took a position in the literature department of the University of Tehran, but, in 1981, after refusing to wear her veil as the new rule demanded, she was forced to give up her post. Nafisi went on to teach elsewhere, but she retired in 1995 and began to teach in private. In *Reading Lolita in Tehran*, she writes about reading forbidden books with a group of seven women students who gathered secretly at her home to discuss them. The works included Vladimir Nabokov's *Lolita* as well as *The Great Gatsby* by F. Scott Fitzgerald and *Daisy Miller* by Henry James. She memorably describes the period of the Iran-Iraq War, during which she became a mother – to a daughter, Negar and son, Dara. Nafisi left Iran in 1997 and currently lives in the United States where she teaches at John Hopkins University in Washington DC. She is the author of numerous works of criticism, including a study of the novels of Vladimir Nabokov.

NASDIJJ (1950–) Native American writer. *The Blood Runs Like A River Through My Dreams: A Memoir* (2000)

The writer Nasdijj was born in the American south-west in 1950, his mother a Navajo, his father a white cowboy. His powerful first memoir, excerpted in this compendium, was written after Nasdijj published an article in *Esquire* magazine about his adopted son, who died at the age of six from fetal alcohol syndrome. As father and son take their last fishing trip together, Nasdijj also evokes the harshness of his own early years, growing up on the reservation and in migrant camps across America. In his second book of memoirs, *The Boy and the Dog are Sleeping* (2003), Nasdijj writes about his next adopted son, already dying of AIDS when he comes to live with his new father. A third volume of memoirs, *Geronimo's Bones*, is about the author's relationship with his brother, and how their bond helped to redeem the adversity of their growing up. Nasdijj has worked as a journalist, migrant labourer and teacher. He presently lives in North Carolina. Nasdijj means 'to become again' in the Athabaskan language.

PABLO NERUDA (1904–1973) Chilean poet. *Memoirs* (1974)

Pablo Neruda began writing his autobiography towards the end of his life and although his death in 1973 interrupted the editing of the manuscript, he did manage to complete its final pages. His last words form a response to the coup and assassination of his friend President Salvador Allende – Neruda died 12 days after the coup, at the age of 69. He was born Neftalí Reyes Basualto in Parral, Chile, and took his pen name in tribute to the Czech poet, Jan Neruda. The *Memoirs* include Neruda's lyrical descriptions of his motherless childhood and follow his progress to Santiago, where he studied at the University of Chile, becoming the quintessential poet-student – dressing in black, writing all night, and discovering politics. His most famous collection, *Twenty Love Poems and a Song of Despair* (1924), was published while he was still at the university. In 1927 Neruda was appointed Chilean consul to Burma, later being stationed in Ceylon, Java, Singapore, Argentina, Spain, France and Mexico. His period in Spain, which coincided with the Spanish Civil War, confirmed him as a republican. Two years after his return to Chile in 1943, Neruda was elected to the country's senate, until his opposition to the president forced him to go into hiding. He escaped across the Andes on horseback in 1949. After migrating through Europe, Russia and China, he was permitted to return to Chile in 1952. During the Chilean election of 1969, he was the Communist Party candidate until Allende replaced him. Neruda took a new position as ambassador to France. He was awarded the Nobel Prize for Literature in 1971 and returned to Chile in 1972.

SHERWIN B. NULAND (1930–) American surgeon and writer. *Lost in America: A Journey With My Father* (2003)

Dr Sherwin B. Nuland's memoir explores his relationship with his Russian-Jewish father, Meyer Nudelman. Meyer, who came to America in the early part of the 20th century. The book begins with the author's description of his crippling mid-life depression and then charts a course back to the immigrant community of the Lower East Side in New York, where Nuland was born Sherwin Nudelman. As he recounts his earliest memories, images of his father as a potent and terrifying presence reverberate; and after the death of his beloved mother when he is 11, Nuland and his brother are then left alone with their frequently violent and irascible father. The last third of the book deals with Nuland's decision to become a doctor, his time at Yale medical school, the trials of assimilation and his decision to change his name so that it would sound less Jewish, a period where he all but abandoned Meyer. The book is simultaneously an attempt to render the struggle between father and son while trying to come to terms with that relationship. The author's previous books include *How We Die: Reflections on Life's Final Chapter* (1994), as well as a biography of Leonardo da Vinci. He is clinical professor of surgery at Yale and also teaches bioethics and medical history.

NUALA O'FAOLAIN (1940–) Irish writer. *Almost There: The Onward Journey of a Dublin Woman* (2003)

Nuala O'Faolain never meant to write her memoirs. In 1996 she was asked by a small publishing house to compile a collection of her weekly columns for *The Irish Times*. O'Faolain offered to write an introduction to the edition and while she was working on it, the narrative grew until it became a meditation on her life to that point: her Irish childhood, her frequently absent father and neglectful, alcoholic mother, the forces that shaped her as a person. The introduction was later published as *Are You Somebody?: The Accidental Memoir of a Dublin Woman* (1998). It became an inadvertent best-seller, and the author, at the age of 56, found herself famous. After this success, O'Faolain was asked to write a novel and she decided to leave Ireland and move to America to do so – the period that's recounted in the second volume of her memoirs, *Almost There: The Onward Journey of a Dublin Woman*. O'Faolain was born in Dublin in 1940. After studying literature at universities in Dublin, Hull and Oxford, she lectured, worked as a producer for the BBC, wrote for newspapers, and later became a columnist for *The Irish Times*. O'Faolain finds love again with a man she meets in New York, and *Almost There* becomes, as the author has described it, 'a parable about miracles that might happen to anyone in middle age'. O'Faolain lives in New York and Dublin.

MARGARET OLIPHANT (1828–1897) Scottish-English writer. *The Autobiography of Margaret Oliphant* (1864–1894)

Margaret Oliphant Wilson was born in Midlothian, Scotland, in 1828 and grew up in Scotland as well as in Cheshire, England. She published her first novel, *Passages in the Life of Margaret Maitland*, in 1849 at the age of 21 and continued to write for the rest of her life, becoming one of Queen Victoria's favourite writers. Her oeuvre includes over 100 books, including novels, stories, biographies, travel books and articles, as well as her posthumously published memoir. The bulk of Oliphant's autobiographical manuscript was written during times of extraordinary grief and over a period of 30 years, beginning with the death of her eldest daughter Maggie, at age ten, in 1864. Oliphant's husband had died five years earlier of tuberculosis, leaving his wife to support their young family through her writing. Her two remaining sons died young, before their mother. The *Autobiography* is filled with moving accounts of intense sorrow relieved by moments of remembered joy in the ordinary details of life. The author died in 1897, and despite her wishes that her autobiography should be for family use only, it was published two years later, its fragments pieced into chronological order, and with many sections discarded. Even in its abridged form, Virginia Woolf praised the work, describing it as 'a most genuine and moving piece of work'. It was only in 1990 that Oliphant's *Autobiography* was published in its entirety.

MICHAEL ONDAATJE (1943–) Canadian writer. *Running in the Family* (1982)

Michael Ondaatje is the author of ten collections of poetry and four novels as well as his 1982 memoir, *Running in the Family*. He was born in Colombo, in what was then Ceylon, now called Sri Lanka. His father was a superintendent at a rubber plantation, his mother was a dancer, but the two separated in 1954 and after his parents' divorce, Ondaatje moved to England with his mother. In 1962 Ondaatje went to live into Canada, where he attended university and began a teaching career. As he describes in *Running in the Family*, 25 years since leaving Sri Lanka, at the age of 40, he decides to go 'home'. What follows is an impressionistic patchwork of description: encounters with eccentric relatives, reconstruction of family history, the flood of childhood memories that inevitably return to him while travelling through a strangely familiar landscape, and Ondaatje's attempt to understand his flawed father and his roots in Asia. The author went on to publish his most famous book – *The English Patient* – in 1992, and *Anil's Ghost* in 2000. He currently teaches literature at York University in Toronto, Canada, where he lives. Together with his wife, Linda Spauling, he edits the literary journal *Brick*.

GEORGE ORWELL (1903–1950) English Writer. *'Such, Such Were the Joys ...'* (1952)

George Orwell was born Eric Arthur Blair in Bengal, India, in 1903, the son of an English civil servant. While still a baby, he was brought by his mother and sister to England. After failing to win a scholarship to university he travelled to Burma to take up a post with the Indian Imperial Police, a period he later wrote about in the volume of autobiographical essays, *Shooting an Elephant* (1950). In 1927 Orwell resigned from his post and returned to Europe, living as a vagrant and migrant labourer, experiences that inspired his early autobiographical work, *Down and Out in Paris and London* (1933), published under his pen name, George Orwell. He is lastingly famous for his anti-Stalinist allegories *Animal Farm* (1945) and *Nineteen Eighty-Four* (1949) – although a devoted democratic socialist who fought on the republican side in the Spanish Civil War, he was fervently opposed to the extremes of Communism. During World War Two Orwell served in the Home Guard, and worked as a journalist and editor before succumbing to tuberculosis. After his death in London in 1950, his second wife and executor, Sonia Orwell, arranged for the publication of 'Such, Such Were the Joys ...', written in 1947 and found amongst the author's papers. The essay reveals Orwell's experiences at St Cyrian's preparatory school in Sussex – 'Crossgates' in the essay – where he was beaten for wetting his bed. It seems Orwell delayed publishing during his lifetime to avoid a potential libel suit by his alma mater.

PETER O'TOOLE (1932–) Anglo-Irish actor. *Loitering With Intent: The Child* (1992)

Peter O'Toole's first volume of memoirs encompasses the first 20 years of his life. The sequel, *Loitering With Intent: The Apprentice* (1997), begins when O'Toole is 21 and deals with his time training to be an actor at the Royal Academy of Dramatic Art in London. Rambunctious, digressive and marvellously anecdotal, O'Toole's autobiographies employ a stream of consciousness style that owes something to James Joyce and an equal debt to the ramblings of the original actor Colley Cibber. In the first volume O'Toole describes his earliest years, from his birth into a working-class family in County Galway to his boyhood in Leeds and London during World War II. He left school at 14 and tried various professions, including a stint in the navy, before deciding he wanted to act. After attending RADA, O'Toole made his stage debut in 1955 at Bristol's Theatre Royal. His breakthrough in film came seven years later, with his portrayal of T.E. Lawrence in David Lean's *Lawrence of Arabia* (1962). He has appeared in over 70 films, and continues to perform.

EMMELINE PANKHURST (1857–1928) English suffragette. *My Own Story* (1914)

Emmeline Pankhurst was born Emmeline Goulden in Manchester in 1857. Her parents were supporters of women's rights, and their daughter grew up attending radical meetings. In 1879 she married Richard Pankhurst, a barrister more than 20 years her senior, and a man who helped to draft the property acts allowing married women greater control of their finances. Richard Pankhurst died in 1898, leaving his wife to fend for herself and their three children. Soon afterwards, Mrs Pankhurst founded the Women's Social and Political Union, along with her daughters Christabel and Sylvia. In 1905 the organization became militant and its members made headlines for starting fires, smashing windows, slashing pictures and going on hunger strikes. Pankhurst's autobiography is still shocking for its descriptions of the brutal treatment the suffragettes received at the hands of the government, the police, the courts and prison wardens. It is also a lasting testament to the energy, imagination and determination of the indomitable Pankhursts and the suffragettes – Mrs Pankhurst herself was imprisoned 12 times in a single year. She lived to see women receive the vote on the same basis as men in 1928, the year of her death.

THOMAS DE QUINCEY (1785–1859) English writer. *Confessions of an English Opium-Eater* (1856)

Thomas De Quincey was born in Manchester in 1785. His father died when he was seven and at 15 De Quincey was sent to Manchester Grammar School. In the account of his life, *Confessions of an English Opium-Eater*, he describes how he ran away from school at the age of 16, tramping through Wales before arriving in London, where he lived with a prostitute until his family tracked him down. In 1803 De Quincey went up to Oxford, and it was while he was a student that he first took opium, according to his account, to help dull the pain of a toothache. De Quincey married in 1816, and began working as an editor and journalist to support his family. In 1821 he was encouraged to write about his opium addiction for a London magazine. When published, De Quincey's descriptions of his struggles and eventual triumph over the drug caused such a sensation that a book was immediately prepared. In 1845 a sequel to the *Confessions*, *Suspiria De Profundis*, was published, and later followed by *Autobiographic Sketches* (1853). Shortly before his death, in 1856 De Quincey published a revised edition of his original autobiography – an excerpt from this version is included in this compendium – where he admitted that he had lapsed back into addiction numerous times. He died in Edinburgh in 1859.

GWEN RAVERAT (1885–1957) English wood engraver, illustrator and writer. *Period Piece: A Cambridge Childhood* (1952)

Gwen Raverat was in her 60s when she wrote her classic memoir – a book this artist described as 'a drawing of the world when I was young'. She was born Gwen Darwin in Cambridge in 1885, the granddaughter of Charles Darwin – although her famous forebear had died three years earlier. *Period Piece* is a beguiling portrait of a turn-of-the-century childhood, its manners and mores, illustrated throughout with Raverat's drawings. As a young woman Raverat was determined to become a professional artist, and from 1908 to 1911 she attended the Slade School of Fine Art in London. She contributed her engravings and illustrations to a number of books and was a member of the Bloomsbury Group. In 1911 she married the French painter Jacques Raverat in a neo-pagan ceremony attended by, amongst others, Rupert Brooke and Lytton Strachey. The Raverats went to live in France for the sake of Jacques' health, but when he died of multiple sclerosis in 1925, Gwen returned to England with her two young children. She went on to design scenery and costumes for the ballet, worked as an art critic, exhibited her artworks and illustrated books, and achieved especial prominence for her wood engravings. Soon after completing *Period Piece*, Raverat suffered a debilitating stroke. She took her own life, in Cambridge, in 1957.

MARY DARBY ROBINSON (c.1758–1800) English actress and writer. *Memoirs of the Late Mrs Robinson, written by herself* (1801)

When Mary Darby Robinson died in 1800, she left an unfinished draft of her autobiography to her daughter Maria, with a request that it should be published. *Memoirs of the Late Mrs Robinson, written by herself* appeared in 1801 and it tells the story from the time of her birth in Bristol in 1758 (although recent research shows she was probably born two years earlier). At the age of 16 she married a lawyer, Thomas Robinson, and their daughter was born that same year. Robinson soon discovered her husband was a gambler who had fallen into terrible debt and so, in an attempt to raise funds, she published her first book of poems. Despite her best efforts, Robinson's husband was thrown into a debtors' prison and she dutifully accompanied him there. After their release, she began to support her family through her acting, making her debut as Juliet in 1776. Her greatest success came at the age of 21, as Perdita in *A Winter's Tale*. The teenage Prince of Wales, the future King George IV, spotted her on stage and soon afterwards 'The Prince and Perdita' – as the press dubbed them – began a scandalous and very public affair. After the relationship ended, Robinson became involved with a colonel in the British army, suffering a miscarriage that left her an invalid. She continued to write into her 40s, publishing poems and later a series of highly successful novels. In 1799 she completed 'A Letter to the Women of England, on the Injustice of Mental Subordination', where she argued that women should be allowed to leave their husbands, as she herself had done. Robinson died the following year.

JEAN-JACQUES ROUSSEAU (1712–1778) French philosopher. *The Confessions* (1782–1789) and *The Reveries of The Solitary Walker* (1782)

Jean-Jacques Rousseau began writing *The Confessions* while exiled in England in 1766 and would continue to work on them for the next four years. Although he gave his *Confessions* the same title as St Augustine's autobiographical masterwork, Rousseau was quick to point out to readers that his project was very different: 'My purpose is to display to my kind a portrait in every way true to nature, and the man I shall portray will be myself. Simply myself.' Unlike Augustine, Rousseau does not seek to define himself in relation to God, but rather as an autonomous individual. The book begins in 1712 in Geneva, Switzerland, where Rousseau was born and brought up by his father after the death of his mother in childbirth. Largely self-educated, Rousseau left home in 1728. He began to write his great works of political philosophy while in his 20s and published *Discourse on the Origin and Basis of Inequality Among Men* in 1755 and *The Social Contract* in 1762. Rousseau left France for England due to the outraged reaction to his novel, *Emile, or Education* (1762), in which he argued for radical educational reform as well as the necessity of a personal and minimal religion. In 1770 Rousseau returned to Paris, where he continued to work on *The Confessions*, although under the terms of his return he was forbidden to publish. When he was 64, in 1776, he began work on *The Reveries of The Solitary Walker*. In this final book, Rousseau re-creates his thought processes over the course of ten walks. The tenth walk-essay was left unfinished at the time of his death in 1778. Both *The Confessions* and *The Reveries* were published posthumously, beginning in 1782.

JOHN RUSKIN (1819–1900) English writer, critic, art historian. *Praeterita: Outlines of Scenes and Thoughts Perhaps Worthy of Memory in my Past Life* (1885–1889)

John Ruskin was born in London in 1810, an only child of a wealthy merchant father. His mother was an Evangelical Christian who forbade her son toys and disallowed him from playing with other children. He published his first poem at the age of 11 and later attended Oxford University where he began to produce criticism on architecture. The year he graduated (1843), Ruskin published his first volume of *Modern Painters*, written in defence of the art of J.M.W. Turner. He went on to write four subsequent volumes, as well as numerous works on architecture, establishing a frame through which Victorian art and European architecture could be viewed. Ruskin had his first mental breakdown in 1875 and for the rest of his life he struggled to maintain stability. *Praeterita: Outlines of Scenes and Thoughts Perhaps Worthy of Memory in my Past Life*, his autobiography, was published in instalments between 1885 and 1889, the writing interrupted by Ruskin's declining mental and physical health. Its title is taken from the Latin word for 'things past', and using his diaries for inspiration, Ruskin described not only his bizarre upbringing and many travels throughout Europe, but also the development of his aesthetic and spiritual sensibility. An impressionistic work, told in discreet, vivid sections, with major omissions (such as his marriage), *Praeterita* was particularly beloved of Marcel Proust. Ruskin died at his home in the Lake District in 1900.

BERTRAND RUSSELL (1872–1970) English mathematician, philosopher, logician. *The Autobiography of Bertrand Russell* (1967–1969)

Written over a period of years and first published in three volumes between 1967 and 1969, Bertrand Russell's memoir begins with his childhood and traces the events of its author's long and distinguished lifetime. He was born Bertrand Arthur William Russell in 1872, and became the third Earl Russell in 1931. His parents died when he was a boy and he was brought up for the most part by his grandmother. Russell attended Cambridge University where he rapidly distinguished himself as a philosopher and mathematician. He was opposed to the First World War and was imprisoned as a result in 1918. Russell went on to become one of the founders of analytic philosophy and to take his place amongst the most influential mathematicians of the modern era. He won the Nobel Prize for Literature in 1950. From the late 1940s, he was a supporter of nuclear disarmament and went on to become a dissenting voice in the war with Vietnam. When the *Autobiography* was published, it became a best-seller and caused a scandal due to Russell's unabashed descriptions of his sexual life. He continued to work for social causes until his death at his home in Wales in 1970.

LORNA SAGE (1943–2001) English academic and literary critic. *Bad Blood: A Memoir* (2000)

Lorna Sage published her memoir just before her death from emphysema at the age of 57. The book was originally commissioned in the early 1990s and Sage repeatedly rewrote it, with the result that it seems close to perfect. Part personal history, part social document, Sage dissects her early years, the milieu of her childhood, growing up in the village of Hamner on the English-Welsh border, where her grandfather was the clergyman. She was born there, Lorna Stockton, in 1943. In Bad Blood Sage decribes her grandparents, and her parents' marriages as well as her own young marriage after she becomes pregnant at the age of 16. Eventually Sage's love of books and of study offered her a way out of her family's saga and into intellectual liberty. She attended Durham University, where she became the youngest student mother ever to graduate with a first. Sage taught English literature at British and American universities, producing numerous academic studies, including *The Cambridge Guide to Women Writers* (1999). She was professor of English at the University of East Anglia from 1994.

EDWARD W. SAID (1935–2003) Palestinian-American academic and writer. *Out of Place: A Memoir* (1999)

In 1991, when Edward Said learned that he was dying of leukaemia, he decided to write down the story of his childhood and coming of age. *Out of Place* transports the reader to the lost world of Said's early years, growing up in a dispossessed but wealthy Palestinian-American family. He was born Edward Wadie Said in Jerusalem in 1935, lived in the Lebanon, attended school in Egypt and America, and went to Princeton and Harvard Universities. The book reveals Said coming to terms with his fractured identity as a Christian of Palestinian birth who is also an American citizen, and who grew up speaking Arabic, English and French. It is also about a son's difficulties establishing himself as an individual under the auspices of loving yet overbearing parents. Said moved to New York in 1963, taking up a position at Columbia University as a professor of English and comparative literature. He became a prominent spokesperson for the Palestinian cause, writing on a wide range of subjects, including literature, politics, history, music and philosophy. His most famous works, *Orientalism* (1978) and *Culture and Imperialism* (1993), have forever altered our perception of the effects of European imperialism on the modern world. After becoming ill, Said withdrew from public life and concentrated on his memoir and his love of music, founding the West-Eastern Divan Orchestra with Daniel Barenboim in 1999. He died in New York in 2003.

GEORGE SAND (1804–1876) French writer. *Story of My Life* (1854–1855)

Story of My Life is George Sand's epic five-volume autobiography, written over a period of eight years and encompassing not only her own history, but the history of her family and her nation. We witness the French Revolution and the entire Napoleonic era before we even get to Sand's birth: 'The actual details of each human existence are like brush strokes on the larger picture of the collective life,' she wrote in the first volume. Sand was born

Amandine Aurore Lucie Dupin in Paris in 1804, and grew up for the most part at her grandmother's chateau, Nohant, in central France. She inherited Nohant in 1821, just before her marriage to Baron Casimir Dudevant. She had two children – Maurice in 1823 and Solange in 1828. Two years after the birth of her daughter, Sand separated from her husband and went to Paris to become a writer, living with the author Jules Sandeau who helped to inspire her pen name. Sand achieved immediate success following the publication of her first novel, *Indiana* (1832), and quickly gained financial autonomy through her writing: her oeuvre includes over 70 novels, more than 20 plays, and thousands of letters in addition to *Story of My Life*. She died at Nohant in 1876, at the age of 72. After it first appeared in 1854 and 1855, *Story of My Life* remained out of print in France for almost a century – it was never popular, disappointing readers with its failure to mention intimate details of Sand's love affairs with the poet Alfred de Musset and the composer Frederick Chopin, amongst others. The book was reprinted in France in 1970 and the first full-length translation in English did not appear until 1991.

JEAN-PAUL SARTRE (1905–1980) French philosopher and writer. *The Words* (1964)

Jean-Paul Sartre's autobiography, written when the author was in his 50s, describes the first decade of his life, growing up in France before the First World War. He was born Jean-Paul Charles Aymard Sartre, in Paris, in 1905. His father died while he was an infant and Sartre was brought up by his mother, grandparents, and later a stepfather. As he describes in *The Words*, his principal influences during childhood came from books and his memoir charts the development of his young consciousness and intellect. Sartre went on to study at Paris's École Normale Supérieure, where in 1929 he met Simone de Beauvoir – a relationship that would last for the rest of his life. He published his first novel, *Nausea*, in 1938, and the book served to demonstrate the existential philosophies for which he would become famous. During the Second World War, Sartre was imprisoned in Germany and after his release took part in the

French Resistance. In 1943 he published his most famous work of philosophy, *Being and Nothingness*, and founded the journal *Les Temps Modernes* soon afterwards – both helping to place him at the heart of French intellectual life. He continued to write and work for social causes, including opposition to the Vietnam War, into his old age. He died in Paris in 1980.

MRS SCOTT JP: See entry for Co-operative Working Women.

FLORIDA SCOTT-MAXWELL (1883–1979) American-British writer and psychologist. *The Measure of My Days* (1968)

At the age of 85, Florida Scott-Maxwell published her best-known work, *The Measure of My Days*. The book is a personal meditation on the pleasures and frustrations of old age, an eloquent description of how the dwindling of physical powers coincides with an increased excitement of mind as death approaches. Scott-Maxwell was born Florida Pier in 1883, in Florida, and was brought up in Pennsylvania. She attended drama school as a teenager, beginning to act professionally at the age of 16. Her writing career commenced in 1903, when she started to produce short stories for magazines. She later became the first woman staff member of the *New York Evening Sun*. In 1910 she married and moved with her husband to Glasgow, Scotland, where she lived for the next 16 years, becoming a mother to four children and joining the women's suffragette movement. Although she wrote a play during this time, it was not until her divorce in 1929 that she took up her writing career in earnest. In 1933 she began training under C.G. Jung to become an analyst, and she practised as such for the remainder of her professional life. Her understanding of Jungian psychology led to two books, *Toward Relationship* (1939) and *Women and Sometimes Men* (1957), on the role of women in a patriarchal society. Scott-Maxwell died at her home in Exeter, England, at the age of 96.

DAVID SEDARIS (1956–) Writer and radio contributor. *Something for Everyone* (1997)

David Sedaris was born in New York State in 1956 and grew up in North Carolina. His career as a writer began in 1992, with an essay produced for America's National Public Radio about his experience working as a department store elf in Santa's grotto. 'The SantaLand Diaries' introduced listeners to Sedaris's signature tone: self-deprecating, bitingly sad and very, very funny. The author's first book, *Barrel Fever*, appeared in 1994, followed by *Naked* in 1997 – a collection of Sedaris's autobiographical essays written for the radio (the title takes its name from an essay dealing with the author's visit to a nudist colony), the collection includes 'Something for Everyone' about being a directionless college graduate. With *Naked*, Sedaris introduced listeners and readers to his family, presided over by a chain-smoking mother who is dying of cancer and a loving but ineffectual father. *Naked* was succeeded by two more best-selling collections, *Me Talk Pretty One Day* (2000) and *Dress Your Family in Corduroy and Denim* (2004). After living in Paris for a number of years, Sedaris recently settled in London.

MANNY SHINWELL (1884–1986) British politician. *Lead With the Left: My first Ninety-Six Years* (1981)

Emmanuel Shinwell's autobiography comprises three volumes and tells the story of the first 96 years of his life and long political career: *Conflict Without Malice* (1955), *I've Lived Through It All* (1973) and *Lead With the Left* (1981). Shinwell was born in London in 1884, the son of a tailor. When he was 11, his family moved to Glasgow and he left school soon afterwards to begin working for his father. Shinwell's socialist convictions were born as a young man – he started working for the Scottish Wholesale Co-operative Society in 1909 and was elected to the Glasgow Trades Council in 1911. After the First World War, he was instrumental in the fight for the 40-hour working week and was elected as a Labour MP in 1922. When Ramsay MacDonald became Prime Minister in 1929,

Shinwell served as Secretary for the Department of Mines and Financial Secretary for the War Office. When Labour won the 1945 general election, Clement Attlee made Shinwell Minister of Fuel and Power, and subsequently Secretary of State for War and Minister of Defence. From 1964 to 1967, Shinwell was chairman of the Parliamentary Labour Party. He was made a Labour peer in 1970, and continued to play his part in the House of Lords into his late 90s. He died, aged 101, in 1986.

SEI SHōNAGON (C.965–C.1010) Japanese courtier and writer. *The Pillow Book of Sei Shōnagon* (C.990–C.1000)

Very little is known about Sei Shōnagon. Her name, Shōnagon, refers to the position of minor counsellor that she held at court during the Heian period in 10th-century Japan, and Sei is her family name. We know that she became an attendant to Empress Sadako Teshi in 990 and remained a loyal servant to her mistress until Sadako's death in 1000. After 1001, records of Shōnagon disappear. *The Pillow Book* was written over a period of years, beginning around the time of Shōnagon's arrival at court – at which point she seems to have been given a bundle of empty notebooks by her mistress – and finishing around the time of Sadako's demise. It is made up of 320 sections – some of which are dated, although nothing is in chronological order and it has never been established in which order the sections are meant to appear. Included are diary-style entries, reminiscences, observations, court gossip, opinions, musings on nature, descriptions of her lovers, as well as highly amusing lists of Shōnagon's likes and dislikes. Nonetheless, Shōnagon's voice resonates across a thousand years – witty, opinionated, poetic and clear, filled with the daily details of a life at times foreign and at others startlingly familiar.

MRS F.H. SMITH: See entry for Co-operative Working Women.

WOLE SOYINKA (1934–) Nigerian writer. *Aké: The Years of Childhood* (1981)

Wole Soyinka's autobiographical account encompasses the first 11 years of his life. He grew up in the west Nigerian town of Aké, where he was born in 1934. A rare example of the African memoir, *Aké* teems with Soyinka's family, his headmaster father, shopkeeper mother, his schoolfriends, neighbours and members of his community. *Aké* also traces the tension in his upbringing – although Soyinka attended a European-style Christian boarding school, outside of formal education he was learning the traditions of his native Yoruba tribe. In 1954 Soyinka left Nigeria to do research at the University of Leeds in England. His earliest plays were staged at London's Royal Court Theatre. He returned home in 1960 to found his own theatre group and began lecturing in English and drama at Nigerian universities. During the civil war in Nigeria, Soyinka was accused of assisting rebel forces and was held as a political prisoner: he spent 15 months in solitary confinement, on unproven charges. He was released in 1969, and his memoir, *The Man Died: Prison Notes* (1972), describes his survival in jail. In 1986 he became the first black African to be awarded the Nobel Prize for Literature. Despite his standing in the world, he was later sentenced to death in Nigeria for his part in the bomb attacks that took place against the army in 1996. Under amnesty, Soyinka returned again to his home in 1998. He is currently professor of comparative literature at the University of Ife in Nigeria.

GERTRUDE STEIN (1874–1946) American writer. *Everybody's Autobiography* (1937)

In 1937, at the age of 63, Gertrude Stein published *Everybody's Autobiography*, a sequel to her best-selling account of her Parisian years, *The Autobiography of Alice B. Toklas* (1933). Whereas the first autobiography had famously been written from Toklas's point of view, the sequel switched the perspective to Stein, who was, after all, the subject of the original. By the time Stein came to write her second volume of memoirs, she had finally achieved literary celebrity and had also earned a considerable sum of money from the Toklas book – after three decades of relative obscurity as a writer. She was born in Pennsylvania in 1874, educated in California and Massachusetts, and moved to Paris in 1903. Stein and her brother collected modern art, becoming early champions of Pablo Picasso, Henri Matisse and André Derain, amongst others. She met Toklas in Paris in 1907 and the two became inseparable, living openly as a couple. Stein's novels, plays, stories and poems were written in her own experimental style – usually plotless, she relied on playfulness, humour, repetition and ambiguity for her effects – although she deliberately made her autobiographies more accessible in the hope of bolstering sales. After the First World War, Stein's salon attracted the great artists and writers of the day, including Ernest Hemingway and F. Scott Fizgerald. During the Second World War, Stein and Toklas, who were both Jewish, escaped persecution – probably due to their friendship with a prominent Vichy collaborator. Stein died from stomach cancer soon after the end of the war.

STENDHAL (1783–1842) French writer. *Memoirs of an Egotist* (1892)

When Stendhal began to write his memoirs it was 1832 and he had recently published his masterpiece, *The Red and the Black* (1830). He was serving as a French consul in Cittavechia, in the Papal States (now Italy), and as a result of his duties was forced to write in his spare time. Sadly, Stendhal abandoned his memoir only two weeks after beginning it, and the unfinished manuscript was not published until after his death. *Memoirs of an Egotist* forms a lively if irregular portrait of the man, his many love affairs and intrigues, as well as offering a glimpse into the glittering Paris of the day. (It also sees the introduction of the word *égotisme* into the French language.) Stendhal was born Marie-Henri Beyle in Grenoble in 1783. His mother died when he was seven and at the age of 16 he moved to Paris. After leaving Napoleon's army, where he had served for a year, he was admitted into government service. He left his position in 1814 and settled in Italy, where he began to write, taking the pen name Stendhal. From 1821 to 1830 – the period described in *Memoirs of an Egotist* – he lived in Paris and worked as a journalist. His *Life of Henry Bruard*, also published posthumously in 1890, is a semi-fictionalized account of Stendhal's life. Like the *Memoirs*, it was written while he was in Cittavechia and also remained unfinished. After a stroke, the author died in Paris in 1842. *Memoirs of an Egotist* was first published in 1892.

WILLIAM STYRON (1925–) American writer. *Darkness Visible: A Memoir of Madness* (1990)

William Styron's poignant memoir of depression and recovery began as a lecture given in 1989 to the psychiatry department of The John Hopkins University School of Medicine in Baltimore. Next, Styron expanded it into an essay for *Vanity Fair* magazine and in 1990 it appeared in book form. *Darkness Visible* describes the summer of 1985, a period when 60-year-old Styron's unhappiness became such that he contemplated suicide. After seeking help, the author was hospitalized and received psychiatric treatment. He was born in Virginia in 1925. His mother died when he was 13 and his father, a shipyard worker, also suffered from depression. Styron served with the Marines during the Second World War and then attended Duke University, graduating in 1947. After college, he worked as an editor in New York before publishing his first novel, *Lie Down in Darkness* (1951) at the age of 26. His novel about a Holocaust survivor and a young writer living in Brooklyn, *Sophie's Choice* (1979), was later made into a film. Styron lives in Connecticut.

ST TERESA OF AVILA (1515–1582) Spanish mystic. *The Life of St Teresa of Avila by Herself* (1562–1565)

St Teresa was born Teresa Sanchez Cepeda Davila y Ahumada in Avila, Old Castile (now Spain), in 1515. Her mother died when she was 13 and her sister married, at which point she was sent to an Augustinian convent. As a young woman, she read the letters of St

Jerome and decided to lead a religious life. Without her father's consent, she entered Avila's Carmelite convent in 1534. Frequently ill, Teresa began to have religious visions. At the age of 47, and under the direction of her confessor, Pedro Ibanezis, she began work on the story of her life. She was most likely one of the first readers in Spanish to encounter St Augustine's *Confessions* and her *Life* was evidently written under its influence – Teresa recounts her youthful sins and uncertainties, before describing the turning-points and awakenings that led her to a more perfect religious life of contemplation and prayer. She portrays ecstatic visions of Christ and his angels, while also relating her struggles to found a new convent for Carmelite nuns that would restore the order to its former austerity. In 1562, in Avila, Teresa founded the Convent of St Joseph, which became her home. She completed her *Life* around 1565 and died at Alba de Tormes in 1582. Her *Life* was first published in 1588. She was canonized in 1622.

MARGARET THATCHER (1925–) English politician. *The Path to Power* (1995)

In the second volume of her memoirs, Margaret Thatcher looks back on her earliest years – her time as a student, her marriage, and her journey from backbencher to leader of the Conservative Party. Although she dealt with her years as Prime Minister in the first volume of her memoirs, *The Downing Street Years* (1993), this second book encompasses the period after her resignation as Prime Minister. She was born Margaret Hilda Roberts in Grantham in 1925, the daughter of a grocer, and studied chemistry at Oxford where she became chairman of the university's Conservative Association. After graduating, she worked as a chemist and in 1950 became a Conservative candidate. She also took a second degree in law and was called to the bar in 1953. She met and married Denis Thatcher in 1951, and won her first seat to the House of Commons in 1959. Thatcher was made a Conservative peer in 1992.

DYLAN THOMAS (1914–1953) Welsh poet. *'Holiday Memory'* (1954)

Dylan Marlais Thomas was born in Swansea in 1914, the son of an English teacher. He began writing at a young age, leaving school to become a trainee reporter on the local newspaper. In 1934, at 20, Thomas published his first collection of poems and by the time his second collection appeared in 1936, he had established himself as a vital voice in English poetry. Just before his death in 1953, Thomas began work compiling autobiographical sketches and essays that he often read aloud at his frequent lectures and radio appearances, produced over a period of ten years. *Quite Early One Morning* (1954), published posthumously, includes many tales from his boyhood and young adulthood in Wales, including the delightful 'Holiday Memory' about a family outing to the beach. As with his poetry, Thomas's prose is characterized by its extreme musicality of language and sensuality of image. Thomas died in New York, where he had gone on a lecture tour, after a drinking binge, at the age of 39.

HENRY DAVID THOREAU (1817–1862) American writer and naturalist. *Walden, or Life in the Woods* (1854)

In his classic memoir, Henry David Thoreau describes the period from 1845 to 1847 when he lived alone in the small cabin he built on Walden Pond, near to Concord in Massachusetts. The famous first-person account of this experiment in simple living and isolation is essentially an argument for reduction – the author spends his days in communion with nature, working on his vegetable plot or reading, a society of one. Through the medium of personal reflection, Thoreau sought to inspire his readers to reconsider their own lives, and to bring about spiritual, economic, political, environmental and moral reform by example. He was born David Henry Thoreau in Concord in 1817. After graduating from Harvard he worked as a teacher and in his father's factory. In 1841 he met the philosopher Ralph Waldo Emerson, who became his champion and mentor. His first book, *A Week on the Concord and Merrimack Rivers* (1849), was not well received and he spent nine years revising *Walden* for publication to ensure this book's happier fate. Although he never earned a living from his writing, Thoreau's works number many volumes. He died from tuberculosis in 1862 and was buried in his beloved Concord.

LYNNE TILLMAN (1947–) American writer. *'Hole Story'* (1992)

Lynne Tillman was born in Brooklyn in 1947 and grew up on Long Island from the age of five. She decided to become a novelist at eight. Her first novel, *Haunted Houses*, was published in 1987. Tillman is the author of three further novels, three collections of short stories, a collection of essays and two other non-fiction books. She has also written extensively on films, literature and culture. For art catalogues and books she writes stories relating to art, often in the voice of a fictional character, Madame Realism. When Tillman draws from her life, she tries to find ways 'to use experience and make it not hers'. Her brief autobiographical essay, 'Hole Story', appears in this anthology in its entirety. It was first published in New York's *Village Voice* in 1992 and was later included in her essay collection, *The Broad Picture*, in 1997. Tillman presently lives in New York, where she has recently completed her fifth novel, and is professor and writer in residence at the University of Albany.

LEO TOLSTOY (1828–1910) Russian writer. *My Confession* (1884)

Towards the end of the 1870s when Leo Tolstoy was almost 50, with the writing of his masterpieces *War and Peace* (1863–1869) and *Anna Karenina* (1875–1877) behind him, he suffered a mid-life crisis that left him so depressed he contemplated suicide. In the autobiographical essay 'My Confession', completed in 1881, Tolstoy describes this period of despair and also justifies the life changes he made in its aftermath. He was born Count Leo Nikolayevich Tolstoy at his family estate outside Moscow in 1828. His parents died when he was a boy and he was brought up by relatives. In 'My Confession', Tolstoy writes about how he rejected his Russian

Orthodox faith as a teenager, but during his crisis decided that he needed to find a new and wholly spiritual way of life. From now on, he resolved, he would live in seclusion on his estate, wear peasant clothing, make his own shoes, work in the fields, eat only vegetables and hold himself to the highest standards of non-violence, celibacy and asceticism. More troubling for his family, he would also attempt to give away his fortune and forgo fiction-writing in favour of producing moral tracts that he hoped would bring about the complete transformation of the Russian people. 'My Confession' was one of these, first circulated illegally in Russia in 1882, and published in 1884. Tolstoy's new way of life mostly served to alienate him from his wife, Sofia, and their nine children, and although he would write a further handful of fictional works before his death, family conflicts eventually caused him to leave his home at the age of 82. He died a week later of pneumonia, at a remote railway station in Astapovo.

ANTHONY TROLLOPE (1815–1882) English writer. *An Autobiography* (1883)

Anthony Trollope wrote *An Autobiography* between 1875 and 1876 and on the understanding that it would not be published until after his death. He was born in London in 1815. In his memoirs he describes at length the period of his childhood and the effect of his father's descent from relative wealth into poverty while his son was still at school, a source of embarrassment for the young Trollope. At the age of 19, Trollope went to work for the Post Office – and stayed there for the next 33 years, writing to supplement his income, often while on long train journeys for his work. In 1855 Trollope published the first of his six Barchester chronicles, thereby inventing the serial novel. The author resigned from the Post Office in 1867 and devoted himself to writing, becoming the most successful novelist of the Victorian era. He died in London in 1882 and his autobiography was published the following year. Trollope's admission in his memoirs that he wrote a thousand words a day in the hour before breakfast, and also that he wrote primarily for financial gain, led to his detraction by critics who deemed him too prolific. More than a century after his death, Trollope's 47 novels continue to sell well.

MARK TWAIN (1835–1910) American writer. *Mark Twain's Autobiography* (1924)

Mark Twain was born Samuel Longhorn Clemens, in Missouri, in 1835. He started his professional life working as a typesetter but soon developed a successful career as a newspaper writer. Twain's first book was *The Innocents Abroad* (1869) and shortly afterwards he abandoned newspaper work to focus on a literary career, using his pen name Mark Twain. The year that Twain published *The Adventures of Huckleberry Finn* (1884), he also jotted down his memories of meeting General Ulysses Grant, the earliest fragments of his future autobiography. Twelve years later, with his literary career at its peak, Twain spent time in Vienna where he began work on a series of writings about his childhood years. These personal writings grew incrementally, without their author paying much attention to chronology or consistency of narrative. In 1906 Twain's friend and biographer, Albert Bigelow Paine, suggested that a stenographer attend their meetings – and Twain used the transcriptions to expand on his memoirs. He was adamant that his autobiography should not be published until a hundred years after his death, ensuring that anyone he spoke about would be dead by the time the book went into print. In fact, 25 of the more innocuous chapters were published in *The North American Review* during his lifetime. Twain died at his Connecticut home in 1910 and his memoir was finally published in its entirety in 1924. Since then, a number of editors have tried to make sense of its experimental and rambling format, and it is not counted among Twain's most famous works. Despite its relative obscurity, it remains amongst the most innovative and original autobiographies.

KURT VONNEGUT (1922–) American writer. *Fates Worse Than Death: An Autobiographical Collage of the 1980s* (1991)

Kurt Vonnegut Junior was born in Indianapolis in 1922. In 1943, after studying biochemistry at Cornell University, he enlisted in the army, surviving the Battle of the Bulge and the bombing of Dresden. After the war, Vonnegut returned to university to study anthropology. He subsequently had a variety of jobs, including running a car dealership, working as a police reporter, and in public relations. His first novel, the futuristic *Player Piano*, appeared in 1952. *Slaughterhouse-Five* (1969), a quasi-autobiographical novel, dealt with his imprisonment under a slaughterhouse during the Dresden bombings. Vonnegut has published two books of autobiographical essays, *Palm Sunday: An Autobiographical Collage* (1981) and *Fates Worse Than Death: An Autobiographical Collage of the 1980s* (1991). The first book he describes as 'a collection of essays and speeches by me, with breezy autobiographical commentary serving as connective tissue and splints and bandages'. The second is 'real life and opinions made to look like one, big preposterous animal not unlike an invention by Dr Seuss, the great writer and illustrator of children's books, like an oobleck or a grinch or a lorax, or like a sneech perhaps'. In *Fates Worse Than Death*, Vonnegut's ostensible subject is the 1980s, but he also returns to his childhood in Indianapolis – his father's depression and his mother's struggles with her mental illness – as well as his experiences during the war. The author lives in New York.

MARY AUGUSTA WARD (1851–1920) English writer. *A Writer's Recollections* (1918)

This volume is a traditional memoir in the sense that it includes very few details of the author's own life. Instead, Ward devotes herself to describing the people and places she has known in her lifetime, with only an occasional diversion into personal anecdote, including the musing on old age excerpted in this compendium. Ward was best known to Victorian readers under her pen name, Mrs Humphry Ward. She was born Mary Augusta Arnold in Hobart, Tasmania, to English parents – her uncle was the Victorian poet-critic Matthew Arnold. In 1856 the family moved back to England, where she was educated. She began to write and publish before the age of 20, contributing stories and articles to magazines. In 1872 she married the writer and editor Thomas Humphry Ward and was instrumental in the founding of Oxford's Somerville

College for women the following year. Her first novel, *Miss Bretherton*, was published in 1884, and her greatest success, *Robert Elsmere*, in 1888. A prolific novelist, Ward was also devoted to her social work, establishing a settlement for working-class men and women in London that became home to the first children's play centre in the country, as well as England's first school for the physically handicapped. Despite her own manifold achievements, Ward was opposed to women having the vote, and in 1908 was made president of the Anti-Suffrage League – she simply believed that men were better suited to solving political, legal, financial and military problems than women. Even so, she was convinced that women should have a role in local government and in the press, and during the First World War she reported from the Front. Shortly before her death in 1920, she became one of the first female magistrates in Britain.

EUDORA WELTY (1909–2001) American writer. *One Writer's Beginnings* (1984)

Eudora Welty's memoir of her formative years is comprised of three sketches. Called 'Listening', 'Learning to See' and 'Finding a Voice', each sketch finds Welty looking back and pinpointing the early influences that made her a writer. Welty introduces us to the world of her childhood and youth – the American South, where she was born in Jackson, Mississippi, in 1909 – the sights and sounds of her parents' house, first books, visits to grandparents in West Virginia, and early attempts at writing while at college. Welty published her first book of stories in 1941, and is the author of three subsequent collections, five novels, her memoirs, a collection of book reviews, and a children's book. For most of her life, Welty lived in Jackson. She worked briefly in radio, as a journalist and as a publicity agent for the Works Progress Administration founded by Franklin Roosevelt, before devoting herself to writing. She was also an accomplished photographer. She died at her home in Jackson, at the age of 92.

WALT WHITMAN (1819–1892) American poet. *'Specimen Days'* (1882) and *'Memoranda'* (1891)

Born Walter Whitman in New York in 1819, he grew up on Long Island and in Brooklyn. After leaving school at the age of 12 he became apprenticed to a printer, and later worked as a teacher, journalist and speechwriter. In 1846, Whitman was made editor of *The Brooklyn Eagle* newspaper and continued to work in newspapers for the next decade. His life's work became the writing of a poem that would contain and convey the new energy, optimism and complexities of his contemporary America, *Leaves of Grass*. In 1855 he published the first edition of the poem and he would revise it repeatedly throughout his lifetime. During the Civil War, the poet worked as a clerk in Washington and was a nurse to soldiers. After a stroke in 1871, he was forced to lead a quieter life, and settled in Camden, New Jersey, where he spent the rest of his days. A collection of his autobiographical jottings written in Camden – *Specimen Days and Collect* – in which Whitman speaks about his youth, his time in newspapers, his travels and his war experiences, was published in 1882 and later revised as *Specimen Days in America* (1887). In 1891 Whitman published his *Complete Prose Works*, including his 'Specimen Days' and 'Memoranda'. A final version of *Leaves of Grass* was prepared just before his death in 1892.

ELIE WIESEL (1928 –) Romanian-American writer and humanitarian. *All Rivers Run to the Sea: Memoirs* (1994)

Elie Wiesel's *Night* was one of the first and most important Holocaust memoirs, originally published in French in 1958. In *All Rivers Run to the Sea*, also written in French, he revisits the subject matter of *Night* – the time leading up to his capture and deportation, and his survival in the concentration camps as a 15-year-old boy. It also expands the story to encompass the years after his release. He was born Eliezer Wiesel in Sighet, Transylvania (now Romania) to Jewish parents. Wiesel's mother and younger sister were killed immediately after their capture in 1944 by the

Nazis. Wiesel's father perished at Buchenwald. After the liberation of the camps in 1945, Wiesel was placed in a French orphanage. He studied at the Sorbonne in Paris, but unable to finish his thesis due to lack of funds, he began to work as a translator and journalist. In 1954, Wiesel broke his silence about his experiences in the camps and began to write. With his memoir in progress he moved to New York in 1956, to take a position as the United Nations correspondent for an Israeli newspaper. After *Night*'s publication, Wiesel turned to writing novels as well as plays, essays and articles. Wiesel was involved in the founding of the State of Israel, has held positions at major American universities, and continues to devote himself to memorializing Holocaust victims. He was awarded the Nobel Peace Prize in 1986, not only for his work for Jewish causes, but also for his humanitarian efforts on behalf of people the world over. Along with his wife, he founded the Elie Wiesel Foundation for Humanity in 1986. In 1996 he published the second volume of his autobiography, *And the Sea is Never Full*. He lives in New York.

OSCAR WILDE (1854–1900) Irish writer. *De Profundis* (1905)

Oscar Wilde's most personal work, *De Profundis* ('from the depths'), is in the guise of a letter addressed to his lover, Lord Alfred Douglas. It was written while the author was serving his two-year prison sentence in Pentonville, Wandsworth and then Reading gaols for 'gross indecency'. In it, Wilde describes the sorrow and privations of captivity, bitterly accusing Douglas of abandoning him, and managing, despite his sombre tone, to sound notes of the elegance and wit that had made the author a literary celebrity. Born Oscar Fingall O'Flahertie Wills Wilde in Dublin in 1854, he was the son of Ireland's leading eye surgeon and a writer mother. Wilde attended Trinity College, Dublin, where he proved to be a brilliant student. At Oxford he was known for his flamboyance, growing his hair long, dressing in velvet breeches and decorating his rooms with flowers and feathers. He briefly returned to Dublin before settling in London where he began to lecture on aestheticism. He married in 1884, had two sons, and worked as a journalist and editor to provide for his family. In 1891 Wilde published his first and only novel, *The Picture of Dorian Gray*, but from this point onwards, his literary efforts were focused on playwriting. From 1892 to 1895 he produced at least one play a year. At the height of his fame he sued Douglas's father, the Marquis of Queensberry, for libel – but instead, his homosexual relations came to light and he was charged and sentenced to hard labour. On his release from prison, Wilde spent the last three years of his life in exile in France – without money or friends, and very ill. He died in a Paris hotel of meningitis in 1900, at the age of 46. Four years after Wilde's death, an edited version of *De Profundis* was published, and in 1949, Wilde's son authorized a complete version.

HARRIETTE WILSON (1786–1846) English courtesan and writer. *Harriette Wilson's Memoirs* (1825)

One of 15 children, Harriette Dubochet was born in London to a Swiss clockmaker. At the age of 15, she became mistress to Lord Craven, and for the next two decades managed to have affairs with some of the most important men in Regency Britain – the Duke of Argyll and the Duke of Wellington amongst them. Wilson was her professional name, and during her reign as England's most notorious courtesan, she charged men £50 for as much as an introduction. Beautiful, intelligent, ambitious and unscrupulous – as one of her rivals observed, she changed lovers as easily as she changed her shoes. At the age of 35 Wilson retired, moving to Paris with a promise of £500 a year from her former lover, the Marquis of Worcester. When the marquis reneged, Wilson wrote her *Memoirs* in revenge and in the hope of paying off some of her husband's debts. Before starting to write, she wrote a letter to each of her prominent lovers, informing them that unless they provided her with £200, she would write about them in her book. When Wellington learned of Wilson's scheme, he told her: 'Publish and be damned!' although the story is probably apocryphal. The book caused a scandal and became a best-seller. Wilson later turned her hand to writing novels. She died in London in 1846.

P.G. WODEHOUSE (1881–1975) English writer. *Over Seventy: An Autobiography With Digressions* (1957)

Pelham Grenville Wodehouse was born in Guildford in 1881 and educated at Dulwich College. In his memoir, Wodehouse dismisses his childhood as 'a breeze from start to finish' – in fact, he rarely saw his parents and was brought up by aunts, although he does seem to be one of the few English writers who genuinely enjoyed his time at public school. Unable to attend university, due to financial constraints, he worked for the Hong Kong and Shanghai Bank before taking up a career as a writer, to the great displeasure of his father. Wodehouse went on to become the author of 96 books – his most famous creations being Jeeves and Bertie Wooster, and the characters of the Blandings Castle novels and short stories. In the early part of his career, he wrote lyrics for Broadway musicals and worked as a successful screenwriter in Hollywood. He was in France when World War II began and was captured by the Germans in 1940. After his release, Wodehouse naively made a series of radio broadcasts for the Germans, giving rise to charges of collaboration. Libraries in England banned his books, and Wodehouse was persuaded to move to the USA to escape a possible trial for treason. He became an American citizen in 1955 and never returned to England, living for the rest of his life at his estate on Long Island. He died there in 1975, at the age of 94. *Over Seventy* is his extended musing on his years as a septuagenarian.

TOBIAS WOLFF (1945–) American writer. *In Pharaoh's Army: Memories of a Lost War* (1994)

Tobias Wolff is credited as one the pre-eminent of American memoirists of these times. Through his teaching work in the creative writing department of American universities, he has also nurtured a new generation of memoirists, including Mary Karr. He is the author of two influential works of autobiography: *This Boy's Life* (1989), about his childhood growing up outside Seattle, and *In Pharaoh's Army*, which deals with his experiences as an officer during the Vietnam War. In this classic of war testimony, Wolff describes how he was trained to speak Vietnamese and was put in charge of South Vietnamese soldiers. He also relates his experience of the Tet Offensive, writing with a surreal detachment that effectively allows the reader to fully register the inhumanity and horror of conflict. Wolff was born in Seattle in 1945. After an itinerant childhood, his father mostly absent and his stepfather increasingly brutal – circumstances described in *This Boy's Life* – Wolff decided he wanted to be a writer. He studied literature at Oxford and Stanford Universities. He is the author of short stories and most recently a novel, *Old School* (2004). Wolff is currently professor of English and creative writing at Stanford University.

VIRGINIA WOOLF (1882–1941) English writer. *'A Sketch of the Past'* (1939–1940)

Adeline Virginia Stephen was born in London in 1882. Her mother died when she was 13, and she had her first breakdown soon afterwards. When her father died in 1904, she moved with her sister Vanessa and their two brothers to a house in Bloomsbury. Here the Stephen family began to gather the writers and artists around them who later became known as the Bloomsbury Group. When her brother Toby died in 1906, Virginia suffered another breakdown. In 1912 she married Leonard Woolf, and her first novel was published three years later. Throughout her professional life, she was a prolific essayist, often writing in distinctly personal terms and in the first person. At the beginning of the Second World War, concerned for her mental stability and, in the event of a German invasion, her life, she decided to set down some autobiographical details structured in the manner of a diary. Although she never finished the memoir, she did leave a highly evocative sketch of her earliest memories as well as the revelation that she and her sister Vanessa were sexually abused by their half-brothers. In 1941 Woolf walked into the River Ouse in Sussex, where she drowned. 'A Sketch of the Past', as the memoir fragment was later called, along with an earlier reminiscence written for her sister and three autobiographical essays written for the Bloomsbury Group's Memoir Club (a regular gathering where works of memoir were read aloud) all appeared in the posthumous collection *Moments of Being*, published in 1976.

Mrs WRIGLEY: See entry for Co-operative Working Women.

MALCOLM X (1925–1965) African-American civil rights leader. *The Autobiography of Malcolm X* (1964)

The Autobiography began life as an interview conducted with Malcolm X by the journalist Alex Haley for *Playboy* magazine, after which Haley suggested that his subject expand the work into a complete autobiography. The begins with his childhood in Omaha, Nebraska, where he was born Malcolm Little in 1925. His father was killed by a white supremacist group in 1931 and his mother was declared insane soon afterwards. Malcolm grew up in a series of foster homes, and after a spell in a detention centre, moved to Boston. Next, Malcolm went to live in Harlem where, in 1946, at the age of 20, he was sentenced to eight to ten years in prison. While incarcerated he discovered the Muslim organization, the Nation of Islam, whose members were advocating for a separate black nation within the United States. He was released in 1952 and went immediately to meet Elijah Muhammad, the leader of the Nation of Islam, who gave him his name 'X' to symbolize his rejection of the white name given to his family by slave-owners. Malcolm became a preacher for the Nation of Islam and a powerful and eloquent voice of the Civil Rights movement. In 1963 he was suspended from speaking after he made incendiary comments about the assassination of John F. Kennedy. Due to tensions within the organization he broke from the Nation of Islam soon afterwards, deciding to convert to orthodox Islam. He travelled to Mecca in the spring of 1964, returning with a new name, El-Hajj Malik El-Shabazz. During the period his autobiography was being written, Malcolm began receiving death threats. On 21st February 1965, he was shot dead at a rally in Harlem. Three Nation of Islam members were convicted of his murder. His autobiography was published that year.

W.B. YEATS (1865–1939) Irish poet. *'Reveries Over Childhood and Youth'* (1915)

William Butler Yeats was born in Dublin in 1865 and grew up in London, Dublin and at his grandparents' home in Sligo. His father was the portrait painter John Butler Yeats, and the younger Yeats attended Dublin's Metropolitan School of Art, leaving in 1886 to pursue a career in literature. His first book of poems was published that same year. He was prominent in the Irish National Movement and co-founded the Irish Literary Theatre in 1899, which five years later led to the founding of the Abbey Theatre where Yeats became director. He was awarded the Nobel Prize for Literature in 1923 and died in the South of France in 1939. His autobiographical writings were published under the title *Autobiographies* in 1926, and as *The Autobiography of William Butler Yeats* in 1938, although the earliest of these, 'Reveries Over Childhood and Youth', was first published in 1915. 'I have changed nothing to my knowledge,' Yeats wrote in his preface to his autobiographical writings, 'and yet it must be that I have changed many things without my knowledge; for I am writing after many years and have consulted neither friend nor letter, no old newspaper, and describe what comes oftenest to my memory.' In the excerpt from 'Reveries' included in this compendium, Yeats writes about his teenage sexual awakening – in fact he would not lose his virginity until many years later, at the age of 31.

～ CREDITS AND SOURCES ～

Every effort has been made to secure permission to reprint the materials included in this book. If for any reason permission has not been given or has been given in error, please contact the publisher and amendments will be made in a future edition.

ACKERLEY, J.R., from Chapter 12, *My Father and Myself* (Bodley Head, London, 1968). Copyright © 1968 by the Executors of the late J.R. Ackerley, reprinted by permission of David Higham Associates Ltd.

ADAMS, HENRY, from 'Boston': *The Education of Henry Adams* (First Vintage Books/The Library of American Edition, 1990).

ALI, MUHAMMAD, from 'Shorty is Watching' and 'The Prophecy of Sell-Out Moe': *The Greatest: My Own Story* (Random House, New York, 1975). Copyright © 1975 by Muhammad Ali, Herbert Muhammad and Richard Durham, reprinted with permission.

ARENAS, REINALDO, from 'The Grove': *Before Night Falls: A Memoir* translated by Dolores M. Koch (Penguin, 1994). Copyright © 1993 by the Estate of Reinaldo Arenas, translation © by Dolores M. Koch, reprinted by permission of Viking Penguin, a division of Penguin Books (USA) Inc.

ASHBRIDGE, ELIZABETH, from *Some Account of the Fore-Part of the Life of Elizabeth Ashbridge*: in The Norton Anthology of American Literature Volume 1 (W.W. Norton & Company, New York, 1989).

ASHWORTH, ANDREA, from Chapter 1: *Once in A House On Fire* (Picador Macmillan, London, 1998). Copyright © Andrea Ashworth, 1998, reprinted by permission of Henry Holt and Company, LLC, and Macmillan London, UK.

ST AUGUSTINE, from Book First, Chapter VI; Book Second, Chapter I; Book Fourth, Chapter IV; and Book Eighth, Chapter XII: *The Confessions Of St Augustine* (Boni & Liveright, New York, 1927). Translated by J.G. Pilkington (1876).

BALDWIN, JAMES, from 'The Devil Finds Work': *James Baldwin Collected Essays* (The Library of America, 1998). Copyright © 1976 by James Baldwin, copyright renewed, reprinted by permission of the James Baldwin Estate.

BARNUM, P.T., from 'My Early History', 'A Batch of Incidents' and 'Side-Shows – Buffalo Hunt etc': *The Life of P.T. Barnum written by himself* (University of Illinois Press, 2000).

BEAUVOIR, SIMONE DE, from Chapter 1: *The Prime of Life* (World Publishing Company, Cleveland & New York, 1962). Copyright © 1960 by Editions Gallimard; English translation by Peter Green, copyright © 1962 by The World Publishing Company, reprinted by permission of Penguin Books Ltd and Editions Gallimard, Paris.

BEAUVOIR, SIMONE DE, from 'Epilogue': *Force of Circumstance* (G.P. Putnam's Sons, New York, 1964). Copyright © 1963 by Editions Gallimard, English translation by Richard Howard, copyright © 1965 by G.P. Putnam's Sons, reprinted by permission of G.P. Putnam's Sons, a division of Penguin Group (USA) Inc. and Editions Gallimard, Paris.

BENNETT, ALAN, from 'The Treachery of Books': *Writing Home* (Faber & Faber, London and Boston, 1994). Copyright © 1994 by Alan Bennett, reprinted by permission of SLL/Sterling Lord Literistic, Inc. and Faber & Faber Ltd.

BERGMAN, INGMAR, from Chapter 1 and Chapter 20: *The Magic Lantern* translated by Joan Tate (Penguin Books, 1988). Copyright © 1988 by Joan Tate. Original copyright © 1987 by Ingmar Bergman. Reprinted by permission of Viking Penguin, a division of Penguin Group (USA) Inc. and Penguin Books Ltd.

BESANT, ANNIE, from 'Early Childhood', 'Girlhood', and 'Marriage': *Annie Besant: An Autobiography* (The Theosophical Publishing House, Adyar, 1893).

BIERCE, AMBROSE, from 'What I Saw Of Shiloh' in *Shadows of Blue & Gray: The Civil War Writings of Ambrose Bierce* edited by Brian M. Thomsen (Tom Doherty Associates, New York, 2002).

BOGARDE, DIRK, from Chapter 5: *An Orderly Man* (Alfred A. Knopf, New York, 1983). Copyright © 1983 by Dirk Bogarde, reprinted by permission of Alfred A. Knopf, a division of Random House, Inc.

BONNIN, GERTRUDE SIMMONS or ZITKALA-SA, from 'The Beadwork' in 'Impressions of an Indian Childhood': *American Indian Stories* (Hayworth Publishing House, 1921).

BOWLES, PAUL, from Chapter I: *Without Stopping* (G.P. Putnam's Sons, New York, 1972). Copyright © 1972 by Paul Bowles, reprinted by permission of HarperCollins Publishers Inc. and Peter Owen Ltd.

BRANDO, MARLON, from Chapter 1: *Brando: Songs My Mother Taught Me* (Random House, New York, 1994). Copyright © 1994 by Marlon Brando and Robert Lindsey, reprinted by permission of Random House, Inc.

BRITTAIN, VERA, from 'When the Vision Dies': *Testament of Youth* (The MacMillan Company, New York, 1933). Copyright © 1933, 1970 by the literary executors of Vera Brittain, reprinted by permission of Mark Bostridge and Rebecca Williams, her literary executors and Victor Gollancz, a division of The Orion Publishing Group.

BRODKEY, HAROLD, from *This Wild Darkness: the Story of My Death* (Metropolitan Books, Henry Holt and Company, New York, 1996). Copyright © 1996 by the Estate of Harold Brodkey, reprinted by permission of Henry Holt and Company, Inc. and HarperCollins Publishers Ltd.

BROWN, CHRISTY, from 'The Pen': *My Left Foot* (Mandarin, London, 1989). Copyright © 1954 Christy Brown. Reprinted by permission of The Random House Group.

CAPOTE, TRUMAN, from 'Self-Portrait': *The Dogs Bark: Public People & Private Places*. Copyright © 1957, 1965, 1966, 1968, 1969, 1971, 1972, 1973 by Truman Capote, reprinted by permission of Random House, Inc. and The Truman Capote Literary Trust.

CARDANO, GIROLAMO, 'Prologue' and 'Stature and Appearance': *The Book of My Life* (New York Review Books, 2002). Translation by Jean Stoner, 1929.

Noel Coward, 1937, reprinted by permission of Methuen Publishing Ltd.

COWLEY, ABRAHAM, from 'Of Myself': *Essays* (Thomas Nelson and Sons Ltd. London, 1937).

COWLEY, MALCOLM, from Chapter 1: *The View From Eighty* (Viking Press, New York, 1980). Copyright © 1976, 1978, 1980 by Malcolm Cowley, reprinted by permission of Viking Penguin, a division of Penguin Group (USA) Inc.

COWPER, WILLIAM, from *Memoir of the Early Life of William Cowper Esq, written by himself* (R. Edwards, London, 1816).

CRISP, QUENTIN, from Chapter 4: *The Naked Civil Servant* (Jonathan Cape, London, 1968). Copyright © Quentin Crisp, 1968, reprinted by permission of HarperCollins Publishers Ltd. and Dutton Signet, a division of Penguin Group (USA) Inc.

CRISP, QUENTIN, from 'The Beginning': *How to Become A Virgin* (Gerald Duckworth & Co. London, 1981). Copyright © 1981 by Quentin Crisp, reprinted by permission of HarperCollins Publishers Ltd. and Radala & Associates.

DAHL, ROALD, from 'The Bicycle and the Sweet Shop': *Boy: Tales of Childhood* (Farrar, Straus, & Giroux, New York, 1984). Copyright © 1984 by Roald Dahl, reprinted by permission of Farrar, Straus & Giroux, LLC and David Higham Associates Ltd.

DAIBU, LADY, from Part 3 Poem 60, and Conclusion: *The Poetic Memoirs of Lady Daibu*, translated by Phillip Tudor Harries (Stanford University Press, California, 1980). Copyright © 1980 by the Board of Trustees of the Leland Stanford Jr. University, reprinted by permission of Stanford University Press.

DALAI LAMA OF TIBET, HIS HOLINESS THE, from 'The Quest for Enlightenment': *My Land and My People* (Warner Books Edition, New York, 1997). Copyright © 1962 by His Holiness the Dalai Lama of Tibet, copyright © renewed 1990 by His Holiness the Dalai Lama of Tibet, reprinted by permission of Warner Books, Inc.

DALI, SALVADOR, from Prologue, Chapter 1, and Epilogue: *The Secret Life of Salvador Dali* translated by Haakon M. Chevalier (The Dial Press, New York, 1961). Copyright 1942, © 1961 by Salvador Dali.

DANIEL, JEAN, from 'Dwelling on Images': in *An Algerian Childhood: A Collection of Autobiographical Narratives* edited by Leila Sebbar (Ruminator Books, St Paul, Minnesota). Originally published as *Une Enfance Algerienne* by Editions Gallimard. Copyright © 1997. English translation © 2001 by Ruminator Books, reprinted by permission of Ruminator Books.

DARWIN, CHARLES, from 'An Autobiographical Fragment', and 'Recollections of the Development of My Mind and Character'. *Autobiographies* edited by Michael Neve and Sharon Messenger (Penguin Books, London, 2002). Reprinted by permission of Cambridge University Press, the Syndics of Cambridge University Library and William Darwin.

DICKENS, CHARLES, from the autobiographical fragment included in 'Hard Experiences in Boyhood 1822–1824': *The Life of Charles Dickens* by John Forster (Cecil Palmer, London, 1928).

DORFMAN, ARIEL, from 'A Chapter Dealing With the Discovery of Life and Language at an Early Age': *Heading South, Looking North: A Bilingual Journey* (Penguin Books, 1999). Copyright © Ariel Dorfman 1998, reprinted by

DOUGLASS, FREDERICK, from Chapter 1: *Narrative of the Life of Frederick Douglass, An American Slave* (Penguin Classics, 1986).

DUNCAN, ISADORA, from Chapter 2, Chapter 19: *My Life* (Boni and Liveright, New York, 1927). Copyright © 1927 by Horace Liveright, Inc. Copyright © renewed 1955 by Liveright Publishing Corporation, reprinted by permission of Liveright Publishing Corporation.

DURRELL, GERALD, from 'The World in a Wall': *My Family and Other Animals* (Penguin Books, 1959). Copyright © The Estate of Gerald Durrell, 1956. Reprinted by permission of Curtis Brown Ltd, London, on behalf of the Estate of Gerald Durrell.

EDWARDS, JONATHAN, from 'Personal Narrative': in *The Norton Anthology of American Literature, Volume 1* (W.W. Norton, New York, 1989).

EGGERS, DAVE, from 'Acknowledgements': *A Heartbreaking Work of Staggering Genius* (Simon and Schuster, New York, 2000). Copyright © 2001 by Dave Eggers, reprinted by permission of Simon & Schuster Adult Publishing Group.

EINSTEIN, ALBERT, from *Autobiographical Notes* (Open Court Publishing, La Salle and Chicago, 1979). Copyright © The Albert Einstein Archives, the Hebrew University of Jerusalem, Israel, reprinted by permission of Open Court Publishing Company, a division of Carus Publishing Company, Peru, Illinois and The Albert Einstein Archives.

EQUIANO, OLAUDAH, from Chapter 2 of 'The Interesting Narrative of the Life of Olaudah Equiano, or Gustavus Vassa, The African written by himself': in *The Norton Anthology of American Literature* (W.W. Norton, New York, 1989).

FISHER, M.F.K., from 'Winding down' in 'Last House: Reflections, Dreams, and Observations 1943–1991': From the *Journals of M.F.K. Fisher* (Pantheon Books, New York, 1999). Copyright © 1995 by Robert Lescher, as Trustee of the Literary Trust u/w/o M.F.K. Fisher, reprinted by permission of Pantheon Books, a division of Random House, Inc.

FRAME, JANET, from 'Hark Hark the Dogs Do Bark' and 'Imagination': *To the Island* (George Braziller, 1982). Copyright © 1982 by Janet Frame, reprinted by permission of George Braziller, Inc. and A.M.Heath & Co Ltd.

FRANKLIN, BENJAMIN, from Part One and Part Two: *The Autobiography* in *Benjamin Franklin: Writings* (The Library of America, 1987).

FREUD, SIGMUND, from Chapter 1: *An Autobiographical Study* (W.W. Norton & Company Inc., New York, 1952) translated by James Strachey. Copyright © 1952 by W.W. Norton & Company. Renewed © 1980 by Alix Strachey. Copyright © 1935 by Sigmund Freud renewed © 1963 by James Strachey, reprinted by permission of W.W. Norton & Company, Inc. and Sigmund Freud Copyrights.

FRY, STEPHEN, from 'Falling In': *Moab is My Washpot: An Autobiography* (Random House, 1997). Copyright © 1997 by Stephen Fry, reprinted by permission of Random House, Inc. and David Higham Associates Ltd.

FU, SHEN, from 'The Pleasures of Leisure' and 'The Joys of the Wedding Chamber': *Six Records of a Floating Life* translated by Leonard Pratt and Chiang Su-Hui (Penguin Books, 1983). Copyright © 1983 by Leonard Pratt and Chiang Su-Hui, reprinted by permission of Penguin Books Ltd.

GANDHI, MAHATMA, from 'Stealing and Atonement': *An Autobiography:*

The Story of My Experiments With Truth translated by Mahadev Desai (Beacon Press, Boston, 1957). Reprinted by permission of the Navajivan Trust.

GIBBON, EDWARD, from: *Memoirs of My Life and Writings* edited by A.O.J. Cockshut and Stephen Constantine (Ryburn Publishing, Keele University Press, 1994).

GORKY, MAXIM, from Chapter 13: *My Childhood* translated with an introduction by Ronald Wilks (Penguin Classics, 1966). Translation copyright © Ronald Wilks, 1966.

GORKY MAXIM, from Chapter 5: *My Apprenticeship* translated with an introduction by Ronald Wilks (Penguin Classics, 1974). Translation copyright © Ronald Wilks, 1974.

GOSSE, EDMUND, from Chapter 2, Chapter 4 and Chapter 12: *Father and Son* (Penguin Modern Classics, 1949).

GRAVES, ROBERT, from Chapter 6 and Chapter 16: *Good-bye to All That:* (Berghahn Books, 1995). Copyright © by the Trustees of the Robert Graves Copyright Trust, reprinted with permission.

GRAY, SPALDING, from *It's A Slippery Slope* (The Noonday Press, 1997). Copyright © Spalding Gray, reprinted by permission of Farrar, Straus and Giroux and William Morris Agency, Inc. on behalf of the author's estate.

GREENE, GRAHAM, from Chapter 6, part 2: *A Sort of Life* (Bodley Head, London, 1971). Copyright © 1971 by Graham Greene, reprinted by permission of David Higham Associates Ltd.

GUINNESS, ALEC, from 'Full Moon in Connemara': *Blessings in Disguise* (Alfred A. Knopf, New York, 1986). Copyright © 1985 by Alec Guinness, reprinted by permission of Hamish Hamilton, an imprint of Penguin Books Ltd and Alfred A. Knopf, a division of Random House, Inc.

HATTERSLEY, ROY, from 'The Broken Circle': *A Yorkshire Boyhood* (Chatto & Windus, The Hogarth Press, London, 1983). Copyright © Roy Hattersley, 1983, reprinted by permission of the author.

HEPBURN, KATHARINE, from 'Bryn Mawr': *Me: Stories of My Life* (Alfred A. Knopf, New York, 1991). Copyright © 1991 by Katharine Hepburn, reprinted by permission of the Estate of Katharine Hepburn.

HOFFMAN, EVA, from 'Paradise': *Lost In Translation: A Life in a New Language* (E.P. Dutton, New York, 1989). Reprinted by permission of Dutton, a division of Penguin Group (USA) Inc. and William Heinemann, a division of the Random House Group Ltd (UK).

HOGG, JAMES, from 'Memoir of the Author's Life': *Altrive Tales* (J. Cochrane, London, 1832).

HOLIDAY, BILLIE, from 'I Must Have That Man': *Lady Sings The Blues* with William Dufty (Penguin Books, 1984). Copyright © 1956 by Eleonora Fagan and William F. Dufty, reprinted by permission of Doubleday, a division of Random House.

HUME, DAVID, from: *The Life of David Hume, Esq. written by himself* (W. Strahan and T. Cadell, London, 1777).

HUXLEY, T.H., from 'Autobiography': *Charles Darwin and T.H. Huxley, Autobiographies* edited and with an introduction by Gavin de Beer (Oxford University Press, London, 1974).

JAMES, HENRY, from *The Middle Years* (W. Collins Sons & Co. Ltd., London, 1917).

JAMES, HENRY, from Chapter 1: *A Small Boy and Others* (Charles Scribner & Sons, New York, 1913).

JUNG, C.G., from Prologue: *Memories, Dreams, Reflections* recorded and edited by Aniela Jaffe, translated from the German by Richard and Clara Winston (Vintage Books, New York, 1965). Copyright © 1961, 1962, 1963 by Random House, Inc., reprinted by permission of Pantheon Books, a division of Random House, Inc.

KARR, MARY, from 'Texas 1961': *The Liars' Club* (Penguin, 1996). Copyright © 1995 by Mary Karr, reprinted by permission of Viking Penguin, a division of Penguin Group (USA) Inc and Pan Macmillan Ltd.

KAVANAGH, P.J., from Chapter 1, Chapter 11, and Chapter 13: *The Perfect Stranger* (Chatto & Windus Ltd., London, 1966). Copyright © P.J. Kavanagh, 1966, reprinted by permission of PFD on behalf of P.J. Kavanagh.

KEENAN, BRIAN, from 'Into the Dark': *An Evil Cradling* (Hutchinson, 1992). Copyright © Brian Keenan 1992, reprinted by permission of the Random House Group, Ltd and the Elaine Steel Agency.

KELLER, HELEN, from Chapter 2: *The Story of My Life* (Signet Classics, New York, 1988). Reprinted by permission of the American Foundation for the Blind, Helen Keller Archives.

KEMPE, MARGERY, from Chapter 1, The First Book: *The Book of Margery Kempe, A Modern Version* edited by W. Butler-Bowdon (Jonathan Cape, 1940).

KUROSAWA, AKIRA, from 'Congenital Defects': *Something Like An Autobiography* translated by Audie E. Beck (Alfred A. Knopf, New York, 1982). Copyright © 1982 by Akira Kurosawa, reprinted by permission of Alfred A. Knopf, a division of Random House, Inc.

LEE, LAURIE, from 'London Road': *As I Walked Out One Midsummer Morning* (Andre Deutsch, 1969). Copyright © 1969 by Laurie Lee, reprinted by permission of P.F.D. on behalf of The Estate of Laurie Lee.

LEHMANN, ROSAMOND, from Part 3, Section 3: *The Swan in the Evening: Fragments of an Inner Life* (Virago, London, 1985). Copyright © Rosamond Lehmann, 1967, copyright renewed, 1982.

LENNON, JOHN, from 'Two Virgins': *Skywriting by Word of Mouth and Other Writings including the Ballad of John and Yoko* (Harper & Row Publishers, New York, 1986). Copyright © 1986 by The Estate of John Lennon and Yoko Ono, reprinted by permission of HarperCollins Publishers Inc. and Yoko Ono Lennon.

LEVI, PRIMO, from 'The Journey': *Survival in Auschwitz* translated from the Italian by Stuart Woolf (A Touchstone Book, New York, 1996). Copyright © 1958 by Giulio Einaudi SpA; English edition copyright © 1959 by The Orion Press, reprinted by permission of Viking Penguin, a division of Penguin Group (USA) Inc.

LYNCH, HANNAH, from 'Looking Backward': *Autobiography of A Child* (Dodd, Mead & Company, New York, 1898).

MAHFOUZ, NAGUIB, from 'A Prayer': *Echoes of an Autobiography* translated by Denys Johnson-Davies (Doubleday, New York, 1997). Copyright © 1994 by Naguib Mahfouz; English translation copyright © 1997 by the American University in Cairo Press, reprinted by permission of Doubleday, a division of Random House, Inc.

MANDELA, NELSON, from '100': *The Long Walk to Freedom* (Little, Brown & Company, New York, 1994). Copyright © 1994 by Nelson Rolihlahla Mandela, reprinted by permission of Little, Brown & Company, Inc.

MARCUS AURELIUS ANTONINUS, from Book 1: *The Meditations of Emperor Marcus Aurelius Antoninus* translated by George Long (A.L. Burt Company, New York 189–).

MARTINEAU, HARRIET, from Period 1, Section 1; Period 2, Section 1; Period 3, Section 3: *Harriet Martineau's Autobiography Volume 1* edited by Maria Weston Chapman (James R. Osgood and Company, New York, 1877).

MARX, HARPO, from 'Confessions of a Non-Lady Harpist' and 'The Education of Me': *Harpo Speaks!* with Rowland Barber (Victor Gollancz, London, 1961). Copyright © 1961, Harpo Marx and Rowland Barber, reprinted by permission of Amadeus Press / Limelight Editions.

MAYNARD, JOYCE, from *Looking Back: A Chronicle of Growing Up Old in the Sixties* (Doubleday & Company, Inc., New York, 1973). Copyright © 1972, 1973 by Joyce Maynard, reprinted by permission of the author.

McCARTHY, MARY, from Chapter 3: *How I Grew* (Harcourt Brace Jovanovich, San Diego, New York, London, 1987). Copyright © 1987, 1986 Mary McCarthy, reprinted by permission of Harcourt Inc. and A.M. Heath & Co. Ltd.

MEAD, MARGARET, from 'On Being A Grandmother': *Blackberry Winter: My Earlier Years* (Simon & Schuster, New York, 1972). Copyright © 1972 by Margaret Mead. Reprinted by permission of HarperCollins Publishers Inc, William Morrow & Company Inc.

MILL, JOHN STUART, from 'A Crisis in My Mental History. One Stage Onward': *Autobiography* (Penguin Classics, 1989).

MILLER, ARTHUR, from Chapter 2: *Timebends: A Life* (Grove Press, Inc. New York, 1987). Copyright © 1987 by Arthur Miller.

MILOSZ, CZESLAW, from 'War': *Native Realm: A Search for Self-Definition* translated by Catherine S. Leach (Doubleday & Company, New York, 1968). Reprinted by permission of Doubleday and Company.

MONET, CLAUDE, from 'An Interview': published in *Le Temps* newspaper, November 26, 1900. Translated from the French by Christopher Durrance and Eve Claxton.

MONTAIGNE, MICHEL DE, from 'Of the Education of Children', 'Of Presumption' and 'Of Experience': *Selected Essays of Montaigne*, The Charles Cotton–W.C. Hazlitt translation, edited by Blanchard Bates (The Modern Library, Random House, 1949).

MORRISON, BLAKE, from 'And When Did You Last?': *And When Did You Last See Your Father?* (Granta Books, London, 1993). Copyright © 1993 by Blake Morrison, reprinted by permission of Granta Books and Picador USA.

MORTIMER, JOHN, from Chapter 21: *Clinging to the Wreckage: A Part of Life* (Penguin Books, 1983). Copyright © 1982 by Advanpress Limited, reprinted by permission of Weidenfeld & Nicolson, an imprint of The Orion Publishing Group and SLL/Sterling Lord Literistic, Inc.

MUIR, JOHN, from 'A Boyhood in Scotland': *Nature Writings: The Story of My Boyhood and Youth* (The Library of America 1997).

MURRAY, MARGARET, from 'Still Looking Forward': *My First Hundred Years* (William Kimber, London, 1963). Copyright © 1963 by William Kimber & Co Ltd.

NABOKOV, VLADIMIR, from Chapter 1, section 2; and Chapter 15, section 2: *Speak, Memory: An Autobiography Revisited* (Penguin Books, 1969). Copyright © 1947, 1948, 1949, 1950, 1951, 1967 by Vladimir Nabokov, reprinted by permission of Vintage Books, a division of Random House, Inc.

NABOKOV, VLADIMIR, from the notes for a second volume of *Speak, Memory: Speak On, Memory* (1968–1971). Manuscript in the Berg Collection of the New York Public Library. Reprinted by permission of the Estate of Vladimir Nabokov.

NAFISI, AZAR, from Part 3, section 5: *Reading Lolita in Tehran: A Memoir in Books* (Random House, New York, 2003). Copyright © 2003 by Azar Nafisi, reprinted by permission of Random House, Inc.

NASDIJJ, from 'Flying Solo': *The Blood Runs Like A River Through My Dreams: A Memoir* (Houghton Mifflin, 2000). Copyright © 2000 by Nasdijj, reprinted by permission of the author and Houghton Mifflin Company.

NERUDA, PABLO, from 'Lost in the City': *Memoirs* translated by Hardie St Martin (Farrar, Straus & Giroux, New York, 1977). English translation copyright © 1977 by Farrar, Straus & Giroux, LLC, reprinted by permission of Farrar, Straus & Giroux, LLC.

NULAND, SHERWIN B., from Chapter 2: *Lost in America: A Journey With My Father* (Alfred A. Knopf, New York, 2003). Copyright © 2003 by Dr Sherwin B. Nuland, reprinted by Alfred A. Knopf, a division of Random House, Inc.

O'FAOLAIN, NUALA, from 'After All': *Almost There: The Onward Journey of a Dublin Woman* (Riverhead Books, 2003). Copyright © 2003 by Nuala O'Faolain, reprinted by permission of Michael Joseph, an imprint of Penguin Books Ltd and Riverhead Books, an imprint of Penguin Group (USA) Inc.

OLIPHANT, MARGARET, from Chapter 1 and Chapter 2: *The Autobiography and Letters of Margaret Oliphant* (Dodd, Mead and Company, 1899).

ONDAATJE, MICHAEL, from 'Asia': *Running in the Family* (McClelland and Stewart, Toronto, 1982). Copyright © 1982 by Michael Ondaatje, reprinted by permission of Alfred A. Knopf, a division of Random House, Inc. and Ellen Levine Literary Agency / Trident Media Group.

ORWELL, GEORGE, 'Such, Such Were the Joys …': *Such, Such Were the Joys* (Harcourt, Brace and Company, New York 1953). Copyright © by Sonia Bronwell Orwell, 1952, renewed 1980, reprinted by permission of Harcourt Brace & Company and A.M. Heath & Co. Ltd.

O'TOOLE, PETER, from *Loitering With Intent: The Child* (Hyperion, New York, 1992). Copyright © 1992 by Peter O'Toole, reprinted by permission of Hyperion and Pan Macmillan Ltd.

PANKHURST, EMMELINE, from 'The Making of A Militant': *My Own Story* (Hearst's International Library Co., New York, 1914).

QUINCEY, THOMAS DE, from 'The Pleasures of Opium': *Confessions of An English Opium-Eater* (J.M. Dent & Sons, London, 1961).

RAVERAT, GWEN, from 'Society': *Period Piece: A Cambridge Childhood* (Faber and Faber Ltd, London, 1952).

ROBINSON, MARY DARBY, from *Mrs Mary Robinson, written by herself* with the *Lives of the Duchesses of Gordon and Devonshire*, by Grace and Philip Wharton. (Grolier Society, London 19—).

ROUSSEAU, JEAN-JACQUES, from Book 1, Book 4, and Book 7, *Les Confessions*

(1782–1789). Translated from the French by Christopher Durrance and Eve Claxton.

ROUSSEAU, JEAN-JACQUES, from 'Third Walk': *Les Rêveries du Promeneur Solitaire* (1782). Translated from the French by Christopher Durrance and Eve Claxton.

RUSKIN, JOHN, from Volume 1, 'The Springs of Wandel' and Volume 2, 'Crossmount': *Praeterita: Outlines of Scenes and Thoughts Perhaps Worthy of Memory in My Past Life* (Ryburn Publishing, An Imprint of Keele University Press, 1994).

RUSSELL, BERTRAND, from Prologue and 'Adolescence': *The Autobiography of Bertrand Russell* (Bantam Books, New York, 1968). Reprinted by permission of The Bertrand Russell Peace Foundation and Taylor & Francis

SAGE, LORNA, from 'School' and 'Sunnyside': *Bad Blood: A Memoir* (Fourth Estate, London, 2000). Copyright © 2000 by Lorna Sage, reprinted by permission of HarperCollins Publishers Inc. and HarperCollins Publishers Ltd.

SAID, EDWARD W., from Chapter XI: *Out of Place: A Memoir* (Alfred A. Knopf, New York, 1999). Copyright © 1999 by Edward W. Said, reprinted by permission of Alfred A. Knopf, a division of Random House, Inc. and The Wylie Agency (UK) Ltd.

SAND, GEORGE, from Part IV, Chapter ix and Part V, Chapter xiii: *Histoire de Ma Vie* (1854–1855). Translated from the French by Christopher Durrance and Eve Claxton.

SARTRE, JEAN-PAUL, from 'Writing': *The Words* translated by Irene Clephane (Penguin Books, 2000). Copyright © 1964 by Editions Gallimard, English translation copyright © 1964 by Hamish Hamilton Ltd, reprinted by permission of Penguin Books Ltd and Editions Gallimard, Paris.

SCOTT-MAXWELL, FLORIDA, from *The Measure of My Days* (Alfred A. Knopf, New York, 1968). Copyright © 1968 by Florida Scott-Maxwell, reprinted by permission of Alfred A. Knopf, a division of Random House, Inc.

SEDARIS, DAVID, from 'Something for Everyone': *Naked* (Little, Brown & Company, New York, 1997). Copyright © 1997 by David Sedaris, reprinted by permission of the author and Don Congdon Associates, Inc.

SHINWELL, MANNY, LORD, from 'The View from the Nineties': *Lead with the Left: My First Ninety-Six Years* (Cassell, London, 1981). Copyright © 1981 by Lord Shinwell, reprinted by permission of the Shinwell family.

SHŌNAGON, SEI, from 'The Pillow Book of Sei Shōnagon': *Anthology of Japanese Literature* edited by Donald Keene (Grove Press, New York, 1955). Copyright © 1955 by Grove Press, Inc, reprinted by permission of Grove/Atlantic, Inc.

SOYINKA, WOLE, from Chapter 2: *Aké: The Years of Childhood* (Vintage Books, New York, 1983). Copyright © 1981 by Wole Soyinka, reprinted by permission of Random House, Inc and Methuen Publishing Ltd.

STEIN, GERTRUDE, from 'What Was the Effect Upon Me of the Autobiography': *Everybody's Autobiography* (Random House, New York, 1937). Copyright © 1937 and 1965 by Alice B. Toklas, reprinted by permission of Random House, Inc.

STENDHAL, from Chapter 1: *Souvenirs D'égotisme* (1892). Translated by Christopher Durrance and Eve Claxton.

STYRON, WILLIAM, from Chapter 6: *Darkness Visible: A Memoir of Madness*

(Random House, New York, 1990). Copyright © 1990 by William Styron, reprinted by permission of Random House, Inc.

ST TERESA, from Chapter 2 and Chapter 9: *The Life of St Teresa of Avila by herself* translated with an introduction by J.M. Cohen (Penguin Classics, 1957). Translation copyright © J.M. Cohen, 1957.

THATCHER, MARGARET, LADY, from 'Beginning Again': *The Path to Power* (HarperCollins, New York, 1995). Copyright © 1995 by Margaret Thatcher, reprinted by permission of HarperCollins Publishers Ltd.

THOMAS, DYLAN, from 'Holiday Memory': *Quite Early One Morning* (New Directions, New York, 1960). Copyright © by New Directions, reprinted by permission of New Directions and David Higham Associates Ltd.

THOREAU, HENRY DAVID, from 'The Bean Field': *Walden, Or Life in the Woods*; in *The Norton Anthology of American Literature Volume 1* (W.W. Norton & Company, New York, 1989).

TILLMAN, LYNNE, 'Hole Story': *The Broad Picture* (Serpents Tail, London, 1997). Copyright © 1992 by Lynne Tillman, reprinted by permission of the author.

TOLSTOY, LEO, from Chapter 1 and Chapter 4 of 'My Confession': *My Confession and the Spirit of Christ's Teaching* (Walter Scott, London, 188-).

TROLLOPE, ANTHONY, from 'My Education', 'The General Post Office' and 'The Way We Live Now – Conclusion': *An Autobiography* (Trollope Society, London, 1999).

TWAIN, MARK, from 'Early Days, written 1897–8': *Mark Twain's Autobiography Volume I* (Harper & Brothers Publishers, New York and London, 1924). Copyright © 1924 by Clara Gabrilowitsch, renewed 1952 by Clara Clemens Samossoud. Reprinted by permission of HarperCollins Publishers Inc.

VONNEGUT, KURT, from Chapter 20: *Fates Worse Than Death: An Autobiographical Collage of the 1980s* (G.P. Putnam's Sons, New York). Copyright © 1991 by Kurt Vonnegut, reprinted by permission of G.P. Putnam's Sons, a division of Penguin Group (USA) Inc.

WARD, MARY AUGUSTA, from Chapter 1: *A Writer's Recollections* (Harper & Brothers, New York, 1918).

WELTY, EUDORA, from 'Listening': *One Writer's Beginnings* (Harvard University Press, Cambridge and London, 1984). Copyright © 1983, 1984 by Eudora Welty, reprinted by permission of Harvard University Press.

WHITMAN, WALT, from 'Specimen Days' ('Paumanok, and My Life on It As Child and Young Man', 'Growth–Health–Work', 'Through Eight Years') and 'Memoranda' ('Some Personal and Old Age Jottings'): *Complete Prose Works* (Literary Classics of the United States, New York, 1982).

WIESEL, ELIE, from 'Childhood' and 'Darkness': *All Rivers Run to the Sea: Memoirs* (Alfred A. Knopf, New York, 1995). Copyright © 1995 by Elie Wiesel, reprinted by permission of Alfred A. Knopf, a division of Random House, Inc.

WILDE, OSCAR, from 'De Profundis': *The Collected Works of Oscar Wilde Volume XI*, edited by Robert Ross (Routledge/Thomemmes Press, 1993).

WILSON, HARRIETTE, from Chapter 1: *Harriette Wilson's Memoirs* edited by Lesley Blanch (Phoenix Press, 2003).

WODEHOUSE, P.G., from 'Introducing J.P. Winkler' and 'Healthward Ho!': *Over Seventy: An Autobiography With Digressions* (Herbert Jenkins, London, 1957).

~ INDEX OF CONTRIBUTORS ~

Biographies are in *bold italic*